*English Pottery
and Porcelain*

# English Pottery and Porcelain

AN HISTORICAL SURVEY

Edited by Paul Atterbury

*A Main Street Press Book*

**Universe Books**  New York

Articles included in this volume are printed as they appeared in the following issues of *The Magazine* ANTIQUES:

*Part I:* North Devon Pottery in the Seventeenth Century, July, 1962; The Rise and Fall of English White Salt-Glazed Stoneware—Part I, February, 1970, Part II, March, 1970; English Earthenware with Dutch Painting, October, 1929; Who Made Creamware?, April, 1940; Some Recent Gifts of Creamware to Colonial Williamsburg, July, 1974; Pearlware: Forgotten Milestone of English Ceramic History, March, 1969; Castleford Pottery for the American Trade, October, 1967.

*Part II:* Battersea and Bilston Enamels, July, 1929; Worcester Porcelain of the Doctor Wall Period, May, 1947; "Powdered Blue" in English Porcelain, January, 1928; The Identification of Liverpool Porcelain of the Early Period, 1756-1765, December, 1964; Lowestoft Porcelain, June, 1922; English Lowestoft in the Chinese Taste, May, 1957; Identifying Early English Soft Porcelain, February, 1954; Early Coalport Porcelain, December, 1950; An English Porcelain Collection at Williamsburg, January, 1965; Bristol Hard-Paste Porcelain, April, 1972; Some Unusual Examples of English Blue and White Porcelain, June, 1950; Examination of English Eighteenth-Century Porcelains by Transmitted Light, August, 1966.

*Part III:* Josiah Wedgwood, Industrialist, August, 1934; Flaxman's Work for Wedgwood, December, 1955; From the Nile to the Trent, Wedgwood "Egyptian" Wares, October, 1949; Cream Color, Alias Queen's Ware, August, 1943; Jasperware and Some of Its Contemporaries, February, 1947; Some Age Tests for Wedgwood, August, 1931; Wedgwood: What's in a Mark?, May, 1970.

*Part IV:* Staffordshire Pew Groups, September, 1936; Staffordshire Figures of the Eighteenth Century, January, 1927; Toby Jugs, May, 1947; Victorian Staffordshire Portrait Figures, August, 1956; A Peaceable Kingdom of Staffordshire Animals, April, 1976; Possibilities in Ceramic Portraiture, November, 1931.

*Part V:* Staffordshire Ware in a Nutshell, March, 1936; Designs in Old Blue, April, 1943; A Chronology of Spode Patterns, May, 1929; Staffordshire Views of American Universities, October, 1933; Some Idiosyncrasies of the Staffordshire Potters, July, 1931; Sources of Staffordshire Designs, September, 1938; History on Staffordshire, August, 1947; Staffordshire and Steam, June, 1964; The Truth About Andrew Stevenson, November, 1934; James and Ralph Clews, Nineteenth-Century Potters, Part I—The English Experience, February, 1974; James Clews, Nineteenth-Century Potter, Part II—The American Experience, March, 1974; Enoch Wood Earthenware Found in St. Paul's Church, Burslem, July, 1977; Children's Mugs, September, 1950.

*Part VI:* A Collection of Swansea and Nantgarw Porcelain, October, 1971; Diversity in Old Spode, September, 1959; English Yellow-Glazed Earthenware from the Eleanor and Jack L. Leon Collection—Part I, Rarities, July, 1971, Part II, American Subjects, August, 1971; Banded Creamware, September, 1966; Pink Lustre, December, 1922; Who Made Old English Luster and When?, April, 1951; Stoneware Gin Flasks: Legacy of the Damned, February, 1975; Mason's Patent Ironstone China: An Underrated Ware, June, 1959; Pratt's Color Prints on Staffordshire Ware, August, 1952; Continental Decorators of English Ceramics in the Victorian Era, August, 1960; English Parian Wares, October, 1960; Minton Porcelain in the Style of Sèvres, June, 1968; Chelsea Today, The Porcelain Figures of Charles Vyse, April, 1945.

First Edition

All Rights Reserved. No part of this publication may be reproduced, stored in a retrieval system, or transmitted, in any form or by any means, electronic, mechanical photocopying, recording, or otherwise, without written permission of the publisher.

Introductory material copyright © 1978 by Paul J. Atterbury.

Original articles copyright © 1922, 1927, 1928, 1929, 1931, 1933, 1934, 1936, 1938, 1940, 1943, 1945, 1947, 1950, 1951, 1952, 1954, 1955, 1956, 1957, 1959, 1960, 1962, 1964, 1965, 1966, 1967, 1968, 1969, 1970, 1971, 1972, 1974, 1975, 1976, 1977 by Straight Enterprises, Inc.

Library of Congress Catalog Card Number 78-59173

ISBN 0-87663-984-8, paperback edition
ISBN 0-87663-314-9, clothbound edition

*Published by* Universe Books
381 Park Avenue South
New York City 10016

*Produced by* The Main Street Press
42 Main Street
Clinton, New Jersey, 08809

# Contents

GENERAL INTRODUCTION

I  ENGLISH POTTERY, 1650-1800

North Devon Pottery in the Seventeenth Century,
    *C. Malcolm Watkins*    12
The Rise and Fall of English White Salt-Glazed Stoneware, Parts
    I and II, *Ivor Noël Hume*    16
English Earthenware with Dutch Painting,
    *Bernard Rackham*    30
Who Made Creamware?, *Edna Donnell*    34
Some Recent Gifts of Creamware to Colonial Williamsburg,
    *John C. Austin*    37
Pearlware: Forgotten Milestone of English Ceramic History,
    *Ivor Noël Hume*    42
Castleford Pottery for the American Trade,
    *Patricia R. Guthman*    50

II  ENGLISH EIGHTEENTH-CENTURY PORCELAINS

Battersea and Bilston Enamels, *G. Bernard Hughes*    56
Worcester Porcelain of the Doctor Wall Period,
    *Marcel H. Stieglitz*    60
"Powdered Blue" in English Porcelain, *Bernard Rackham*    63
The Identification of Liverpool Porcelain of the Early Period,
    1756-1765, *Knowles Boney*    67
Lowestoft Porcelain, *Frederick Litchfield*    71
English Lowestoft in the Chinese Taste,
    *Geoffrey A. Godden*    76
Identifying Early English Soft Porcelain, *George Savage*    79
Early Coalport Porcelain, *Franklin A. Barrett*    83
An English Porcelain Collection at Williamsburg,
    *John M. Graham II*    86
Bristol Hard-Paste Porcelain, *John K. D. Cooper*    91
Some Unusual Examples of English Blue and White Porcelain,
    *Stanley W. Fisher*    103
Examination of English Eighteenth-Century Porcelains by Transmitted Light, *J. L. Dixon*    105

III  WEDGWOOD

Josiah Wedgwood, Industrialist, *Joseph H. Park*    110
Flaxman's Work for Wedgwood, *Jean Gorely*    113
From the Nile to the Trent, Wedgwood "Egyptian" Wares,
    *Elizabeth Chellis*    118
Cream Color, Alias Queen's Ware, *Jean Gorely*    122

Jasperware and Some of Its Contemporaries,
   *Alice Winchester*   125
Some Age Tests for Wedgwood, *Joseph H. Park*   128
Wedgwood: What's In a Mark?, *Geoffrey A. Godden*   131

IV   CERAMIC FIGURES AND PORTRAITS

Staffordshire Pew Groups, *John E. Lerch*   138
Staffordshire Figures of the Eighteenth Century,
   *Mrs. Gordon-Stables*   143
Toby Jugs, *Edward Wenham*   148
Victorian Staffordshire Portrait Figures, *Bryan Latham*   151
A Peaceable Kingdom of Staffordshire Animals,
   *Jerome Irving Smith*   153
Possibilities in Ceramic Portraiture, *Albert Lee*   159

V   BLUE PRINTED WARES

Staffordshire Ware in a Nutshell, *Gregor Norman-Wilcox*   166
Designs in Old Blue, The Development of Staffordshire Transfer-
   Printed Wares as Seen by an English Potter and Collector,
   *Gresham Copeland*   171
A Chronology of Spode Patterns, *n.a.*   175
Staffordshire Views of American Universities,
   *Arthur H. Merritt*   179
Some Idiosyncrasies of the Staffordshire Potters,
   *Ellouise Baker Larsen*   184
Sources of Staffordshire Designs, *Sydney B. Williams*   188
History on Staffordshire, *Ellouise Baker Larsen*   190
Staffordshire and Steam, *Randall J. LeBoeuf, Jr.*   193
The Truth About Andrew Stevenson,
   *Ellouise Baker Larsen*   198
James and Ralph Clews, Nineteenth-Century Potters, Part I: The
   English Experience, *Frank Stefano, Jr.*   202
James Clews, Nineteenth-Century Potter, Part II: The American
   Experience, *Frank Stefano, Jr.*   207
Enoch Wood Earthenware Found in St. Paul's Church, Burslem,
   *Pamela D. Kingsbury*   210
Children's Mugs, *Katharine Morrison McClinton*   216

VI   VICTORIAN AND LATER POTTERY AND PORCELAIN

A Collection of Swansea and Nantgarw Porcelain,
   *Aubrey Niel Morgan*   219
Diversity in Old Spode, *Edgar and Elizabeth Collard*   225
English Yellow-Glazed Earthenware from the Eleanor and Jack
   L. Leon Collection, Part I, Rarities, and Part II, American Sub-
   jects, *J. Jefferson Miller II*   229
Banded Creamware, *Susan Van Rensselaer*   240
Pink Lustre, *Daniel Catton Rich*   245

Who Made Old English Luster and When?, *W. D. John*   249
Stoneware Gin Flasks: Legacy of the Damned,
   *Ivor Noël Hume*   253
Mason's Patent Ironstone China: An Underrated Ware,
   *Stanley W. Fisher*   263
Pratt's Color Prints on Staffordshire Ware, *n.a.*   267
Continental Decorators of English Ceramics in the Victorian Era,
   *Geoffrey A. Godden*   271
English Parian Ware, *Geoffrey A. Godden*   275
Minton Porcelain in the Style of Sèvres,
   *Geoffrey A. Godden*   278
Chelsea Today, The Porcelain Figures of Charles Vyse,
   *Frank Stoner*   282

Index   285

# Publisher's Note

An interest in English ceramic history is one of the strongest bonds linking collectors on each side of the Atlantic. Since the 17th century, utilitarian and decorative wares have moved through channels of trade to reach North America. By the mid-19th century, the export market had become nearly as large as the domestic. Research into the origins and development of English-made pottery and porcelain has become similarly well-organized and ambitious. North American and British experts freely share their finds and publish new material in periodicals on both sides of the Atlantic. *The Magazine* ANTIQUES has been a special forum for contributors since 1922 and has included among the British experts Geoffrey A. Godden, Bernard Rackham, Frederick Litchfield, George Savage, Stanley W. Fisher, Bryan Latham, and Pamela D. Kingsbury. Prominent scholars resident in America have included Ivor Noel Hume, Joseph H. Park, Ellouise Baker Larsen, Randall J. LeBoeuf, Jr., Frank Stefano, Jr., and J. Jefferson Miller II.

Paul R. Atterbury, historical advisor to the Royal Doulton Group in England, at our request, has selected and edited the present collection of articles—never before reprinted—which we feel are of inestimable value to the collector and scholar wherever English ceramics are enjoyed and studied. A member of the English Ceramic Circle, he is a regular contributor to *Connoisseur* and *Antique Collector* and served for two years as the antiques correspondent of *Tatler*.

The commentaries to the six sections of this volume provide the reader with basic information on the development of ceramic styles, forms, and methods of manufacture. Both British and North American readers will find particularly interesting the editor's remarks on the trade in historical blue Staffordshire wares and on the new appreciation of Victorian porcelains. As in other fields of the decorative arts, that which is "old" is constantly being reinterpreted and up-dated.

# Introduction

Of the enormous range of subjects that interest collectors today, probably none has a greater pedigree than pottery and porcelain. In the Middle Ages when pottery was little more than a basic domestic material, the rare examples of Chinese porcelain that came into Europe via the Middle Eastern trade routes were regarded as precious and miraculous jewels, to be finely mounted in silver and gold. Later, as the domestic product improved and the imports became more frequent, collecting pottery and porcelain became an established pastime. For a long period this pastime was dominated by the fascination for porcelain, and there were many attempts at producing this rare oriental material from the 17th century onwards. By the 18th century the production of this material was established in Europe, and at the same time many of the more basic earthenwares and stonewares had been developed to a point of considerable sophistication. Despite the keen collector interest, there was little serious research into the history of ceramic production. Collections were developed, catalogued, and then dispersed, only to be collected and catalogued once again, aided of course by the continual traffic passing through the new salesrooms. However, the collecting and cataloguing was always of a rather personal and non-academic form, the collector or dealer being prepared to accept criteria and standards of aesthetic judgement that left much to be desired. The whole field developed, therefore, a consciously amateur approach, which in fact has plagued the study of ceramics ever since.

The pattern of development of English ceramics was not greatly different from other countries of Europe, and yet the English collector has always been characterized by his severely limited horizons. By the second half of the 19th century these had been limited first to the study of the 18th century and, second, to the study of the porcelains of that period. In the large country houses, the fine porcelains and earthenwares of Europe were represented in major collections amassed by generations of traveling and marriage. However, the ordinary collector of more limited means kept his sights firmly on the local product. As a result, there developed in England an essentially chauvinistic method of studying ceramic history, reflecting perhaps England's traditionally isolated position beyond the European mainland.

In artistic and stylistic terms, however, England was very much a part of Europe. Most European art movements eventually affected England, while England's position as the leading industrial and trading nation in Europe encouraged their development and popularity. The collectors of ceramics have tended to disregard this background by concentrating on the domestic product at the expense of the European; this was a short-sighted approach because, with one or two exceptions, the English product was generally inferior to its European rivals, at least until the 19th century. In any case, the internationalism of ideas in Europe has always made the study of the art or design of any one country in isolation an unwise principle, to say the least.

In the 19th century, when English potters could, for the first time, claim with justification to dominate the design and manufacture of ceramics in Europe, the collector was at least aware of current styles and trends. The popularity of new Victorian ceramic techniques such as parian porcelain, majolica-glazed earthenware, pâte-sur-pâte, and multicolor printing, focused attention for a time on the present. During this inventive period the past was studied more assiduously than ever before, partly because the proliferation of the new museums, art galleries, and art schools made such a study necessary, and partly because the past was seen as a vital source of ideas for the present. During the mid-Victorian period the first serious studies were produced on Italian majolica, German stoneware, English slipware, Dutch Delftware, medieval tiles, French faience, and many other hitherto ignored pre-18th-century ceramic forms. That many of these studies were produced by European authors, such as the French designer and collector L. M. Solon, merely underlined the true internationalism of the period. Indeed, many of these early studies have hardly been improved on since.

In the early 20th century the pattern altered. For various reasons the close relationship between art and industry that had dominated the Victorian period fell apart. Partly as a result of the war of 1914-1918, England became both economically and artistically isolated once again. The impact on the English ceramic industry is obvious, for it failed completely to keep abreast of the new artistic movements emanating from the European centers such as Sèvres, Copenhagen,

Berlin, and Holland. The impact on collectors was more subtle, but potentially just as harmful. There was an immediate concentration of interest on the English porcelains of the 18th century. This period, which in European terms is only of limited technical and artistic interest, was studied at the expense of all others. This narrow philosophy was rapidly adopted as official policy by many collectors and museums, and was underlined by the formation of a national society of porcelain collectors which took the deliberately narrow and chauvinistic title of the English Porcelain Circle. Later this organization did change its name, becoming the English Ceramic Circle, but even today it still exists in an ivory tower of its own construction, refusing adamantly and arrogantly to pay any attention to wares produced after 1830. Instead it prefers to bury its head in the trivial minutiae of the 18th century, holding back thereby the progress of worthwhile and academic ceramic studies in Britain.

Luckily in America this self-imposed blindness has not applied, and so American collectors and historians have been able to fill many of the gaps in our knowledge. The selection of articles in this book underlines the many areas of study about which we would otherwise be ignorant; they also have made it possible for English 18th-century porcelains to be seen in context as only a small part of a much wider story. This broad approach has, of course, been made possible by the vast export trade established from England to North America in the 1830s and 1840s, a trade which has long created in North America an appreciation of contemporary products quite lacking in their country of origin.

This selection has therefore been designed to give an overall picture, not only of ceramic manufacture in England, but also of the nature and status of collecting. If it reflects the lively, imaginative, and questing, if sometimes erratic, nature of the American collector at the expense of the English, then that is merely a reflection of the true position today. The articles published in *The Magazine* ANTIQUES have therefore reflected, over many years, the broad history of English ceramics more accurately than their equivalent in England. By selecting a cross-section of these articles, it has been possible to show both the wide range of English ceramic forms and styles, and to give a true picture of collector interests over the last fifty years.

The articles have been arranged in six sections. The first, *English Pottery 1650-1800,* shows the contribution made by both simple and sophisticated earthenwares in the history of English ceramics, emphasizing the importance of both lesser-known regions, such as North Devon, and lesser-known materials such as pearlware and white stoneware. The second, *English 18th Century Porcelains,* attempts to put English porcelain-making in its historical context, by showing both the unbalanced nature of research and the dependence upon erratic methods of attribution. By failing to judge between the trivial and the significant, the collector has merely reduced the impact of the first-class productions of the period. The third is devoted to *Wedgwood,* whose name and reputation has inspired so many articles that little must remain to be said. However, these articles reflect not only the continuing international reputation of Wedgwood, but also consider his products in the light of contemporary art history, an approach that lifts them, quite correctly, far above the normal level of ceramic study. The fourth, *Ceramic Figures and Portraits,* reflects the traditional role of the potter as an image maker, a role that links the present with the primitive civilizations of the past. The Staffordshire maker of Toby jugs was probably unaware that he was continuing a tradition with roots in ancient Greece, pre-Columbian South America, and medieval Europe, for the tradition in this case was always more powerful than the styles and guises imposed on it by each period. The fifth, *Blue Printed Wares,* shows the importance of an artistically humble, but economically vital basic product of the 19th century. The millions of tons of cheap printed earthenwares shipped to North America from Staffordshire, Bristol, Glasgow, and other British centers helped to create the wealth and stability in the industry that were necessary for the production of the expensive art wares of the period. These articles also show both the dependence of the potter upon printed and engraved sources for his designs, and his ability to reflect both historical and contemporary themes. The final section, *Victorian and Later Pottery and Porcelain,* serves as a reminder that the 19th century was really the most inventive and exciting period in English ceramic history. Disregarded and casually dismissed for so long by ill-informed and opinionated collectors, these wares are now receiving the attention they deserve, at least in North America if not in England.

# I English Pottery, 1650-1800

The concentration by collectors and others on the porcelains of the 18th century has meant that many aspects of English ceramic production have been inadequately studied. For many years it was widely believed that only peasant wares were produced before the 18th century, and so these periods were only rarely given any serious attention. Since the 1900s this attitude has changed, and so, although the porcelain factories still receive a disproportionate amount of attention, there is now a basic understanding of the fact that pottery has always been a far more vital force in England than the better known porcelains.

In the Middle Ages, a pattern of pottery making was established whose life, originality, and decorative traditions were to form a background upon which subsequent generations of potters could build. Although limited technically, the potters of the 16th and 17th centuries were able to make the most of their simple materials in very dynamic ways. The greatest productions of this period are the slipwares, so called because their decoration was achieved either by trailing the surface with patterns and designs drawn in liquid clay, or slip, or by incising or carving through a coating of slip to reveal the contrasting color of the earthenware beneath. This powerful form, drawing its decorative inspiration from sources as diverse as heraldry, mythology, religious symbolism and printed ephemera such as contemporary tobacco wrappers, was developed in many parts of Britain. However, the most important centers were probably Staffordshire, where potters such as Thomas Toft and Ralph Simpson produced their stylish chargers on a quasi-industrial level, and North Devon. At Bideford, Barnstable, and other West Country ports there were colonies of slipware potters who developed their own quite distinctive regional styles. This area was also important for the export trade it built up with the new settlements in North America, a trade that reached proportions which many 20th-century manufacturers would envy. Traditions of slipware manufacture continued to thrive in many rural areas of Britain until the late 19th century, although its social and artistic significance had largely been superceded by the mid 18th century.

Another English material dating back to the 17th century was stoneware. Introduced originally from Germany, the basic brown stoneware was a popular material that has remained in production for domestic use until the present day. However, after considerable refinements had been made to the material by potters such as John Dwight and the Elers brothers, high quality red and white stonewares were produced, capable of emulating many of the qualities of oriental porcelain. The Staffordshire potters, being essentially practical and hard-headed men, did not waste their time and money by trying to make porcelain in the 18th century. Instead, they mastered the manufacture of adequate substitutes, first the fine white stonewares, and later the creamwares and their derivatives such as pearlware. These new materials were able to take advantage of both technical and economic advances. The basic clays were prepared more carefully and were blended with materials such as flint and the newly-discovered Cornish china stone which served to increase their strength and whiteness. At the same time, advanced mechanization plus increased production enabled these wares to be made cheaply, thus satisfying demand in both home and export markets.

Of course, the potters of Staffordshire were not the only ones to benefit from this technical and economic revolution. The new materials were made at many centers of pottery production, and particularly in Yorkshire, where Leeds creamware and Castleford stoneware continued to show the world that Britain did not yet need to worry about the manufacture of porcelain.

# North Devon pottery in the seventeenth century

BY C. MALCOLM WATKINS, *Curator, division of cultural history, Smithsonian Institution*

THE NORTH DEVON towns of Barnstaple and Bideford, then among England's foremost ports, were vitally concerned with American trade in the seventeenth century. When the American colonies were once established and prospering, North Devon merchants established agencies with resident factors in Newfoundland and New England and, according to Bideford's eighteenth-century chronicler John Watkins (*An Essay Towards a History of Bideford in the County of Devon, Exeter*, 1792, p. 65), "Some of [Bideford's] chief merchants had very extensive possessions in Virginia and Maryland."

What has not generally been recognized is the fact that one of the industries most stimulated by this combination of economic forces was the manufacture of earthenware. In Barnstaple and the neighboring parish of Fremington pottery has been made apparently since the Middle Ages. Barnstaple is located on the westward-flowing river Taw, some six miles upstream from its entry into the Bristol Channel. A series of rich clay deposits lies along the south shore of the Taw in Fremington, between Barnstaple and the Taw estuary; it was doubtless their proximity to a navigable river that attracted the early potters.

Bideford is on the river Torridge, which flows north to join the Taw where both enter the Bristol Channel. John Watkins tells us that "Bideford rose so rapidly as to become a port of importance at the latter end of Queen Elizabeth's reign . . . when the trade began to open between England and America in the reign of King James the First, Bideford early took a part in it." Although, like Barnstaple, it engaged heavily in the Newfoundland fishing trade, "the principal part of foreign commerce that Bideford was ever engaged in, was to Maryland and Virginia for tobacco . . . Its connections with New England were also very considerable." By the early eighteenth century, Bideford was second only to London in amount of tobacco imported.

In Barnstaple, C. H. Brannam's Litchdon Street pottery is the only one of the North Devon potteries to survive to the present day. It has operated continuously, although under a variety of proprietorships, since medieval times. In Fremington a pottery was carried on by the Fishley family from the late eighteenth century until 1912. In Bideford the earliest record of pottery making noted thus far is a 1659 mention of one John Berryman as the owner of a pottery works. Crocker's pottery is said to have been established in 1668, continuing in the same family under the same name until it closed in 1896.

The later North Devon potters have been remembered principally in association with a handful of individual, elaborately decorated sgraffito harvest jugs. Consequently, they have been regarded merely as peasant potters who expressed the vitality of English rural folk life. However, archeological and documentary evidence now indicates that whatever vigor the potters may have been endowed with naturally was stimulated commercially by the demand for large-scale production to supply the growing settlements of North America. The increas-

Gravel-tempered pan. *Except as noted, all objects illustrated were excavated at the site of Jamestown and are published by courtesy of Colonial National Historical Park.*

July, 1962

12

Gravel-tempered chafing dish.

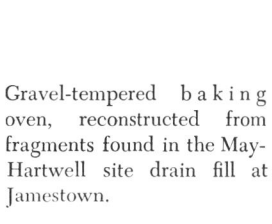

Gravel-tempered baking oven, reconstructed from fragments found in the May-Hartwell site drain fill at Jamestown.

ing absorptive powers of those distant markets transformed the cluster of North Devon potteries into a highly productive ceramic center, able to compete successfully against the potteries of Bristol and Somersetshire in the west of England as well as those of South Wales and southern Ireland. The sgraffito harvest jugs, full of peasant vitality though they may be, were thus the by-products of a much larger and in many ways more significant phenomenon. Because they were presentation pieces, they have survived in North Devon households, while the commercial wares, put into daily use and soon broken, have disappeared from the face of the earth if not from below its surface. It was this commercial production that established the contemporary reputation of the North Devon wares in distant markets.

The first modern awareness of this seventeenth-century commercial product came in 1935 as a result of excavations by the National Park Service at the site of Jamestown, Virginia, the first permanent English settlement in America. In the fill around a drain laid there on the property of Henry Hartwell between 1689 and 1695 were found hundreds of shards of red earthenware, coated with white slip, gaily decorated with sgraffito designs, and glazed with an amber lead glaze which imparted a butter-yellow color to the white slip. Numbers of plates, platters, deep dishes, globose jugs, wine cups, and a candlestick were reconstructed, revealing a remarkable series of one-of-a-kind geometrical and floral designs. Park Service excavations at the site of the John Washington house in Westmoreland County, Virginia, also yielded numerous examples, and scattered findings have been made elsewhere in Virginia, in Maryland, and at Kingston, Massachusetts.

There was little in the ceramic literature to explain this splendid pottery. Its color, when compared with the eighteenth-century harvest jugs, if not the style and design, hinted at a relationship with North Devon. The likelihood of a North Devon source was greatly strengthened when J. C. Harrington, who excavated the Hartwell site, saw at Brannam's pottery at Barnstaple a seventeenth-century shard discovered under the pottery's foundations. This was decorated in sgraffito style and was obviously related to the Jamestown pieces, although slight stylistic differences were noticeable.

Also found in the Hartwell drain fill were countless fragments of an extraordinarily crude utilitarian ware, characterized by a heavy admixture of coarse sand or gravel. The forms included large jars with reinforcement strips under the rims, a chafing dish, cooking pots, bowls, three-legged pipkins, and rectangular baking pans. A few slip-coated fragments matched the sgraffito ware in color. There was also a large and heavy baking oven of this ware. At first it seemed impossible that such crude pottery should ever have been shipped across the ocean, and it was thought that the ware must have been locally made. However, it began to appear in numerous sites other than Jamestown, from Massachusetts to Hampton Roads. A fragment of an oven was found in Kingston, Massachusetts, and a whole oven may be seen *in situ* in the John Bowne House at Flushing, Long Island, built in 1661. Clearly, this pottery had a common source in a large center of distribution.

It was the ovens which first suggested a link with North Devon. Llewellyn Jewitt (*The Ceramic Art of Great Britain*) in 1883 illustrated sketches of ovens resembling the one at Jamestown. He described their manufacture as a specialty of North Devon, stating that those made in the Crocker pottery in Bideford "are, and for generations have been, in much repute in Devonshire and Cornwall, and in the Welsh districts . . ." Today in and around Barnstaple and Bideford may be seen seventeenth-and eighteenth-century examples in their original settings, while others are preserved in museums in Bideford, Taunton, and Plymouth. All, despite minor variations, belong to the same family as the ovens in Jamestown and Flushing.

The gravel used to temper the coarse ware and the ovens is never seen in other types of earthenware used in British America (although it occurs more typically in English medieval pottery). Microscopic comparison of shards from oven and utensil fragments found in America with those from Bideford confirms the supposition that Bideford—or at least North Devon—was almost surely the source. Where the gravel came from is explained in an article about Bideford which appeared in *The Gentlemen's Magazine* in 1755: "Just above the bridge is a little ridge of gravel of a peculiar quality, without which the potters could not make their ware."

British *Port Books*, in the Public Record Office in London, give us a picture of the extent of the North Devon earthenware trade. As early as 1601 Barnstaple shipped to "Dublyn—100 dozen Earthen Pottes of all

Sgraffito-ware shard from Jamestown.

Sgraffito-ware shards recovered from trench near the site of the Crocker pottery (1668-1896), Bideford. *Smithsonian Institution.*

sorts." Large cargoes to Irish ports followed all through the century. In 1635, the earliest shipment of earthenware to New England was recorded. Subsequently other cargoes were sent to America, but it was not until after the Stuart restoration in 1660 that these were frequent. There were several shipments from Barnstaple in 1665. In 1680 and 1681, hundreds of tons were evidently sent from the two towns to Virginia, Maryland, and New England. On October 11, 1688, for example, when the *Eagle* arrived in Boston from Bideford, her entire cargo consisted of nine thousand parcels of earthenware. Each parcel probably weighed two hundred pounds or more.

It is noteworthy that Bideford exceeded Barnstaple in the export of this earthenware after 1680; the establishment of the Crocker pottery in 1668 may have been a factor. In any case the recent salvage in Bideford by Reginald Lloyd of sgraffito-ware kiln wasters from a utilities trench dug close to the site of the Crocker pottery proves conclusively that most of the sgraffito ware thus far excavated in America was made in Bideford, probably at Crocker's.

Presumably the overseas export of pottery stopped about 1760. The sgraffito tableware had long since ceased to be produced; indeed, no known examples of the Bideford type have survived above ground. Essentially a product of seventeenth-century taste, it was bound to succumb to competition from the more sophisticated delftware made in Bristol and London. The gravel-tempered wares, on the other hand, medieval though they were in all but date, survived longer because they filled a widespread need. In America the growth of colonial earthenware manufacture during the eighteenth century, with stoneware centers increasing as well, reduced the need for this archaic ware.

Yet in nonindustrial western England and southern Wales, the markets for it persisted. The anonymous writer on Bideford in *The Gentlemen's Magazine* noted in 1755 that "Great quantities of potters ware are made, and exported to Wales, Ireland, and Bristol." As late as 1824, eight separate potteries were still in business in Bideford. The last of these, established by 1760, closed its doors in 1917. In 1829, one hundred and forty-eight coastwise vessels were engaged in shipping earthenware from Bideford to Wales. Ovens were among the cargoes of these ships, we may be sure. In 1750, Dr. Richard Pococke observed that in Devonshire and Cornwall "they make great use here of Cloume [*i.e.*, earthenware] ovens" and in 1786 "Barnstaple ovens" were advertised in Bristol. In 1851, Brannam's exhibited an oven at the Crystal Palace Exhibition where it was described as "generally used in Devonshire for baking bread and meat." At Brannam's, ovens continued to be produced until 1935, when the last potter who could make them retired.

Excavations in England, conducted mainly by John G. Hurst, assistant inspector of Public Monuments, Ministry of Works, reveal a wide distribution of the same class of Bideford sgraffito ware in the west of England and South Wales, primarily in sites dating from the late seventeenth and early eighteenth centuries. Its occurrence in Bristol and Exeter is supported by *Port Book* records of shipments of earthenware to those ports in 1681. No wonder, then, that John Watkins could write of Bideford, "The profits to the manufacturers of this article [*i.e.*, earthenware] are very great, which is evidenced by several persons having risen within a few years, from a state of the greatest obscurity and poverty, to wealth and consequence of no small extent."

The production of sgraffito tableware of the type found at Jamestown was apparently short lived. American archeological dating evidence fails to show any deposit of it later than 1700, or much earlier than 1680. None, for example, has been found in Williamsburg, Virginia, which was laid out as a town in 1700 and is probably the most thoroughly excavated eighteenth-century town site in England or America. The gravel-tempered ware, which has been found in deposits dated as early as 1650, has a much longer range: a pan found in the Coke-Garrett House site in Williamsburg was left there between 1740 and 1760. It was about 1760 that the wars with France closed the North Devon ports and brought about a decline from which the region never recovered.

This article is based on the author's monograph "North Devon Pottery and its Export to America in the 17th Century," published as Paper 13, United States National Museum Bulletin 225 (*Contributions from the Museum of History and Technology*).

Sgraffito-decorated plates.

Sgraffito-decorated jug and cups.

# The rise and fall of English white salt-glazed stoneware   Part I

BY IVOR NOËL-HUME, *Director, department of archaeology, Colonial Williamsburg*

THE DEVELOPMENT OF English white salt-glazed stoneware was one of the eighteenth century's most significant ceramic advances, not only because it marked the advent of a new body, but because it brought along with it a new design capability that was subsequently reflected in other wares. There can be few students of English pottery who have not learned that delftware was followed by salt glaze, salt glaze by creamware, and cream by pearl. Actually the chronology was neither so simple nor so clearly defined, and in this two-part article I propose to examine the complicated history of the birth of white salt glaze, and then to review its demise and the legacy it left behind.

It is widely supposed that "the regular manufacture of the white stoneware did not begin until the 1730's" (Honey, *English Pottery and Porcelain,* London, 1952, p. 70) and that it was on its way out in the 1760's. There is, however, ample documentary and archaeological evidence that both dates are wide of the mark. As early as 1724, William Randall "in the middle of Cross-Street," Boston, was advertising "white stone Tea-Cups and Saucers." Indeed, Randall's notice in the *Boston News-Letter* (January 17, 1724) may have offered a greater diversity of white salt glaze than mere cups and saucers, listing as it did "Hogsheads of Earthen Ware, white stone Tea-Cups and Saucers, Bowls, Plates, Salts, Milk Pots, handsome cut Salts, cotton, silk. . ." Advertisements can, unfortunately, be very misleading, and as the cut salts were clearly not of white salt glaze, it is possible that the bowls and plates were also of another material, for there is as yet no unequivocal evidence that white salt-glaze plates were made before the early 1740's.

Newspaper advertisements, though often frustrating, are generally more informative than household inventories, as the writers of the former made their descriptions as full as possible in order to attract customers. The compilers of inventories, on the other hand, were concerned only with the appraisal of the objects, and gave no fuller description than was necessary for visual identification. Consequently the man who, in July 1728, listed the household effects of Nathaniel Harrison of Williamsburg recorded "5 stone Tea Potts" and "3 do. Milk Potts" in the sideboard in the hall, but failed to say whether they were of Nottingham brown stoneware, Elers-type redware, or white salt glaze. That appraiser was no more informative when he got to the dining room, where he found "1 stone slop bason." Nevertheless, there is good reason to believe that Harrison's teapots, milk pots, and slop basin were as likely to have been of white salt glaze as of any other ware.

There is archaeological evidence that three different types of white salt glaze were reaching the American Colonies in the 1720's, the cheapest of them having only a dipped white

Fig. 1. Fragmentary cups of refined white salt glaze and a cream pitcher of dipped ware found in the ruins of Robert Carter's Corotoman, which burned in 1729. Cup height, 2⅝ inches. *Collection of James Wharton.*

February, 1970

Fig. 2. Teacup of dipped white salt glaze, the lip decorated with a brown iron-oxide slip, c. 1725. Found in Williamsburg excavations. The pin used as a scale in this and other illustrations measures one inch. *Colonial Williamsburg.*

Fig. 3. A dipped white salt-glaze mug, the engobe made from a mixture of flint and pipe clay, and covering a buff body (two views). The incised decoration is filled with brown slip (scratch brown) similar to that around the lip, and the design appears to be the work of a sgraffito slip-ware potter. Dated 1723, this is the earliest documented example of dipped white salt glaze yet recorded. Height 5¼ inches. *City Museum, Stoke-on-Trent.*

slip, or engobe, over a gray to buff body. (The term engobe is here used to distinguish between a coating of white-firing clay that totally covers the body, and slips, which can be of various colors and which do not necessarily conceal all of the body clay.) Next to the engobe-covered ware in refinement was a rather coarse off-white ware, flecked with small black particles and coated with a thick salt glaze which generally lacked the fine surface pitting associated with the more lightly glazed ware common in the mid-eighteenth century. This last represents the third category reaching America prior to 1730. Figure 1 shows shards of three cups of the evolved white salt glaze that were found in the ruins of Robert Carter's great Virginia mansion Corotoman, which burned in 1729. Found with them was a small milk pitcher of the dipped ware (Fig. 1, *right*), this characteristically decorated with a band of iron oxide at the rim and with another patch on the crest of the handle. The use of the brown was not entirely ornamental: it served to conceal the engobe's embarrassing tendency to drop away from rims, spouts, and handles during firing, leaving the gray core exposed.

The dipped ware has long been supposed to have been no more than an evolutionary step on the way to the true white salt glaze. Although it probably was the first to be marketed, it did not die out when the solid white ware was perfected; on the contrary, this cheaper variant continued in use until the 1770's. The best-preserved example yet found in this country is a mug retrieved from one of the British vessels sunk at Yorktown in 1781.

After about 1730 the dipped ware seems to have been reserved for coarse tavern mugs and occasionally for pitchers. Prior to that date it was much used for tea ware, as the Corotoman pitcher and a teacup from Williamsburg (Fig. 2) remind us. The earliest dated example is a mug in the Hanley museum at Stoke-on-Trent (Fig. 3) with incised decoration filled with iron-oxide slip. This enormously important 1723 piece was almost certainly the work of a sgraffito slip-ware decorator, suggesting the nature of the potter's principal occupation at the time he turned his hand to the new ware.

Before discussing other early and diagnostically important

Fig. 4. Examples of dipped, coarse, and refined white salt glaze from Williamsburg excavations. *Left:* Dipped mug with iron-oxide band at its rim; discarded c. 1770. Height 6⅛ inches. *Center:* A seemingly unparalleled coarse salt-glaze teapot coated above the girth with a thin iron-oxide slip; from a context of c. 1730-1740. Height 3¾ inches. *Right:* A typical regular white salt-glaze tankard, discarded c. 1759. Height 6⅜ inches. *Colonial Williamsburg.*

pieces, it is necessary to try to untangle the rather complicated and contradictory historical evidence about the birth of white salt glaze. According to Simeon Shaw (*History of the Staffordshire Potteries,* Hanley, 1829, reprinted in London, 1900, p. 109), the first step in the direction of white salt glaze was made when "About 1685, Mr. Thomas Miles, of Shelton, mixed with the whitish clay found in Shelton, some of the fine sand from Baddeley Hedge [Edge], and produced a rude kind of WHITE STONE WARE." In a letter of July 19, 1777, addressed to his partner, Thomas Bentley, Josiah Wedgwood gave his account of the ware's development, stating that "Glazing our common clays with salt . . . was improv'd into White Stone Ware by using the White Pipe Clay instead of the common clay of this Neighbourhood, & mixing with it Flint Stones calcin'd & reduc'd by pounding into a fine powder." The letter did not explain how the pipe clay and flint were used; for that we turn again to Simeon Shaw (*ibid.,* p. 129), who reveals that the flint was at first used "in a mixture with water to a thick pulp, as a *wash* or *dip,* which he [Astbury] applied to give a coating to the vessels, some time before he introduced it along with the clay into the body of his ware." In an earlier passage (*ibid.,* p. 126) Shaw described Astbury's [John? 1688-1743] experiments in the use of "the Pipe Clay, from Biddeford [in North Devon], mixed with water . . . the pipe clay was levigated until only the finest particles were suspended in the water, forming a liquid substance like cream; he also tried

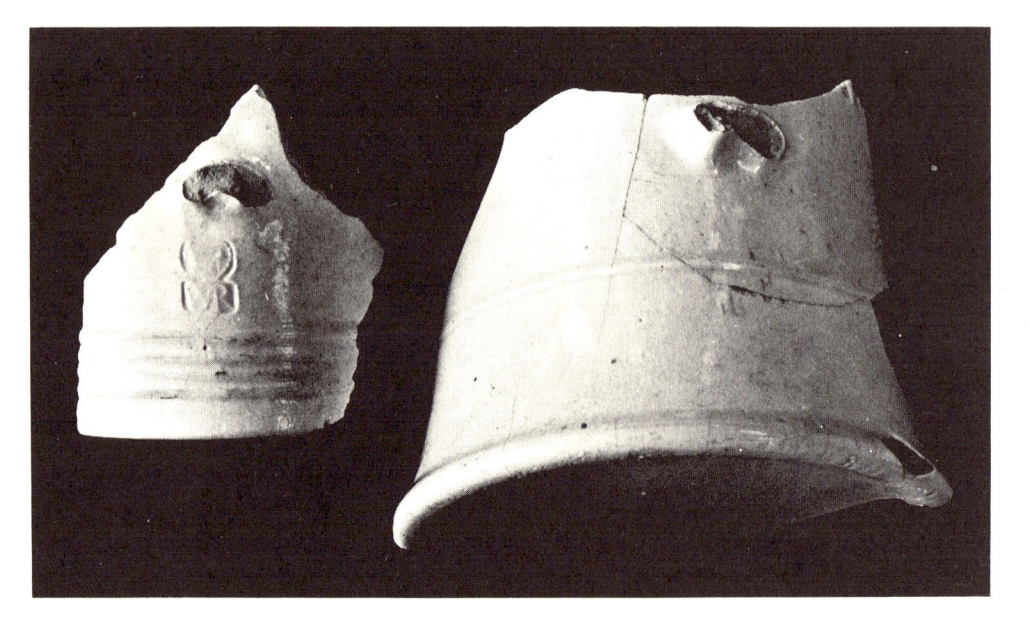

Fig. 5. Lower body and basal fragments from early and later dipped white salt-glaze mugs excavated in Williamsburg. That on the left is cordoned above the base in the manner of the Hanley museum's 1723 example, and is impressed below the handle with a crowned *WR* excise stamp, a mark in use long after the death of William III. The shard at right has a flaring foot copying a style common in regular white salt glaze in the mid-century. Note that the body-revealing chip on the foot is covered with the glaze and so occurred before firing. *Colonial Williamsburg.*

this clay and the Shelton marl, for his white ware, with such success, that he soon rejected the native clays entirely, and made *White Dipped* or *White Stone Ware,* by a very easy transition from the Crouch ware."

The proper identification of Shaw's "Crouch" ware has given rise to endless speculation, and some collectors have contended that he was referring to the dipped white salt glaze. However, it is clear from the above quotation that he was not. In his *Chemistry of Pottery* (London, 1837, reprinted in 1900, p. 416) Shaw went further and stated that "the *crouch-ware* was first made of common potter's clay and grit from Mole Cob, and afterwards, the grit and canmarle, by A. Wedgwood, of Burslem, in 1690." It is clear, therefore, that crouch ware contained neither pipe clay nor flint, and it is much more likely that the term related to the palish gray-bodied brown stoneware made from local Staffordshire clays, and now loosely described as Burslem stoneware. Because of Shaw's statement that the white dipped ware was made "by a very easy transition from the Crouch ware," it seemed possible that the gray core of the dipped ware was the same as that used for the crouch ware; certainly they look very similar in both color and texture. However, an analysis of their composition failed to support this theory. Two Williamsburg shards examined by the British Ceramic Research Association were shown to differ in that the dipped specimen was found to contain "a higher proportion of quartz and to be microstructurally of a coarser texture" than the Burslem stoneware fragment. Furthermore, the interior of the latter was covered with a flint slip—which, as we shall see, precluded it from dating prior to about 1720.

According to Josiah C. Wedgwood (*Staffordshire Pottery and its History,* London, n.d., p. 46), Astbury first used the Devonshire clay only as a wash or dip to whiten the surface of the ware. "Then he developed the use of the white sands of Baddeley Edge and Mow Cop [in Staffordshire on the border of Cheshire] to harden the body; and, in 1720, according to tradition, he made the really vital discovery of the value of calcined flint stones . . . to whiten and harden the clay body. . ." This statement (largely derived from Simeon Shaw) would lead us to believe that Astbury first used the Devon clay as a dip; then, when flint was introduced, he mixed it into the body, eliminating the engobe. In theory, therefore, if this were true, the white coating of the dipped ware should contain no flint. However, an analysis of four samples (one dipped, two coarse, and one regular white salt glaze), provided by the British Ceramic Research Association, revealed that all four contained flint, though that in the dipped sample was confined to the surface engobe. It is true that one analyzed fragment does not prove that all dipped white salt glaze contains flint, but it does prevent us from contending (as one might on the basis of Josiah C. Wedgwood's statement) that dipped ware necessarily predated the introduction of flint—or that after white salt glaze was fully developed, it continued to be made only by potters who eschewed the cost, trouble, and danger to life (they could contract silicosis) of using flint. On the contrary, and as archaeological evidence cited has shown, the dipped ware (with flint in the engobe) continued to be made well into the second half of the eighteenth century (see Figs. 4, 5).

Determination of the correct date for the introduction of flint as a stoneware ingredient is of considerable significance because most available evidence indicates that a solid, really white-firing body had not been achieved in Staffordshire prior to its discovery. Rebuttals, such as they are, are derived from Simeon Shaw's reference to Thomas Miles' uncertain achievement in 1685, and from Josiah Wedgwood's list of

Fig. 6. The earliest known dated piece of white salt glaze, inscribed *Mrs. Mary Sandbach her Cup anno dom 1720.* The body is off-white and contains small black flecks characteristic of the early coarse ware. Height 6 inches. *Nelson Gallery-Atkins Museum, Burnap collection.*

Fig. 7. Posset cup of white salt glaze, the body slightly flecked with black. The inscription states that the piece was made by Cornelius Toft in 1727/8. Height 6⅛ inches. *Central Museum and Art Gallery, Northampton.*

Fig. 8. Posset cup made from white stoneware of uncertain quality, marked *W.A.* on one side, and dated *1735* on the other, the inscription in brown(?) slip. Height 5 inches. This important piece was in the Earle collection in 1915, and is reproduced from the catalogue of that date.

Fig. 9. Posset cup inscribed *Mary Cowdal/ of Frolsworth ∴ 1750*, exhibiting the clean lines characteristic of the regular white stoneware of that date, but with handles that are unusually simple. Height 4⅜ inches. *British Museum.*

"Pot Works in Burslem about the year 1710 to 1715," which included Aaron Shaw as a maker of "stone & dippt white." However, Wedgwood made his list in 1765 and based it on the memories of aging potters whose recollections of the period from 1710 to 1715 could easily have been colored by events occurring in 1720, the date Shaw gave for the introduction of flint. Shaw described how, while on a journey to London in that year, Astbury's horse developed an ocular complaint, and how a tavern hostler "burned a flint stone till quite red, then he pulverized it very fine, and by blowing a little of the dust into each eye, occasioned both to discharge much matter and be greatly benefited." Observing the ease with which heated flint could be ground, and "its clayey nature when discharged in the moisture from the horse's eyes," he wondered whether it could be used to whiten his pottery (Shaw, *op. cit.*, p. 129).

Virtually the same story was related by Josiah Wedgwood in his previously cited letter to Bentley (July 19, 1777), except that he gave no credit to "a Mr. Heath of Shelton" who "brought some of the stones home with him, mix'd them with Pipe Clay, & made the first *White Flint Stone Ware.*" Wedgwood did not say anything about Mr. Heath's product being a dipped ware, but he did state unequivocally that he mixed the flint simply with pipe clay. Wedgwood also failed to give a date for Mr. Heath's revelation. However, Shaw's 1720 seems reasonable enough, particularly in view of the fact that in 1726 Thomas Benson of Staffordshire secured the first known patent for the grinding of flint. That patent stated that flint was the "chief ingredient" in making "white pots," and that the stone had previously been prepared by "pounding or breaking it dry, and afterwards sifting it through fine lawns [linen cloth], which has proved very destructive to

Fig. 10. Flask of early off-white stoneware, the body containing numerous small black flecks. This, the earliest recorded example of scratch brown on the coarse white stoneware, is decorated on the other side with a simple bird motif. Height 3⅝ inches. *British Museum.*

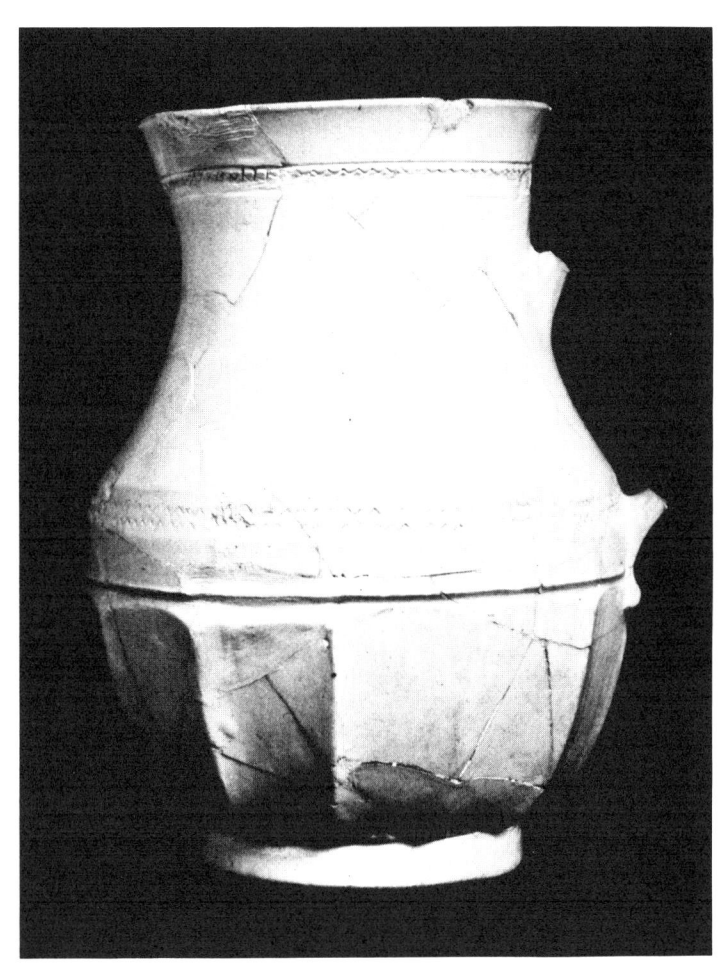

Fig. 11. An as yet unparalleled coarse white salt-glaze pitcher, decorated at the girth and rim with incised zigzag ornament, and with panels or facets on the lower body possibly emulating a metallic shape. Found near the Brush-Everard House in Williamsburg in an archaeological context dating no later than 1728. Height 6½ inches. *Colonial Williamsburg.*

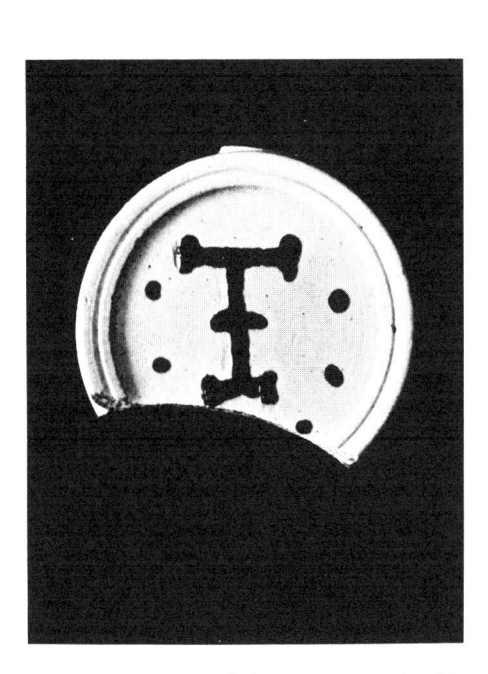

Fig. 12. Part of a flask of coarse, yellowish white stoneware, the side recessed and decorated in thick brown slip with the contemporary version of the letter J. The vessel had a very small capacity and was filled through a short, threaded mouth at the top. Found near the James Geddy House in Williamsburg in an archaeological context of c. 1770. *Colonial Williamsburg.*

Fig. 13. Pitcher and can of dark brown stoneware coated on the interior with a white salt-glazed engobe, the result paralleling Ralph Shaw's 1733 patent. In addition to the usual trailed pipe-clay lines around the outside, the pitcher is decorated with sprigged devices, including the British royal arms. These features, plus the white-slipped rim and the spot on the crest of the handle, are paralleled on the lead-glazed redwares loosely attributed to John Astbury and to Samuel Bell; c. 1740. Pitcher height, 4⅜ inches. Can height, 2⅝ inches. *Colonial Williamsburg.*

mankind" (Jewitt, *The Ceramic Art of Great Britain,* London, 1878, Vol. I, p. 109). We may conclude, therefore, that the dry grinding of flint had been practiced for some years prior to 1726. Actual ceramic documentation is provided by the Hanley museum's 1723 mug (Fig. 3), whose white engobe has been found to contain flint. Potentially more important, though not yet tested for flint, is the two-handled posset cup in the Burnap collection dated 1720 (Fig. 6). The cup is of the rather coarse, black-flecked and off-white salt glaze frequently found in archaeological contexts of the second decade of the eighteenth century, and its incised inscription reads: *Mrs. Mary Sandbach her Cup anno dom 1720.* It thus proves that if, as Simeon Shaw suggests, the use of the flint and pipe-clay engobe began in 1720 and preceded the manufacture of solid white salt glaze, it did so by only a matter of months.

The number of recorded white salt-glaze pieces (dipped, coarse, or refined) bearing dates in the 1720's—or in the 1730's, for that matter—is very small. The 1723 mug in the Hanley museum has already been discussed. Next comes a flask in the British Museum, decorated with a bird in scratch brown on one side and marked *IM 1724* on the other (Fig. 10). The ware is similar to that of the Sandbach cup, off-white and flecked with black. Also decorated in scratch brown (incised decoration filled with iron-oxide slip in the same manner as cobalt was later used to make scratch blue) is a perfume bottle inscribed *1727 S·S.* Unfortunately, the present whereabouts of this piece is not known to me, but it was described by Charles Luxmoore (*Saltglaze with the Notes of a Collector,* Exeter, 1924, p. 62) as "cream-coloured," thus strongly suggesting that the body was of the coarse intermediate ware.

Another posset cup rather similar in form to the Sandbach example, in the collection of the Central Museum and Art Gallery in Northampton, is dated 1727 (Fig. 7). The full inscription reads, on one side: *C martha Barlar T/1727:8,* and on the other, *WB marthar Barlar CT/Cornelius Toft 1727/8 hand,* the lettering incised without coloring into a white body containing small black flecks. Next comes yet another posset cup with a heavily cordoned and chevron-rouletted body marked *W.A.* on one side and *1735* on the other, the lettering applied in brown slip without previous incising (Fig. 8). This cup differs from its predecessors in that its handles are much less securely anchored to the body, and exhibit the pinched and pressed lower terminals characteristic of white salt glaze in the mid-century (see Fig. 4, *right*). Although I have yet to see this type of handle in use before the 1730's, it does not follow that simpler handles were thenceforth abandoned. There is, for example, a fine posset cup in the British Museum, with relatively simple handles, yet bearing the incised inscription *Mary Cowdal/ of Frolsworth ∴ 1750* (Fig. 9). Frolesworth, incidentally, is a village in Leicestershire close to the Staffordshire border. Simple though the cup's handles are, they differ from the early examples in that they are not wedged or tooled tightly into the body at the base of the loops. Furthermore, regardless of its handles, the Mary Cowdal cup could hardly be mistaken for an early piece, for the body lacks the fussy cordoning and chevron, or zigzag, ornament so characteristic of its ancestors.

Three important examples of the early, coarse, off-white salt glaze have been found in recent Williamsburg excavations, the best documented being a pitcher decorated with incised zigzag lines, and with the lower body faceted (as are some of the earliest salt-glaze teapots), excavated near the Brush-Everard House in a context that could date no later than 1728 (Fig. 11). Small, but no less interesting, is half of a thin flask with a threaded mouth, the side decorated with the brown-slipped initial *I* (Fig. 12). Such objects are usually described as powder flasks, but as this one would hold no more than enough to prime one pan, it may be more logical to think of it as a perfume flask. Nevertheless, it was found near the workshop of James Geddy I, gunsmith and brass founder (see ANTIQUES, January 1969, p. 106). The third new find is also from the same property: a seemingly unparalleled teapot coated above its girth with a thin iron-oxide slip (Fig. 4, *center*). Although found in a context of about 1730-1740, it seems likely that the teapot was manufactured in the early 1720's and that it may parallel the "5 stone Tea Potts" listed in Nathaniel Harrison's 1728 inventory.

Both the flask and the teapot are markedly yellow in color and the ware is distinctly granular in fracture. It seems reasonable to deduce that both features were the products of underfiring. A test sample refired in the salt-glaze kiln at the Williamsburg Pottery, at a temperature close to 2300° F (higher than would have been reached in the eighteenth century), lost its yellowish color and emerged as hard and as white as the refined ware. Another experiment reproduced the thick and sometimes crazed glaze common to many early pieces, an effect achieved by greatly increasing the time that the ware was exposed to the salt. Thus it would appear that the *coarse* ware was not a consciously different class of white salt glaze, but merely an interim product manufactured while potters were experimenting with body component proportions, with the time and quantity of salting, and with kiln temperatures.

It would be cheating to leave the genesis of white salt glaze without saying a word or two about a variant which, though not in the mainstream of the story, certainly added useful punctuation. In 1733 Ralph Shaw of Burslem obtained a patent for the making of "a curious ware . . . whose outside will be a true chocolate colour, striped with white, and the inside white, much resembling the brown China ware, and glazed with salt" (Simeon Shaw, *op. cit.,* p. 146). Figure 13 shows two examples of this ware in Colonial Williamsburg's furnishings collection, while Figure 14 illustrates fragments found in Williamsburg excavations. The shards clearly show that the body of the ware is dark brown and that the white interior is an engobe—instead of the other way round, as both museums and collectors have so frequently supposed.

More important to the history of salt glaze than the 1733 patent was the suit brought against it three years later by Ralph Shaw's competitors. Simeon Shaw tells us that "witnesses proved Astbury's invention and prior usage, of the practice," *i.e.,* of lining the body with an engobe (*ibid.,* p. 147). In his decision, the judge told the plaintiffs to "make whatever kinds of Pots you please," and declared Shaw's patent void. In doing so he unwittingly supported Astbury's claim to the discovery of the potential of ground flint over Wedgwood's candidate, "Mr. Heath of Shelton." Unfortunately, no dated examples fitting Ralph Shaw's description are known from the three years of his patent's validity. There is, however, a privately owned mug of the same general character, bearing the name *John Shaw* and the date *1742*—six years, according to Simeon Shaw, after Ralph and his family moved to France to begin again in a less hostile atmosphere.

---

In the interest of brevity, acknowledgments
are listed at the end of the article's second part,
which will appear next month.

---

Fig. 14. Rim fragments from a dark brown stoneware mug coated on the interior with a thick white salt-glazed engobe (see Fig. 13). Found in a Williamsburg archaeological context of c. 1750. *Colonial Williamsburg.*

# The rise and fall of
# English white salt-glazed stoneware  Part II

BY IVOR NOËL-HUME, *Director, department of archaeology, Colonial Williamsburg*

---
Part I of this two-part article appeared
in ANTIQUES for February 1970.

---

IN THE 1720's, when white salt glaze was in the process of development, the ware had very little competition. Contemporary English stonewares were relatively clumsy, delftware could not be potted sufficiently thinly (without chipping) to compete with the increasingly popular Oriental porcelain, and the porcelain itself was still too costly for the poorer households and too elegant for common use. White salt glaze, on the other hand, achieved both thinness and durability. Although enamelers' efforts to embellish it with polychrome *chinoiserie* were never very successful, the hitherto unparalleled plasticity of the highly refractory white salt-glaze body enabled its potters to emulate not only porcelain shapes but also those of the metalsmiths, to which they and their blockmakers added their own details, notably in handle terminals, spouts, plate-rim decoration, and relief body modeling on mugs, tureens, sauceboats, pitchers, and teapots.

In the period when white salt glaze was getting into its stride (c. 1720-1740), John and Thomas Astbury, Ralph Shaw, Thomas Wedgwood, and others were developing new ceramic fabrics that could be potted as thinly as salt glaze, and which, when lead glazed, provided relatively inexpensive alternatives to the stark whiteness of the stoneware. Among them were the lead-glazed redwares pioneered by the Astburys and by Samuel Bell of Newcastle-under-Lyme, agate wares in which red- and yellow-burning clays were blended to create a marblelike appearance beneath the glaze, and a red- to purple-bodied ware coated with a thick black glaze, popularly though not always correctly known as Jackfield ware. These and other innovations provided new colors, but the potters were generally content to retain the established white salt-glaze shapes.

By mid-century white salt glaze was at its zenith and its

Fig. 1a. White salt-glaze plate reflecting British popular support for Frederick the Great after his victory at Rossbach on November 5, 1757. The *Boston Gazette* (November 13, 1758) advertised "White Stone, Prussian & Basket work'd Plates and Dishes," and it is likely that they continued to be sold throughout the remainder of the Seven Years' War. Diameter 9 5/16 inches. *Except as noted, illustrations are from Colonial Williamsburg.*

Fig. 1b. Cream-color *King of Prussia* plate; clouded lead glazes in brown, yellow, and green on the front, and mottled manganese on the back. The plate exhibits the same mold idiosyncrasies as does the salt-glaze example shown in Fig. 1a. Diameter 9 1/16 inches. *British Museum.*

Fig. 2. Plate-rim shards in barley, queen's, and milled designs. *Left:* Above, barley in salt glaze, and below in Wedgwood's green-glaze cream-color ware. *Center:* Queen's shape, similar to the preceding but with the barley panels removed; above in white salt glaze, and below in creamware. *Right:* The raised, milled edge in salt glaze, and below in lead-glazed tortoise shell on cream-color earthenware. The green barley cannot date before 1759 or the queen's shape apparently before c. 1765, while the milled edge seems to have been popular in the period from 1755 to 1765. The pin shown here and elsewhere measures one inch.

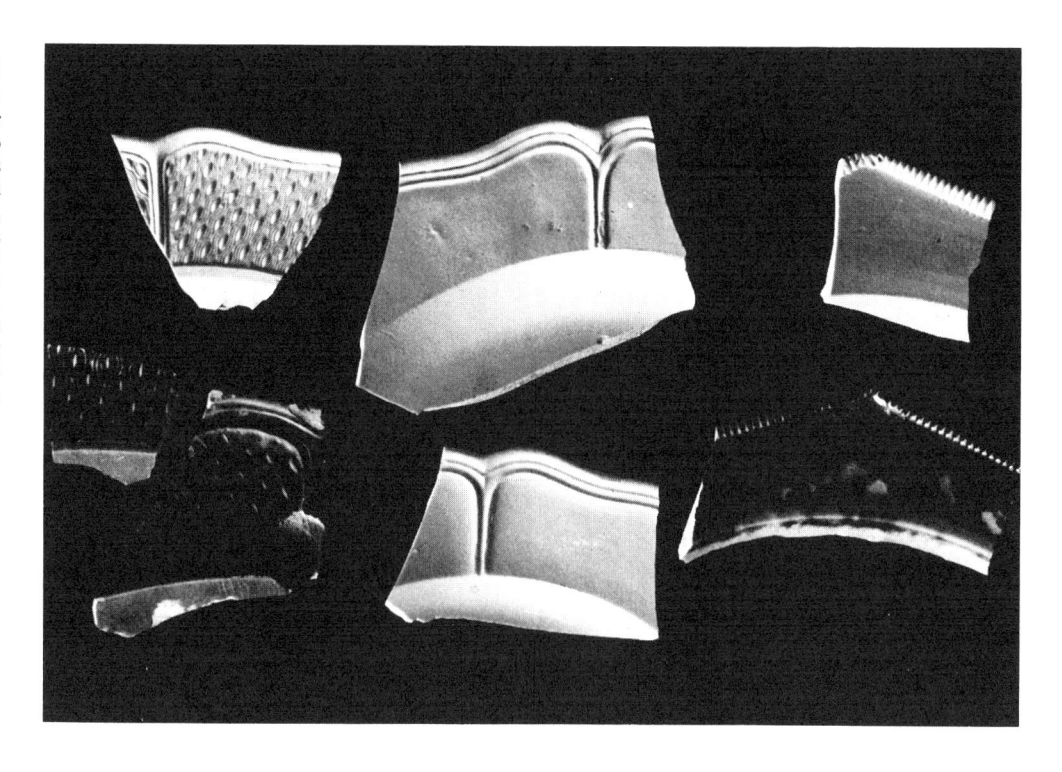

manufacturers were asking themselves: what next? It was true that the ware's cold whiteness could be relieved by painting it in enamel colors or by adding incised scratch-blue decoration, but both were time-consuming operations and the former required skilled workers, always in short supply. What was needed was a new body whose ornament could be molded and which, at the same time, could take on new color through glazing or by means of pigments beneath the glaze that could be applied by relatively untalented decorators. The salt-glaze potters' solution was not as revolutionary as we have sometimes been led to believe; they simply took their white salt-glaze body, fired it to biscuit in an oxidizing atmosphere, then dipped it in a fluid lead glaze, and fired it again in the kilns used for lead-glazed earthenware. The result eventually became the creamware that was to dominate the Staffordshire trade from about 1765 until at least 1780, when it began to share the utilitarian market with pearlware (see ANTIQUES, March 1969, p. 390).

Just how early cream-color earthenware began to be made is still hotly debated, but there is evidence in the shape of a bowl marked E*B *1743* that a lead-glazed yellow body was being made by the early 1740's. Up to that time lead glazes were dusted onto the green ware in powdered (galena) form; but around 1740 Enoch Booth of Tunstall —probably the E*B of the 1743 bowl—developed a fluid glaze into which the once-fired ware could be dipped. It was a step that brought lead glazing back to the prominence it had enjoyed prior to the invention of English stoneware.

According to a bill quoted by Donald Towner in his *English Cream-coloured Earthenware* (New York, 1957, p. 6), Thomas Whieldon was selling tortoise-shell and cream-color plates as early as November 1749, while Simeon Shaw gave credit to the Warburton family of Hot Lane, Cobridge, for having made, in 1751, "the last improvements of Cream Colour (prior to those of the late Mr. Wedgwood)." Be that as it may, creamware in shapes developed by Josiah Wedgwood did not appear until about 1763, while archaeological studies have so far failed to establish the presence of its predecessors, the tortoise-shell- and clouded-glaze wares, in American homes before the mid-1750's.

The contention that the earliest creamware body was identical to that used for white salt glaze has sometimes been disputed—probably because the mixture was later changed to include feldspathic Cornish stone. However, seemingly irrefutable evidence was provided by A. H. Church in his *English Earthenware* (London, 1904, p. 87). There he described a large creamware dish enameled in red on its back, signed by Enoch Wood in 1826: "The dish was made at Etruria by Messrs. Wedgwood and Bentley, the first year after Messrs. Wedgwood and Bentley removed from Burslem to Etruria [1770] . . . I preserve this to show the quality of common cream ware before the introduction of growan or Cornwall stone. This body is formed of flint and clay only, the same as used for salt-glazed ware at that time, and flint and lead only instead of a salt-glaze, and it is fired in the usual and accustomed way and manner as usual for glazed tea-pots, tortoiseshell, mottled, and agate, and cauliflower, etc."

In an attempt to determine whether, if fired to a higher temperature in the reducing atmosphere of a salt-glaze kiln, the cream-color body would indeed resemble the eighteenth-century white stoneware, a creamware plate fragment (c. 1770) was broken in two and the lead glaze removed from one shard which was then refired to a temperature of 2300° F. in the salt-glaze kiln at the Williamsburg Pottery. The result was an excellent piece of white salt glaze similar in color to the contemporary white stoneware—but it had shrunk by no less than twelve per cent. This revelation came as a considerable shock, for it seemed to deal a serious blow to an otherwise well-founded belief that when the salt-glaze potters began to make cream-color earthenware, they used the old salt-glaze molds. Indeed, Simeon Shaw (*History of the Staffordshire Potteries,* Hanley, 1829, reprinted in London, 1900, p. 165) was quite clear on that score. "There are specimens," he wrote, "of Table Plates

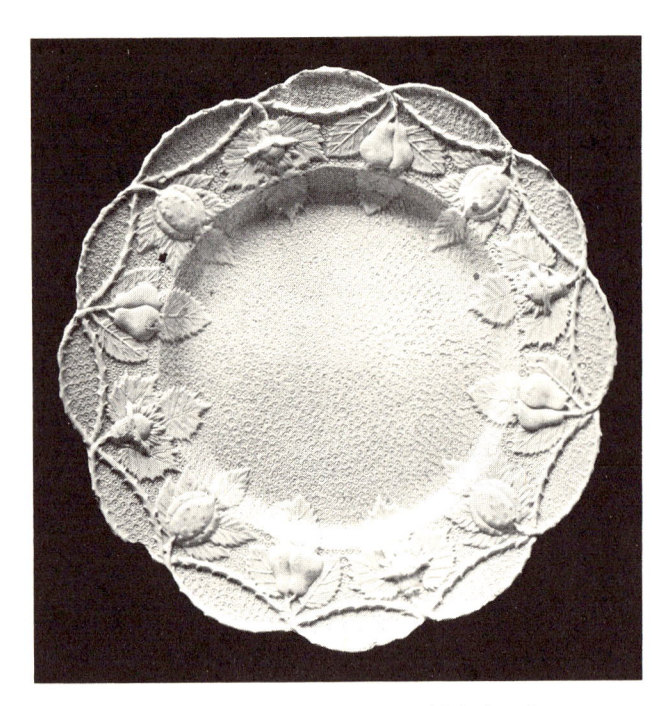

Fig. 3a. White salt-glaze plate decorated with fruit and leaves in high relief and with multiple impressed circles and dots, the latter usually associated with green- and clouded-glaze cream-color wares. C. 1755-1765. Diameter 8 11/16 inches. *Author's collection.*

Fig. 3b. Green-glaze cream-color earthenware plate with fruit and ring-and-dot decoration similar in character to that of the salt-glaze examples shown in Fig. 3a. Found in a Williamsburg context of c. 1765-1770. Diameter 9 1/4 inches.

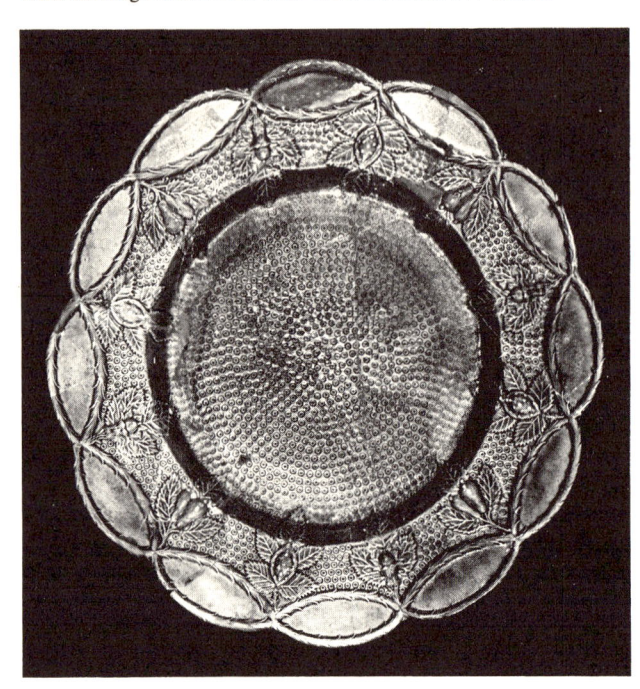

and Fruit Dishes, made of flint and clay, in old moulds of the White Stone ware, which after being dipped in the lead and flint glaze for washing the insides of Tortoiseshell, and fired in the old lead glaze ovens, form exactly and identically the first *Cream Coloured* Pottery."

R. L. Hobson in the British Museum's *Catalogue of the Collection of English Pottery* (London, 1903, pp. 188, 198) illustrated a clouded-glaze plate with a molded border commemorating Frederick the Great's contribution to the Seven Years' War (Fig. 1b) and stated that it was from the same mold as another in white salt glaze whose measurements were identical. The British Museum's clouded-glaze plate is certainly from the same mold as another salt-glaze example in the collection of Colonial Williamsburg (Fig. 1a), and the latter is only a quarter of an inch larger. Yet, on the basis of the recent experiment, casting the cream color and the salt glaze in the same mold should have resulted in a salt-glaze plate at least an inch larger than the creamware after both were fired.

Salt-glaze table plates (as opposed to dishes having diameters of 10 inches and up) generally measure 9½, 9¼, 8½, and 7½ inches in diameter—sizes not far removed from those listed in Hartley, Greens, and Co.'s Leeds catalogue (1783), which offered queen's, feather, shell-edge, and royal pattern "Table Plates, 9½ Inches, Soup ditto same Size, Smaller ditto called Twisters, 6, 7, 8 and 9 Inches." After measuring literally dozens of comparable plates in white salt glaze, clouded-glaze cream color, and plain creamware, I am forced to the conclusion that the test shard's dramatic shrinkage was caused by the firing of the Williamsburg Pottery kiln at a considerably higher temperature than the eighteenth-century salt-glaze potters used. Support comes from Dr. A. E. Dodd of the British Ceramic Research Association, who states that "salt-glazed stoneware can be achieved as low as 1100° C. (2012° F.) depending upon the alumina content and certain other features of the clay concerned," a temperature no higher than would have been needed for firing good creamware biscuit.

Had shrinkage been such that the new ware required new molds, we would have to assume that the potters made a conscious decision to continue with old patterns rather than to offer the public new designs in the new ware. Such an argument is readily assailed when we recall that when the first potters began making the plain yellow ware (queen's ware, cream color, or creamware) they did not, with rare exceptions, use the old patterns, but instead followed Wedgwood's lead in removing the barley-rim decoration from a once-popular salt-glaze design to create what came to be known as the queen's pattern (Fig. 2).

When Wedgwood ended his partnership with Whieldon in 1759, he had only recently developed an even green variety of the fluid lead glaze with which to cover the cream-color body, and it was to produce this new green ware that he first set up in business on his own (Fig. 3b). The ware continued to be made throughout the 1760's, most of it in old salt-glaze patterns. Thus we have it in the green in the dot, diaper, and basket; the barley; bead and reel; and variations on elaborate fruit patterns for plates and pickle leaves—all with their salt-glaze parallels (Figs. 2, 3b, 4, 5). The same is true of the clouded- and tortoiseshell-glaze plates, as well as of similarly glazed teapots and related hollow wares (Figs. 1b, 2, 4, 5). It was not, however, an entirely one-way street, for designs allegedly created for creamware (*e.g.* the queen's, featheredge, and royal patterns: Figs. 2, 6, 7) occasionally occur in white salt glaze, adding considerable weight to the argument that the molds were interchangeable. In this connection it is interesting to note that the largest number of featheredge salt-glaze plates yet found in Williamsburg was discovered in a well shaft believed to have been filled around 1765—some three or four years before the creamware it was copying seems to have reached Virginia. The first records of queen's ware reaching the colony are found in inventories and advertisements of 1769, the same year that it appeared among the domestic inventories of Providence, Rhode Island (see ANTIQUES, October 1968, p. 574). Nevertheless, we know that Wedgwood was shipping cream-color mugs to Boston as early as 1764, for in that year he filled an order from "a very careful Man, who has sent us Cash to pay for them" (Thomas Bentley to Wedgwood, September 25, 1764). The order read as follows:

4 dozen of flint white dishes
6 dozen pineapple teapots
5 dozen Colly flower cannisters
6 dozen white flint mugs of round sizes
4 dozen cream coloured do. do.
2 dozen small muggs cream coloured, pencilled
10 dozen small ware of several colours such as pickle leaves
2 dozen Black Coffee pots of several sizes
2 do pineapple coffee pots do. do.

It is significant that the bulk of the order related to the so-called Whieldon-Wedgwood wares—and to white salt glaze. Very few collectors associate Wedgwood with the latter, and it sometimes comes as a shock to discover that until the early 1770's white stoneware was one of his major production lines. In 1772, when experimenting with the body and glaze that would later become pearlware, Wedgwood wrote: ". . . if it is not superior to our white stoneware in whiteness, it would be esteemed a degradation of *cream-colour* into *white stone ware*. . ." (Wedgwood to Bentley, April 18, 1772).

It is safe to assume that whereas creamware straddled the period of the American Revolution, plain white salt glaze ceased to be imported when the war began, and pearlware started to arrive soon after it ended. On July 11, 1776, Joseph Stansbury of Philadelphia inserted a long advertisement in the *Pennsylvania Evening Post* offering: "Plain, blue and white and enamelled white stone" teapots, sugar dishes, tea and coffee cups and saucers, half-pint bowls and saucers, and bowls of several sizes. The references to "blue and white" are certainly to white salt glaze decorated with incised scratch-blue ornament, a ware frequently encountered in archaeological contexts of Revolutionary date (Fig. 9). The quality of the decoration was rarely as fine as that of the mid-century, but it was far superior to that on a coarser variety of white (or off-white) stoneware used for pitchers, mugs, and chamber pots from

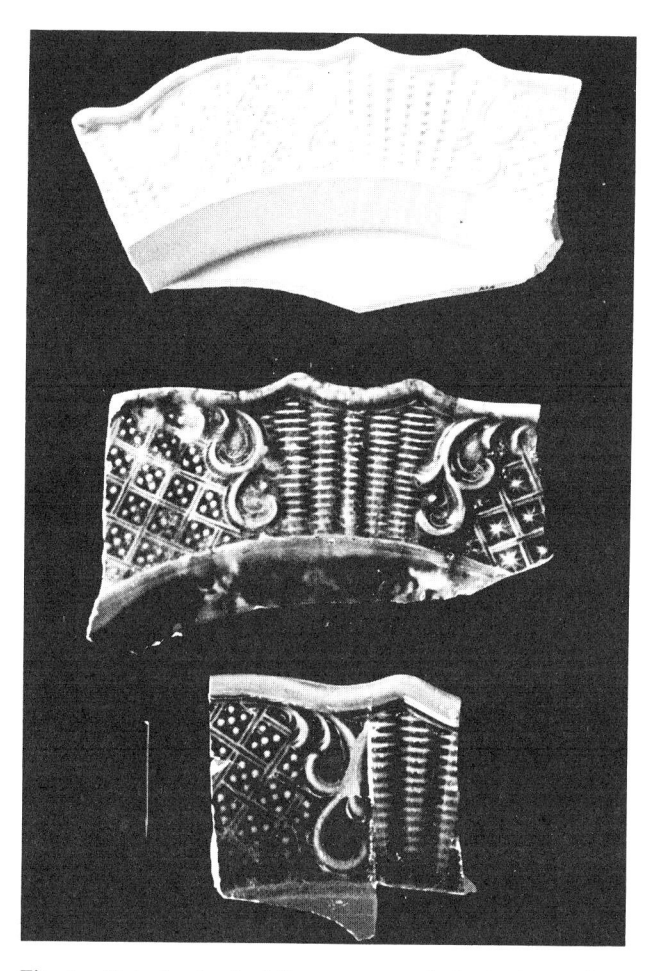

Fig. 4. Plate-rim shards of the commonest of all salt-glaze designs, the dot-diaper-and-basket pattern. It is here used on white salt glaze, clouded-glaze cream-color earthenware, and the green-glaze ware developed by Wedgwood in 1759. The original salt-glaze pattern may date as early as 1745.

Fig. 5. Plate-rim shards of the bead-and-reel pattern, a silver style common in the mid-eighteenth century; seen here in white salt glaze, tortoise shell, green glaze, and plain creamware. The fragments span the years from c. 1755 to 1775.

the 1760's to around 1790 (see ANTIQUES, December 1965, p. 834, and October 1966, p. 520). The inferior ware, often called debased scratch blue, was made in imitation of the Rhenish gray stonewares so widely marketed in England and her colonies in the first half of the eighteenth century and specifically excluded from the British embargoes on foreign pottery imposed in 1672 (see ANTIQUES, September 1967, p. 353). The debased scratch blue left much of its cobalt on the surface of the ware, giving the exterior a bluish gray cast akin to that of the Rhenish products. In some instances the British potters did not bother to use the white salt-glaze body formula but made do with local clays that fired to a pale gray. This debasement of the once delicate scratch blue represented the last white salt-glaze innovation, one that was itself in decline by the time the American Revolution was resolved. It is evident, however, that the British potters took a philosophical view of the outcome, manfully smiling through their tears to welcome a new foreign market. The proof is provided by a debased scratch-blue mug in the Colonial Williamsburg collection embellished with a crude rendering of the Great Seal of the United States (post September 16, 1782) in place of the usual cipher or portrait of George III.

Covering the salt-glaze body with solid blue was a technique originally borrowed from the Rhineland, where it was applied to the vessels in slip form. According to tradition, the stoneware and porcelain manufacturer William Littler of Longton Hall developed a blue dip into which the ware could be immersed, a discovery reputedly made about 1750. It has often been contended that the so-called Littler's blue was applied after the vessels had been fired in the salt-glaze kiln, but experiments made at the Williamsburg Pottery have shown that there was no need for that extra trouble and expense. Indeed, there was really no need for the Williamsburg experiments either—if only we could have brought ourselves to admit that Simeon Shaw sometimes knew whereof he wrote. In his *History of the Staffordshire Potteries* (p. 168) he stated that, using "Mr. Astbury's method of *washing* or *dipping,* Messrs. Littler and Wedgwood first introduced a compound of very fusible materials —of certain proportions of ground zaffre with the flint and the clay that composed the body of the pottery; mixed with a determined quantity of water . . . Into this liquid the vessels were dipped, while in the state of clay very little dried, and absorbing the water, received a very thin coating of the materials in solution, which when dried and fired in the salt glaze oven, appeared of a fine glossy surface, free from those minute inequalities observable on all the Pottery glazed with salt only."

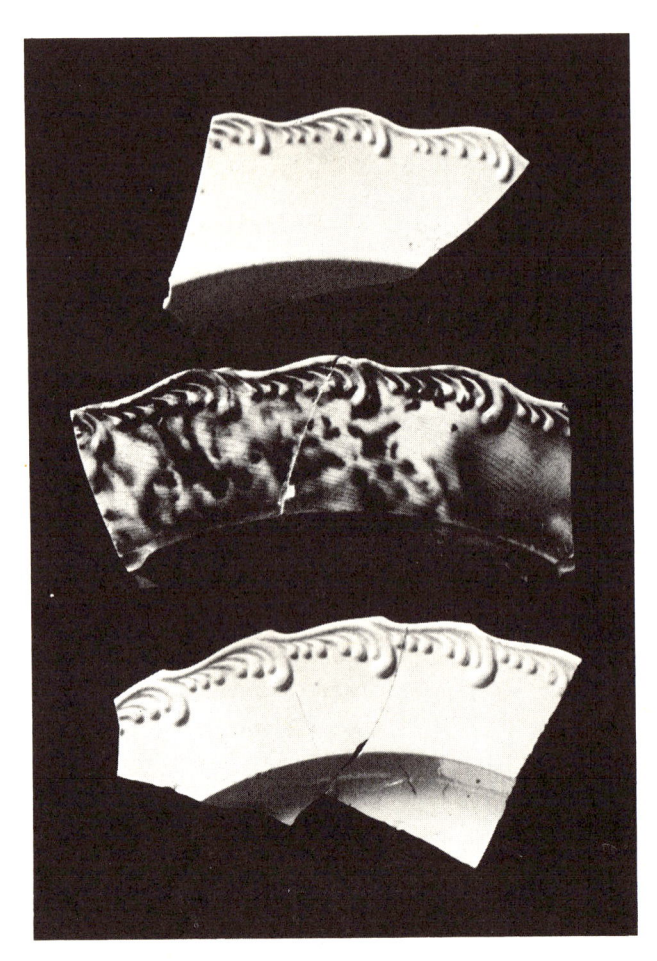

Fig. 6. Plate-rim shards of the featheredge pattern, seen here on white salt glaze, tortoise-shell-glaze cream-color earthenware, and the plain creamware from which it was borrowed. C. 1765-1770.

Fig. 7 Variations on the royal pattern. *Top:* The shape that correctly bears that name: a creamware soup-plate fragment transfer printed for Phillip and Anne Barraud of Williamsburg, who were married in 1783. *Center*: A popular white salt-glaze plate form of c. 1755-1765, with an edge comparable to that of contemporary silver and pewter, but also like the creamware royal pattern. *Bottom*: A salt-glaze plate rim akin to the royal-pattern creamware; essentially the same as the center example, but without the raised floral decoration. This shard was found in a context dating no earlier than 1770.

Fig. 8. Sauceboats in white salt glaze and green-glaze cream-color earthenware, both with bead-and-reel rims, and with wall panels divided as are those on the rims of plates in the queen's pattern. Similar design features occur on silver of the 1750's. Both pieces were found in Williamsburg, the salt glaze in a context of c. 1770-1775, and the green-glaze example in another of c. 1780.

Although I knew of no recorded examples, it seemed reasonable to expect that if Littler's blue was a popular color for salt-glaze teaware, it might also have been used on creamware—providing the glaze could be made to mature at the lower creamware temperature. The conjecture became fact when a fragmentary cream-color teapot coated with blue glaze was found near Wetherburn's Tavern in Williamsburg, proving that yet another salt-glaze innovation was passed on to its successor.

The terminal date for the importation of white salt glaze may have been many years earlier than that of its disappearance from American homes. Occasional shards turn up in archaeological contexts of the 1820's, but, as I have suggested, it is unlikely that much, if any, of the plain white ware was imported after the Revolution. That does not mean, however, that it had by then ceased to be made in England. We know, for example, that John Graham Jr. of Burslem was making "white stone, and enamelled white and cream earthenware" in 1787 (see ANTIQUES, March 1969, p. 391). In the absence of evidence to the contrary, it seems probable that such mundane items as chamber pots, close-stool pans, wash basins, and pharmaceutical ointment pots continued to be made in this ware until about 1800. Its decline was dictated not solely by the fickleness of fashion, but also by a desire on the part of the potters to be rid of a ware whose high-temperature firing, coupled with the destructive qualities of the salt, made kiln life short and the replacement of kiln furniture both frequent and costly. As James E. Maloney of the Williamsburg Pottery (one of the very few factories making white salt glaze today) has pointed out, lead-glazed wares such as creamware and pearlware were infinitely kinder to kilns and their equipment.

As I stated at the outset, the role of white salt glaze in British ceramic history was both long and complex, and I am all too aware that I have made numerous generalizations that could have been qualified and expanded into articles on their own. I have said nothing about the development of transfer printing, or about the relationship between salt-glaze and early creamware enameling; nor, for that matter, have I discussed the plethora of factories from Devonshire to London, and London to Glasgow, where white salt glaze was manufactured. My excuse is simply that I have already been allowed much more than my fair share of space.

---

I am greatly indebted to Mr. Maloney for his many experiments undertaken to reproduce the eighteenth-century salt-glaze fabrics, as well as to Arnold Mountford, of the City Museum at Stoke-on-Trent, for analytical assistance and for the provision of illustrations; also to Colonial Williamsburg; to the Central Museum and Art Gallery, Northampton; to Hugh Tait, of the British Museum; and to Ross E. Taggart, of the Nelson Gallery-Atkins Museum, Kansas City, for the use of photographs of objects in their collections. I am also grateful to J. Palin Thorley of Williamsburg for sharing knowledge acquired through many years of creamware manufacturing.

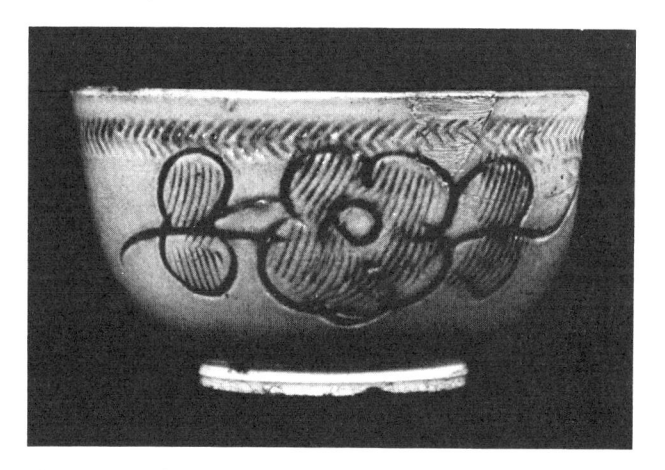

---

Fig. 9. Scratch-blue salt-glaze tea bowl of a simple type often encountered in contexts of c. 1765-1780. Excavated in Williamsburg. Diameter 3 inches.

# English Earthenware with Dutch Painting

By Bernard Rackham

*Keeper of the Department of Ceramics, Victoria and Albert Museum*

IN THE history of pottery, as in political history, certain periods stand out as times of great change. Such a period in Europe was the second half of the eighteenth century. During the centuries immediately preceding, the dominant type of Continental pottery had been a tin-glazed or enameled earthenware, known in certain of its national variations as maiolica, faïence, or delft. About the middle of the eighteenth century, however, a new type of pottery was being perfected in England, namely, the fine, lead-glazed, white-bodied earthenware known, from the pale yellowish color of its glaze, as "cream-colored earthenware," or, more simply, as "creamware." To his improvement and commercial exploitation of this class of ware, more than to anything else, Josiah Wedgwood owed his great reputation as a master potter.

So obvious, from both utilitarian and hygienic points of view, were the advantages of this creamware over the tin-enameled earthenwares, liable as these latter were to unsightly chipping, that the public quickly bestowed their favor on the newer product. Thus, English creamware soon commanded a ready sale, not only in home markets, but also on the Continent, where its way had, to some extent, been prepared by the trade in Staffordshire salt-glaze ware, which had been at the height of its success as an article of commerce during the fifth and sixth decades of the eighteenth century. There can be no doubt that the English wares mentioned in advertisements and other records of that time as being sold in France and Holland were salt-glaze stonewares, which must have commended themselves as a cheap and excellent substitute for porcelain.

*Fig. 1* — ENGLISH PLATE WITH DUTCH DECORATION
Portraits of William V, Prince of Orange, and Princess Frederica Sophia Wilhelmina. Unmarked.
*In the Victoria and Albert Museum*

Salt-glaze, however, suffered from the disadvantages of brittleness and of liability to crack when suddenly heated; whereas lead-glazed creamware was known to combine the attractions of neat, cleanly appearance, with comparative freedom from the serious drawbacks of salt-glaze. In the hands of such enterprising business men as Wedgwood in Staffordshire, and the proprietors of the Leeds pottery in Yorkshire, creamware quickly made headway in Continental markets. The results, in almost all countries, were artistically regrettable. The native tin-glazed wares, with their gay coloring and vigorous designs, were crowded out of existence by the imports from England; while their makers, in most instances, saved themselves from financial extinction only by adapting their factories to the production of lead-glazed wares in imitation of the English — under such names as "faïence fine," "Steingut," "steengoed," or "steen," and "faïence anglaise."

The Delft potters suffered as severely as their fellows in other countries. The blue-and-white and polychrome delft survived only as peasant pottery, *boerendelftsch*, for sale to country purchasers. In fashionable circles and town markets, the exquisitely painted *delft-doré*, and other superior classes of tin-glazed ware, fell from favor. The enamel-painters of Delft who had been engaged in the decoration of these wares were mostly thrown out of employment. Some, however, found occupation as painters of the English wares imported "in the white"; for, while English pottery was esteemed, English decorations were too austere in their plainness to suit all Dutch customers. Thus some of the muffle-kilns at

October, 1929

30

*Fig. 2 —* ENGLISH TEAPOT WITH DUTCH DECORATION
Portraits of the Prince and Princess of Orange. Probably Leeds.
*In the Victoria and Albert Museum*

*Fig. 3 —* ENGLISH TUREEN WITH DUTCH DECORATION
The Prince and Princess of Orange, and an orange tree. Unmarked.
*In the Victoria and Albert Museum*

Delft were kept busy covering the foreign pieces with Dutch designs, wrought in popular patterns and gay colors.*

Examples of these Dutch-enameled English wares are fairly numerous. The blank pieces were supplied by several English manufacturers. Many are unmarked, and their attribution to a particular firm, or even to a specific place of origin, is risky, in view of the fact that the same shapes and molded details were employed in different factories. Among marked pieces, however, the names most commonly found are those of Turner of Lane End, near Stoke-on-Trent, in Staffordshire; Heath, also of Staffordshire; the Herculaneum Pottery, Liverpool (opened in 1796 — on the site now occupied by the Herculaneum Dock — and named in emulation of Wedgwood's famous Etruria); and Sewells and Donkin of St. Anthony's, near Newcastle-on-Tyne. Some items may be attributed, with tolerable certainty, to the Leeds pottery. A plate in private possession in England bears, im-

---
* These colors are, of course, applied entirely over the glaze. — *Ed.*

*Fig. 4 —* ENGLISH SOUP TUREEN WITH DUTCH DECORATION
Portraits of William V, Prince of Orange. Unmarked.
*In the Victoria and Albert Museum*

pressed, an unidentified mark WHITENING. The majority of wares of this class may be assigned to the end of the eighteenth, or the first decade of the nineteenth, century.

The colors used by the Dutch enamelers are a dominant iron-red, green, yellow, and black, with — less often — grayish blue and pinkish crimson. The decoration is sometimes confined to bunches or sprays of flowers rendered in a summary but not unattractive manner. More often, flowers or formal borders are subsidiary to pictorial or allegorical designs, as a rule accompanied by titles or longer inscriptions. A large group is made up of wares with patriotic motives — portraits of William V, Prince of Orange, with or without his wife, Frederica Sophia Wilhelmina of Prussia, niece of Frederick the Great; or orange trees laden with fruit. An unmarked soup plate in the Victoria and Albert Museum (*Fig. 1*) shows busts of the Prince and Princess, with the initials PVOR (for Prins van Oranje) and FSW, and a lighted candle between them. Below appears the

*Fig. 5 — ENGLISH PLATE WITH DUTCH DECORATION*
*Extreme Unction.* Unmarked.
*In the Victoria and Albert Museum*

*Fig. 6 — ENGLISH PLATE WITH DUTCH DECORATION*
*Confession.* Mark TURNER (impressed).
*In the Victoria and Albert Museum*

legend: *ik brand Ligt voor de Pruis zyn nigt En ook voor de Oranje spruit. Die het niet wil zien die blaast het uit.* (I burn a light for the Prussian's niece and also for the Orange sprout. He who will not see it blows it out.)

A teapot (*Fig. 2*), probably from Leeds, in the same museum, has similar portraits, with these legends: on one side, *Siet wat hier van agteren staat* (See what is here on the back); on the other, *bid voor ū vorst wenst hem gen kwaad* (pray for your prince, wish him no harm). Similar political allusions appear on a tureen (*Fig. 3*) with portraits of the same persons, and a symbolical orange tree between them, accompanied by the initials PWDV (for Prins Willem de Vijfde). On the reverse, the tureen is inscribed *Nu ziet man wier Als in oude daagen De Oranje Stam weer vrugte draagen.* (Now we see the Orange stem bear fruit again as in the old days.) A large soup tureen and stand (*Fig. 4*), also at South Kensington (in the Schreiber collection), has portraits of William V. of Orange and Frederick the Great of Prussia, in medallions flanked by lions, ships, and military trophies.

Many of the subjects are of a religious character. There is, first, the series of the Seven Sacraments. In the Victoria and Albert Museum are two plates, one unmarked, the other, with the mark of Turner's factory in Staffordshire, bearing the respective subjects *Het Oliesel* (Extreme Unction) and *Den Biegt* (Confession) (*Figs. 5 and 6*). The plate marked WHITENING, above referred to, has the subject *De Communie* (Holy Communion).

Another series is that illustrating the parable of the Prodigal Son, the figures being dressed in eighteenth-century costume. Three examples are in

*Fig. 7 — ENGLISH PLATE WITH DUTCH DECORATION*
*The Prodigal's Departure.* Mark, L (impressed).
*In private possession*

32

*Fig. 8* — ENGLISH PLATE WITH DUTCH DECORATION
*The Madonna of Kevelaer.* Mark: HEATH (impressed).
*In the possession of the author*

*Fig. 9* — ENGLISH PLATE WITH DUTCH DECORATION
Dutch verses of welcome. Mark: HERCULANEUM (impressed).
*In the Ryksmuseum, Amsterdam*

private possession in the United States. One of these (*Fig. 7*), entitled *Den Verlooren Zoon*, shows the prodigal, dressed as a fop of the end of the eighteenth century, receiving his patrimony from his father, who sits, in embroidered dressing-gown and full-bottomed wig, beside a table, on which reposes a bag labeled *50 Gulden;* another of the trio, *Zyn Berouw* (His Repentence), represents the young man welcomed by his father on his return home. (*See Cover.*)

A plate with the mark HEATH, belonging to the author, bears a picture entitled *Maria van Keevelaar* (*Fig. 8*). This is the famous Madonna in the church of Kevelaer, in Dutch-speaking territory—now across the German frontier — a much venerated seventeenth-century image, which is the object of pilgrimages. We notice here, as in all these figure-subjects, how white patterns on the costumes are executed by scratching, probably with the stick of the paint brush, through the layer of enamel pigment.

Some pieces carry, in addition to floral ornament, merely the names of their owners; for example, a plate in the Victoria and Albert Museum, dated *1819*, from the factory of Sewells and Donkin at Newcastle-on-Tyne. It is inscribed *Jan Oordwyn Wyntje Iding Dunning*. A Herculaneum plate in the Ryksmuseum at Amsterdam (*Fig. 9*), the second in a numbered series, bears verses of welcome to a guest:

> Mÿn vrint ik ben verblijt
> Dat Gij gekomen sijt
> Om ons eens te besoeken
> Ik heb u lang verwagt
> Ja menig dag en nagt
> Uijt vergelegen hoeken

(My friend, I am glad that you are come to visit us for once. I have long expected you, yes, many a day and night, from out-of-the-way corners.)

It remains to ask by whom these English wares were decorated. None has the signature of a painter; but Professor Ferrand Hudig tells us, in his newly published work, *Delfter Fayence*,* of two firms, those of Sanderson and Bellaert, and of H. A. Piccardt, proprietors of the old factory of the *Porcelain Bottle* (*Porceleyne Fles*), that made — apparently with only indifferent success — imitations of English earthenware. The latter exhibited some of his products in an exhibition at Haarlem, in 1825; and, on a plate of cream-colored earthenware in private possession, we find the name PICCARDT DELFT impressed in a sunk oblong cartouche.

This plate has a painting of *Marriage* (*Het Huwelyk*) in colors decidedly inferior to those of the class we have been discussing. We find dull blue, brownish purple, yellow, brown, and sage green — all of rather dirty tones — whilst the fresh red so conspicuous in the earlier decorations is entirely lacking. We may, perhaps, conclude that this piece represents the decline of the same establishment in which the English wares had previously been painted, and that Piccardt, who was already in possession of the factory in 1800, was responsible for the earlier as well as the later work.

*Berlin, 1929, p. 287.

# WHO MADE CREAMWARE?

## By EDNA DONNELL

AMONG late eighteenth-century American importations from England none received more frequent contemporary mention than creamware or queen's ware. George Washington and Benjamin Franklin collected it. Washington in 1769 wrote his London agent to send him a large order of "ye most fashionable kind of Queens ware." The vogue it enjoyed in the colonies was doubtless largely due to its novelty: we find that merchants always advertised queen's ware as "Just imported from England." For example, Henry Wilmot advertised, November 7, 1771, that he had "just imported in the last vessel from London . . . a large assortment of the newest fashioned plain and enamelled Queens and white stone Ware . . ." China collecting in the colonies began early. Inventories give proof of it before 1700. Margaret Van Varick, widow of the minister of the Reformed Church, left when she died, "three East India cups, three East India dishes, three Cheenie pots, one Cheenie pot bound in silver two glassen cases with thirty nine pieces of small china ware." However, not until some thirty years later (May 5, 1737) do we find any advertisement of length for a merchant with a large stock of chinaware:

By Mehitabel Kneeland at the Kings Arms a choice sortment of Delph, Stone and glass ware, viz. Bowles of divers & colours Plates of sorts & sizes, Tea Potts Cups and Saucers, strayners, . . . Baskets, Punch Ladles, cream Pots, Pencil'd and plain, Bird Fountains, Tankards and Salvers etc. wholesale or Retail."

Fine pottery and porcelain were probably made in this country in the second half of the eighteenth century, though proof is difficult to find. But in 1792 Ridgely and Evans advertised "A good Assortment of Green and blue edged and white Queensware . . . in daily inspection of our assortment of china from Philadelphia."

To Washington and his contemporaries queen's ware was queen's ware and the maker was not important. But to the twentieth-century collector the maker of a piece of pottery matters almost as much as the piece itself. Who made this queen's ware? Wedgwood, of course. But not exclusively. Only in the last few years, thanks to the collecting of Lady Charlotte Schreiber, have we realized that a large portion of this ware was manufactured at Leeds. Little by little examples of it have been gathered together, but even now the only sizable collection is in the York Museum. The Victoria and Albert has not one marked piece of Leeds queen's ware, though there are a number of marked pieces in private collections in this country. But it was not until very recently that we became aware of the existence of a third important creamware factory — Castleford (*Fig. 1*). Diligent search has been rewarded with two marked pieces of Castleford creamware, a plate with colored border design, and a plate with pierced rim (*Fig. 8*).

FIG. 1 (*top*) — CREAMWARE PLATE WITH CASTLEFORD MARK. *From the Victoria and Albert Museum*

FIG. 2 — LEEDS POTTERY. *Above, right*, design from Leeds catalogue of 1794. *Left*, creamware covered dish, unmarked. *From the Victoria and Albert Museum*

The Leeds and Castleford catalogues are in the collection of the Metropolitan Museum, the Wedgwood catalogue in the British Museum

FIG. 3 — *Left to right:* design from Leeds catalogue of 1794; design from 1814 revised edition of 1794 Leeds catalogue; design from Castleford catalogue of 1796; creamware vase, unmarked. *From the Victoria and Albert Museum*

April, 1940

34

Fig. 4 — *Left to right:* design from Leeds catalogue; design from Castleford catalogue; creamware vase, unmarked. *From the York Museum*

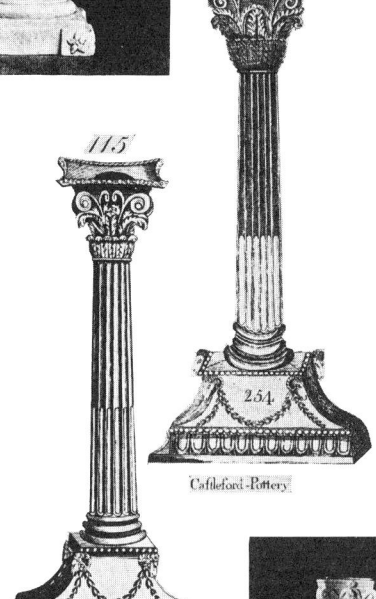

Fig. 5 (*below*) — Design from Leeds catalogue; design from Castleford catalogue; creamware candlestick, unmarked. *From the Victoria and Albert Museum*

How shall the collector know whether his piece of creamware is Wedgwood, Leeds, or Castleford? The answer is easy if it is rightly marked. The Wedgwood mark is *Wedgwood*. Leeds marks are LEEDS*POTTERY; L.P.; LEEDS*POTTERY twice repeated in the form of a cross; HARTLEY, GREENS, & CO. LEEDS*POTTERY; HARTLEY, GREENS, & CO. LEEDS POTTERY in the form of a horseshoe. Castleford marks are D.D. & CO. CASTLEFORD; D.D. & CO. CASTLEFORD POTTERY.

But, fortunately or unfortunately, the great mass of queen's ware was turned out unmarked. Some writers claim that this was because the manufacturers wished it all to be mistaken for Wedgwood, in the hope that it would sell better. If a piece is not marked, the collector must decide what to call it on the basis of glaze and paste. The consistency of the paste depends on the clay. But there is nothing to hinder one manufacturer from using the same clay as another. Furthermore, over a long period of years, clay varies. Hence we may find in the consistency of the paste of pieces produced at different dates by one factory the same variations as are discernible between pieces made by different factories in the same year or even in the same month. Great store has been set on the glaze as the determining element. Wedgwood pieces are said always to have been on the creamy side, and Leeds always to have a greenish cast in the grooves where the glaze puddled. For years I believed these generalizations, but after examining all the examples of Leeds and Wedgwood in the Victoria and Albert and in the Metropolitan Museum of Art, I find they do not hold. A marked Wedgwood basket dish has a glaze with greenish tinge, and a covered Leeds dish, also marked, has a glaze that is uniformly deep cream with no vestige of green in the puddles. But the criterion by which we have never judged these pieces is the pattern book of designs which potters issued for their customers to consult in placing orders.

In 1744, Josiah Wedgwood started his apprenticeship to his brother, Thomas, at the Churchyard Works. At the close of his apprenticeship he accepted a partnership, which lasted a very short time, with John Harrison, a tradesman of Newcastle-under-Lyme. A second partnership was offered to him in 1754, when he was 24 years old, this time with Thomas Whieldon who had started a pottery at Fenton Low in 1740. The firm made many experiments for the improvement of earthenware. In 1759 Wedgwood started out in business alone. He developed the cream-colored ware which became known as queen's ware after it had received the patronage of Queen Charlotte. In 1767, Wedgwood wrote to Bentley: "The demand for this sd. Cream color, alias Queensware, alias Ivory, still increases. It is amazing how rapidly the use of it has spread all most over the whole Globe & how universally it is liked."

The original catalogue of creamware issued by Wedgwood about 1780 consisted of nine engraved plates showing 35 articles, accurately enough to give a fairly good idea of their shape and ornamentation. It contained a numbered list of the objects illustrated and a foreword as follows: "It being impossible to send specimens . . . and the Names conveying but a very imperfect Idea of the Forms, it has been thought proper to send a few Prints of the Pieces, which will explain their Uses, and show their Forms better than could be done by Words alone."

Tradition says that the Leeds Pottery was founded in 1760 by two brothers named Green. In 1774 a flourishing pottery was being operated at Leeds by a firm called Humble, Green and Company. The annals of Leeds quote from a newspaper of the time: "On Sunday, July 31st, 1774, the sails of the windmill belonging to the Leeds Pottery fell down with a tremendous crash; which being looked upon as a judgment for the desecrating of the Sabbath, the proprietors resolved that the mill should never be allowed to be worked afterwards on the Lord's Day." Between 1775 and 1781 William Hartley joined the firm, which became known as Humble, Hartley, Greens and Company. In 1781 the following advertisement appeared in the Leeds *Intelligencer*:

Leeds Pottery, 19th February, 1781
Notice is hereby given that the Partnership in the Leeds Pottery Between Richard Humble, William Hartley, Joshua Green, John Green, Henry Akeroyd, John Barwick, Saville Green, and Samuel Wainwright, under the firm name Humble, Hartley, Greens, & Company, is amicably dissolved, and that the said William Hartley, Joshua Green, John Green, Henry Akeroyd, John Barwick, Saville Green, and Samuel Wainwright, will hereafter trade under the name of Hartley, Greens, and Company.

In 1783 the first edition of the catalogue of designs made by

35

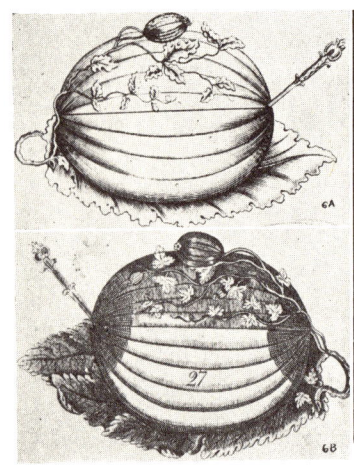

Fig. 6 — *Above:* design from Leeds catalogue; design from Castleford catalogue; creamware covered dish, unmarked. *From the Victoria and Albert Museum*

Fig. 7 — *Left,* design from Wedgwood catalogue; *right,* creamware dish, marked *Leeds Pottery. From the collection of Mrs. John D. Williamson*

Fig. 8 — CASTLEFORD WARE. The creamware plate with pierced rim bears the impressed Castleford mark. Pitcher and teapot are of the stoneware usually associated with Castleford. *From the collection of Charles Marshall*

Castleford. The Castleford pottery was established about 1790 by David Dunderdale, who was born at the "Crosse," Leeds, in 1772. Dunderdale was churchwarden and overseer of the poor for Methley at various periods between 1799 and 1814. He retired from the pottery works and died at Trafalgar Street, Leeds, in May 1824. The factory was closed in 1820. The Castleford catalogue, which was issued in 1796, consists of 57 numbered plates illustrating 259 objects. On each page is the inscription *Castleford-Pottery*. The index and title are in both French and Spanish.

the Leeds Pottery appeared. Later editions appeared in 1785, 1786, 1794, and 1814. In the 1794 catalogue the title page and the list of objects illustrated was in German, French, and English: "Designs of Sundry Articles of Queens or Cream colour'd Earthenware, manufactured by Hartley, Greens and Co. at Leeds Pottery; with a great variety of other articles, The same Enamel'd Printed or Ornamented with Gold to any Pattern; also with coats of Arms, Cyphers; Landscapes &c.&c. Leeds, 1794." Then follows the explanation of the plates, which show 152 items on 38 plates, and 32 items on plates 39–45 labeled *Tea Ware*. A re-issue of this catalogue, with a French title page and no list of objects illustrated, is dated 1794, but printed on paper watermarked 1814. It shows 221 objects on 60 plates, followed by the illustrations of Tea Ware — 48 objects on plates 61–71. The name *Leeds Pottery* in an oval has been added to the plates, which have been reworked.

Until recently the name Castleford has never complicated the creamware problem. If you had creamware you had Leeds or Wedgwood. But a rather poorly engraved design book issued by Dunderdale and Company in 1796 rises as a dark cloud on the horizon, and with it the marked creamware plates which have been discovered (*Figs. 1 and 8*). Now you may no longer be sure that you have either Leeds or Wedgwood; very likely you have Castleford. Though Castleford ware has hitherto been known as a paste of blue-white stoneware, creamware was made at the Castleford factory, and all the shapes that were made at Leeds were copied at

After indicating that the pattern book more or less determines the maker of a piece of unmarked creamware, I offer a final confrontation (*Fig. 7*). This shows a piece of marked Leeds ware, brittle, highly glazed, and conforming to all the accepted Leeds criteria — and the design corresponds exactly with a design in the Wedgwood pattern book! Which goes to show that all the potters copied the designs of all their competitors, and any reasoning is false which leaves out of consideration such a pertinent fact.

# Some recent gifts of creamware to Colonial Williamsburg

BY JOHN C. AUSTIN, *Curator of ceramics and glass*

CREAMWARE WAS MADE in large quantities in the potting district of Staffordshire and at the cities of Liverpool and Leeds; many people have considered these the sole areas of manufacture of the refined cream-color earthenware often referred to in the eighteenth century as "Queen's Ware," "creamcolour," or "Queen's China," as it was usually called in Williamsburg. Through research and archaeological excavations, it has become apparent that there were also many other centers of creamware manufacture not only throughout Great Britain, but as far away as America and Russia.

French *faïence fine*, a type of creamware made "à l'imitation de celles d'Angleterre,"[1] copied the English salt-glaze and ceramic forms (Fig. 1). That produced at Pont-aux-Choux is renowned. Many Continental faïence factories had to change their wares to compete with the great influx of creamware from England. Most of this Continental ware is distinctive enough that it cannot be confused with its English prototypes; however, Continental pieces posing as English creamware can be found in collections today.

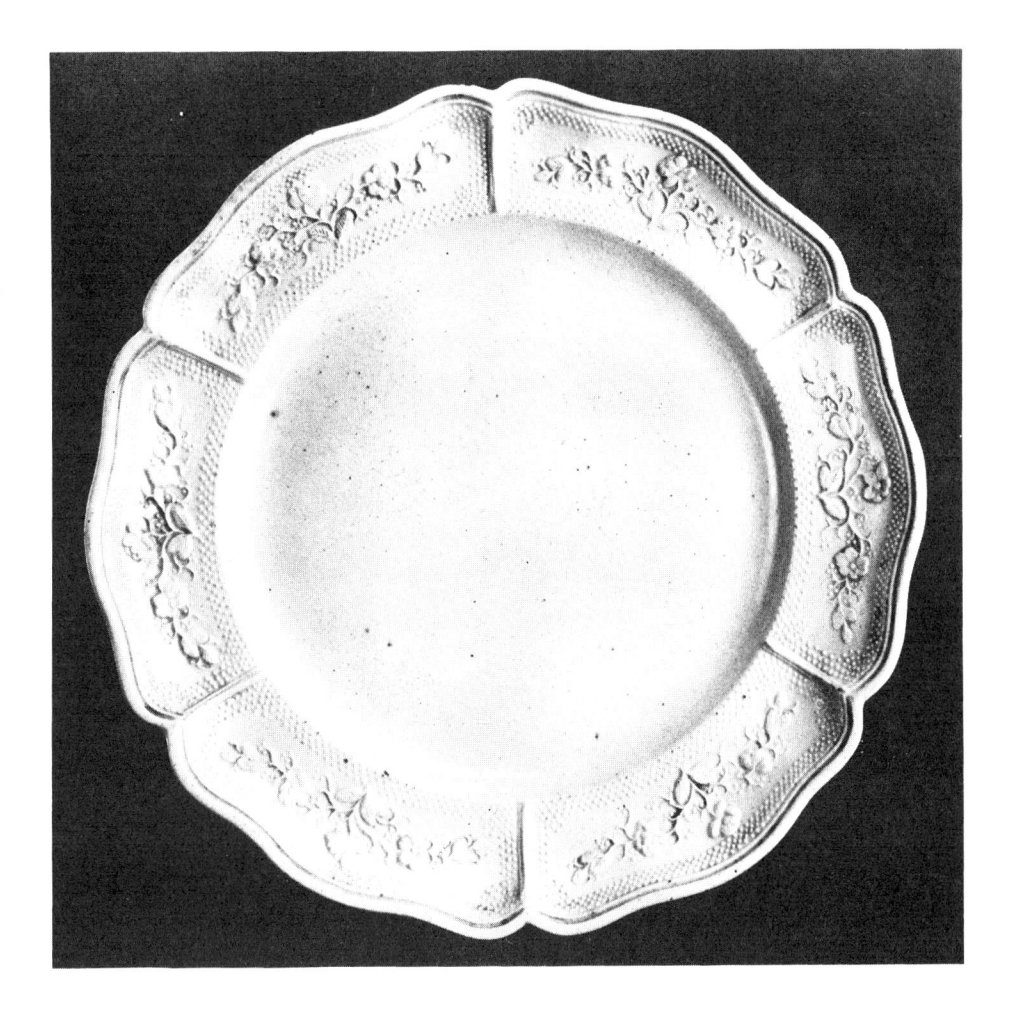

Fig. 1. Creamware, or *faïence fine*, plate made in France, possibly at Pont-aux-Choux, c. 1765-1775. A typical example, this plate illustrates well the influences of both salt-glazed stoneware and creamware imported from England. The rim is molded in the Queen's pattern, a shape adopted by Josiah Wedgwood and used on services made for Queen Charlotte and Catherine the Great (see Figs. 6a, b, c). The raised flowers on this plate, seen more often on English salt glaze, appear to be molded with the piece rather than applied. Diameter 9¼ inches. *Gift of Shila Sol.*

*Except as noted, illustrations are from the Colonial Williamsburg Foundation.*

Fig. 2. Creamware plate, c. 1770, transfer printed in black with birds reminiscent of those found on wares from Liverpool. Donald C. Towner attributes the plate to the Melbourne factory, a small pottery in Derbyshire (*English Ceramic Circle Transactions*, Vol. 8, Part 1, p. 22). A small double slash in the foot-rim, perhaps a method of counting, appears to be unique to this factory. The molded border of a raised-diamond pattern is frequently found among the shards excavated at the pottery. However, the pattern is also found on fragments from Staffordshire. Diameter 9¾ inches. *Gift of Donald C. Towner.*

Fig. 3. Among the largest and most intricate forms produced at the Leeds Pottery was the cockle pot. When Donald C. Towner published his monograph *The Leeds Pottery* (London, 1963), only three of these vessels had been recorded. Since then several more have come to light, including this unmarked example of c. 1780 (shown without its perforated outer cover). Mr. Towner states that other examples are marked LEEDS-POTTERY or LP. There appears to be only one other recorded example which still has both its covers (see ANTIQUES, November 1973, p. 735). Over-all height, 16⅛ inches.

Fig. 3a. This plate from *Designs of Sundry Articles of Queen's or Cream-colour'd Earthen-Ware manufactured by Hartley, Greens and Co. at Leeds Pottery* . . . (first published at Leeds in 1783) illustrates a "Cockle Pot or Potpouri, from 15 to 18 and 22 Inches high." The name probably indicates that the vessels were used as potpourris and were decorated with shells, since in the eighteenth century the term cockle was sometimes used for shellfish in general. In this case the inner, or solid, lid would have been used except when the scent of the dried leaves was to perfume the room. Then it would have been replaced by the perforated lid. It has also been suggested that the vessels were used both as potpourris (with the perforated lid) and containers for shellfish soup or stew (with the solid cover).

Fig. 4. This partial creamware tea service of c. 1770, with strong yellow-cream ground and splotchy manganese and green decoration, is attributed on stylistic grounds to the Rothwell Potworks, four miles southeast of Leeds. Little is known about the Rothwell pottery, but it must have been in existence longer than 1770 to 1774, which is the span of notices that were published about it by Towner in *The Leeds Pottery*. The discovery of the Rothwell pottery site is so recent that examples are only now being identified; a few terminals and other molded details have been recovered. Tentative attributions can be based only on the yellow-cream body and the splotchy decoration. Teapots related to the one illustrated here include a straight-sided example at Temple Newsam House, York; one at the Treasurer's House, National Trust, York; and one in the collection of David Zeitlin, Philadelphia. Height of pot, 6 inches.

Although most examples of English creamware are still attributed to Leeds, Liverpool, or Staffordshire, information concerning creamware made in other centers is continuously coming to light. We know that creamware was made in the town of Bristol by, among others, Joseph Ring, a delftware potter. Ring announced in December 1786 that he had "established a manufactory of Queen's and other earthenware which he can sell at on as low Terms Wholesale and Retail as any of the best Manufactory in Staffordshire, can render the same to Bristol."[2] In Scotland the Delftfield Pottery of Glasgow also kept up with the times and began to manufacture creamware about 1770, much of which was exported to America. These are only two

Fig. 5. This molded sauceboat of c. 1770, with the pineapple-in-the-basket motif, is attributed to the Derby Pot Works at Cockpit Hill in Derby owing to its similarities to shards found on the site. Two other sauceboats apparently from the same mold, one in white salt glaze, the other creamware with overglaze green, are in the Derby Museum and Art Gallery. Similar sauceboats with a variation of the pineapple motif are believed to have been made in Staffordshire, and may have been the inspiration for the mold maker who designed this sauceboat. Transfer-printed creamware teapots have been attributed for many years to the Cockpit Hill pottery because of inscriptions incorporated with the prints, but only since recent excavations have simple, molded, undecorated examples been attributed to this factory. According to Towner, the Cockpit Hill factory was in existence for about thirty years, closing in 1780 due to bankruptcy. The factory produced the brown salt glaze more typical of Derbyshire and Nottingham as well as creamware and white salt glaze. Length $5^{15}/_{16}$ inches.

Fig. 6a. Creamware plate from the service made by Josiah Wedgwood for Catherine the Great of Russia. Wedgwood wrote to his partner Thomas Bentley in May of 1770, "Mr. Rhodes has hands who can do husks, which is the pattern of the table service. I shall not wait for your reply to send you two or three for flowers . . . in order to complete the Russian service in due time" *(Metropolitan Museum of Art Bulletin,* May 1964, p. 298). The purple husks were painted on the standard Queen's pattern. (The husk motif was by no means used exclusively on this service. It was a standard Wedgwood pattern and was also used at other factories and in different colors. Fragments of a lid to an octagonal tureen, decorated with the husk motif, have been excavated at Williamsburg). Diameter 9$^{15}/_{16}$ inches. *Gift of the Wedgwood Company.*

Fig. 6b. Creamware plate made in Moscow as a replacement in the Wedgwood husk service for Catherine the Great. The plate bears the impressed mark L:o, for the Otto Factory which was in operation from 1801 until 1812, and was made for Catherine's grandson Alexander I. Diameter 9¾ inches. *Gift of Mrs. Richard P. Carter.*

of many potteries scattered throughout Britain of which little or nothing is known except that they existed. Recent excavations have brought about the identification of the wares produced in other creamware factories, including ones in Derbyshire (Figs. 2, 5) and Yorkshire (Fig. 4).

Over the past several years Colonial Williamsburg has received a number of pieces of creamware as gifts. Some are important to the collection because of their relationship to pieces used in Williamsburg in the eighteenth century. Other, more unusual wares range from the sophisticated products of well-established and documented factories, such as the Leeds cockle pot shown in Figure 3, to simple pieces that are rare only because they can be attributed to recently identified pottery sites—for example, a partial tea service attributed to Rothwell (Fig. 4), and a sauceboat attributed to the Derby Pot Works at Cockpit Hill (Fig. 5). Other interesting and unusual gifts include plates made in Russia as replacements in a Wedgwood service made for Catherine the Great (Figs. 6b, c), and late nineteenth- and early twentieth-century examples made in the town of Leeds in forms reminiscent of eighteenth-century creamware (Figs. 7, 8).

Fig. 6c. Creamware plate made in St. Petersburg, also as a replacement piece in the Catherine the Great husk service, for either Alexander I or his successor Nicholas I. According to the Russian State Museum at Leningrad, the plate was made at the factory owned by Sergei Yakovlevich Poskochin between 1817 and 1842. The plate bears the impressed mark СП. Diameter 9$^{15}/_{16}$ inches.

---

[1] Emil Hannover, *Pottery and Porcelain,* London, 1925, Vol. 1, p. 293.

[2] ANTIQUES, June 1935, p. 225.

Fig. 7. Pair of reticulated mantelpiece jars made at the beginning of this century. These reproductions have the impressed mark LEEDS POTTERY, and were made at the factory of James and George Senior and John Thomas Morton. They can generally be distinguished from eighteenth-century creamware by their slightly gray tone and severe crazing. The factory was particularly skilled at reticulation and many of their pieces, like these, are highly decorated. Height 10¼ inches.

Fig. 8. Pair of creamware stands marked LEEDS POTTERY, early twentieth century. These reproductions and the mantelpiece jars shown in Fig. 7 were made at the same factory and show the same color, crazing, and reticulation. Length 7¾ inches. *Gift of J. Ricks Wilson.*

# Pearlware: forgotten milestone of English ceramic history

BY IVOR NOËL-HUME, *Director, department of archaeology, Colonial Williamsburg*

Your idea of the *creamcolor* having the merit of an original, & the *pearl white* being consider'd as an imitation of some of the blue & white fabriques, either earthenware or porcelain, is perfectly right, & I should not hesitate a moment in preferring the former if I consulted my own taste and sentiments: but you know what Lady Dartmouth told us, that she & her friends were tired of creamcolor, & so they would of Angels if they were shewn for sale in every chandlers shop through the town. The pearl white must be considered as a *change* rather than an *improvement*, & I must have something ready to succeed it when the public eye is pall'd, or it comes upon the town.

SO WROTE JOSIAH WEDGWOOD to his partner Thomas Bentley on August 6, 1779, thus establishing (after a fashion) a generic name for a class of earthenware that did, indeed, come upon the town—where it remained for more than half a century. However, Wedgwood's name for it was not adopted by the majority of potters, and in the absence of a neat label for collectors to hang around its neck, the ware has received surprisingly little attention. In truth, pearlware represented one of the landmarks in the evolution of English earthenwares, providing a bridge between creamware, which was introduced in the early 1760's, and the bone china, ironstone, granite, and porcelaneous wares of the nineteenth century. In the chronology of British domestic wares it became the last major step forward in the eighteenth century: delft, white salt glaze, creamware, then pearlware.

For the purposes of this article I propose to use the term pearlware to describe a whitened creamware body whose glaze was treated with a small quantity of cobalt to create the slightly bluish tint that characterized much of the China Trade porcelain of the period. It is true that the name pearl has been applied to other, less common fabrics, and that Wedgwood called his product Pearl White and not pearlware. But for the sake of brevity I shall here use pearlware to parallel that creamware—which Wedgwood actually referred to as "cream coloured" (or cream colored) or as "Queen's ware."

The history of English ceramics is blessed with more than its fair share of misnomers and misconceptions, not the least of them being the belief that Wedgwood *invented* creamware. However, the cream-color body had been in use for more than a decade before the first of Wedgwood's queen's ware appeared. A letter published in the *Virginia Gazette* for June 30, 1768, describing the wonders of the great Staffordshire potting center at Burslem, contained the following surprising statement: "The Ladies go to Warburton's to buy the Queen's sets of cream coloured ware." The reference is to the Mrs. Warburton of Hot Lane whom Simeon Shaw (*History of the Staffordshire Potteries*, 1829) credited with having "made the last improvements of Cream Colour, (prior to those of the late Mr. Wedgwood,)" in 1751.

Be this as it may, much of Wedgwood's early fortune rested on the success of his creamware, and on his ability to produce and market it in prodigious quantities. He was an extremely skillful promoter, and he possessed the all-important ability to keep one step ahead of his customers' taste. It is not surprising, therefore, that even before creamware was at the height of fashion, Wedgwood was asking himself what next?

As early as March 6, 1765, Josiah wrote to John Wedgwood telling him that he had "just begun a Course of experiments for a white body & glaze which promiseth well hitherto," adding that he did not intend to make the new ware at his Burslem factory. However, it would seem that he did not then go on to make it anywhere, for on July 2, 1770, he wrote to Bentley: "I have given over the thoughts of making any other colour but Queen's ware. The white ware would be a great deal dearer, & I apprehend not much better liked; and the Queen's ware, whilst it continues to sell, is quite as much business as I can manage."

Wedgwood's change of mind was apparently not shared by other creamware potters, and two years later, on April 18, 1772, he wrote to Bentley describing a newly developed body having "a small quantity of limestone which is intermix'd with all this Chert [a flintlike rock], so that the *Pottery in general* will now make their Cream-colour nearly as white as the white stone-ware, at least it will in a little time, when the Mills are all supply'd with this stone . . ." He added that "if it is not superior to our white stone-ware in whiteness, it would be esteemed a degradation of *cream-colour* into *white stone ware*, rather than an improvement of it into *Porcelain* . . ."

On the last day of December 1775, Wedgwood was still vacillating. He then wrote to Bentley wondering "whether I should be content still with the good old

March, 1969

Creamcolour, painted, & varied in every way we can invent. Or whether I should have a tryal in earnest at Porcelain, or white ware—or what I should do next." He was still wondering two weeks later when he wrote again, saying: "You know very well that from the moment a finer ware than the Cream-color is shewn at our Rooms, the sale of the latter will in a great measure be over there. The consequence then of my shewing them a little, before I am certain of being able to supply their wants, would be tantalising them & ruining my own business." Nevertheless, by the beginning of 1779 Wedgwood had produced a white ware and on February 25 he told Bentley that he had "Settled my white body and glaze" and asked him to suggest a name for it. At the same time Wedgwood expressed his fear that it might turn into porcelain (it contained Cornish china clay) and might thus infringe the porcelain patent held by Richard Champion of Bristol.

Bentley told Wedgwood that he would want to see the baby before he baptized it, and added his own warning against letting it fuse into porcelain, to which Wedgwood replied on March 8: "I find to my grief that I cannot make any great improvement in my present body but it will be china, though I have endeavoured all in my power to prevent it. However to give the brat a name you may set a cream-color plate & one of the best blue & white ones before you, & suppose the one you are to name another degree whiter and finer still, but not transparent, & consequently *not china*, for transparency will be the general test of china." By June 19, the new ware had been named Pearl White and the Queen had already expressed her approval of it.

This, then, is the history of the development of pearlware in so far as it related to Josiah Wedgwood. However, there remain a number of unanswered questions regarding other manufacturers' progress in this direction. What became of the use of limestone which Wedgwood had been sure would enable his competitors to whiten their creamware "nearly as white as the white stone-ware"? What had he meant when he told Bentley to think of a name for a ware one step whiter than "the best blue & white"? Did this refer to a flint and china clay or to a limestone and Derbyshire chert composition already being used by other potters? Unfortunately, the records of Wedgwood's competitors have rarely survived—which is one reason why any research into the history of Staffordshire potting begins with Wedgwood and ends with him shortly thereafter.

Our principal clue as to who did what, and how soon, is provided by a *Survey of the Counties of Stafford, Chester and Lancaster* made in 1787 by William Tunnicliffe, a study that includes a "Directory of the principal merchants and manufacturers." The following extracts from the list of potters are extremely revealing:

**Burslem.**

Wm. Adams & Co. Cream-coloured ware and China glaze ware painted.

John Bourne, China glaze, blue painted, enamelled and cream coloured earthenware.

Bourne & Malkin, China glaze, blue painted, enamelled and cream coloured earthenware.

John Graham jun., white stone, and enamelled white and cream earthenware.

John Robinson, enameller and printer of cream colour and china glazed ware.

John & George Rogers, china glazed, blue painted, and cream coloured ware.

Chas. Stevenson & sons, cream coloured ware, blue painted.

Thos. Wedgwood, (Big House), cream coloured ware, china glazed, painted with blue etc.

**Cobridge.**

Thos. & Benj. Goodwin, Queens ware and china glazed ware.

**Stoke.**

Hugh Booth, china, china glazed, and Queens ware in all its branches.

**Fenton.**

Edw. Boon, Queens ware and blue painted.

**Lane End.**

John Barker, cream colour, china glaze and blue wares.

On reading these extracts one fact immediately becomes apparent: something called China glaze was sharing the spotlight with creamware and, in some instances, was edging it out. Although the wording and punctuation vary from entry to entry, it is evident that China glaze was not descriptive of a type of creamware. There was a definite distinction between the two. Whether "blue painted" when used without "China glaze" meant the same thing is less certain, though Edward Boon was cited as being maker of "Queens ware and blue painted." However, other entries seem to refer to creamware and China glaze as painted in blue.

The next question, of course, is what was meant by China glaze. Before answering, one must first pose another: what was meant by "China"? Nathaniel Bailey's *English Dictionary* (1749 edition) listed "China-Ware, a fine sort of Earthen-ware made in *China*." Chambers' *Cyclopaedia* (1738 edition) went one better: "China or China-Ware, a fine sort of earthen-ware, properly called *porcelain*." Nevertheless, the term seems to have been used more loosely to describe wares that did not look in the least like porcelain and that had been nowhere near China.

On July 6, 1765, Josiah Wedgwood wrote to John Wedgwood describing a visit to the seat of the Duke of Bridgewater, who had shown him "a Roman urn, fifteen hundred years old at least, made of red china, which had been found by his workmen in Castle Field, near Manchester." There is little doubt that the urn was of Gaulish Samian ware (terra sigillata), an opaque red ware coated with a high-gloss red slip which, though looking not at all like porcelain, might, if stripped of its gloss, have passed for Chinese red stoneware. My point is that the word china was not reserved for true porcelain, but could be applied to other quality wares that might or might not resemble the products of China.

In the case of China glaze it is reasonable to conclude that the potters were referring to a ware whose surface, if not structure, resembled that of porcelain, and, as we have seen, Wedgwood was concerned lest his Pearl White should step beyond earthenware into porcelain. It is therefore equally reasonable to deduce that

43

Wedgwood's Pearl White and the other potters' China glaze were approximately the same, and that they became the popular white ware of the closing years of the eighteenth century. This thesis gains strength when one considers the meaning of "blue painted," and the interpretation of John Robinson's craft as an "enameller and printer of cream colour and china glazed ware."

By 1770 Wedgwood was devoting much of his energy to obtaining painters to decorate his creamware, as he felt that the plain ware had lost its sales appeal everywhere but on the lowest rungs of the social ladder. The majority of his designs have no bearing on the pearlware story, but one is of some significance. Number 83 in Wedgwood's first pattern book (begun in 1774) shows a blue-painted shell-edge-rim style (not to be confused with the featheredge—see Fig. 1) which was to become the most popular of all pearlware borders. However, the design was not a Wedgwood innovation; it had been used on Bow porcelain as early as 1755, a fact that may have prompted pearlware potters to adopt it. The date at which the shell edge was first used on creamware is uncertain, but an important clue is provided by a plate illustrated by Jean Gorely in her book *Wedgwood* (New York, 1950; Fig. 32) decorated with enameled profiles of the Prince and Princess of Orange, and seemingly commemorating their marriage on October 4, 1767. Although this shell-edge creamware plate is unmarked, the painting has been attributed to Dutch enamelers working at Mrs. Warburton's Hot Lane factory. One is tempted, therefore, to attribute the plate itself to Hot Lane.

We know that creamware potters besides Wedgwood used the shell-edge design, for Hartley, Greens & Co. of Leeds included it in their 1783 creamware catalogue. Nevertheless, there is strong evidence—archaeological evidence—that it was not a particularly popular style. Of the tens of thousands of shell-edge plate fragments excavated in Williamsburg, only one is of creamware (and that unpainted); all the rest are blue or green shell-edge pearlware.

There is no denying that on occasion underglaze blue decoration could look extremely handsome on creamware (Fig. 1), particularly on tureens and coffee-pots; but for the earthenware potter who was striving to compete with porcelain, blue on yellow fell far short of the goal, while the man who made creamware for creamware's sake had only to turn to the wares of Thomas Whieldon and Josiah Wedgwood to see that other colors looked better on it. If this argument is valid, it follows that Tunnicliffe's repeated juxtaposition of "China glaze" and "blue painted" was no accident: China-glaze ware was painted blue. As there appears to be no such thing as totally white pearlware, one more building block is set in place to support the conclusion that China glaze and pearlware are one and the same.

At first, blue seems to have been the only color used

Fig. 1. Featheredge creamware plate decorated in underglaze blue with Chinese house design, the brushwork markedly superior to that usually seen on pearlware. Diameter 9½ inches; c. 1770. *Except as noted, illustrations are from the author's collection.*

Fig. 2. Pearlware teapots, both with Chinese house designs in underglaze blue. *Left:* Early example with Leeds-type knop and handle terminals; c. 1785. *Right:* Miniature. Height 3⅜ inches; c. 1790-1800.

Fig. 3. Serving or tureen platter of shell-edge pearlware, with elaborated Chinese house design painted in underglaze blue. Length 18¾ inches; c. 1800.

in the decoration of pearlware, and the styles of ornament—generally a pseudo-Chinese design comprising a house, flanking pieces of picket fence, and a tree or two—were equally limited. On small items, such as the miniature teapot in Figure 2, there was room for little more than the house; but when there was more space, as in Figure 3, the painters spread themselves to include mountains and additional arboreal embellishments. Laying some claim to being the earliest documented example of the house pattern on pearlware is a jug in the Victoria and Albert Museum inscribed *A Butcher* and *A D 1777,* but as the black letters were applied after firing, it must be assumed that the date was retrospective and that both it and the name were added later. Otherwise one would have to suppose that pearlware was fully developed two years before Wedgwood first put his Pearl White on the market.

Regardless of their inviting expanses, most early pearlware plates were decorated only around their shell edges, and on the evidence already outlined it is fair to suppose that they first appeared around 1779. If this is so, the shell edge had an extraordinarily long life of about half a century. At the outset, the painting of the rims harmonized with the grooved modeling of the shell edge, the brush strokes being carried toward the center so that a feathery effect was achieved (Fig. 4)—thus creating subsequent confusion among collectors between the shell edge and the relief-molded featheredge of creamware.

Before long, many painters did not take the time to build up the borders from a multitude of carefully placed brush strokes, and instead simply placed the brush at right angles to the rim and applied a stripe as the plate was rotated. This technique was still being used well

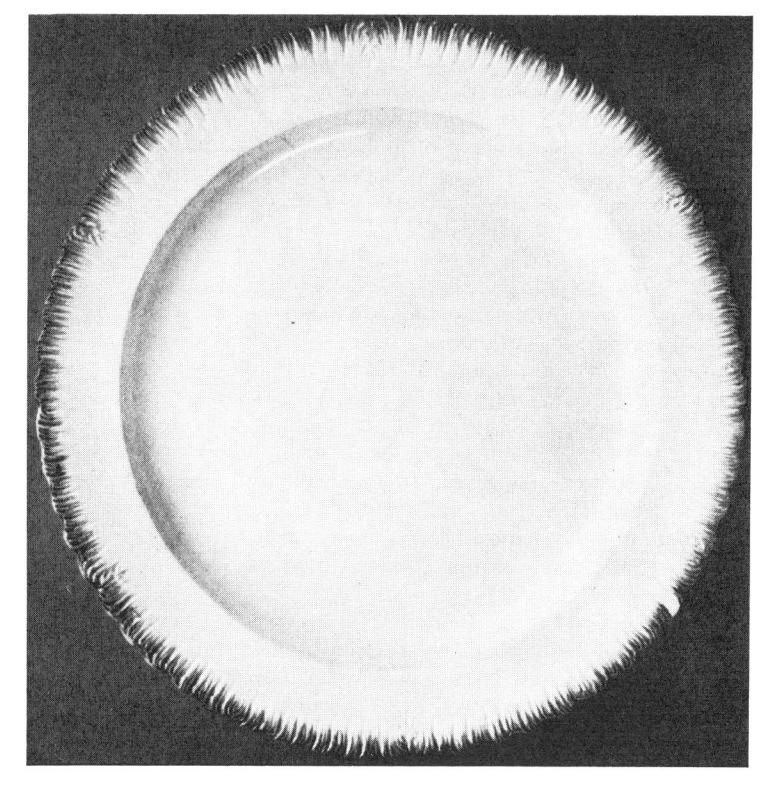

Fig. 4. Pearlware plate with well-executed blue-painted shell edge; marked ENOCH WOOD & SONS, BURSLEM, so post-1818. Diameter 10 inches.

45

Fig. 5. Pearlware mug decorated with the tools and produce of the farmer, painted in blue, yellow, orange-brown, green, and dark purple. Height 4½ inches; c. 1795-1805.

through the second quarter of the nineteenth century, though the latest examples were generally not on pearlware but on a harder and coarser white ware that succeeded it. Careful modeling of the shell-edge grooves is a better indication of an early piece, though good quality molds and careful painting were both used on pieces dating as late as the 1820's.

The vast majority of shell-edge pearlware pieces are not marked, but even when they are, close dating is rarely possible, as some of the marks are unrecorded and others were in use for very long periods; or we may know when the marks were first used but not when they were superseded. The principal impressed marks on plain (presumably shell-edge) fragments found in Williamsburg are as follows: HERCULANEUM (1793-1841), PHILLIPS LONGPORT (1822-1834), DAVENPORT (post-1805), CLEWS (1818-1834), T. MAYER, STOKE (1826-1836), and ENOCH WOOD (1818-1840). Hand-painted pieces are marked HERCULANEUM and ADAMS (1804-1840?), while transfer-printed shards offer ROGERS (1784-1836), STUBBS (1822-1835), and ENOCH WOOD. In addition to the many Staffordshire potteries, the ware was made at numerous other places, notably at Leeds and Swansea. Many of the potters produced batches specifically for the American market, and some, like Enoch Wood & Sons (1818-1846), included the American eagle in their marks when impressing export pieces. It is worth noting, incidentally, that some of this factory's products were also marked *Pearl China*.

To both collectors and archaeologists, the question of how early pearlware reached America is of considerable importance. It may or may not be relevant to note that although creamware was fashionable in England by 1765, the earliest documentary reference to it yet found in Virginia dates four years later, suggesting that in that colony, at least, there was an appreciable time lag between the ware's appearance in England and its arrival in Virginia. There is reason to suppose that there was a comparable delay in popularizing pearlware on this side of the Atlantic—partially explained by the intervention of the Revolutionary War which so severely damaged the British export trade. In any case, it is unlikely that the makers of the new ware would have paid much attention to foreign markets until their production outpaced home consumption. If so, about 1785 would have been a likely date for the first consignments to reach American ports.

The ware seems to have been available at Rhinelander's Store in New York in 1786, in which year an advertisement in the *New-York Packet* (April 17) offered "A large and general assortment of plain, enameled and blue and white earthen-ware." Another New York merchant was more explicit in his advertisement in the *New-York Daily Advertiser* for January 1, 1791: he listed "An assortment of green and blue edged ware in sets or separate." A later subscriber to the same paper (April 11, 1796) invited customers to buy "two hundred and eight Crates Staffordshire Earthenware, assorted, consisting of cream coloured, blue and white cups & saucers, bowls, plates, dishes, tureens, chambers, wash basons, teapots, mugs, jugs, &c.: green edged table services compleat, suitable for genteel, private families." Three days later a competitor (again in the same paper) offered "from England . . . complete dining table setts of brown, wine, blue, green edge ware." All these colors (with the possible exception of the brown) are known on shell-edge pearlware (I am assuming that the wine color refers to a purple). In addition, a reddish pink is sometimes encountered.

In his book *Wedgwood* (London, 1953) Wolf Mankowitz listed what he considered to be the 1774 patterns, and among them were both blue and green shell edge. The author assumed (rightly or wrongly) that design Number 83 (blue) was inserted in 1774 when the pattern book was started; his evidence for including the green with it is not cited. Nevertheless, the latter was certainly in production ten years later (presumably on pearlware) when William Absolon advertised in the English *Norwich Mercury* for July 10, 1784, that he had just returned from London "with a large quantity of foreign and Salopian China, some Blue and Green-edge Table Services of two Sorts . . . which he is enabled to sell on the cheapest Terms, at his Shop" in Yarmouth.

Although the foregoing evidence indicates that green-edge pearlware was available in English shops before the first blue-edge pearlware was shipped to the United States, the virtual absence of green-edge shards from archaeological contexts prior to 1800 and their comparative scarcity thereafter suggest that the green was never as popular as the blue, or was perhaps more expensive. No examples of the wine, brown, or pink edges have been found in Williamsburg excavations.

The elaborate floral decoration of pearlware in polychrome seems to have become popular around 1800 and to have continued in bright and busy motifs for about twenty years. These designs, generally with yellow, green, and orange predominating, also occur in silver-luster resist, and they are most common on pitchers and mugs. Many ceramics historians ungenerously dismiss them as "peasant" styles, and while it is true that they belonged in village homes rather than in aristocratic town houses, designs, shapes, and thinness of potting are frequently all of a high standard. The polychrome mug (Fig. 5) decorated with the tools and products of the farmer is an excellent example of the pleasing and lively character of pearlware painting at the close of the eighteenth century.

At the outset, pearlware was decorated with the same, often elaborate and mechanical, devices used on creamware, such as engine-turned checker patterns cutting through underglaze blue, green, or red-brown. Marbleized surfaces in green and brown were common, and a little later the white body was almost entirely hidden beneath brown and green slips; sometimes banded (annular ware) in green, brown, blue, yellow, or black, the black frequently incised to create a black and white checker border. In addition the pearlware body was often disguised behind the swirling, so-called finger-painted, decoration, or the tobacco fronding of mocha. Copies of the debased scratch-blue salt-glaze designs (ANTIQUES, October 1966, p. 520), including their relief-molded medallions, were used to beautify pearlware chamber pots, a technique that persisted into the second quarter of the nineteenth century.

Because early pearlware designs were so akin to those used on creamware, collectors sometimes have difficulty distinguishing between the two wares. The clue is provided not by the body but by the glaze: the lead glaze used on creamware has an inherent yellowness and appears slightly green where it has pooled in crevices around foot rings, under handles, and beneath rims. The thickened pearlware glaze found in these same traps appears blue, as a result of the cobalt used to counteract the yellowness. One word of warning: rather similar bluish pooling of the glaze under foot rings occurs on many run-of-the-mill pieces of Liverpool porcelain. However, the latter are generally decorated in underglaze-blue designs reminiscent of Worcester, and I have yet to see these on pearlware.

Examples of pearlware dating from the first quarter of the nineteenth century are plentiful and are collected under a variety of aliases: Leeds, annular ware, mocha ware, early Staffordshire, and the like. Much more difficult either to date or to identify are the pieces made in the last twenty years of the preceding century. The problem is well illustrated by a fine jug decorated in underglaze blue in the collection of Colonial Williamsburg (Fig. 6). Were it not for the fact that it is dated 1792 one might be tempted to attribute it to the first decade of the nineteenth century. Conversely, the group of examples excavated in Alexandria (Fig. 7) might have been assumed to date a year or two before 1800 had they not been found in quantity in an archaeological context

Fig. 6. Pearlware jug decorated in underglaze blue with a floral garland around the cipher *WR* over the date 1792; on the side, the tools of the carpenter's trade. Attributed to Liverpool. Height 11⅛ inches. *Colonial Williamsburg.*

Fig. 7. Examples of English hand-painted pearlware from a privy pit at the rear of Arell's Tavern in the market block of Alexandria, Virginia, discarded c. 1810. *Top, left to right:* Bowl with dark brown bands at rim and foot, the body decorated with a fruit motif in orange, green, and brown. Bowl with rouletted decoration at the rim, painted with brown lines and a geometric border in green, blue, yellow, and brown. Bowl with engine-turned annular decoration of alternating bands of solid olive and light blue, and alternating rows of lozenges in light blue and dark brown. *Bottom, left to right:* Tea bowl decorated with brown lines, and a band of yellowish green above green swags and orange tassels. Green shell-edge plate with American eagle painted in polychrome: wings, arrows, and stars in brown, head and stripes golden yellow, leaves green, and upper part of shield, blue. Small mug, or can, decorated over all in orange brown, with brown horizontal lines and vertical incised stripes revealing the pearl body, alternating with stripes filled with blue. Diameter of plate, 6¼ inches. *City of Alexandria, Virginia; photograph by courtesy of the Smithsonian Institution, where these pieces are currently on loan.*

of about 1810 and had they not closely paralleled another group from Williamsburg containing coins of 1816 and 1817.

One of the most historically important functions of pearlware was its ushering in of underglaze-blue printing on earthenware, the best remembered being, of course, the so-called willow pattern said to have been designed at Thomas Turner's Caughley factory by Thomas Minton. Whether it was Minton or Turner himself who conceived it remains debatable, but it must be assumed that the original 1779 engraving was intended for printing on Salopian porcelain. Just how early it was used on pearlware is uncertain, though it is reasonable to conclude that it, or comparable *chinoiserie* prints, were employed by the 1790's. It will be recalled that William Tunnicliffe's 1787 directory listed John Robinson of Hill Top, a man who had previously worked for the celebrated creamware printers John Sadler and Guy Green of Liverpool, as an "enameller and printer of cream colour and china glazed ware." Dated examples of the willow pattern on pearlware are infinitely rare. The Victoria and Albert Museum has one bearing the name *Thomasine Willey* and the date *1818*, but this is too late to be significant.

Occasionally the prints themselves exhibit datable features, as does the small plate shown in Figure 9. On the evidence of its thinness, its well-molded rim, and the quality of its painting, one might be tempted to date it around 1800. However, the lines of verse it carries are from one of Thomas Moore's *Irish Melodies*, which were first published in 1808; while the pictorial elements are characteristic of the reviving enthusiasm for neo-Gothic melancholy of the second decade of the century.

Vast quantities of pearlware were shipped to the United States in the period from 1790 to 1830, and although until about 1810 most of it was decorated only with the standard shell edge, some was designed specifically for the erstwhile colonial market. Shell-edge plates were adorned with the American eagle and shield in polychrome, and others displayed prints of American ships flying polychrome flags. Later, blue transfer prints of engraved American landmarks were applied to plates, dishes, chamber pots, and pitchers, but by that time pearlware's tide was ebbing, giving way to the whiter wares that flourished alongside the stone and granite "chinas" of the Victorian era. However, the Wedgwood factory was still making pearlware in 1865, at which date Llewellynn Jewitt observed that it was "not 'a pearl of great price,' but one for ordinary use and of moderate cost."

The transition occurred without either fanfare or regret. Pearlware's contribution had been more technical than decorative, and may be compared to the invention of a better canvas for painters, an achievement appreci-

Fig. 8. Pearlware soup plate transfer printed in pale underglaze blue, the design akin to the so-called willow pattern. The unusual rim print occurs on pieces attributed to Swansea. Diameter 9½ inches; perhaps as early as 1810.

ated by artists but unnoticed by art lovers. Although "New Pearl White" was chosen for Wedgwood's Royal Jubilee service of 1809, the factory's 1810 price list featured "Cream colour" and "New white ware" but made no specific reference to the old Pearl White; nor, for that matter, did the term China glaze survive. Indeed, so quickly were the early names forgotten that Shaw (*op. cit.*) described "Pearl" only as the unglazed white ware "introduced . . . by Messrs. Cheatham [Chetham] and Woolley, of Lane End," which was "to the white Pottery, what Jasper is to the Coloured." It is small wonder, therefore, that few modern collectors have given Wedgwood's "brat" much thought or attention.

Fig. 9. Shell-edge pearlware plate with well-painted blue rim and Gothic revival underglaze-blue transfer print in center. The lines of verse, by Thomas Moore, were first published in 1808. Diameter 6½ inches.

Fig. 10. *Left:* Typical pearlware saucer painted with the Chinese house design in underglaze blue; c. 1790-1810.
*Right:* Pearlware saucer with willow pattern transfer print, also in underglaze blue. Diameter 5 inches; c. 1815-1825.

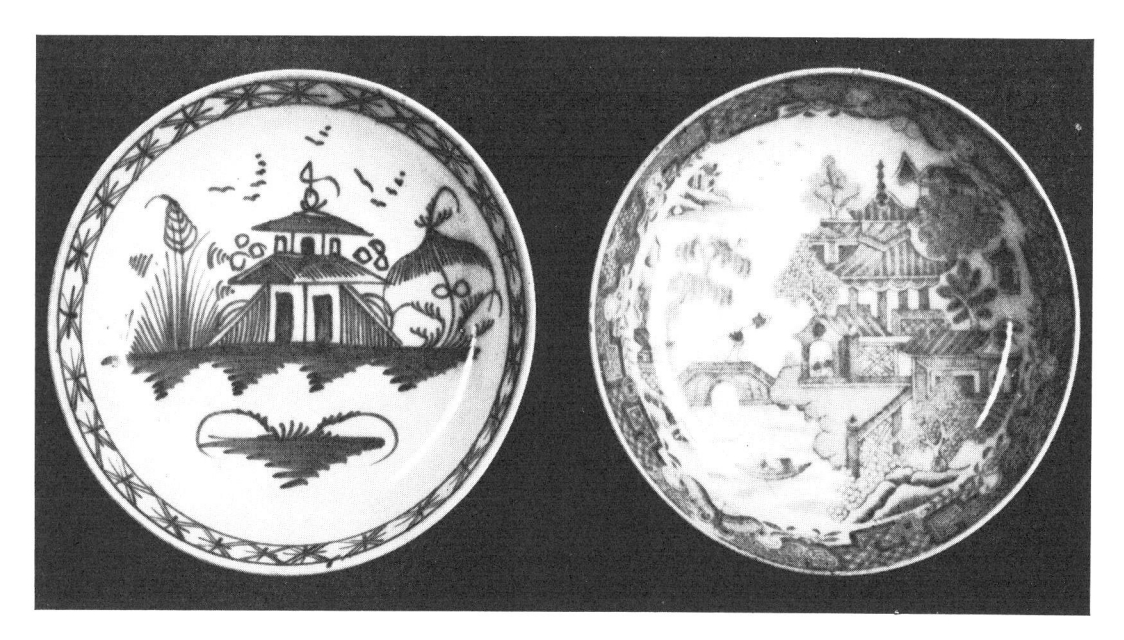

49

# Castleford pottery for the American trade

BY PATRICIA R. GUTHMAN

Blue-decorated white teapot with hinged lid and applied armorial eagle in center panel; Liberty head on reverse. This lid, secured by a metal pin, is a distinctive feature of Castleford ware. Also included in our collection is a teapot of this same type, with 36 impressed on the bottom, but with a lid that slides out over the handle, another feature characteristic of Castleford. *All illustrations are from the collection of Mr. and Mrs. William H. Guthman; photographs by Taylor and Dull.*

IN THE EARLY 1790's David Dunderdale established the Castleford Pottery about fifteen miles southeast of Leeds in Yorkshire, England. During the thirty years the factory was in operation several types of wares were made. Creamwares were one of Dunderdale's main products and it is evident from his pattern book, issued in several languages in 1796, that he intended to copy the creamware of Leeds, where he had been apprenticed. The 259 creamware designs he illustrated are merely inferior imitations of those in the Leeds pattern book. A black basalt of the type perfected and widely distributed by Wedgwood was another of Dunderdale's principal products.

But what Castleford is best known for—and indeed what the name Castleford means to most people nowadays—is the smooth white jasperlike stoneware produced there. Vitreous, translucent when held to the light, this was mainly used for teapots and other tea wares and was decorated with raised ornaments. Blue—or occasionally green or brown—was frequently used to outline panels and borders. Some pieces are lightly covered with a "smear" glaze, achieved by a process in which the biscuit is refired in saggers smeared with glaze. This vaporizes and leaves a waxy film over the objects. Others, which have been "dipped," have a thicker glaze. Pots were made in one of two ways: either the clay was pressed into molds, or slip was poured into molds, which produced thinner pieces. Three types of lids appear on the teapots: a sliding one, a hinged one secured with a metal pin, and the usual lifting lid.

According to A. Hurst's *Catalogue of the Boynton Collection of Yorkshire Pottery*, 1922, there are three marks which can be definitely assigned to Castleford:

| 1) D.D. & Co. CASTLEFORD POTTERY | 2) D.D. & Co. CASTLEFORD | 3) CASTLEFORD POTTERY |

L. M. Bickerton ("What is Castleford Pottery," *Apollo*, July 1948, p. 18) states that none of the three marks has been found on Castleford made for the American trade. These wares, from the same molds as pieces meant for the European market but with American patriotic motifs replacing classical scenes and figures in the center medallions, sometimes do have a number impressed on the bottom. The most common impressed number is 22, but 36, 34, and 13 are also recorded. The numbers do not always insure a given pattern, but in our collection of Castleford decorated with patriotic American motifs,

Blue-decorated teapot with sliding lid; applied Liberty head in center panel and eagle on reverse. The decorative borders were formed by the mold in which the teapot was made, but the center medallion—eagle, Liberty head, or classical figure—was separately molded and applied (see broken eagle on cream pitcher, facing page, top).

October, 1967

Blue-decorated unnumbered teapot and matching creamer. The panels and border designs, the handles, and the crisscross rim of the teapot are unlike those of any other examples I have seen, but the daisy knob and the spout are familiar. Eagle and Liberty head, on both pieces, are identical to those on numbered pieces.

Two blue-decorated cream pitchers, each with applied eagle and Liberty head. These are identical, except in size (the one at right is about ¾ of an inch taller than the other). The decoration here suggests that the eagle and the Liberty head were always made in the same molds and applied to the piece at hand, regardless of size. In the larger pitcher the seals are neatly framed in the panels, but in the smaller, they overlap the bottom border. Though both creamers are in the pattern associated with pieces numbered *36*, the larger example is marked *24* and the smaller one has no mark at all. The Victoria and Albert Museum has a creamer, numbered *30*, in the same pattern but with a classical scene instead of the patriotic symbols in the center panel. It is therefore clear that the numbers do not always accompany American patriotic motifs, though it is possible that they do indicate a piece intended for export—either to America or to the Continent.

pieces impressed with *22* always have the same leaf design in the border and panels, though some are plain white while others have blue-stripe borders. All our examples numbered *36* have the same border and a dot-and-circle design in their panels, but once again some are plain white, and some have blue or green borders. The applied medallions in the center panels of pieces stamped with a given number vary, however. For example, a sugar bowl which exactly matches a teapot in basic form and in ornament may have different center medallions.

It seems convenient to follow Mr. Bickerton's lead in referring to pieces with one of the three Castleford marks as "marked," and to pieces with only an impressed number as "numbered." No clue to the original purpose of the numbers has yet been uncovered, and though there has been some controversy over whether unmarked pieces could even be assigned to Castleford, Mr. Bickerton believes that the numbered as well as the marked pieces came from that factory. He says, "It seems as though the marked and numbered pieces were for different markets, and it is likely that it was the numbered pots which were exported, since it is only on these that the American device is found." (The reverse is not true, however. At least one pot is known which is decorated with classical scenes and numbered but not marked.) Mr. Bickerton further says that the Castleford Pottery does not seem to have had a consistent marking policy, and there are unmarked and unnumbered pieces which are so similar to identified Castleford wares—in one case a documented unmarked and unnumbered teapot whose companion sugar bowl *is* marked—that they can reasonably be assigned to Castleford. There are one or two other characteristics peculiar to marked pots which we need not go into here, since our theme is the wares intended for the American market, none of which was marked.

Three motifs appear consistently on our Castleford wares. One that occurs in every case is the American bald eagle holding the olive branch in one talon and grasping a bundle of thirteen arrows in the other, denoting respectively peace and war. Stars and stripes decorate the escutcheon on the eagle's breast and a scroll inscribed *E Pluribus Unum* emerges from its beak. Above its head are thirteen stars surmounted by an arc of clouds. This is the American eagle as it appears in the Great Seal of the United States adopted by the Continental Congress in 1782, except that there the position of olive branch and arrows is reversed.

The second motif, which occurs frequently in conjunc-

Three pieces of blue-decorated tea ware that seem to be a set, since their borders, lids, handles, rims and other features are the same. The sugar bowl is decorated with the seated figure, whereas the creamer and the teapot have the Liberty head; all have the eagle as well. Even though it varies in this respect, the sugar bowl has *36* impressed on the bottom. The border designs found on our pieces numbered *36* are a flower-in-circle chain on the side panels and a plumelike leaf around the bottom border. In the upper corners of the main panels are large stylized motifs resembling the caduceus.

Blue-decorated teapot with panels; Liberty head on reverse. This pot shows a different type of panel and a completely different diamond design in the side sections, an elaborate shell border on the shoulder and a repeated arch border around the base—all of which make the piece unique in our collection. The daisy knob and the spout are like those on more usual pieces.

tion with the eagle, is the Liberty head in a Phrygian cap, which was adopted by the French and subsequently by the Americans as a symbol of liberty. It has been convincingly suggested (ANTIQUES, November 1937, p. 228) that the armorial eagle and the head of Liberty which decorate these wares were taken from the American ten-dollar gold piece minted in 1796. Wherever they were made, it is interesting that the American-trade wares of Castleford type invariably bear the very same eagle and Liberty head. There is never the slightest modification.

The third motif, which is substituted for the Liberty head on several of our Castleford pieces, is a seated neoclassical figure. Since she holds an olive branch and has a shield and helmet beside her, she probably represents Britannia. It is noteworthy that all the references I have found to Castleford made for the American trade refer to the coat of arms and the head of Liberty—but not one of them mentions this third figure, which repeatedly shows up on pieces in our collection.

It is obvious that the Castleford Pottery was making a strong bid for the American market by employing the Liberty head and the eagle from the coat of arms of the United States on their tea wares. Since the factory was situated near the seaport of Hull it was natural that Dunderdale was competing for the American trade, but it is curious that although these "Castleford" export wares were quite similar in over-all appearance and color, their sizes, border types and patterns, lids, and the like, were so varied. It is certainly possible—and many authorities believe this to have been the case—that other factories were producing wares of this type, which would account for the variations noted. But since so many Castleford items were unmarked or unnumbered, and since the oddities we have acquired, also unnumbered, do not correspond to the marked pieces of any other factory, I have classified them all as Castleford.

Blue-decorated sugar bowl with Britannia on reverse and *22* impressed on bottom. Pieces stamped *22* have the fernlike border seen here around the bottom, a leafy branch in side panels, and a simple leafy motif in the upper main-panel corners. The applied bail handle does not appear on any other piece of Castleford that I have seen, but the lid, of the lift-top type, is found on all Castleford sugar bowls in our collection.

Blue-decorated rounded teapot with classical figure on reverse. This handsome pot differs from all others in our collection in its oval, swelling shape, its larger size, and its border designs. The form suggests a later date than the octagonal examples. The straight spout, too, is completely different, as are the handle and columned sides. The knob and flower-in-circle rim along with the overall effect of the piece, and of course the patriotic decoration, make us think it is Castleford, though it is unnumbered and may be from another establishment. We have a creamer which matches this in all respects except that it is plain white.

Plain white teapot, *36* impressed on bottom; decorated with same motifs as our other items numbered *36*. Part of a rare three-piece all-white set. This and the matching creamer have the Liberty head on reverse, but the sugar bowl has the figure of Britannia. We also have a matching teapot in a smaller size.

# II English Eighteenth-Century Porcelains

The history of porcelain-making in England in the 18th century is probably the most over-recorded chapter in the story of European ceramics. As such, it is simply a reflection of the narrow-mindedness of the collectors who have largely been responsible for writing it.

Porcelain production came late to England, for it was not until the 1740s that potters in London and elsewhere met with any success in their experiments. The first type of porcelain to be made in England, a soft, soapy, smooth, and semi-opaque material generically known as soft paste, was closer to contemporary French porcelain than to the true oriental or German hard paste variety. Both technically and aesthetically it was more an opaque glass than a true porcelain, and as such was effectively exploited by modelers and decorators who were able to work within the limits imposed by the material. However, it was always a costly, luxurious material, expensive and wasteful in its production and unable to rival the imported oriental and European porcelains in either quality or price. Despite this, factories sprang up in great profusion in the middle of the 18th century in Chelsea, Bow, Derby, Worcester, Liverpool, Lowestoft and elsewhere; some were successful, while others soon found to their cost how expensive, time-consuming, and unpredictable the manufacture of porcelain could be. Although the problems were great and the bankruptcies frequent, the English potters persevered. Later in the century, further experimentation and the development of the china clay deposits in Cornwall led to the manufacture of a type of true hard paste porcelain, at Plymouth, Bristol, and other centers. However, the production of this new material proved to be even more costly and hazardous than the soft paste variety. By the 1780s, procelain was a well established part of the English ceramic industry, although its artistic and social significance was far greater than its economic.

For this reason, it would be wrong to dismiss English 18th-century porcelains too hastily. The factories that did survive, and were successful, at Chelsea, Derby, and Worcester, made a considerable contribution to the development of English taste of the period. Through the efforts of these factories, the making of ceramics changed from an essentially domestic industry into one of considerable artistic quality. For the first time, it became possible to judge ceramics by the same criteria as silver, furniture, and the other applied arts, and thus to see them as part of broad artistic movements such as the rococo and neo-classicism. This was expressed both in the elaborate modeling, and in the enjoyment of both color and ornamentation, neither of which had really been seen in English ceramics before. That this was an alien enjoyment, based on European, oriental and exotic models cannot be denied; however, this was a characteristic of the 18th century as a whole.

As the history of English porcelain has largely been written by collectors, it is full of the curiously individual interpretations, whims, and fancies inevitably associated with collecting. As a result, some comparatively minor factories, such as Lowestoft, have received an extraordinary amount of attention. In the case of Lowestoft, this was probably because of the theory that the factory had produced much of the Chinese export porcelain of the period; this totally bizarre and today unbelievable conceit was still widely supported as late as the 1920s. More unfortunate perhaps is the quite disproportionate amount of study that has been directed towards the Longton Hall factory, the technical and artistic ineptness of whose products resulted in the speedy brankruptcies of its owners. Owing to the serious lack of historical balance to which collectors are frequently prone, this interesting, but very minor experimental factory has achieved a status and renown quite beyond its actual worth. By the same token, important factories, manufacturers, and designers have been inadequately researched simply because the products do not have sufficient collector-appeal.

The serious study of English porcelain has also been adversely affected by both the lack of technical knowledge, and the pseudo-scientific approach of many of the writers. The histories of many factories, such as those in the Liverpool area, have often been written on the basis of casual attribution, unsupported by either documentary or archaeological evidence. Wares have been grouped together in quite arbitrary ways, simply to suit the predilections of particular collectors who have disregarded the basic fact that many factories produced identical products. Similarly the study of techniques such as transfer printing, closely associated with the development of enamels and porcelains in England, has rarely been undertaken in the necessary context of a broad understanding of printing technology. When questioned on his technical background, the collector often falls back on his alchemy, of which a perfect example is the attribution of porcelains by transmitted light. In theory, this method of attribution seems to give very positive results, but it is based on the quite false premise that all porcelains produced at any one factory were made from identical ingredients and fired under precisely identical conditions. Clearly such control and regularity would be hard to achieve today and was certainly quite impossible in the 18th century.

# Battersea and Bilston Enamels

*By* G. Bernard Hughes

THE word "Battersea" as applied to small articles of printed enamel has become a general descriptive term rather than an indication of a specific place of manufacture. Yet it is well for the collector to realize that a goodly number of the dainty candlesticks, patch boxes, inkstands, and the like, of enameled metal, which he finds in the antique shops, though often attributed to Battersea, are, in reality, the product of other places.

The Battersea factory happened to be located in a district of London; its proprietor, furthermore, was a man of aristocratic lineage, a prominent member of the community, and, in 1754, Lord Mayor of London. He eventually failed in business, and the advertisement of the subsequent sale of his effects is still preserved. So it came about that the Battersea establishment attracted greater public attention than its contemporaries, and, even today, receives a perhaps disproportionate recognition from historians of English handicrafts. That is the reason why, to the careless observer, all specimens of painted enamel are known as Battersea, just as all pressed glass is known as Sandwich. It is the purpose of these notes to describe the products of Battersea and other contemporary English factories, and to suggest ways of differentiating one from another.

Painted enamel work, an art invented, so it is said, during the fifteenth century, by a Venetian glass blower, was first made in England by Stephen Theodore Janssen at York House in Battersea about 1750. As already remarked, Janssen was a man of high standing, third son of Sir Theodore Janssen, a French refugee, and fourth and last baronet of his line. At the time of his death, in fashionable Soho Square, he was the close friend of princes and the boon companion of artists. Having acquired York House, onetime residence of the Archbishop of Canterbury, Janssen there organized a factory for the making of enameled wares.* In 1756 he failed,

*Fig. 1 — Battersea Plaque (c. 1752)*
Colored over a transfer print.
*From the collection of Miss Gladys Hall*

\* It is not to be assumed that any process of enamel decoration, unless it be the use of transfer printing, actually originated at Battersea. On the whole, the painted enamels of France were superior to English products. Fine specimens of the art were likewise produced in most of the other countries of Continental Europe and in China. The Battersea establishment and its English contemporaries, however, did much to popularize enamel work, and to bring it within reach of the average purse. This was made possible largely through the use of transfer printing in the decoration. There is reasonable ground for believing that this method was first perfected by the French engraver Ravenet during residence in England, and that it was successfully utilized at Battersea before its exploitation in behalf of porcelain and earthenware by Sadler and Green of Liverpool. — *Ed.*

*Fig. 2 — Battersea Boxes (1750–1756)*
The scrollwork on the sides of the first example, with its enclosed diaper patterns, is evidence of Battersea origin.
*From the collection of Miss Gladys Hall*

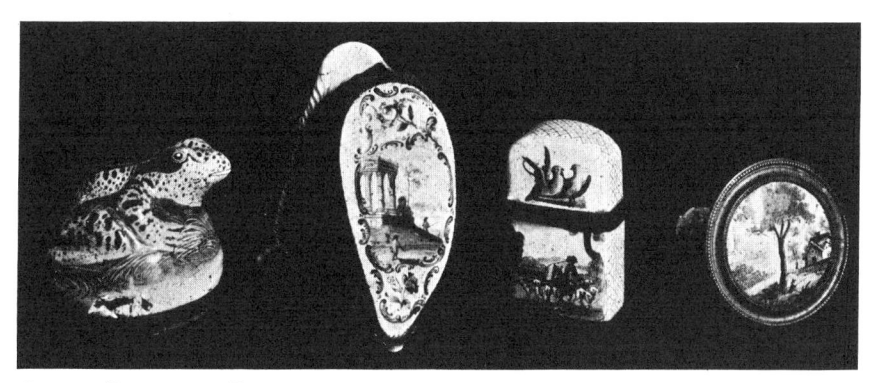

*Fig. 3 — BILSTON AND BATTERSEA*
*a*, Frog-shaped box, Bilston; *b*, rare type of snuffbox made from a cowrie shell with decorated enamel lid, Battersea; *c*, Bilston etui; *d*, Bilston drawer or mirror knob.
*From the Marcus King collection*

and his household effects and stock in trade were sold at auction, as has previously been told.

The characteristic of these wares is a copper base covered with soft white enamel, which, either in the natural color, or as a reserve in a tinted pink or blue ground, offers a surface for decoration — painted by hand or applied by the well-known transfer process.* The high glaze peculiar to these enamels is an indication that lead played an important part in their composition.

As for the nature of the decoration, it was widely diversified. Landscapes, figures, vases, flowers, birds, and portraits of celebrities were favorite motives; but mottoes, sentiments, and verses were likewise popular. Painted designs were usually carried out in full color in imitation of the china decorator's technique; but transfers were usually confined to black or sepia, with occasional exceptions in favor of crimson, mauve, and brick red, save where the transfer served as an outline for full color painting. The transfer method of printing enamels is peculiar to British practice, a point to be remembered when one is trying to determine the origin of a specimen. The true Battersea transfers, moreover, are almost invariably clear and distinct; whereas, those made in other parts of England are frequently obscured beneath a thick surface gloss.

As for color, Battersea boxes were usually covered with pink or blue washes over the white enamel body. Gilt or gold Rococo scrollwork and foliate ornament were applied as a decorative finish. Many of these patterns were in imitation of contemporary French enamel work; yet they were not slavish copies, and something of native English taste and creative genius is perceptible in them all. This fondness of the Battersea decorators for scrollwork, with trellis and diaper patterns by way of variety, gives us another means of identifying the true Battersea product; since precisely similar motives do not appear on the enamels of other English factories of the time.

On the whole, too, the best of the portrait enamels were turned out at Battersea. Among them appear the three Georges, the Gunning sisters, the Duke of Dorset, Admiral Boscawen, Sir Robert Walpole, and Horace Walpole. The latter Walpole, indeed, seems to have had a fancy for Battersea pieces. In 1755 he sent Richard Berkley a snuffbox of the ware "done with copper plates." He mentions similar items in his writings, and his inventory discloses ownership of

*Fig. 4 — BILSTON AND BATTERSEA*
The first three etuis are typical of those made in the South Staffordshire factories. The columned ruin of the fourth points to Battersea production.

*Fig. 5 — BILSTON BOXES*
Sprigged snuffboxes similar to these are fairly common. They are of Bilston manufacture.

---
* It is maintained by some that the basis of all Battersea pictorial decoration is a transfer outline, sometimes colored by hand, sometimes not. It is, however, difficult to verify such sweeping statements.

57

three or four examples.

SOUTH STAFFORDSHIRE FACTORIES

But many of the brilliantly colored enamels attributed to Battersea probably originated in South Staffordshire — at Bilston and Wednesbury — where, until well into the nineteenth century, several factories were devoted to their manufacture. It is quite possible that these establishments antedated the York House project; for it has been definitely established that enamels were produced at Bilston in 1760, and a recently discovered lease refers to a Bilston enamel works as early as 1749. More recent records indicate that, in 1780, there were at least three enamel-box makers established in Bilston — Thomas Perry (d. *1808*), Mary Bickley (d. *1780*), and Isaac Beckett.

Mary Bickley confined her decorating exclusively to hand painting, which she accomplished with exquisite skill and taste. Her favorite motive was a delicate spray of flowers upon a netted or mesh background. Isaac Beckett, on the other hand, utilized transfers extensively, sometimes filling the printed outlines with color so as to achieve delightful effects. It is the Bickley and Beckett enamels among Bilston types that are most liable to confusion with Battersea productions.

In general, Bilston enamels were decorated in all colors;

*Fig. 6* — HISTORICAL ENAMELED BOXES
 *a*, His Majesty Reviewing the Volunteer Corps 4th June 1799; *b*, Princess Charlotte (d. 1817); *c*, The Late Glorious Victory over the Spanish Fleet by Admiral Sir John Jervis, K.B. 1797. All South Staffordshire types.
 From the Marcus King collection

*Fig. 7* — SOUTH STAFFORDSHIRE ENAMELS (*c. 1760*)
 The portraits are typical of South Staffordshire work.

*Fig. 8* — SOUTH STAFFORDSHIRE BOXES
 The first shows the mesh or netted background upon a plain color.
 From the Marcus King collection

but a peculiar rose color known as Rose Pompadour was a special favorite, though it did not come into use until after 1760. The most frequent ornamental motives were small flowers and gilt borders. Candlesticks, round salts supported on three or four feet, snuffboxes, patch boxes, toothpick cases, etuis, and finely modeled toys in the shape of birds, animals, human heads, fruit, and the like, were among the articles manufactured at Bilston.

One of the latest of the enamel factories was that of John Yardley at Wednesbury, where toys and decorated boxes were made even during the 1850's. But these were of crude workmanship, and were finished with a high gloss. To enamels, as to other artistic products, the nineteenth century brought coarseness and technical degradation.

DATING AND ATTRIBUTING ENAMELS

In the dating and attributing of enamels, a few fundamental facts will serve as aids to accuracy. Bear these hints in mind:

*Color* — Dark blue first used as a ground color in 1755.
  Pea green, 1759.
  Turquoise and claret color, 1760.
  When uncolored, the ground of Bilston enamels is hard and very white.

58

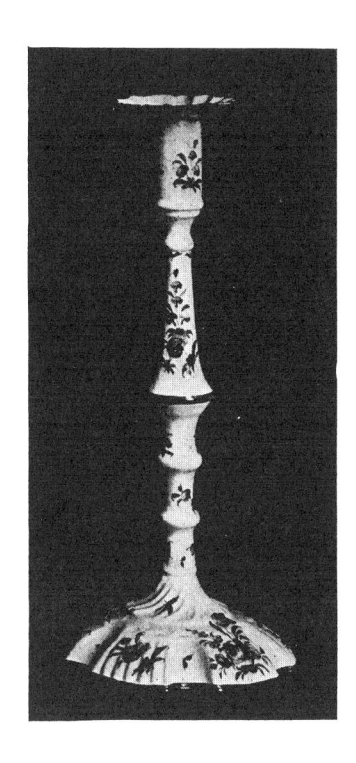

*Fig. 9* — CANDLESTICKS AND DESK TRAY
White enamel with flower sprays in the Bilston manner.
*From the collection of Mrs. Bantock*

In general, though with marked exceptions to the rule, Bilston colors are less refined than those of Battersea. Violent contrasts rather than subtle harmonies characterize Bilston work.

*Form* — Small boxes with corrugated sides did not occur much before 1805.

*Mirrors* — Polished steel mirrors in patch boxes were discontinued about 1785, when glass mirrors were substituted. A patch box with a glass mirror is therefore best attributed to Bilston.

*Character of Design* — Many of the decorations used on Bilston enamels were copied from Pillement's designs in *The Ladies Amusement or the Whole Art of Japanning*, published, 1760. Specimens bearing patterns borrowed from this source definitely originated in the South Staffordshire workshops.

In attributing portrait enamels, it is well to find the date of the original from which the enamel version has been derived. If, as will often be the case, this original was executed after the closing of York House in Battersea, 1756, we must credit Bilston with the copy.* The works of Sir Joshua Reynolds, for example, were reproduced in miniature with great skill by the Bilston enamelers. The so-called Battersea knobs shipped to America and there largely treasured, probably belong in the South Staffordshire category; for they are obviously of late date.

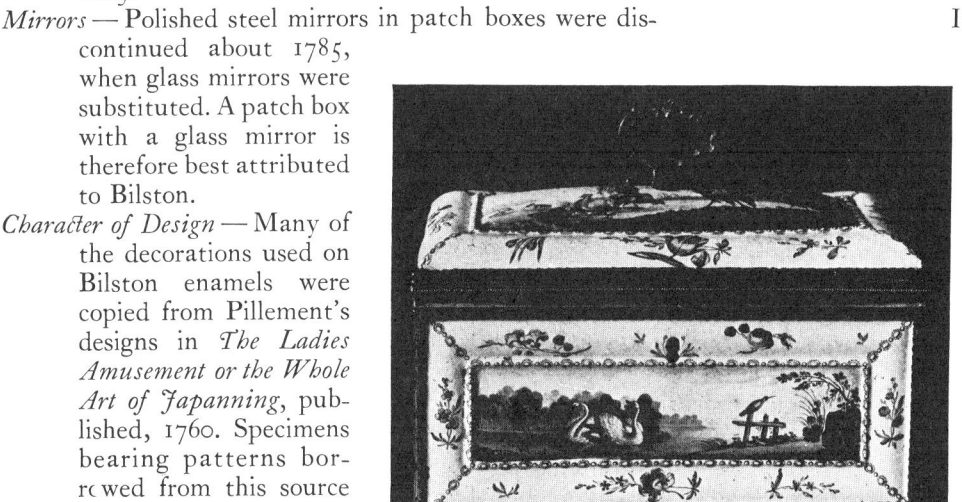

*Fig. 10* — TEA BOX (*c. 1760*)
The design, adapted from *The Ladies' Amusement*, indicates South Staffordshire origin.
*From the collection of Miss Gladys Hall*

IMITATIONS

Among the modern imitator's favorite products are many pseudo-Battersea enamels. The majority of these are made in France, whence they find their way to all the markets of the world. For the most part, they take the form of snuffboxes, conveniently enlarged to cigarette size, patch boxes, and candlesticks. Often they are cleverly aged, and show chips and cracks that would appear to be the workmanship of time alone. Their detection is not easy even to one whose eye is trained to take note of very slight variations in quality. Usually, however, these modern commercial enamels are inferior to their early prototypes. Those which are inscribed with sentiments are not so well lettered as they should be, and those which are more elaborately decorated with landscapes and figures, while effective, lack the fine exactitude of touch which characterizes the eighteenth-century examples. Most of the better grade shops that deal in porcelains carry these modern enamels, which are procurable at reasonable prices. Old-time specimens are not so easily found though they occasionally appear in public sales whence they find their way into regular trade channels.

---
*William Turner, in his *Transfer Printing on Enamels, Porcelain and Pottery* (London, 1907), states that the York House enterprise was continued for twenty years after the Janssen failure. Other writers suggest that former York House workmen maintained small independent shops in the Battersea district. In either case, Battersea enamels appear to have been made subsequent to 1756. — *Ed.*

# WORCESTER PORCELAIN

## Of the Doctor Wall Period

### By MARCEL H. STIEGLITZ

FIG. 1—PAIR OF HEXAGONAL VASES, painted in underglaze blue *(c. 1760)*.

*All of the illustrations are from the author's collection.*

IN THE MANY collections that have been formed of Doctor Wall Worcester porcelain, comparatively little attention has been paid to the collecting of the very early pieces, or to the so-called "penciled" ware. It is quite possible that the reason for the former omission is the fact that only recently have enough research and investigation been done to convince authorities and collectors alike that many specimens usually ascribed to Lowdin's factory of Bristol are actually Worcester. It is fairly well established that when Doctor Wall commenced the manufacture of porcelain at Worcester in June 1751, he did not start from scratch. At any rate, it was announced in July 1752 that he had merged the Lowdin factory, so that many of the very early examples of the Worcester porcelain were manufactured with the molds, workmen, and enamelers of the merged company.

The early pieces of 1752-1755 are of real interest because it was during these formative years that Doctor Wall experimented with the paste and decoration of his wares, and it was through these early experiments that Worcester porcelain became one of the finest porcelains of eighteenth-century England. As an example of this early experimental period, there is illustrated a molded teapot with raised pattern of contrasting designs on either side *(Fig. 2)*. Of interest also is an early three-piece garniture which sagged in the firing *(Fig. 3)*.

Many of the molds used in those days were copied from the silversmiths of that period, and it was only later in the development of the factory that original designs were used. The use of silver designs was probably occasioned by the influence of Samuel Bradley, silversmith, who was one of the original subscribers to the "Worcester Tonquin Manufacture," as the original concern was known.

The enamel painting of this period is a thing of great delicacy, reminding one of the work at York House, Battersea, known as Battersea enamel. In fact, it is quite possible that these early pieces were enameled by men who had worked at the Battersea factory. The workmanship, in my judgment, was never surpassed. The colors are so beautifully blended and the refinement of design so exact that it has often made me wonder whether the artists worked with a magnifying glass. An example of the close connection with Battersea can

FIG. 2—MOLDED TEAPOT, enameled in Chinese taste *(c. 1755)*. Two views.

FIG. 3—THREE-PIECE GARNITURE, enameled in colors after the Chinese taste *(c. 1755)*.

May, 1947

FIG. 4—TEAPOT, molded in low relief with a design which is enameled in lilac *(c. 1755)*.

FIG. 5—*Left*, DEMI-TASSE with design known as *Gypsy Fortune Teller (c. 1758)*; *right*, CREAMER, enameled after the Chinese taste *(c. 1760)*.

be seen in the enameling on a demi-tasse, in *gypsy fortune teller* design *(Fig. 5, left)*. With slight variations, the same design was used at Battersea. From specimens I have seen and collected of that period, none have come to my attention which could be considered ornate, garish or not in perfect taste. Designs are simple and the shapes are beautifully proportioned.

The Oriental influence in color and design was early apparent in Worcester porcelain. An imitation of the Chinese taste is seen in the beautifully formed ewer, a piece which kept its shape *(Fig. 6)*.

About 1760 Worcester was manufacturing services in the rare penciled ware. Penciling was originated in China about 1730, and was merely a means of hand decoration by the use of a very finely pointed brush, using a metallic-base India ink for color. Why these penciled examples are so rare, or why so few collectors have interested themselves in this facet of the Worcester factory, I cannot say. To me, at least, the examples I have collected are a real joy. The design is much clearer, finer, and more brilliant than any pieces of transfer printing that I have seen. The workmanship is meticulous and the patterns most interesting. Unfortunately, very little has been written on this subject and not much is known about it. To the best of my knowledge, Worcester was the only English porcelain factory of the eighteenth century that produced services of this type, although certain European factories did manufacture penciled ware during the Wall period.

The only India inks that I believe were used were black and lake (lilac), as those are the only penciled colors I have seen in my search for these examples. Specimens in lake are really quite rare; I have procured only one, illustrated here, in several years' search *(Fig. 8)*. Strangely, the pattern on this shows no Oriental touch at all, but rather the influence of Robert Hancock, the most prolific of Worcester's engravers for transfer-printed ware. The black penciled examples that have come to my attention, however, definitely show the Oriental influence *(Fig. 9, left)*. Of particular interest are the teabowl and saucer with decorations of flowers and butterflies

FIG. 6—EWER, with wheatsheaf design *(c. 1757)*.

FIG. 7—COVERED BOWL AND SAUCER, enameled with flowers and having flower knob on cover of bowl *(c. 1757)*.

FIG. 8—PLATE with penciled design in lake *(c. 1760)*.

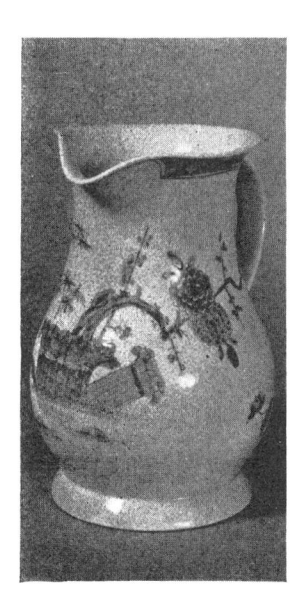

61

Fig. 9—*Left*, Bowl, black pencil decoration shows Oriental influence (*c. 1760*); *right*, Plate, transfer printed after a design by Pillement (*c. 1760*).

Fig. 10—Teabowl and Saucer, penciled in black with touches of gold (*c. 1760*).

(*Fig. 10*). These are possibly among the early penciled pieces. They are slightly enriched in gold, the only instance of this I know in examples of penciled ware. Figure 9 (*right*) shows a combination of the pencil and transfer print techniques. The center decoration, a design after Jean Pillement, is transfer-printed, and is much lighter in tone than the design on the rim of the saucer, which is penciled in black. This offers a good illustration of the brilliance and fineness of penciled work, as compared to the usual transfer pieces.

The next ten years of porcelain manufacture at Worcester were those in which most progress was made in the development of the beautifully decorated and gilded services (*Fig. 11*). The scale-blue and pea-green grounds, the exotic birds, and paintings by Donaldson and O'Neale were all brought to such heights that by the year 1770, I dare say, no porcelain factory in England could compare with Worcester. At about this time Worcester also produced figures, one of which appears on the cover of this magazine. Known as *The Gardener's Wife,* this figure is one of a pair. A mate is in the Lloyd collection at the British Museum. To date there are ascribed to Worcester examples of only two pairs of figures, *The Gardener* and *The Gardener's Wife,* and a man and woman dressed in Turkish costume, known as *The Turks*. It is possible, as time goes on, and we gain more knowledge, other figures now ascribed to other English porcelain works may be reascribed to Worcester.

And now a word or two as to the means of recognizing Wall Worcester; and let me add that although these methods are helpful, they are not infallible. First, the glaze does not craze; second, there is usually a shrinkage of the glaze around the base; third, when seen through transmitted light, the paste takes on a greenish hue. The usual Worcester marks, such as the fretted square, the open crescent, the script *W*, and marks in imitation of Chinese characters, are not proofs of authenticity, since these symbols were imitated by other factories. A great many important and highly sought-after pieces were never marked. It is only through seeing and handling Wall Worcester that one recognizes its characteristics.

Fig. 11—*Left*, Sauce Tureen and Cover with *gros bleu* ground (*c. 1770*); *right*, Dish decorated with fruits and flowers (*c. 1770*).

Fig. 12—Chinese Porcelain Saucer and Worcester Cup, a copy made to match the Chinese original (*c. 1765*).

*Fig. 1* — TEACUP AND SAUCER (*Worcester*)
*Victoria and Albert Museum.*

# "Powdered Blue" in English Porcelain

By BERNARD RACKHAM

*Department of Ceramics, Victoria and Albert Museum*

COLLECTORS of English porcelain will be familiar with a certain class of design which seems to have enjoyed a wide popularity in the sixties and seventies of the eighteenth century. I refer to an arrangement of circular and fan-shaped panels containing landscapes and small floral themes painted in blue, reserved on a "powdered blue" ground. The white panels are effected by covering up those parts of the surface of the piece whilst the blue color is being sprayed on, before the application of the glaze.

These designs are found alike upon teapots, cups and saucers, sugar basins, and the various other items of tea services; upon meat dishes, dinner plates, and shell-shaped fruit dishes; and upon water bottles and basins for the small washstands of the period. They are, of course, not an English invention, but an adaptation from the Chinese. From the time of K'ang Hsi onwards, we find in Chinese porcelain a similar decoration of panels reserved on a sprayed or powdered blue ground, and painted with landscapes or flower motives, either in blue or in enamel colors. This same class of Chinese porcelain inspired the colored grounds, the *Fondporzellan*, of Meissen and other German factories, and later of Sèvres.

The marks on these English wares do not, as a rule, give any help in determining their factory of origin. Only occasionally do we find, as on the cup and saucer in Figure 1, a recognized factory mark. In this particular instance, the origin is doubly established by two of the Worcester marks used together, the crescent and the so-called "fretted square," itself of course an adaptation of a Chinese mark. As a rule, the mark on the pieces we are discussing is a group of characters, four or six, imitating in a rough and ready manner the *nien-hao*, or reign-mark, of Chinese porcelain. The addition, in exceptional cases, of a somewhat faint-hearted forgery of the crossed swords of Meissen confuses rather than helps the issue. To decide the question of origin, therefore, we must generally be guided by technical considerations alone.

In the Schreiber Collection of the Victoria and Albert Museum are several plates of this class, which, in the original catalogue of the collection, published in 1885, were attributed to Worcester. One of them is shown in Figure 2. Plates and dishes exactly resembling them have also been attributed, in my opinion mistakenly, to Lowestoft. There is little doubt in my mind that such pieces were made at Bow, as they show definite Bow characteristics.

The paste is, in some instances, almost opaque; in others, of a dusky brownish translucence, displaying here and there lighter flecks or fissures. These latter

63

January, 1928

*Figs. 2* and *2a* — PLATE (*Bow*)

Decorated in the Chinese manner in reserves on a powdered blue ground. The mark, shown in *2a* — one of several similar marks used by the Bow factory — is an attempt to imitate Oriental characters. Compare Figure 8a.
*Victoria and Albert Museum (Schreiber Collection).*

*Fig. 3* — SLOP BASIN (*Bow*)
*Victoria and Albert Museum (Broderip Gift).*

*Fig. 4* — PLATE *(Caughley, Salopian china)*
*Victoria and Albert Museum (Broderip Gift).*

*Fig. 4a* — MARKS ON PLATE OF FIGURE 4

are due to defective cohesion of the paste, and appear on the surface of a piece, under the glaze, in the form of what may be likened to pockmarks on the human skin, or the small fissures in a lump of uncooked dough.

The glaze is soft and absorbent, and consequently tinged with brown, where a small chip or crack has allowed it to become impregnated with grease in the course of daily use and washing. These qualities of paste and glaze are seen in pieces of ascertained Bow origin.

The plates and dishes sometimes have a projecting foot-ring, but are usually of the Dutch form, with sunk centre under the base (as in *A* in the annexed sections, *Fig. 5*) common in Delft earthenware, but not occurring — or only very exceptionally occurring — on English porcelain other than Bow. This form is found in such unquestioned Bow pieces as plates with the Kakiemon partridge or "quail" pattern, in distinctive Bow enamels, and in plates with *Prunus* reliefs on the rim, authenticated by "wasters" found on the site of the factory.

The marks on one of the plates in the Schreiber Collection are reproduced in Figure 2a. The faint and unconvincing imitation of the Meissen crossed swords will be observed alongside the sham Chinese characters. A much better imitation of the Meissen mark is seen on a pretty slop basin, also at South Kensington (*Fig. 3*).

As regards shapes, we find not only circular but also (as frequently in Bow porcelain) octagonal plates and oblong eight-sided dishes, and bulbous water bottles (*Fig. 6*).

The powdered blue in these Bow examples is definitely speckled, and

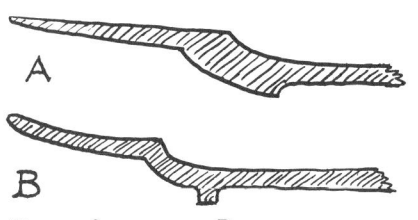

*Fig. 5* — SECTIONS OF PLATES
A. Showing characteristic base of Bow plates and dishes with sunk centre under the base.
B. Showing characteristic *Salopian* base with bold foot-ring.

65

of a strong sapphire tone. A plate in the Herbert Allen Collection, exhibited on loan at South Kensington (*Fig. 8*) is decorated with exotic birds in the panels, in enamel colors including the typical "stale mustard" yellow, slatey blue, and purplish crimson of Bow. The blue ground in this case is lighter than usual in tone and poor in color. The pseudo-Chinese mark on the back of this plate is shown in Figure 8a. Bow plates also occur in which there is no painted design, the entire surface being covered with the speckly "powdered blue."

Pieces which can justly be attributed to Lowestoft show an even greenish cream colored translucence.* The powdered blue ground is generally blotchy and smudgy, and of darker tone than that of Bow. The plate in the British Museum (*Fig. 9*) with a view of Lowestoft Parish Church is an unimpeachable example. The teapot in the Schreiber Collection at South Kensington is also typical (*Fig. 7*).

The pattern was used at Worcester, but here again, even when the factory marks of a crescent, a script *W*, or a fretted square are not present to settle the question, the technical characteristics will be a guide. The paste shows the duck's egg greenish translucence of the first Worcester body, the glaze is tight and even, and free from the stains by which the soft Bow glaze is often disfigured. The blue is of a pleasant dark-greyish tone, almost "navy blue," and

*For an account of English Lowestoft porcelain the reader is referred to an article on the subject by Frederick Litchfield, in ANTIQUES, Vol. I, p. 252.

*Fig. 6 — WATER BOTTLE (Bow)*
*Victorian and Albert Museum (Schreiber Collection).*

*Fig. 7 — TEAPOT (Lowestoft)*
*Victoria and Albert Museum (Schreiber Collection).*

sprayed on so evenly as to form a dense unbroken covering. The foot-ring has the neat Worcester finish of blunt triangular section, and within it, as a rule, will be found a narrow circle bare of glaze, as usual in Worcester porcelain. Figure 1 shows a typical Worcester example.

Lastly we pass to the examples of this pattern on "Salopian china," the porcelain made, from 1772 onwards, at the Shropshire factory of Caughley. A plate at South Kensington (*Fig. 4*), with the name *Salopian* impressed in small neat characters on the back (*Fig. 4a*), will serve very well as a criterion. The paste is of a fairly even creamy translucence. The powdered blue is granular, and much like that of Worcester as regards tone. In addition to the impressed mark, the plate shows some feathery imitations of Chinese characters in blue, in a form making no sort of pretence to be decipherable, and recalling the disguised Arabic numerals which are the recognised mark of a certain other class of Salopian china. The plate has a bold foot-ring, of rectangular section (as in *B* of Figure 5).

So far as I am aware, this decoration was not used at Chelsea or Derby, or at Longton Hall, and if it should appear on Liverpool porcelain, the usual poor quality of Liverpool as regards pigment and glaze should make it easy to recognise. It seems, to judge from the number of specimens surviving, that its popularity was greatest at Bow, probably from about 1760 onwards to the closing of the factory in 1776.

66

# The identification of Liverpool porcelain of the early period, 1756-1765

BY KNOWLES BONEY

IN THE YEAR 1755 Richard Chaffers, Liverpool potter, entered into partnership with Philip Christian of Liverpool and Robert Podmore of Worcester to make porcelain. No marketable product appeared until December 1756, but for fifty years after that date many other Liverpool potters followed their example and turned to the manufacture of soft-paste porcelain.

The study of this porcelain has advanced considerably during the last twenty years (a letter in *Apollo* for March 1951, signed Collington Bishop, sheds much light on the state of our knowledge on this subject as recently as twelve years ago), and some of the difficulties attending its recognition have disappeared. Those that remain affecting the early wares chiefly result from the resemblances which we might expect to find between these and the wares of the parent factory, Worcester. Not every difficulty, however, disappears with the waning of Worcester influence, which probably set in before the death of Chaffers in 1765. The latter part of the eighteenth century was a time when the manufacture of porcelain in England was still in the experimental stage and potters copied the successful lines of their competitors without scruple. As a result it is difficult to distinguish between the later products of Liverpool and those of New Hall and Caughley, not to mention others of more doubtful Staffordshire parentage (*e.g.*, Baddeley & Fletcher), of which we are still lamentably ignorant. We should also remember that the use of bone ash was constantly increasing, bringing the product closer and closer to today's

Fig. 1. Teapot of flattened globular shape with polychrome decoration "in the Chinese taste." Height 4⅞ inches over all. *All Liverpool porcelain illustrated from the Knowles Boney Collection, Williamson Art Gallery, Birkenhead, England; Figs. 1, 4, 6, from the author's* Liverpool Porcelain of the Eighteenth Century, *by courtesy of B. T. Batsford Ltd.*

Fig. 2. Bell-shape mug brilliantly enameled in *famille rose* colors. Height 4¾ inches.

Fig. 3. Tea bowl of eggshell porcelain painted with "peony and dots" pattern in blue. Height 1¾ inches.

Fig. 4. Bell-shape mug printed in black with portrait of Pitt; Signed *I. Sadler Liverpool Enaml.* Height 6½ inches.

Fig. 5. Coffeepot painted with the arms of Isley impaling Piggott. Height 8½ inches over all.

standard porcelain body and thereby making distinctions ever more difficult.

Although we are accustomed to speak of Liverpool porcelain in much the same way as we speak of Derby, Chelsea, or Worcester porcelain, the term in fact covers the wares of almost a dozen potteries over a span of some fifty years. During this time a variety of substances were used in its manufacture in many different ways. While such conditions were not conducive to uniformity, many unifying factors were at work, of which two deserve mention. Firstly, the great size of the pottery community (which of course included the makers of earthenware) provided a pool of labor which permitted easy exchange of ideas and methods. Secondly, the vogue of the outside decorator whose "hand" and stock patterns covered a wide field was a considerable unifying influence. The late Peter Entwistle listed about eighty persons who carried on business in this way in Liverpool at the time; and doubtless there were many of whom there is no record.

The Worcester product now being introduced by Podmore was a soaprock porcelain with an essentially Oriental background. Ware of a phosphatic (bone-ash) type was also made in considerable quantity, not only by Chaffers' competitors but, if we accept traditional attributions, by the partnership itself when for any reason the supply of soaprock fell short. To a limited extent only, therefore, is it possible to distinguish between these two groups; but as we come to know more we shall no doubt be able to do so more readily. The unifying factors just noted were at work here, and the dual role played by Chaffers makes their separation more difficult. The description of the porcelain of the first period (1756-1765) which follows will therefore include both types, phosphatic and soaprock.

*General characteristics.*

The ware is predominantly of gray or grayish-green appearance. It is occasionally green, so green in fact that I once heard it likened to a coat of green paint (no Worcester influence here, yet the group is traditionally attributed to Chaffers). This darkish appearance is a striking feature of the ware, which is well potted although not always well proportioned. It is usually neatly finished and the forms used are simple; articles for domestic use predominate.

Except perhaps on the green ware, the glaze is thin, bluish green, and even, but not infrequently it shows imperfections —minute pitting, peppering due to small black specks, sanding, and darkened areas that look like smudgy finger marks. All these may occur, yet it is remarkable how often these defects are confined to such areas as the bases or the insides of pieces where the disfigurement is of little consequence. Glaze shrinkage inside the foot ring, well known as a Worcester characteristic, is not often seen but may occur. The thick starch-blue glaze which tends to collect in pools belongs to a later date.

The color of the ware by transmitted light may be green or greenish yellow, sometimes greenish blue, and occasionally pure blue. The latter is, rarely, encountered in Worcester wares and therefore possesses limited attributional value. Flaws in the paste sometimes appear as small glaze-filled depressions; and small tears with a linear appearance or shaped like commas may be met with.

*Individual features.*

I. Bases and foot rings yield valuable information.

a. Base flat without foot ring and unglazed except of occasional patchy volatilization. Found on cylindrical mugs, coffee cans, and (more rarely) jugs. Almost a Liverpool trade-mark.

b. Foot ring small and insignificant, at times little more than a bead. Found on teaware and has little attributional value.

c. Foot ring smallish, slightly convex in profile and forming a shallow angle with the belly of the piece. Gives a false impression because viewed from below the inside depth is seen to be one third or less that of the outside. A good Liverpool feature on much teaware (Fig. 1). May be found, but less marked, on cider mugs (Fig. 2).

d. Foot ring undercut. May be—and often is—associated with preceding. Generally confined to cups, saucers, and bowls (Fig. 3). Not met with on jugs or teapots. A Liverpool feature that is sometimes found on Worcester wares.

e. Foot ring flat, as on Worcester-model cylinders, but weight-bearing surface glazed and generally much narrower (Worcester invariably unglazed). Found on cylinders and a few coffee cans. Possesses attributional value.

f. Foot ring surmounted by a scotia molding (concave member of Ionic base molding). Weight-bearing surface of foot ring unglazed, its edge falling sharply to well-recessed glazed base. Found on Liverpool mugs of inverted bell shape (Fig. 4) and (slightly modified) on mugs with different handle generally attributed to Longton Hall. The shape is linked with a coffee cup attributed traditionally to Chaffers, although analysis of this piece shows no soaprock. But the attribution receives support from the salt-glazed Plumper mug of the same shape made by Philip Christian to commemorate the parliamentary election of 1761 (see Boney, *Liverpool Bulletin, Museum and Arts Comm.*, April 1954).

g. A type of grooved foot ring of which the profile is either rounded (Fig. 5) or flat and sloping outward at an angle of roughly forty-five degrees (Fig. 6). In both types the foot ring is usually beveled on the inner side.

II. Handles.

a. Plain, flat, and straplike with neither thumb rest nor grooving. Lower end back-turned, showing depression caused by potter's thumb. Found on large jugs of baluster shape, on many mugs (Fig. 2), and on many coffeepots (Fig. 6). Rarely on coffee cans. A distinctively Liverpool type.

b. Plain round loop (Fig. 1). Common on teapots, mugs, and small jugs, both at Liverpool and elsewhere. Is frequently ribbed on teapots (Fig. 7, where its position high on the shoulder is unusual). Lower end back-turned (never on teapots) indicates later date.

c. Similar to preceding, but the upper end descends about half an inch down the side of the piece. This is found only on small straight-sided mugs.

d. Loop with central grooving on Worcester model. Often found on coffee cups and small jugs, less often on mugs and coffee cans. Is occasionally U shape with the upper and lower portions almost parallel (Liverpool and possibly accidental).

e. Scrolled, round in section, with thumb rest and lower end back-turned. No grooving. Found on some jugs and always on mugs of type shown in Fig. 4.

f. Elaborately scrolled with thumb rest, lateral grooving, and dependent tag at lower end. Herringbone molding between thumb rest and body (Fig. 5). Found towards the end of this period and later, on coffeepots (not teapots) and on jugs and mugs of large size. A Liverpool peculiarity.

g. Scrolled handles on sauceboats are met with in great variety. The comparatively simple form illustrated in Fig. 8 is sometimes found on mugs. Others, sometimes with double C scrolls and generally more elaborate, may be encountered. Examples of an ear-shape handle may be seen on a teapot and a sauceboat in the Williamson Art Gallery, Birkenhead. A peaked handle is frequently associated with custard cups.

III. Spouts, tea- and coffeepot.

a. Plain, curved (Fig. 1).

b. Molded. Generally both scrolled and ribbed (Figs. 5, 7). Occasionally hexagonal.

Spouts, jug.

a. Wide, openmouthed, splayed type. Found on baluster-shape jugs and on some with grooved foot. Something similar found on early Derby jugs, but not in combination with the baluster shape which makes a Liverpool attribution reasonably secure.

b. Pinched lip, or sparrow-beak, type. Found in profusion on jugs of all shapes and sizes, wherever made.

c. Both the mask and the cornucopia are occasionally met with.

IV. Covers, tea- and coffeepot and vase.

a. Conical knop (Figs. 5, 7) most common.

b. Mushroom-shape knop with projecting apex (Figs. 1, 6), of common occurrence.

c. Turreted knop, uncommon.

d. Worcestor-type flower knop, rare. Covers of coffeepots tend to become progressively deeper. Underside of flange almost invariably glazed. Helical turning marks often visible inside towards center.

A few other points concerned with the identification of Liverpool porcelain of the first period may also assist. Teapots are usually globular but the flattened globular shape (Fig. 1) is not infrequently found, while an elongated shape not unlike that of Lowestoft sometimes occurs. The number of spout holes is usually more than five, the magic number which was at one time looked upon—and occasionally still is—as a Worcester characteristic. Cups and saucers may show eversion of the rims, particularly those which have poorly developed foot rings, good translucency, and are thinly potted. These are all features which indicate Oriental influence via Worcester. On the other hand, foot rings of many Liverpool cups and bowls are irregular in outline, whereas their Worcester counterparts are almost invariably perfectly circular (probably due to a potting technicality). Cylindrical mugs often show a tendency to be perfectly straight sided instead of slightly waisted; and they may exhibit a chamfered edge where side and base meet. In small jugs the attachment of the upper end of the handle is occasionally angulated (possibly accidental). Lastly, many sauceboats are elaborately molded, and in flat-based examples a row of acanthus leaves rising from the base is a favorite motif.

It may be said that in a few instances only are attributional values likely to approach the absolute. In the majority of cases a number of points must be taken into account and compared and contrasted before a conclusion can be reached. The result, as always, will be a balanced judgment the value of which will largely depend on the experience that lies behind it.

Fig. 6. Coffeepot painted in blue with English trees. Height without cover, 7⅜ inches.

Fig. 7. Teapot painted in polychrome with peony, rocks, and branch. Height 5½ inches over all.

Fig. 8. Sauceboat, molded and painted in polychrome. Length 8 inches.

*Figs. 1, 2, 3* — LOWESTOFT PORCELAIN  *British Museum*
Centre, round dish with paintings in blue on white panels. In centre medallion, view of old Lowestoft Church. The two canteen-shaped "Pilgrim Bottles" are painted, that to the left with blue on a white ground; that to the right in colors.

# Lowestoft Porcelain

## *By* Frederick Litchfield

[NOTE—Mr. Litchfield is recognized as a leading English authority on all aspects of collecting and expertising. Author, among other books, of *Pottery and Porcelain*, and editor of the eighth edition of Chaffers' monumental work on *Marks and Monograms*, he is particularly eminent in the field of ceramics. In preparing this article for ANTIQUES, Mr. Litchfield arranged for the taking of special photographs from the collections of the Victoria and Albert and the British museums. The courteous permission of the Directors and Secretaries of these institutions is hereby appreciatively acknowledged. The photographs for illustration, Figs. 11 and 12, are supplied by Mr. Albert Amor, London, Antiquary by appointment to H. M. The Queen of England.

The marks and signs found on Lowestoft are reproduced, by permission, from Mr. Litchfield's *Pottery and Porcelain*, published by Truslove & Hanson, London.—ED.]

LOWESTOFT porcelain was, some twenty-five or thirty years ago, the subject of much controversy among collectors: indeed, some of our authorities went so far as to deny its existence. Sir Wollaston Franks, the learned Keeper of the British Museum, considered that the china "termed Lowestoft" was really Oriental; i.e., Chinese porcelain decorated in England. Professor Church in his *English Pottery and Porcelain* omitted any mention of Lowestoft; while Chaffers went to the opposite extreme and gave the factory an importance out of all proportion to its real merit. Chaffers claimed as Lowestoft the Chinese hard paste porcelain table services which had been made to the order of English families, at the latter end of the eighteenth century, and which were, as a rule, decorated with coats of arms and crests, their only other ornament being a neat border to the plates, dishes, or cups and saucers, and the requisite coloring of the knobs on the covers of tureens or jugs.

This claim of Chaffers was accepted by many of the dealers of his time, and, as Lowestoft became the fashion, every plate or cup and saucer bearing a crest or coat of arms was readily sold as Lowestoft at some three or four times the price which such a specimen, in those days, would have realized as an armorial Chinese piece.

In 1895, after Mr. Chaffers' death, I was asked by his publishers to undertake the revision of his great work of reference for an Eighth Edition (his original work having been published in 1863); and I then added to his long notice on Lowestoft my own editorial note, stating the points of difference between us.

Some few years afterwards, in 1902, some excavations took place on the site of the old Lowestoft factory and brought to light a veritable *trouvaille*, consisting of numerous fragments of china in various conditions of finish, several moulds, and such other valuable pieces of evidence in the work of identification as handles of jugs, spouts of teapots, and, *inter alia*, some lumps of the clay which had been used in the factory. This excavation was followed by others in 1903, when many more relics of this old china factory were unearthed. The first discoveries were purchased *en bloc* by Mr. Frederick A. Crisp, an enthusiastic collector, and he had plaster casts made from portions of the moulds and presented them to the British Museum, where they may be seen. The results of the later excavation were purchased by Mr. A. Merrington Smith, of Lowestoft, and sold by him to Mr. W. W. R. Spelman, of Norwich, who published his *Lowestoft China* in 1905 and reproduced by photography over one hundred plates, some of them colored, representing the "finds" and also some specimens which he had collected from other sources. He also reproduced the ground plan of the factory and a view

vases of every shape and color, made in the porcelains of half a dozen different European countries, can be readily purchased, it is difficult to realize the enthusiasm for porcelain production which existed about the middle of the eighteenth century. Bow had started its "New Canton" factory in 1744; Chelsea a year later. Derby and Worcester had followed suit in 1750 and 1751. The discovery, therefore, of a white china clay by Mr. Luson was an event of much greater importance than such a find would appear to be in these latter days. He made plans to commence a porcelain factory on his own estate, and for that purpose

*Figs. 4, 5, 6* — LOWESTOFT PORCELAIN                                                                                                                 *British Museum*
The pitcher is in blue and white, a typical Lowestoft specimen. Left-hand mug is of similar decoration. That on the right, painted in imitation of Chinese, is similar in coloring to Chinese porcelain.

of the buildings. His collection was afterwards sold to Lady Colman.

Information, therefore, is now available to give the reader of ANTIQUES a tolerably full and connected account of the history and productions of this interesting factory. In Gillingwater's *History of Lowestoft*, there is a record of the discovery by Mr. Hewlin Luson, of Gunton Hall near Lowestoft, of some white earth on his estate which he analysed and found suitable for the production of porcelain. This occurred in 1756, when, we must bear in mind, there was, all over Europe, a keen desire to manufacture porcelain of a kind similar to that which had been produced for centuries in China, and which had been imported into England as rare and valued specimens so far back as during the reign of Queen Elizabeth.

In these days, when porcelain tea or dinner services, or

procured workmen from London. But no sooner was this fact known to the factories in London than means were taken, by the bribery of Luson's workmen, to spoil his production and so bring his scheme to an end.

In the year following, however, a second attempt was made by a firm of potters, in which Messrs. Walker, Browne, Aldrich, and Richman were partners, and, to quote Gillingwater's *History of Lowestoft*:

They purchased some houses on the south side of Bell Lane, converted the same to the uses of a manufactory by erecting a kiln and other conveniences necessary for the purpose: but in carrying their designs into execution they also were liable to the same inconveniences as the proprietor of the original undertaking at Gunton was, for being under the necessity of applying to London for workmen to conduct the business, this second attempt experienced the same misfortune as the former one, and very

*Victoria and Albert Museum, F. F. Broderip Loan Collection*
*Figs. 7, 8, 9* — LOWESTOFT PORCELAIN
Small vase and cover with flowers, similar in style to those on old Delft ware. Teapot decorated in Indian red and blue to imitate old Japanese porcelain. Inscribed mug with sprigs of flowers of the kind known to collectors as the "Angouleme" sprig; a favorite Lowestoft decoration.

nearly totally ruined their designs, but the proprietors happening to discover these practices before it was too late, they took such precautions as rendered every future attempt of this nature wholly ineffectual and have now established the factory upon such a permanent basis as promises great success. They have now enlarged their original plan, and erecting additional buildings, have made every necessary alteration requisite for the various purposes of the manufactory. They employ a considerable number of workmen, and supply with ware many of the principal towns in the adjacent counties, and keep a warehouse in London to execute the orders they receive, both from the city and the adjoining towns, and have brought the manufactory to such a degree of perfection as promises to be a credit to the town, useful to the inhabitants, and beneficial to themselves.

Gillingwater's *History of Lowestoft* was published in 1790; it is uncertain when the above account of the factory was actually written, but there is a footnote which gives us some clue, as it quotes an advertisement from a London newspaper of 1770, which is as follows:

Clark Durnford, Lowestoft China Warehouse No. 4 Great St. Thomas The Apostle, Cheapside, London. Where merchants and shopkeepers may be supplied with any quantity of the said wares at the usual prices. N.B. Allowance of 20 per cent for ready money. *March 17, 1770.*

The earliest date which has been found upon any piece of Lowestoft is 1761 and there are a great many examples which are marked 1762 and with subsequent dates.

Mr. Jewitt has told us in his *Ceramic Art of Great Britain* that Robert Browne, one of the partners mentioned above, visited the Bow or Chelsea factory disguised as a workman and secured an engagement. He bribed a fellow-workman to help him to hide himself in an empty hogshead when the paste was being mixed. This was, naturally, a very secret process and Browne returned to the Lowestoft factory, having gained much valuable information by his device.

In addition to the home trade mentioned in the extract given above, the Lowestoft factory appears to have exported a considerable amount of these productions. In 1803-4, however, the works were closed, owing to considerable losses and the successful competition of Staffordshire; but chiefly, it is said, on account of the seizure by Napoleon in Holland of some thousands of pounds worth of their ware.

### The Lowestoft Paste and the Productions of the Factory

The paste of Lowestoft was what is known as soft paste, similar to the paste of the Bow factory during its soft paste period. Mr. Spelman had analysed three specimens of the clay which was found at the excavations. I will here quote the table of ingredients which he has given us. The three examples are described as clay, white biscuit, and lavender jasper biscuit, and they are compared as follows:

|  | Clay | White Biscuit | Lavender Jasper Biscuit |
|---|---|---|---|
| Silica | 38.20 | 41.60 | 37.21 |
| Alumina | 22.22 | 19.14 | 17.32 |
| Bone earth (phosphate of lime) | 28.74 | 25.81 | 32.43 |
| Lime | 7.67 | 10.80 | 8.71 |
| Magnesia | 1.65 | 1.22 | 1.10 |
| Potash | .93 | .41 | 2.25 |
| Soda | .59 | 1.02 | .98 |
|  | 100.00 | 100.00 | 100.00 |

In some specimens there are traces of steatite, or soap rock, which was used very considerably in the old Worcester paste, and it is quite probable that the quantities of bone ash were varied from those given in the analyses above.

These variations in the composition of the paste and also some differences in methods of firing have produced examples of Lowestoft which lead to differences of opinion among collectors. The writer has examined many specimens, where the bottom rim, if unglazed, shows a much harder and more vitreous appearance than is usual. This is probably due to such pieces having been fired at a higher temperature. The earlier examples are decorated with painting or transfer printing in underglaze blue; after 1770 the painting is more generally *over* the glaze.

Mr. Chaffers mentions the manufacture of hard paste at Lowestoft in 1775; but, so far as the writer's investigations have gone,—and his views are confirmed by nearly all authorities on the subject,—really hard paste was never made there. It is almost certain that the hard paste china which

*Victoria and Albert Museum, Schreiber Bequest*
*Fig. 10* — CHINESE PORCELAIN TEA POT
The one mentioned in the text and signed in red script "Allen, Lowestoft."

*Fig. 11* — Lowestoft Porcelain
Covered sugar-bowl and saucer. Decorated in Worcester blue on white ground. These spirals with salmon-scale markings are typical of Lowestoft, although such pieces were formerly attributed to Caughley, or termed "cottage" Worcester. Specimen illustrated was formerly in the Richard Drane collection. Purchased by Mr. Hubert Eccles, a small piece was broken off and analyzed. It was found to be composed of ingredients known to be those of Lowestoft porcelain. Where the flower on the cover joins the cover proper the glaze is thick, as noted in the text.

Chaffers considered to be Lowestoft was really such Chinese porcelain as I have already mentioned, which is decorated with English coats of arms. Some of this Chinese porcelain may have been decorated and refired at Lowestoft.

Lowestoft glaze has a bluish-green tinge and has run into the crevices, and is apparent where the handle or spout joins the body of a piece. There is also this peculiarity, that it has overrun the rims or flanges of teapots, jugs, and their covers. These rims also show signs of unskilful potting, in many cases, being untrue or slightly misshappen. Mr. Spelman considers that figures were made at Lowestoft and he bases this claim chiefly on the evidence of some arms of figures which were found at the excavations. The figures, however, which he illustrates in *Lowestoft China* have much more the appearance of having been made in Staffordshire than at Lowestoft.

The chief Lowestoft productions were table services, or jugs, bowls, small inkstands, teapoys, mugs, and such like domestic ware, with a *specialité* in birthday plaques or medallions. There are many of these, about two inches in diameter, bearing the names of persons who were well known in Lowestoft. For instance:

Martha Redgrave
born Augt, ye 12th
1765

John Gaul
born
April 22
1793

These names are accompanied by some scroll flourishes and a neat border round the edge of the medallion, while on the reverse of some occurs a sprig of forget-me-not, painted in two colors, blue and green. Besides these birthday medallions, several of the jugs, mugs, teapoys, and inkstands have initials with dates, such as R.B.1762, on the little nine-sided inkstand which was made for Robert Browne, one of the partners. Sometimes there are quite lengthy inscriptions with dates which, as a rule, run from 1762 to 1790 odd.

*Fig. 12* — The Sugar Bowl Shown Above
Shows the flange or rim over which the typical blue-green Lowestoft glaze has run. The crescent is a Worcester mark adopted by the Lowestoft factory.

In the British Museum there is a small basin painted in blue on a white ground, also having a delicately worked ornamentation in slight relief. Inside the bowl the following inscription is printed:

> This comes from your heart's delight
> Which thinks of you day and night
> This bowle is round, it is for you
> If you'll be constant, I'le be true.
> Wm. Benney Yarmouth
> Elizth. Mershall.

Flat-shaped flasks known as Pilgrim Bottles, bearing initials and dates, were also in favor. See illustrations, (Figs. 2 and 3).

Generally speaking, it may be said that the better class of Lowestoft resembles what used to be called "Cottage Worcester," and the poorer quality bears a marked similarity to inferior Bow. The painting of flower subjects is, with a few exceptions, generally somewhat crude, and the landscapes, frequently of local districts with a cottage and some cattle and peasants, are of a sketchy character. On some of the teapots and mugs there are copies of Oriental decoration similar to that on Caughley or early Worcester. The blue and white pieces have Chinese dragons, pagodas, and flowers, with the blue color often blurred as if it had run in the firing. There is in the British Museum a dish with powder blue ground color, and a view of Lowestoft Church in the centre, as shown, (Fig. 1).

There was no regular fabrique mark; but the marks of other factories were sometimes copied. Among these the Worcester crescent is the most favored, and also one or two of the imitation Japanese characters, or hieroglyphics, which we also find on some Worcester specimens. Several pieces are marked with one of the following initials: H, S, R, Z, W, and R.P. These are said to indicate various ones among the artists who worked at the factory,—Hughes and Stevenson, both modellers who migrated to the Worcester factory; Stevenson, mother and daughter (?), who painted the blue and white ware; the Redgraves, both John and James, who went afterwards to Worcester. R.P. stands for Richard Philips. The Z and W we have been unable to identify.

Besides these, Mr. Spelman mentions the names of Mrs. Cooper, an artist in blue and white, James Balls and James Mollershead, John Sparham, Richard Powles, Thomas Curtis and Thomas Rose as artists who decorated the ware. On many pieces of Lowestoft there will be found a rose painted somewhat out of proportion to the other flowers which form part of the decoration: this is said to be the work of an artist named Rose. Some pieces bear small signs which are apparently workmen's marks; and many have numerals somewhat imperfectly formed, ranging from 1 to 60. These numerals will generally be found inside the rim on the bottom of pieces.

### Robert Allen's Work

There are a great many specimens of so-called Lowestoft, which, for many years, have puzzled collectors, inasmuch as they are, in many cases, evidently of a paste which could not be identified with that made at the Lowestoft factory; and yet the decoration appears to resemble that of this somewhat elusive establishment. Such inscriptions as "A present from Lowestoft," for instance, are met with; and there appear the initials R.A. on others. The solution of this puzzle is that, after the factory closed in 1803–4, the manager of the works, one Robert Allen by name, who had joined the works as a lad in 1757, kept a shop in Crown Street, Lowestoft, where he had a kiln. He purchased undecorated pieces of china from the Rockingham works at Bramheld and other factories, and also articles of Chinese porcelain. Having redecorated and refired these, he sold them as souvenirs, and this work continued for about 30 years after the factory had closed.

The Rev. Mr. Hallam, an old Lowestoft resident, has written to me, stating that he had a plate bearing Allen's initials and the date 1832. In the Victoria and Albert Museum there is a teapot, evidently of Chinese porcelain, which is marked in red script, "Allen, Lowestoft." It is probable such examples as this, without the explanation here given, which are responsible for the confusion in the attributions of Chinese and Lowestoft wares, to which I have alluded. Allen died in 1835, aged ninety-one.

### Imitations

The craze for collecting Lowestoft, which was particularly marked about thirty years ago, caused a flood of imitations to be put on the market. The sale at an enhanced price of Chinese plates and cups and saucers, tea-pots, jugs, and mugs which were decorated with English coats of arms, has already been mentioned. These, although not Lowestoft, are excellent of their kind and well-worthy the collector's attention as armorial china.

An arch French imitator of the products of many old porcelain factories, one Samson by name, whose works are in Paris, made great quantities of China, in services and in sets of vases, generally decorated with coats of arms, which were extensively sold in England to Lowestoft collectors. If the inexperienced collector will obtain from a dealer of established reputation one or two genuine examples of Lowestoft, he will, by intelligent comparison of these as regards paste, glaze, and decoration, be able to distinguish the French frauds from the real Lowestoft.

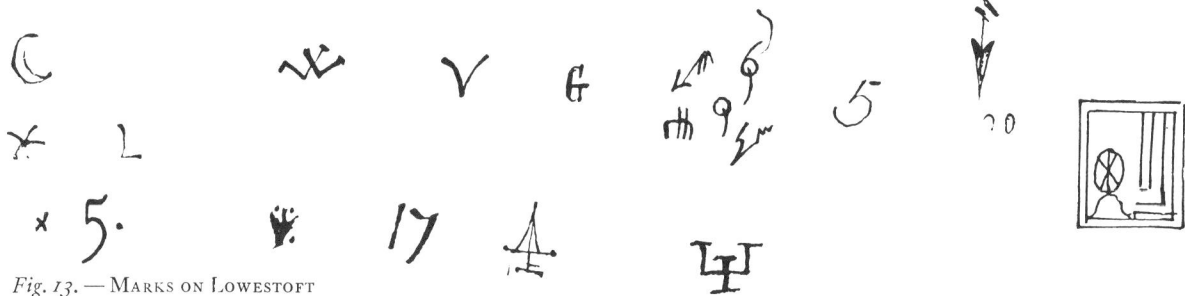

*Fig. 13.* — MARKS ON LOWESTOFT
The marks here shown appear on various Lowestoft specimens. For the most part they appear to be painter's marks.

BY GEOFFREY A. GODDEN

# English Lowestoft in the Chinese taste

Lowestoft teapot in underglaze blue with the royal coat of arms and the date 1772 shows the general resemblance to standard Chinese teapots. On early Lowestoft blue-and-white ware a blue dash is usually found on each side of the handle or spout at the point where it meets the body; this, like other Lowestoft potting customs, is copied from the Chinese. *Castle Museum, Norwich; other illustions, except as noted, are from the author's collection.*

SOME SEVENTY OR EIGHTY YEARS AGO the belief was generally held that all Chinese porcelain bearing European devices had been manufactured, or at least decorated, in the small English fishing port of Lowestoft. However, as readers of ANTIQUES know, soon after the turn of the century this class of porcelain was correctly attributed to the export factories in China which catered to European taste by decorating their wares with armorial bearings and other designs taken from European patterns, drawings, or prints sent out to China. The fact still remains that the small factory at Lowestoft did manufacture armorial, crested, and other porcelain which was as close in feeling to the Chinese as that of any other English factory. (The general background and history of the factory is admirably set out by Mrs. Jacques Noel Jacobsen in ANTIQUES for July 1947, p. 31.)

The English factories were, on the whole, slow to compete with the Chinese trade in armorial porcelain—such large items as dinner services (one of the main Chinese "lines"), while they were produced by the major

Enameled bell-shaped mug made at Lowestoft, decorated with the arms and motto of the Blacksmiths Company and inscribed on the base *James & Sarah Hacon, 1775. Castle Museum, Norwich.*

Both Lowestoft and Chinese potters soon substituted this cylindrical shape for mugs. This is one of two specimens painted in 1778 by Richard Powles, an artist interested in marine subjects who worked at the factory from 1776 until 1784, when he went to Denmark. The large central panel, surmounted by the arms and motto of Trinity House (an ancient body concerned with erection and maintenance of lighthouses, buoys, and so on, around the English coast) depicts the lighthouses at Lowestoft with shipping in the roadstead. Both mugs show a type of light installed in 1778 and were probably made to commemorate the event. *Castle Museum, Norwich.*

May, 1957

Left: saucer in one of the so-called Redgrave patterns, marked on the inside of the footrim with a cross in red enamel which may be a rebus. Center: cup and saucer from the most ambitious of the three recorded Lowestoft tea sets, the Ludlow service; finely decorated with a central crest (lion rampant in gold with gilt initials *E L* below) and black floral festoons hanging from the gilt dentil border. Right: saucer from the tea set made about 1789 for the Reverend Robert Potter, prebendary of Norwich and vicar of Lowestoft. One of the most distinguished scholars of his time, Potter is known today chiefly for his excellent translations of Aeschylus, Euripides, and Sophocles. Small arms in center, crest above, and motto *In Deo Potero*, below; single gilt line border. Only bowls, cups, and saucers of this service have come to light.

potteries, were too costly for the smaller factories to manufacture in their experimental states. These did, of course, produce occasional armorial pieces to order, but their main production was in patterns and ornaments which, though probably Chinese in inspiration, were not restricted to sale to individual families. The illustrations here are of soft-paste porcelain made and decorated at Lowestoft, pieces interesting not merely for their rarity but also for their remarkable similarity to Chinese prototypes.

Three Lowestoft tea services with armorial or crested decoration are recorded, all from the last twenty years of the factory's existence and all following closely in style the Chinese sets of the later crested and initialed type. Parts of two are illustrated; the third, the Townshend service, is decorated with a central crest (a stag trippant) in gold with surrounding floral sprays in black enamel. Charles Townshend was for thirty-eight years member of Parliament for Yarmouth (the near-by fishing port with which the Lowestoft factory carried on a good trade).

William Chaffers (*Marks and Monograms on Pottery and Porcelain*) says that a certain John Bly, who was employed at Worcester after leaving Lowestoft, sent a specimen of a service made for the Duke of Cumberland back to Lowestoft as proof of his continued progress. Chaffers also had a sketch of a coat of arms by this artist which was intended for another Worcester armorial service (page 854, 1946 edition). Probably, then, Bly was responsible for some of the Lowestoft armorial pieces.

The formal Chinese patterns—peonies with conventional rock motifs, cottage and temple designs, birds or animals in landscapes—consisting of small areas of underglaze blue with the pattern completed and touched up with overglaze enamels (notably a pale green and a tomato red, enhanced with slight gilding), are traditionally associated with the Redgrave families at Lowestoft. Three Redgraves are recorded as painters at the factory, and small Lowestoft birth tablets (ANTIQUES for November 1956, p. 464) record this name from one made for *Mary Redgrave, Born Nov. 19th, 1761* to that made for *Ann Redgrave Born Novr. 4th. 1795.*

One of the most ambitious examples of armorial Lowestoft: decorated with the arms of Henry Barton (1737-1818) in full color and gilt. The flower painting is by a well-known Lowestoft painter who did many important pieces, but the armorial bearings and the leaf treatment on the handle are reminiscent of an artist who worked on Bow porcelain and who may have gone to Lowestoft after the Bow works closed in 1776. *Castle Museum, Norwich.*

Special pieces depicting their ships were made at Lowestoft, as at other ceramics factories near ports, for visiting captains. A China-Trade saucer is shown here at left for comparison with a bowl made at Lowestoft; the bowl itself is of Chinese shape. Saucer by courtesy of J. & E. Vandekar, London.

Teapot with simple floral pattern and Fitzhugh-type border, in a manner associated with Lowestoft painter Thomas Curtis, inscribed *John Harm 1789*; and vase from a garniture with unusually ornate decoration and wide shaded diaper borders.

The mandarin patterns, which formed a large proportion of the output of the Lowestoft factory during the final twenty years of its existence, were of course staples of most European ceramics factories of the period. Closely rivaling these in popularity at Lowestoft were the formal floral patterns within wide shaded diaper borders. Variations in these types are illustrated in the ornate vase and the simple floral teapot shown. The teapot is of a type generally associated with Thomas Curtis, one of the Lowestoft painters. The similarity between these and Chinese specimens is self-evident.

Because the Lowestoft factory catered to local trade it produced a good many pieces to special order, inscribed and dated. Like the tea caddy illustrated, these are often similar to their Chinese counterparts; in both cases the potters were striving to follow current European and American fashions. Marriage pieces were also made. A Lowestoft example inscribed *Thos. and Eliza Crafer, Downham 1793* is decorated with a bride and bridegroom supporting a heart—a device also used by the Chinese.

Left. Hitherto unrecorded mug with unusually liberal use of gilding—on initialed shield, lion supporters and crest, handle pattern, and lines around the body (the last two are identical with those on the Trinity House mug). There are gilt floral sprays as well as the usual enameled ones on each side of the body, and the black enamel of the top border is heightened with gilding.

Right. Tea caddy dated 1797, inscribed with initials *M M* on one side and *J D R* on the other.

BY GEORGE SAVAGE

# Identifying early English soft porcelain

THE PURPOSE OF THIS ARTICLE is to discuss the fundamental principles by which English soft (or artificial) porcelain of the eighteenth century is attributed to its factory of origin.

The translucency of both Chinese porcelain and that of Meissen was the property which the English manufacturer sought most to achieve. Since the commonest transparent substance of the period was glass, the idea of using clay for plasticity and glass to confer the translucent quality provided a natural basis for the first experiments in English porcelain manufacture.

There seems little doubt that the first production on a commercial scale was at Chelsea in London, and the body used was primarily a glass mixed with clay. It is significant that this earliest Chelsea porcelain (period of the triangle mark, 1745-1750) has been mistaken for the milk-white glass of Bristol. The ingredients used seem to have been crushed lead glass mixed with clay. Chemical analysis reveals a lead oxide content of around 7 per cent. Held to the light this porcelain is usually highly translucent, and appears to be specked with tiny pinholes of bright light.

There are few other English porcelains which have so high a percentage of lead oxide as these early Chelsea examples. The only exception is the rare Girl in a Swing class (named after a group represented both in the Victoria and Albert Museum, London, and in the Museum of Fine Arts, Boston) which is commonly attributed to the Chelsea factory about 1751. These show the massive amount of approximately 17 per cent.

Immediately following this early type a distinctly different porcelain was made at a number of factories between 1750 and 1755. This body is still glass-like in many ways, but lacks any significant percentage of lead oxide. Such domestic wares as plates and dishes, however, show peculiar patches of greater translucency when the specimen is held up to the light. These are the aptly-named "moons," small flattened cavities in the body which developed during formation.

This type of porcelain was made at Chelsea between 1750 and 1755, at Derby between 1750 and about 1770, and at Longton Hall from 1752 to 1758. These dates are approximate, but correct to within a year or two. Some early French soft pastes also contain moons and the body would appear to have been made from much the same ingredients. Generally, Derby moons are somewhat smaller than those in either Chelsea or Longton Hall.

The wares of Chelsea at this period show a body of fine quality, of close grain, and cream-white in color, though the earlier pieces are more inclined to the color of skimmed milk. If a mark is present, it is either an anchor raised on a medallion, an anchor in red, or an anchor in blue (the last is extremely rare). Nearly all domestic wares show three or four defective points in the glaze on the base where the piece stood in the kiln on "stilts." The complete absence of these stilt marks, also called spur marks, is suspicious, and suggests either a mistaken attribution or a reproduction.

Derby porcelain is not so fine in quality, or so white in color, during this early period. Until 1760 the glaze of domestic wares was often tinged with a slight yellowish green which may have been due to the presence of traces of iron. The first figures (1750-1755) have a peculiar dry edge around the base where the glaze has

Figure in a tricorn hat, possibly an actor (Derby, prior to 1755). One of the earliest examples of Derby porcelain. "Dry-edged" type.

retracted upwards, and some have a funnel-shaped hole on the underside. Others have what looks like a countersunk screw hole from which the screw has been removed.

From about 1755 on, nearly all figures, and some domestic and decorative wares, exhibit patches on the base which are bare of glaze. Though termed "thumbprints," these were caused by the use of clay pads as kiln supports. This was a Derby practice for many years, and can be noticed on late figures as well as early.

While the confusion between Chelsea figures of the gold-anchor period (1758-1770) and those made at Derby during the same period has largely been resolved, Derby figures of 1755-1760 are often wrongly attributed to Longton Hall. No doubt this is due to the fact that an opacifying substance—probably tin oxide—was added to the glaze at both factories, producing a surface which has been well described as similar to paraffin wax or candle grease. The colors, too, are often so alike as to give rise to the conjecture that some Longton figures were enameled at Derby. There is no doubt, moreover, that some early Derby domestic wares are masquerading as Chelsea of the red-anchor period.

Longton Hall porcelain, apart from the presence of moons in many pieces, has a number of peculiarities which ought to make it fairly easy to distinguish from Derby. It is usually wrought more clumsily, and is likely both to have fire-cracks, particularly in the base, and to have warped somewhat. Most bases have been ground to remove surplus glaze and to level them up. It is heavier than Derby porcelain. Many pieces will show three or four spur marks about half an inch long and an eighth of an inch wide where they have rested in the kiln. Domestic wares—plates, basins, and so forth—often have a flat ground base instead of the conventional footring. Despite its faults, Longton porcelain of this period is generally to be preferred to that of Derby on artistic grounds, and is considerably scarcer.

These glass-like porcelains had a number of serious drawbacks. The tea bowls and teapots could not stand boiling water without cracking. They were likely to collapse and melt in the kiln if the maximum permissible temperature was exceeded even slightly. Pieces which have sagged are not uncommon, and must have constituted a large percentage of the total output.

Two easily separated variations on the original glass-like porcelain were elaborated, of which that made at Bow will be discussed first.

The first patent granted to the Bow firm in 1744 refers to the use of Cherokee china clay under the name of *unaker*. It is virtually certain that this was supplied by Andrew Duché of Savannah, Georgia; evidence indicates that he was in London in 1744 offering to sell Virginia

Figure of Isabella d'Andreini, an Italian Comedy actress (Chelsea, c. 1750). A fine example of figure modeling of the early period. Raised-anchor mark outlined in red. *Burrell collection, Glasgow Art Gallery and Museum.*

*Except as noted, illustrations from the collection of Mr. and Mrs. Sigmund J. Katz.*

Ballad singer (Longton Hall, c. 1755). Unmarked. Characteristically decorated.

Bone-ash porcelain figure of Kitty Clive as the Fine Lady from Garrick's farce *Lethe* (Bow, c. 1750). Unmarked. An early model on a very unusual base.

Figure group (Derby, c. 1760). Unmarked. Representative of Derby's middle period. "Thumbprints" on underside of base.
G. M. Garforth-Bles

china clay to the Bow patentees, Edward Heylyn and Thomas Frye, and this probably formed the basis for the enterprise.

Nothing certainly dating from this period is at present known to exist, although there are a number of problem pieces which may belong here. The factory first becomes important in 1749 with the registration of a patent in the name of Thomas Frye for making porcelain from "calcined animals, vegetables, and fossils"—in other words, undoubtedly, bone-ash.

Early bone-ash porcelain is somewhat different in appearance and texture from those thus far discussed. It is generally heavier and less translucent, and where unglazed is noticeably absorbent. A chip or fracture will exhibit a granular appearance, somewhat similar to the surface of a fine sugar lump or a close-grained sandstone. Early figures in this medium have less refinement of modeling, due in part perhaps to primitive workmanship but also to the character of the material. It can be identified by a simple chemical test which will not harm the specimen.

From a commercial point of view, bone-ash porcelain represented a distinct advance over the earlier kinds. Kiln wastage was lower due to a greater temperature latitude, and it was markedly easier to handle in other ways. It was therefore adopted by other factories as opportunity offered. The Lowestoft factory manufactured it exclusively from its inception in 1757; Chelsea first used it about 1754, and the major difference between Chelsea porcelain of the late red-anchor and that of the gold-anchor periods is in the more glassy glaze better suited to the use of colored grounds; Derby acquired the formula with the purchase of the Chelsea factory in 1770 and adopted it at once; and Josiah Spode elaborated the modern standard English bone china—a hybrid between feldspathic and artificial bone-ash porcelain—about 1800.

Lowestoft porcelain during its first years is often difficult to distinguish from Bow, and this must be done principally on the basis of differences in decoration. Chelsea bone-ash porcelain is altogether of a finer quality than that of Bow. The paste is whiter, finer, and the glaze usually richer. The period of bone-ash porcelain at Derby mostly comes after the closure of the Bow factory, so that no room for confusion exists.

The second variation for consideration belongs to the west of England. Here soaprock replaced bone ash. This substance, a natural mixture of steatite and china clay, fuses at a comparatively low temperature to form a greenish translucent mass. It lent itself to very precisely potted wares, best seen in the products of the Worcester factory, although both plates and large vases were somewhat subject to warping.

We probably owe the discovery of this substance to the researches of the English inventor of hard paste, William Cookworthy of Plymouth. As early as 1745 he was experimenting with substances likely to provide the feldspathic rock of the Chinese and of Meissen. In its properties, soaprock superficially resembles it, and it is significant that the first porcelain of this nature was made at Bristol at a small factory variously known as Lowdin's, Redcliff Backs, and Lund's. The last name is the most satisfactory. Cookworthy had many connections with Bristol, and later opened a factory for the manufacture of hard porcelain there.

Soaprock porcelain is usually light, thin, and potted with exactness and precision. It was made at Bristol, Worcester, Caughley, and Liverpool, and apart from the fact that some Bristol pieces have a glaze with an opaque quality somewhat similar to that of Longton, the wares made at these factories are often hard to differentiate. The glaze of soaprock porcelains is usually thin and without the crazing so noticeable on the earlier wares of some factories, notably Derby and later Chelsea. Caughley nearly always has an orange translucency, whereas soaprock porcelain from the other factories usually exhibits a greenish color, but this is not an infallible test. Worcester porcelain, particularly black transfer-printed pieces, can be orange on occasion. Liverpool porcelain is inclined to be less precise in manufacture than that of Worcester, but often only differences in decoration determine at which of the two factories a specimen was made. Caughley porcelain is also occasionally difficult to distinguish from Worcester, and, once again, decoration is often the principal determining factor. In fact, decoration is considerably more important in the attribution of soaprock porcelains than of the other types discussed.

Decoration can be, nevertheless, a very unreliable guide, since a number of the factories had their porcelain decorated at London enameling establishments, principally that of James Giles. So it is helpful to realize that, as far as the evidence shows, they did not experiment with a number of formulae, but each kept to a basic receipt. The body and glaze can, therefore, be an extremely good guide to factory of origin.

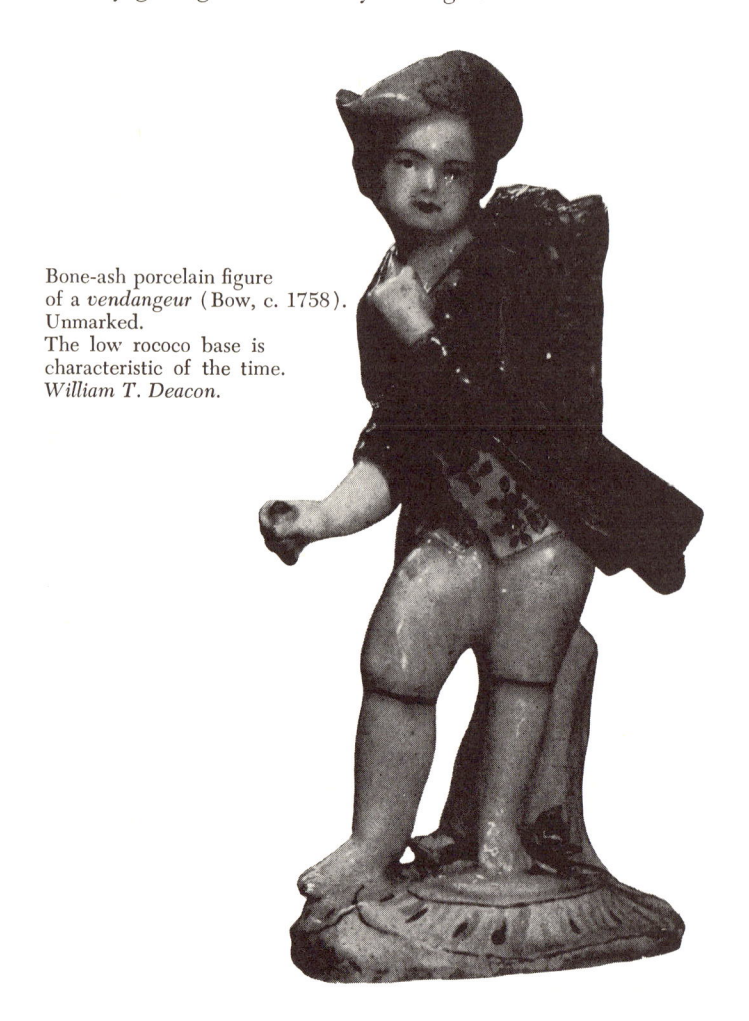

Bone-ash porcelain figure of a *vendangeur* (Bow, c. 1758). Unmarked. The low rococo base is characteristic of the time. *William T. Deacon.*

# EARLY COALPORT PORCELAIN

## By FRANKLIN A. BARRETT

*Mr. Barrett has been interested for some time in various aspects of English ceramics, and has just completed a book on Caughley and Coalport porcelain, to be published shortly in England.*

THE FACTORY OF COALPORT was established early in the nineteenth century amid the foothills southeast of Shrewsbury, and transplanted to Stoke-on-Trent; it still survives, active and vigorous, to the present day. Its founder was John Rose. He was born in 1772, the same year in which Thomas Turner left Worcester and took charge of the Salopian factory at Caughley. It was there that Rose received his early training, and in 1799 he purchased the Caughley factory from his old employer. It appears that he had already set up a small works at Coalport, and in 1814 the manufacture was removed wholly to that place.

The earliest Coalport porcelain remains largely unidentified, though we may guess that for some years Rose continued to make at Caughley the blue-printed china which had been the mainstay of Turner's factory. There exist today a fair number of examples of highly translucent, very white porcelain, printed with the old Caughley patterns, and these in all probability date from this time.

PLATE decorated by William Billingsley prior to his joining the Coalport factory *(c. 1810)*. Flower arrangement in center. Blue border with gilding. Marked in red *Coalbrookdale*, with the letters arranged in a circle. *Victoria and Albert Museum.*

VASE in Chelsea style, painted with long-legged exotic birds similar to those found on Chelsea, Worcester, and Derby porcelain *(c. 1820)*. Marked with an anchor and the letter *C. Victoria and Albert Museum.*

PLATE in imitation of Chelsea. The Coalport mark has been erased, though its "ghost" remains, and a small "Chelsea" gold anchor substituted, surmounted by a letter *C. Author's collection.*

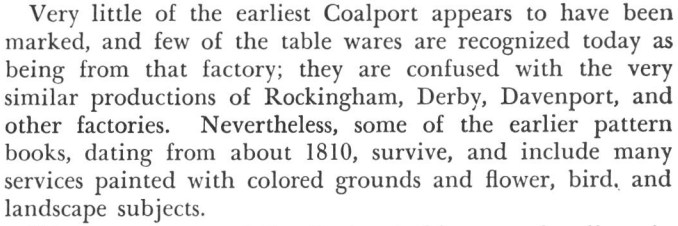

Very little of the earliest Coalport appears to have been marked, and few of the table wares are recognized today as being from that factory; they are confused with the very similar productions of Rockingham, Derby, Davenport, and other factories. Nevertheless, some of the earlier pattern books, dating from about 1810, survive, and include many services painted with colored grounds and flower, bird, and landscape subjects.

The greater part of the Coalport china was, in all probability, decorated in the studios of London china painters, such as Baxter's, Randall and Robins, and others. We know that artists were employed at Coalport, however, from the names recorded in the factory pattern books. Among the best known was John Randall, who became famous for his painting of birds, and who worked at the Shropshire factory for no less than forty-six years. He was born on September 1, 1810, and learned his art from his uncle, Thomas Martin Randall, who had a kiln at Madeley nearby. In 1835 Randall joined the Coalport works and continued to paint there until his sight failed in 1881. He lived to be a hundred, dying in 1910, and was an enthusiastic antiquarian. It is to him that we are largely indebted for the greater part of our knowledge of the Coalport China Works. Bird subjects by Randall are found on services and decorative vases made over the long period of his stay at Coalport, and in the pattern books "Randall's birds" is a frequent annotation.

In 1820 William Billingsley, founder of the Nantgarw factory, was invited to Coalport. This was an astute move on the part of John Rose. designed to put an end to the threat to his London trade represented by Billingsley's fine white Nantgarw porcelain. Rose acquired a good deal of the equipment of the Nantgarw factory, and shortly after Billingsley's arrival Coalport produced many services with molded patterns similar to those made at both Nantgarw and Swansea. The Coalport examples were of a highly translucent porcelain, harder than that of the South Wales factories, but nevertheless so similar as to

JUG in Swansea style, made in the white, very translucent body which was introduced following Billingsley's arrival at Coalport *(c. 1820)*. Unmarked. *Victoria and Albert Museum.*

mislead the unwary collector today. Most of the dessert services were glazed with a newly discovered feldspathic glaze, which earned John Rose and Company the gold medal of the Society of Arts. Some bear the special mark designed to commemorate that event.

Of all the Coalport productions of the early nineteenth century, the specimens chiefly sought today are, perhaps, the vases and other decorative porcelain ornamented with encrusted flowers. The application of flowers modeled in the round to decorative china was, of course, no new thing. Among the eighteenth-century factories, Longton Hall had used the technique on an extravagant scale, and in the early years of the succeeding century Derby turned out vases and other decorative wares embellished in this manner. Most Coalport vases of the 1830's were made in two styles, with and without "raised" flowers, the latter being the more expensive. Other forms which featured encrusted flowers were baskets, inkstands, clocks, flower holders, pastille burners, and pot-pourri jars. Reserved panels were painted with groups of flowers, landscapes, birds, and, more rarely, figure subjects.

The modeling of flowers for encrusted decoration was probably introduced at Coalport by George Cocker, who is said to have done similar work at Derby. Indeed, it is sometimes difficult to distinguish the unmarked Coalport (and most of it *was* unmarked) from the similar product of the Derby factory. Fortunately most Derby was marked at this period, generally with the Bloor stamped mark, though sometimes with the crossed swords of "Dresden." Rockingham also made encrusted wares, often unmarked, and these may sometimes be distinguished from those of Coalport only by the measure of restraint usually, though not invariably, exercised by the Shropshire factory. Rockingham was almost always overdecorated, and the colors heavy. A yellow-green is characteristic of the foliage on Coalport encrusted wares.

Figures were made on a small scale at Coalport, usually of small size, and are often quite charming. Some bear candle sconces, others surmount vases, and a number were made to fit onto the base of ormolu candelabra. From their comparative scarcity today it appears that they were made for a short time only; possibly George Cocker had something to do with this also, for he afterwards made small figures on his own account at Derby.

Gilding during this period of the "revived rococo" was elaborate, reflecting a fondness for scrolling lines which was carried sometimes to fantastic extremes. Great strides were made in the invention of new ground colors that were to attain to their full flowering in the period of the Sèvres revival about the middle of the century. But that was not during the lifetime of John Rose, although it owed to him a great deal of its achievement. Rose died in 1841 and was succeeded first by his brother Thomas, then by his nephew W. F. Rose. This point marked a distinct change in the productions of Coalport.

PAIR OF VASES with underglaze blue ground and Italian landscape views *(c. 1820)*. Unmarked. *Nottingham Castle Museum, England.*

POT-POURRI VASE with periwinkle blue ground and flower group in reserve *(c. 1830)*. Such vases, with pierced covers, formed a large part of the Coalport ornamental wares. Unmarked. *Privately owned.*

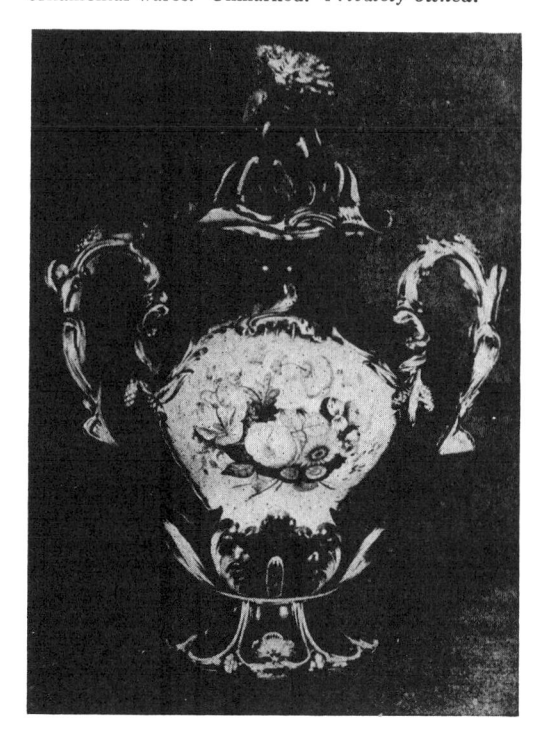

POT-POURRI VASE AND COVER, richly encrusted with raised flowers and painted with a bouquet of flowers in the reserved space on either side *(c. 1825)*. Unmarked. *Victoria and Albert Museum.*

PAIR OF ROCOCO VASES on square base, green ground, with panels of birds painted by John Randall *(c. 1840)*. Unmarked. *Nottingham Castle Museum, England.*

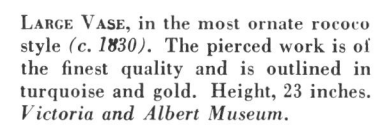

LARGE VASE, in the most ornate rococo style *(c. 1830)*. The pierced work is of the finest quality and is outlined in turquoise and gold. Height, 23 inches. *Victoria and Albert Museum.*

PAIR OF SEATED FIGURES, made for the base of ormolu candelabra *(c. 1820)*. Height, 4 inches. Unmarked. *Collection of N. Blackwell Wood, England.*

85

# An English porcelain collection at Williamsburg

BY JOHN M. GRAHAM II, *Director and curator of collections, Colonial Williamsburg*

BEFORE ITS ACQUISITION by Colonial Williamsburg the M. G. Kaufman collection of eighteenth-century porcelain, perhaps better known in England than in America, was generally conceded to be the best of its kind still privately owned in this country and not scheduled to be given to a museum. It is not a large collection, containing as it does only one hundred and four examples of useful wares and figures. However, it would be difficult if not impossible to assemble such a group today, and its purchase by Colonial Williamsburg happily insures its being kept intact in this country.

The wares included are primarily Chelsea, with Derby, Longton Hall, and Bow represented. The soft-paste Chelsea periods and corresponding marks found in this collection are as follows:

A.  Triangle period (c. 1745-1749)
    Marks:   a.  Incised triangle
             b.  Crown and trident painted in underglaze blue
B.  Raised Anchor period (c. 1750-1753)
    Mark:    a.  Anchor in relief on oval medallion applied
C.  Red Anchor period (c. 1753-1758)
    Mark:    a.  Anchor painted red
             b.  Anchor painted blue
             c.  Anchor in relief on oval medallion painted red—examples bearing this mark may have been made in the earlier period and decorated and sold in the Red Anchor period, or there may have been an overlapping of the Raised Anchor mark into the Red Anchor period
D.  Gold Anchor period (c. 1758-1770)
    Marks:   a.  Anchor painted gold
             b.  Anchor painted brown

Mr. Kaufman's preference was for Chelsea of the Triangle and Raised Anchor periods. One of his objectives was to assemble all known types of the Triangle period—an ambitious aim, but it is believed he came closer to achieving it than any other collector, here or abroad. Twenty pieces from his distinguished collection are illustrated in F. Severne Mackenna's three authoritative books on Chelsea.

Shown here are a few Chelsea pieces, with representative examples of Derby and Bow, from this "collector's collection," now added to the growing Colonial Williamsburg collection of English ceramics.

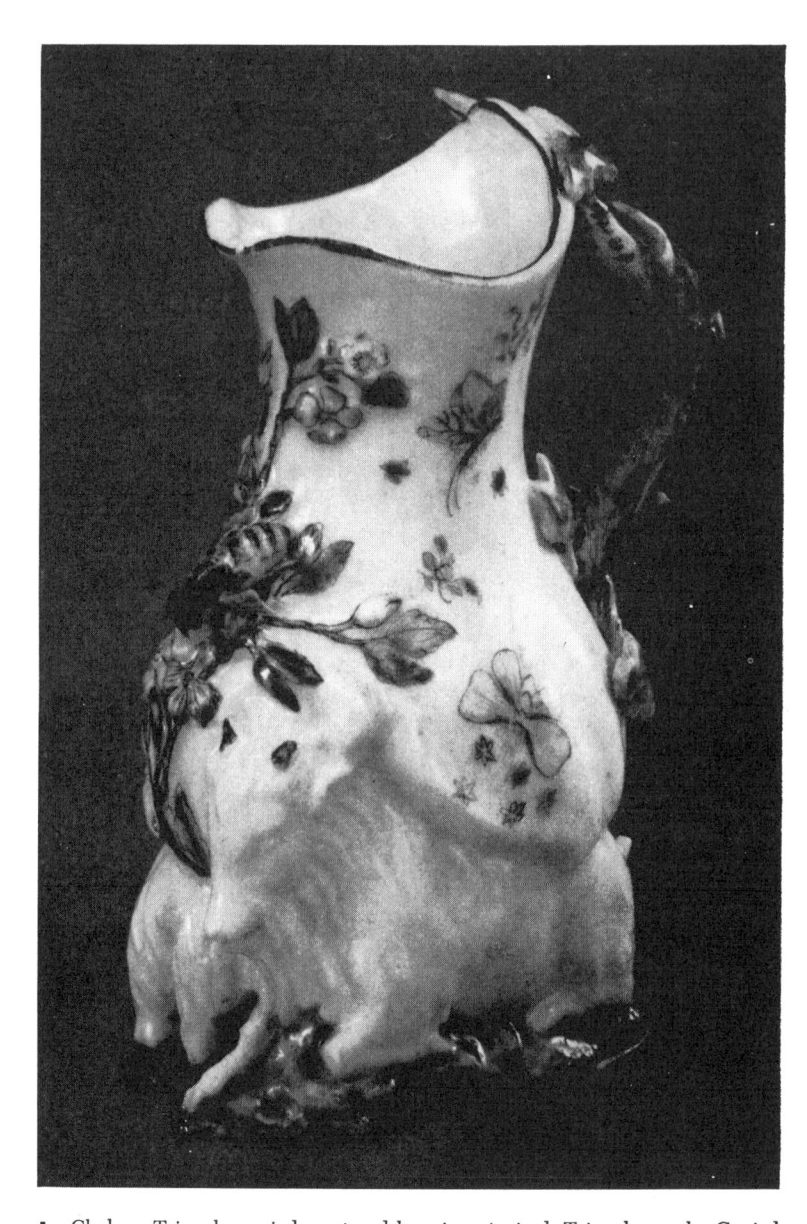

1 Chelsea Triangle period goat-and-bee jug, incised Triangle mark. Copied from an earlier silver shape; one of two examples in the collection. The design has two recumbent goats on the base; under the lip, among flowers, is an applied bee in relief. A few goat-and-bee jugs bear the date 1745. Ex coll. *Wallace Elliott. All photographs by courtesy of Colonial Williamsburg.*

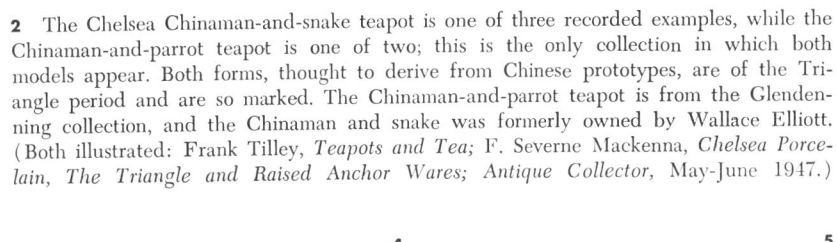

**2** The Chelsea Chinaman-and-snake teapot is one of three recorded examples, while the Chinaman-and-parrot teapot is one of two; this is the only collection in which both models appear. Both forms, thought to derive from Chinese prototypes, are of the Triangle period and are so marked. The Chinaman-and-parrot teapot is from the Glendenning collection, and the Chinaman and snake was formerly owned by Wallace Elliott. (Both illustrated: Frank Tilley, *Teapots and Tea*; F. Severne Mackenna, *Chelsea Porcelain, The Triangle and Raised Anchor Wares*; Antique Collector, May-June 1947.)

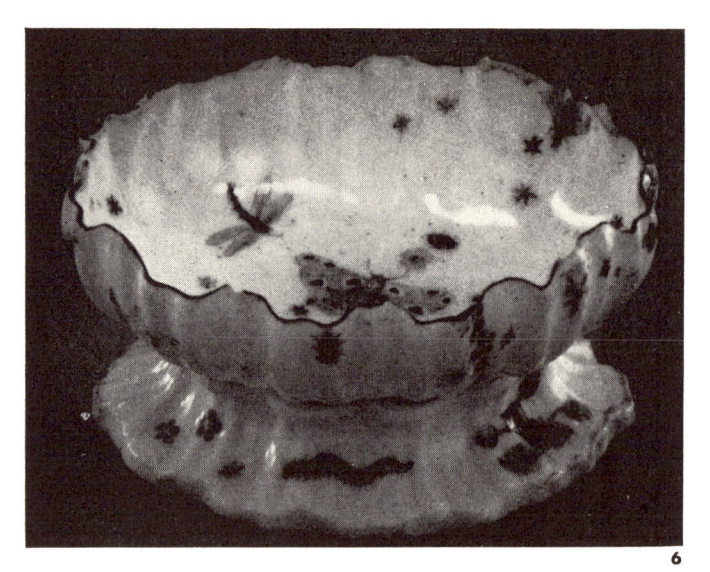

**3** Chelsea oval basket with flaring sides, exterior molded in basketwork design; ormolu rim, handle, and foot. Exterior base has incised Triangle mark. One of three such baskets known. (*Illustrated: English Ceramic Circle Transactions,* Vol. 1, No. 3, 1935; *Connoisseur,* December 1926.)

**4** Chelsea Triangle period acanthus cream jug with crown and trident in underglaze blue; one of two pieces in the collection with this rare mark. Ex coll. *Dr. Glaisher and Frances Dickson.* (Illustrated: *Eng. Cer. Cir. Trans.,* Vol. I, No. 3, 1935; *Connoisseur,* October 1922.)

**5** Chelsea Triangle period cup in the tea-plant pattern with design molded in high relief and painted in brilliant overglaze enamels of turquoise, blue, yellow, purple, red, and black; unmarked. The interior base has a painted design of fruit and leaves. Every form made at Chelsea in this pattern is represented in the collection.

**6** Chelsea Triangle period strawberry dish, so called because applied strawberries are usually found around the base of this model. Decorated with flower forms and insects in overglaze enamel colors. Ex coll. *Glendenning.* (Illustrated: *Eng. Cer. Cir. Trans.,* Vol. I, No. 3, 1935.)

**7** Unmarked teapot attributed by Dr. Bellamy Gardner, in whose collection it once was, to Huguenot silversmith Nicholas Sprimont because the base is fitted into the body of the teapot in a way which suggests a silversmithing technique. Sprimont managed the Chelsea factory at a time when some of its most unusual designs were produced. Copied from a Chinese buccaro model. (Illustrated: Tilley, *Teapots and Tea; Eng. Cer. Cir. Trans.,* Vol. I, No. 3, 1935; Vol. II, No. 6, 1939; Mackenna, *Chelsea Porcelain, The Triangle and Raised Anchor Wares; Antique Collector,* August 1937, August 1938, August 1947.)

**8** Unmarked Chelsea portrait bust of William Augustus, Duke of Cumberland (1721-1765), third son of George II, who was a patron of the Chelsea Porcelain Manufactory; his secretary, Sir Everard Fawkener, was a proprietor. Triangle period. The duke had his state coach redecorated with the arms of Virginia and sent over to his friend Lord Botetourt, the royal governor. It is recorded that this coach was drawn through the streets of Williamsburg by eight white horses. A palace inventory of the governor's effects lists numerous examples of Chelsea.

**9** Chelsea cream jug, or boat, with Raised Anchor mark; decorated with two Chinese figures in overglaze multicolor enamels. Mackenna cites this as one of two "... singularly rare instances of the use of figure decoration at this period." (Illustrated: Mackenna, *Chelsea Porcelain, The Triangle and Raised Anchor Wares; Antique Collector,* November-December 1948 and March-April 1947.)

**10** Three pieces of the Chelsea fable series from the Raised Anchor period, decorated in enamel colors. Cup marked with Raised Anchor; teapot and saucer unmarked. The teapot illustrates *The Lioness and the Fox*, the fable on the tea bowl is *The Fox in the Well*, and the saucer depicts *The Old Hound*. The last two are copied from Francis Barlow's illustrations in a seventeenth-century edition of *Aesop's Fables*. (Saucer illustrated in William H. Tapp, *Jefferyes Hamett O'Neale*.)

**11** Chelsea octagonal plate in Kakiemon style, with birds in overglaze enamels; Red Anchor mark. This is probably one of "Twelve octagon soup plates with a wheat sheaf and pheasants, old pattern" referred to in the 1756 Chelsea sales catalogue. (Illustrated: Mackenna, *Chelsea Porcelain, The Red Anchor Wares*.)

**12** Red Anchor period saucer with Blue Anchor mark; decoration in underglaze blue. An unfired matching cup found at the Chelsea factory site in 1906 is now in the Katz collection. Of four distinct types of decoration found on Chelsea with the Blue Anchor mark, two are in this collection.

**13** Britannia mourning the death of Frederick, Prince of Wales, son of George II and father of George III; unmarked. This belongs to the group classified as "Girl-in-a-swing" figures, believed to have been made at a second factory operating at Chelsea c. 1749-1754.

**14** One of a pair of Chelsea Gold Anchor urns, unmarked. Decorated in underglaze mazarine blue with gilded flowers and scrolls; in the reserves are figures painted in the style of Boucher. (Illustrated: Mackenna, *Chelsea Porcelain, The Gold Anchor Wares*.)

**15** Derby cream jug, pear shape, with applied strawberries and leaves around base. The exterior base has the inscribed mark *Derby*. There are two other recorded examples: one in the British Museum marked with an incised *D* and the other in the Victoria and Albert Museum marked *D.1750*. These jugs are key pieces which prove that the Derby factory was in production by 1750. Ex coll. *Edgerton Leigh, Arthur Hurst, Frank Hurlbutt*. (Illustrated: *Burlington Magazine*, December 1926.)

**16** Figure of James Quin the actor, in the character of Falstaff; Bow, 1760-1765. Quin wears a large plumed hat, ruffled collar, red coat, orange belt and breeches, and gold-figured waistcoat. Hanging from one waistcoat pocket is a bill inscribed:

| | |
|---|---|
| Jack | 1.0. |
| Anchovey | 0.1.0 |
| Capon | 0.0.2 |
| Bread | 0.0.½ |
| Brandy | 2. |
| | 1.3.2½ |

13

14

15

16

# Bristol hard-paste porcelain

BY JOHN K. D. COOPER

THE YEAR 1768 was momentous in the history of true porcelain manufacture in Europe: in that year deposits of kaolin from Saint-Yrieix near Limoges were used for the first time to produce *pâte dure* at Sèvres, and William Cookworthy (Fig. 1), a Quaker chemist of Plymouth, patented his formula for the first English hard paste. The two events, occurring relatively late in the eighteenth century, had somewhat different repercussions. Sèvres was able to purchase the Saint-Yrieix quarries outright, which naturally helped reduce its production costs. The Cornish deposits of kaolin and petuntse discovered by Cookworthy were available only after harsh terms had been negotiated with the landowner, Thomas Pitt—a vital factor in the ensuing fortunes of both the Plymouth and Bristol undertakings. In brief, English hard paste was to be expensive to make; moreover, the factories lacked the experienced personnel that their Continental rivals could count on.

By the late 1760's, the soft-paste wares of Derby and Worcester, as well as those of the declining factories at Chelsea and Bow, were widely accepted. Prices were reasonable and were soon to be made more so by amalgamations resulting in large, efficient factories and by the economic use of labor and materials. The rich not unnaturally remained true to imported wares, while the thriving middle classes were content with both blue-and-white from the Orient and acceptable English soft pastes. By 1768, habits were established; any attempt to change them would be a gamble, as Cookworthy must have realized.

When the Plymouth factory was founded Cookworthy's partners included two strong Bristolian interests in the persons of Thomas Frank, whose family had long been connected with the delftware industry, and a younger man, Richard Champion (Fig. 2), who was then twenty-five. Cookworthy himself was sixty-three and had been engaged in ceramic research probably since soon after J. B. du Halde's *History of China* appeared in English in 1738. This book, which included accounts of porcelain making at Ching-tê Chên, must have inspired Cookworthy, a chemist by profession, to explore the Devon and Cornwall countryside in the hope of finding the rocks and clays required for the manufacture of hard paste.

Two to three years of naïve and often faulty porcelain production followed the opening of the Plymouth factory. It was too remote not only from Bristol, with its long-standing ceramic tradition (including "Lund's" soft-paste factory, which had transferred to Worcester in 1752), but

Fig. 1. William Cookworthy, founder of the Plymouth Factory and proprietor of the Plymouth and Bristol undertakings from 1768 to 1773. After John Opie, R. A. *Plymouth City Museum and Art Gallery.*

especially from other centers of fashion and commerce which were better sources of skilled craftsmen. Perhaps, the partners thought, hands could be attracted from Bow and Chelsea, whose fortunes were uneasy at this time. In 1770, Cookworthy gave in and by midyear the Plymouth factory had been moved to Bristol. Sometime before that Champion went to Plymouth and drew a diagram of the enameling kiln for adaptation in the new factory. Soon after the move, advertisements were published in Worcester to tempt discontented blue-and-white painters to the Bristol factory. Cookworthy brought at least two of his best decorators, William Stephens and Henry Bone, the factory manager, John Brittan, and a large quantity of

Fig. 2. Richard and Judith Champion.
*From a miniature in the collection of Phyllis Rawlins.*

Fig. 3. Typical Plymouth, or early Bristol, hexagonal vase and cover with exotic birds in landscapes, a style attributed traditionally to a Monsieur Soqui; c. 1770. *Privately owned.*

molds to the new premises at 15 Castle Green, Bristol.

The wares of the "Plymouth New Invented Porcelain Manufactory" were the subject of a large exhibition held in 1970 at the City Art Gallery, Bristol, to mark the bicentenary of the transfer. The objects on view confirmed that in general character the porcelain produced at Bristol while Cookworthy remained in charge differed little from what had been made at Plymouth. When Cookworthy retired and his young, ambitious partner, Richard Champion, assumed control in 1773, the rococo was replaced by the neoclassical, particularly in wares of higher quality. To raise Bristol's standards to those of Champion's rivals in Worcester and Derby more capital was needed, to be derived from new partners, and this resulted in an almost complete break with Plymouth methods.

It cannot be denied that many of Cookworthy's Plymouth and Bristol prestige pieces—for the most part chimney garnitures of hexagonal vases (Fig. 3)—were decorated with great precision and style, however *retardataire* they may have been in design. Other wares probably continued to bear the old Plymouth tin mark until Champion introduced a deliberate imitation of the Meissen crossed-swords mark and the more frequently used blue cross. The new marks were intended for a new type of porcelain: a whiter paste, more evenly potted, and decorated with a new sophistication. Significantly, an advertisement for Bristol hard-paste porcelain of November 1772 called attention to the "old Stock, which will be sold very cheap." In 1773 or soon afterwards a fourth mark, occasionally and confusingly accompanying one or another of these three, made its appearance—a capital B, presumably for Bristol. The numerals from 1 to 26 which normally accompany the blue-cross mark have caused great confusion. Quality of decoration is generally high when the number is below ten, and undistinguished or low thereafter, especially above 16. It is probable that the painters and gilders were numerically graded on merit at certain stages, but there is as yet no thoroughly satisfactory explanation for this system of coding. Numerals from 1 to 8 accompany the B mark in surviving examples, and, again, pieces bearing the higher numbers—6, 7, and 8—are of lesser quality. Unfortunately no pattern books survive from either Plymouth or Bristol, and the site of the Bristol works is so well built over that no excavations have been possible to throw light on this intriguing problem.

The full inscription *Mr Wm Cookworthy's Factory Plym: 1770* appears on the base of several pieces of polychrome porcelain, quite possibly as a form of epitaph for that factory during its last months in production. To this group should be added the earliest known documentary piece—the British Museum's small blue-and-white mug (Fig. 4) inscribed *Plymouth Manufacy* and, on the base, *March 14 1768 CF* (three days before Cookworthy's patent was granted)—and a most interesting mug with che-lin (or kylin) decoration also in the British Museum, inscribed *November ye 27th 1770*. This same date appears on Champion's drawing of the kiln following the remark "The Last Burning of Enamel." The coarse quality of these two mugs is apparent again in a third mug in the same collection that is inscribed on the base *JBRC 1772* (Figs. 5, 5a), which lends weight to the argument that the Plymouth style lasted well into Bristol's lifetime. The *JBRC* mug is the only dated piece of the years 1771 and 1772.

The bicentenary exhibition was used as an opportunity to assemble as many figures of the more sophisticated Plymouth and Bristol types as possible. As it happened, few of the spectacular Plymouth shell pieces and other larger wares could be borrowed, but almost every type of square- or mound-based Bristol figure (as opposed to the usually scroll-based figures from Plymouth) was exhibited. Among these were pieces of the period 1770 to 1774 marked T°, indicating the presence at Bristol of the ubiquitous modeler and repairer Mr. Tebo (or Thibault). Earlier than his usually well-assembled figures were the better-known scroll-based Continents (Fig. 6). These were originally taken from Longton Hall molds said to have been purchased by Cookworthy in a moment of foresight at the Longton closing-down sale in 1760. Other groups, notably those of boys playing with a goat, were also taken from Longton molds. During the Champion period, however, Derby was to play a more prominent role. Perhaps the most successful groups were those ordered by Champion from an unidentified Derby modeler (possibly Pierre Stephan), whose attributes are fully specified in a letter of 1772. The resulting Classical Seasons and Four Elements (Fig. 7) are clearly the work of the same skilled hand. At about the same date Champion produced his larger and more sentimentalized Rustic Seasons. These are also just as accomplished as comparable Derby groups designed to cater to quite a different taste.

An exciting discovery made after the exhibition closed is that of a figure of Milton, originally paired with a similar Shakespeare, bearing the mark *X 10*; this is the first figure found to bear a numbered mark hitherto known only on tablewares. A pair of Sphinxes decorated in polychrome and marked with a blue cross has also been found in a private collection; up to now the Plymouth plain white versions have been the only examples known.

Plymouth's tablewares included a high proportion of blue and white, much of the blue of a peculiar blue-black tint. What little X-marked Bristol ware survives is for the

Fig. 4. The *Plymouth Manufacy* mug, dated March 14, 1768, on the base. *British Museum.*

Fig. 5. The *JBRC* mug, 1772. *British Museum.*

Fig. 5a. The *JBRC* mug, showing inscription on bottom.

Fig. 6. Set of Four Continents adapted from Longton Hall molds of c. 1755 but made by Cookworthy in hard-paste porcelain, c. 1770. The figures shown are from two different sets. *City Art Gallery, Bristol.*

Fig. 7. Figure of Air from the Elements, c. 1772-75. *Royal Scottish Museum, Edinburgh.*

most part a noticeably purer blue in shade; however, only one large lobed teapot, a type of shallow circular cream dish, and a quantity of tall cups are available for comparison. Blue-and-white is mentioned in two early advertisements but it seems that Champion, in common with the Chelsea proprietors, did not approve of this cheaper class of ware and had little time for transfer printing. None of the underglaze-blue printed hard paste is marked, and the more common overglaze and sometimes enameled output, some of it marked with the crossed swords, is usually irregular in quality and frequently smoke stained. From these facts it may be argued that some of the underglaze printed wares which are not in typical Bristol shapes may have been produced by one of the soft-paste factories, such as Caughley, which are now known to have made a limited amount of hard paste. It is also true that overglaze printing and decoration could well have been done in another center—Liverpool has been suggested—on plain white porcelain purchased during the Bristol factory's decline in the late 1770's.

A distinctive feature of English hard-paste wares, provided that they have been thrown on a potter's wheel, is the presence of a curious technical deficiency called spiral wreathing: a perceptible ridging in the body of vessels probably resulting from difficulties in working the clay and later accentuated in the firing processes. The wreathing appears to have been caused by the potter's drawing up his fingers in a final shaping of the object, and then being unable to smooth down the surface owing to the density of the clay and possibly to a tendency for it to dry out too quickly. The jug illustrated in Figure 8 shows this fault quite clearly.

Champion's new style of classical decoration was heralded in the dated John Brittan jug of 1773 (Fig. 9) now in the E. MacGregor Duncan Collection at the City Art Gallery, Bristol. It was soon followed by a series of tea, coffee, and dessert services (Fig. 10) intended as serious rivals to Worcester and Derby and even to the best Sèvres porcelains. Many patterns were copied and adapted from these sources, and much of the painting and the very fine gilding, some of it intricately tooled, was especially well executed by the Bristol decorators. Henry

Fig. 8. Cream jug painted in enamel colors and bearing the crossed-swords mark in underglaze blue, c. 1775. Notice the spiral wreathing, or ridging, of the body. *Royal Scottish Museum.*

Fig. 9. Bristol figure of a "bachelor," c. 1775; the John Brittan jug dated 1773, and a coffee can and saucer decorated in the Sèvres style; c. 1775. *City Art Gallery, Bristol.*

Fig. 10. Sauce tureen from a dessert service of high quality, of which only three pieces are known to survive. *City Art Gallery, Bristol.*

Bone and William Stephens, the best known of these decorators, had been with Cookworthy in Plymouth, but none of the work they did before Champion took control is reasonably distinguishable. A teapot in the Victoria and Albert Museum, for example, is inscribed below the spout *HMB* and may quite possibly have been painted by Bone for his Cornish parents, Henry and Mary (Pl. I). The fine landscapes painted on this vessel compare well with those on the superb armorial service presented by Champion and his wife, Judith, to Jane Burke on the election of her famous orator husband, Edmund, as a Whig member for Bristol in November 1774 (Fig. 11, Pl. II). The figure style of the supporters of the Burke-Nugent coat of arms is remarkably similar, also, to that of Henry Bone's miniatures of Champion's children, which are of the same period. Bone became a Royal Academician in 1811, and then painter in enamels to King George IV.

It is most likely that William Stephens specialized in flower painting, as a number of pieces from a tea service still in the possession of the Stephens family are painted with polychrome festoons only. He may well have been responsible for decorating a possibly unique tea service that survives in the MacGregor Duncan and other collections (Fig. 12). It shows flowers drawn with botanical accuracy.

Among the best-known Bristol tea services were those decorated with stock patterns of oval and circular gilt medallions containing the armorials, crests, or initials of individual customers and linked by laurel festoons. Among these is the Chough service, which is also the most complete, although the (probably) West Country family for which it was made has not yet been identified (Fig. 13). Other services in this stock pattern were made for the Edwards family; Sarah Smith, whose husband was host to the Burkes in the election period of 1774; Sir Robert Smyth—this one thought to be a wedding present datable to 1776; the Duke of Leinster; and William Plumer, a Whig Member of Parliament for Hereford. The Harfords and the Frys received services of different designs, possibly in return for the financial support they afforded the factory as partners. A tea-and-coffee service (Fig. 14) was only recently identified by Robert Williams, by means of its

Fig. 11. Teapot from the Burke service, presented in 1774 by Richard and Judith Champion to Jane Burke, wife of the famous orator and Member of Parliament for Bristol. *Royal Scottish Museum.*

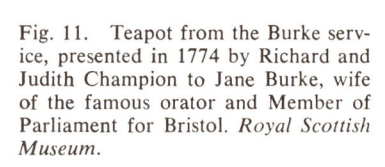

Fig. 12. Teapot and stand from a Bristol service possibly decorated by William Stephens. *City Art Gallery, Bristol; E. MacGregor Duncan collection.*

very modest-size coat of arms, as having been made for Thomas Pitt, later Lord Camelford, and part of a tea service inscribed *TMH* came to light only in February of this year.

The less well-off customer had to be content with festoon or bouquet-and-sprig patterns for his dessert or tea service, with gilt, lake, or plain edging according to his pocketbook. The most common pattern, which exists in many varieties, is the Green Festoon—but it was consistently well executed. Cheaper and later wares with scantily painted floral decoration clearly allowed the reputation of the factory to fall and have earned the unfortunate nickname of "cottage Bristol" for their class.

The range of wares produced at Bristol had its limitations. No large tureens or dishes were made, probably owing to the difficulty of controlling the weight of the paste and its consequent tendency to sag. Some circular dessert plates have inner foot rings, and some longer shaped dishes are supported on S-shape ridges to prevent them from sagging between potting and firing. Vases and figures were also liable to misbehave in this way, although in some pieces the faults and fissures could be disguised with enamel decoration. Among the most vulnerable of Champion's output were ungainly table centerpieces consisting of three Vestal Virgins grouped around a central pedestal supporting a classical urn. Most of the urns have been broken and detached from their bases, and at present only one such unit, the property of an Australian collector, survives intact (Fig. 15).

Some of the larger combined tea-and-coffee services are notable because they include spoon trays of two distinct types and sizes. This is true of a particularly fine armorial service made for Daniel Ludlow of Camden, of which the large spoon tray is in the Bristol Art Gallery and the smaller one in an American private collection (Fig. 16).

On a more modest level, Plymouth and Bristol both produced an unusual range of wares for the household. Rare pairs of toilet bottles and basins, sets of egg cups, and inkwells and pounce pots are known to survive, but until recently, when one pair was reunited by a Bristol collector, it was not realized that the inkwells and sanders must have been made in pairs.

Luxury wares made primarily for the china cabinet included a number of finely decorated breakfast services complete with trays. Usually made for one or two people, these services appear to have been fashioned to meet individual requirements. The milk jug of a service in the Bristol Art Gallery, decorated in a banded laurel pattern, was always thought to have been missing until the small

Fig. 13. Covered *sucrier* and teapot from the Chough service, c. 1775. *City Art Gallery, Bristol.*

Fig. 14. Part of the recently identified Pitt service reassembled in Bristol for the bicentenary exhibition in 1970. The tray is of a large size—possibly for the coffeepot, which also survives.

teapot, *sucrier*, and single cup and saucer were placed on their tray prior to the Bristol exhibition. It was then found that there was no room for anything else, indicating that the owner simply never took milk. The most richly decorated set known, whose tray is illustrated here (Fig. 17), is part of the Lady Binning bequest at the Royal Scottish Museum. There was a similar one, now lost, in the Alfred Trapnell collection, dispersed in 1912.

Most students of European porcelain are familiar with Bristol's unique production of unglazed, or biscuit, porcelain plaques. Originally these ranged in price from several shillings for floral bouquets to several guineas for the large, oval armorial examples generally five and one-half inches high. It is clear that Champion sought to use the plaques as evidence of the quality and fine workmanship of Bristol porcelain. The first were probably produced in 1774, when Champion seems to have secured at least one craftsman from Derby, Thomas Briand, to bring the technique of biscuit porcelain to his factory. Not one of the plaques is, however, dated, and the only evidence for this *terminus post quem* is the decoration with biscuit flowers of the lids of teapots, *sucrier,* and milk jug of the 1774 Burke service. The latest documentary piece with biscuit decoration is a teapot in the Bristol Art Gallery inscribed *IEW 1777*. A superb unrecorded gilt potpourri vase and cover (Fig. 18) similarly embellished with biscuit flowers and festoons is illustrated here so that its decoration may be compared with that of the plaques.

Fig. 15. Table centerpiece of Vestal Virgins type, as illustrated in the Trapnell Collection catalogue published by Amor, 1912. *Privately owned.*

The most common type of biscuit plaque is the small circular or oval flower piece, usually in its original glazed gilt or black frame. About twenty of the armorial plaques survive, no two of which are identical. Many were made for influential friends with Whig leanings like Champion's own, and could well have been presented in return for favors. Of the members of the House of Lords who were in a position to help Champion, the Marquis of Rockingham, the Earl of Bessborough, and the Duke of Montagu owned plaques showing their own coats of arms within a gilt laurel wreath and a chaplet of intricately modeled flowers. Among the others, Mark Harford probably received his plaque as a sometime partner in the undertaking; Charles Fox of Plymouth as Champion's close friend and future brother-in-law; Isaac Elton as master of the Society of Merchant Venturers in Bristol from 1773 to 1774, and Edmund Burke as his great friend and supporter in the Commons (Fig. 19). Two plaques are known with the coat of arms painted in enamel colors on a glazed oval medallion but framed, as were the others, in biscuit flowers. One of these bears Champion's arms; the original owner of the other has not been identified.

Only four monogrammed plaques are known, and these are very similar to the armorial examples described above except for the center, where the shield of the owner is replaced by a monogram within a rayed gilt border. The most important of these (Fig. 20) was made for Gabriel Goldney, a member of a prominent Bristol family, and bears on the back the contemporary inscription *Specimen of Bristol China modeled by Thomas Briand of Derby 1777* (Fig. 20a). The remaining three are inscribed *JB* for Jane Burke, *SC* for Champion's sister Sarah, and *EP* possibly for Ellin Peach, the daughter of a Quaker friend.

Portrait plaques are rare and were clearly intended to rival those that Wedgwood and Bentley produced at Etruria from about 1775. The most splendid example is undoubtedly the Benjamin Franklin plaque (Pl. III), which is known to have been in the great American's possession by 1778. A letter dated July 3 of that year refers to Franklin, then representing the United States of America in Paris, as finding a "good likeness" between Champion's profile and one that Wedgwood and Bentley had made. Another example, also in the British Museum, shows a classical bare head of Washington within a wreath of flowers and trophies of arms. Champion and Burke were very sympathetic to the American cause and especially to the freedom of trade across the Atlantic which was so severely curtailed during the War of Independence. No other portrait plaques are now known, although Champion did present a pair bearing their likenesses to George III and Queen Charlotte—hoping, of course, for favors as a result. Like Champion's cause, however, both of these were eventually lost. Three surviving plaques are decorated with classical figure subjects, two molded in relief and the other painted in enamels. Many more of all types must have been produced, according to old sale records, but these have probably been smashed or remain unrecognized.

Little has been said about the fortunes of the factory itself after Richard Champion took it over. Although it still had seven years to run, Champion undertook to renew Cookworthy's patent for a second term of fourteen years. This could only be done by presenting a bill to Parliament, which Champion did in February 1775. Already embarrassed by trading losses, Champion now met serious op-

Fig. 16. Part of the Ludlow of Camden service reassembled for the bicentenary exhibition, showing the larger-size spoon tray and two of the rare surviving teaspoons.

Fig. 17. Oval plateau or tray from a cabaret, or breakfast, service, which includes teapot, milk jug, *sucrier,* and two cups and saucers. Bristol, c. 1775. *Royal Scottish Museum.*

Fig. 18. Richly gilded potpourri vase and cover of campana shape, with finely modeled biscuit flowers applied on lid and urn. No mark, c. 1775. *City Art Gallery, Bristol.*

position to his "China Bill" in the House of Lords from a strong lobby of Wedgwood's friends who were determined not to allow Champion to retain the monopoly on the use of the kaolin and petuntse deposits. Without wishing to rival Champion, whom he thought unsuited to the ceramic arts, Wedgwood wanted to have access to the kaolinic clays, which could add to the durability and whiteness of his earthenwares and stonewares. Champion had to produce witnesses and show the House some of his finest porcelain to support his case (Pl. IV). The bill was passed in May 1775, but not without the amendments Wedgwood wanted. The whole costly rigmarole considerably weakened Champion's finances and therefore the prospects of the Bristol factory.

Pl. I. The *HMB* teapot, probably painted by Henry Bone for his parents, c. 1774. *Victoria and Albert Museum.*

Pl. II. Tall teacup and saucer from the Burke service, 1774. *City Art Gallery, Bristol; MacGregor Duncan collection.*

Pl. III. The Benjamin Franklin plaque, c. 1777. *British Museum.*

Pl. IV. Coffee can and saucer with painted scenes of Theseus slaying the Minotaur and Theseus in the Labyrinth; shown to Parliament in 1775. Formerly in the possession of Champion's foreman, John Brittan. *British Museum.*

101

Fig. 19. Plaque presented to Edmund Burke c. 1774, showing the arms of Burke impaling Nugent. *British Museum.*

Figs. 20 and 20a. Front and back views of the Gabriel Goldney plaque, dated 1777. *Collection of Lloyd E. Hawes.*

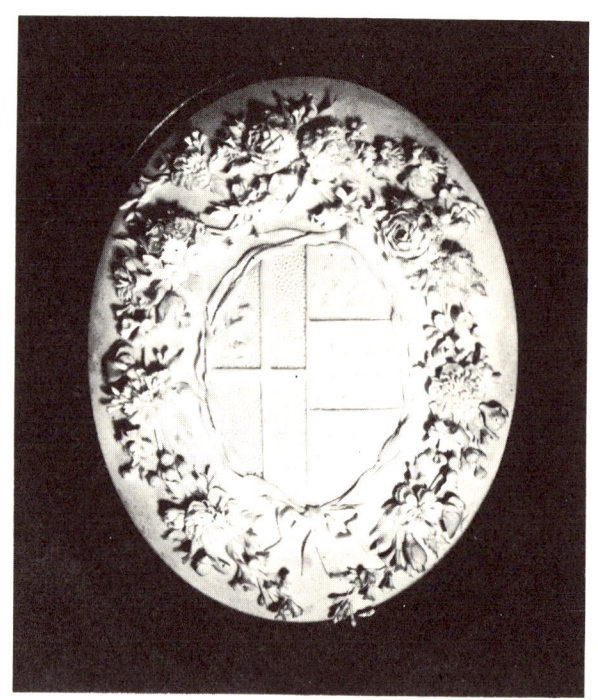

By 1778, Champion's insolvency had become more than apparent. The apprentice lists, relatively full since they had been opened in 1772, included only one new name for that year. It was clear that neither Champion nor any of his very patient partners would see much, if any, of their £15,000 investment again, and in August 1778 a deed of assignment was made in favor of his creditors. The manufacture of porcelain ceased, but decorating was probably carried on until the closure of the works in 1781—although returns must have been disappointing. Meanwhile, Champion's London warehouse continued to try to clear accumulated stocks until 1782, when a final sale was held. A three-day auction had taken place at Christie's in May 1780 but prices were modest considering the obvious quality of the services described. Champion attempted to recoup some of his losses by selling his still-valid patent, but could find little or no enthusiasm at his price of £8,000. A syndicate of Staffordshire potters bought the patent in 1781 and used it to produce hard paste at New Hall. It must have galled Champion to see the wares which resulted. A duller, creamier paste was produced at first and the decoration was clearly hurried in order to cut costs. Within thirty years hard-paste porcelain ceased to be produced in England. It was replaced by bone china, in effect a form of diluted hard paste which includes a high proportion of calcined ox bones, making it both cheaper and smoother in texture. Firing temperature no longer had to be so high and consequently difficult to control, and the formula proved so popular that bone china is the staple porcelain produced in England to this day.

Champion did not remain long in England after New Hall's foundation. He had a brief political career but finally emigrated to America with his family in 1784. After settling at Camden, South Carolina, he took some part in local affairs before he died on October 7, 1791, a broken man.

*Some Unusual Examples of*

# ENGLISH BLUE AND WHITE PORCELAIN

## By STANLEY W. FISHER

*Mr. Fisher's first article for* ANTIQUES *appeared in October 1948, soon after his book,* English Blue and White Porcelain of the Eighteenth Century. *Here he illustrates some more of his favorite ware—unusual examples from his own collection in England.*

THE GREATER PART of the late eighteenth-century English soft-paste ware, painted or printed in underglaze cobalt blue, was utilitarian; it was designed to meet a widespread demand for a durable yet beautiful ware with at least a passable resemblance to the "Nankin" porcelains so popular in Europe at that time. Purely ornamental pieces in blue and white were made in comparatively small quantities, since they could not hope to compete with their more splendid polychrome rivals. Among the utilitarian wares, however, the collector occasionally finds specimens which by reason of their purpose or rarity are lifted out of the ordinary. A few such examples are shown here.

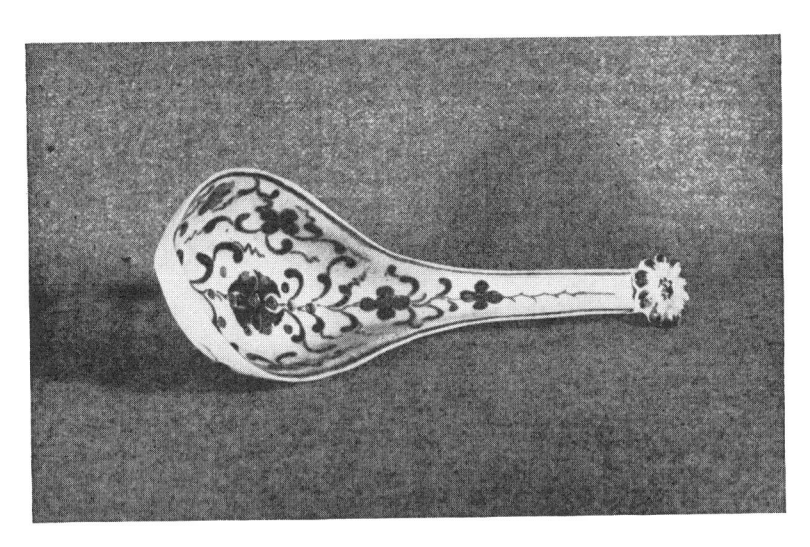

WORCESTER EGG DRAINER *(c. 1755).* The painted decoration, copied from a Chinese original, features the lotus flower. Marked with the open crescent. The purpose of the spoon was to lift an egg from boiling water—an excellent advertisement of the Worcester claim as to the heat-resisting nature of its wares. Caddy spoons of similar design were made, without the piercing.

WORCESTER CANDLESTICK *(c. 1760),* marked with an open crescent. Molded wares, usually in imitation of silver forms, were much favored by this factory. Worcester candlesticks are rare today, though they were made both in the pillar and chamber styles. The painting is restrained and does not detract from the molded shape. The head below the handle is reminiscent of the similar device on certain bell-shaped mugs made at the earlier Bristol factory at Redcliff Backs.

WORCESTER FEEDING CUP *(c. 1775),* transfer-printed in underglaze blue. Noteworthy shape and design, well adapted to its purpose. The dainty molded handles fit snugly into the hand, and the spout and half-cover assure comfort in drinking. Similar cups were made at Caughley, but the shapes are not so satisfactory.

CAUGHLEY TRIAL MUG, dated on base *22nd May, 1787;* otherwise unmarked. Such pieces were intended to try out various mixtures of cobalt pigment in the kiln.

103                                                                 June, 1950

CAUGHLEY CUP AND SAUCER, part of a miniature tea set (*c. 1780*). Marked S for Salopian. Compare the painted decoration with that on the trial mug.

CAUGHLEY EYE BATH (*c. 1775*). Transfer-printed, and marked with one of the disguised numerals peculiar to Caughley.

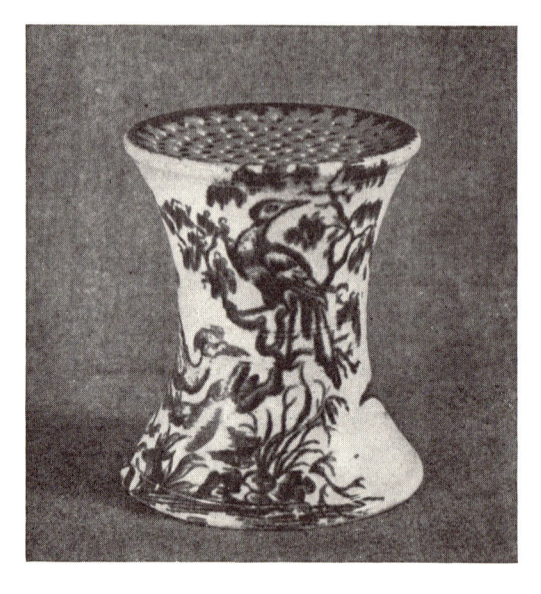

LIVERPOOL POUNCE POT (*1770*). Probably an example of the ware made by Zachariah Barnes. The paste is almost opaque, but in its thinnest parts it shows yellow by transmitted light. Brilliant glaze, and printed decoration in very dark blue, with exotic birds. Pounce, the predecessor of blotting paper, was made of powdered cuttlefish bone.

BOW MUG (*c. 1745*), an early experimental piece. Marked with a script *G*. The decoration is similar to that on a fragment excavated in 1921 at the Bow site by Aubrey J. Toppin. The painting, which is very elementary, is done in an opaque ultramarine, with almost the appearance of overglaze enamel. The handle, made of a roll of clay, is decorated with bars in the same blue. The paste has a pale green translucency, and the glaze is soft and heavily blued.

REDCLIFF BACKS MUG. The earliest dated piece of porcelain from this Bristol factory was made in 1750. Two years later the factory was taken over by Dr. Wall of Worcester. This mug may perhaps be a product of the earlier factory. It shows a green translucency, and has a sanded glaze and pale blue decoration. The handle terminal is in the shape of a head.

# Examination of English eighteenth-century porcelains by transmitted light

BY J. L. DIXON

PORCELAIN IS BY DEFINITION a translucent substance. If you hold a reasonably thin piece of it before a strong light some of the light is transmitted through the porcelain. Now although various porcelains may resemble one another when seen by ordinary, or reflected, light, some surprising differences, especially among the soft-paste porcelains of the eighteenth century, become apparent when the same pieces are examined by transmitted light. This fact has long been recognized as helpful in determining the origin of specimens. The aim of this article is to set down systematically the results of a comparative study of English porcelains by transmitted light, and to describe a simple apparatus that enables such comparative tests to be made.

Collectors, dealers, and others who are constantly handling and identifying porcelain acquire a facility for recognizing the various types and can, in general, make fairly reliable attributions and assign dates on sight. This knowledge must, however, be built up over many years and those who have not had this experience frequently ask themselves how they can be sure that this or that specimen of porcelain belongs to a particular factory or period. Books on porcelain give help in this direction to various degrees. For those who are scientifically inclined there are chemical-analysis tests. These, however, tend to be tedious and expensive, and generally involve the destruction of some part of the specimen. Transmitted-light testing is simple, can be done quite quickly, and does not damage the specimen. It should be remembered, however, that like most simple methods it has its limitations, and only by proper recognition of these can it be usefully employed.

I have developed a simple apparatus (illustrated here) for the study of specimens by transmitted light which enables comparative tests to be made. If one relies on holding a specimen before an electric-light bulb, one has to remember the color, and so forth, in order to make comparisons. The apparatus in question consists of two cinema-projector lamps giving off an intense, concentrated light, connected to a switch and mounted on a small table covered in black velvet, by means of which two specimens can be illuminated at the same time and a direct comparison made, thus permitting recognition of slight differences which might otherwise be difficult to remember. Moreover, by this method a known and accepted specimen can be directly compared with one that is in question.

Translucence and color by transmitted light are subject to fairly wide accidental variations and their value can never be more than contributory: they serve to confirm an attribution based on other evidence, or to suggest one which may in turn be confirmed by other features. Some training of the eye and some practice are necessary to enable one to recognize easily the basic luminous qualities characteristic of the various factories. It is desirable to practice this recognition in a low, ambient light, such as ordinary electric light, rather than in full daylight.

About translucence there need be no difficulty as to different opinions. Given specimens of the same thickness it should be easy to say whether a specimen is 1) highly translucent, 2) very translucent, 3) fairly translucent, 4) slightly translucent, 5) almost opaque, 6) opaque, and by using these terms to distinguish sufficiently clearly the relative translucence of any specimen.

When we come to describe color, however, we find that people do not agree. Eyes vary in sensitivity to different colors. Ordinarily we believe we are seeing the same thing because we are looking at the same thing, and for everyday purposes such a belief is justified, but for the purpose of distinguishing subtle shades of color it may lead to difficulties. This need not be so very important, as the student will soon come to recognize what might be called the basic appearance of each period and factory. What matters is that when pieces of any particular period are examined, we should all agree on the peculiar color and translucence of that factory and period. If, for example, we are looking at a pale greenish Derby specimen, it is important that we should be able to distinguish its color from other greens and to say, "Yes, that is a typical Derby paste."

Examining by transmitted light groups of specimens attributed to known factories, we find that some show a high degree of consistency, the appearance varying very little over the whole group. Such a group is referred to in the tabulation as Consistent (C). Other groups seem to vary considerably, at the same time maintaining a characteristic appearance. These are referred to as Variable (V). The thickness of a piece obviously affects its appearance by transmitted light and here allowance must be made for reduced translucence and deeper color. Sometimes a specimen may be stained, and the almost dark-brown color of specimens in the Bow, Lowestoft, Longton Hall, and Derby groups may be due to some

Device developed by the author for examining porcelain by transmitted light. The light is provided by cinema-projector lamps controlled by a switch; the table is covered with black velvet.

fault in the mixture, or failure in the firing, perhaps associated with insufficient flux in the mixture to ensure complete fusion.

## GLASSY PORCELAINS

Chelsea

*Triangle period.* Triangle Chelsea shows a consistent and characteristic color and high translucence.

*Raised-anchor period.* The appearance of raised-anchor paste is almost perfectly white; it has an alabaster-like quality. There are frequently little bright specks in the paste.

*Red-anchor period.* The use of the red anchor probably marks the change in the paste, which by transmitted light looks greenish yellow in various tints, often, and particularly in the case of plates and dishes, showing the well-known "moons," which are now known to be caused by small bubbles in the paste. Many red-anchor pieces show high translucence with the peculiar smooth whiteness of the gold-anchor period; these would seem to be red-anchor types that were also made in the early part of the gold-anchor period. Intermediate examples of this kind frequently occurred at Chelsea and at other factories as well and must be allowed for.

*Gold-anchor period.* Gold-anchor plates and dishes are often heavy and thick, but when the paste is thin it shows a smooth, almost white appearance, which can generally be easily distinguished from the somewhat crystalline whiteness of raised anchor. Some of the thick pieces are only slightly translucent, but the attribution of these to gold anchor on other grounds is generally not difficult.

Derby

Transmitted light is particularly helpful in the recognition of Derby specimens of the early periods, as these generally show a characteristic color, here referred to as pale misty grayish green. There is, however, another group of Derby pieces which show only slight translucence and a brownish color not peculiar to any one factory.

Longton Hall

There are two fairly clearly marked groups of Longton Hall pieces, one showing a characteristic cold white, the thicker parts being of a cold, icy blue. This is an interesting color by transmitted light, unique and unmistakable.

The second group, which presumably represents the later paste, comes nearer to red-anchor Chelsea in color and not infrequently has moons, but can be distinguished from Chelsea pieces by a bluish tint; and here again the transmitted-light test fails in a number of pieces which are almost opaque and brownish.

## BONE PORCELAINS

Bow

Bow porcelains have their characteristic appearance, and are divided into two groups, one highly translucent and yellowish in color, the other ranging through various degrees of brownish color and opacity. It must be remembered that Bow porcelains stained very easily, taking up organic color. The early dated "New Canton" inkwells show only slight translucence and brownish color, while there are pieces which give every indication of having been manufactured in the early fifties and are highly translucent. Apart from being confused with Lowestoft, Bow pieces are not usually difficult to recognize.

Lowestoft

Lowestoft paste is frequently similar to Bow paste in appearance by transmitted light, but there are many highly translucent pieces which show a cold white to a characteristic pale creamy white. Another group, which is only fairly translucent, shows a streaky, yellowish color. An interesting feature of Lowestoft teapots shows up by transmitted light: sometimes the translucence varies in horizontal bands due to varying thicknesses of the pot, which, although turned smooth on the outside, might be left with the finger grooves on the inside.

## STEATITE PORCELAINS

Worcester

*Lund's Bristol period.* These specimens divide into two groups. The first is very translucent and varies in color from pale to rich cream. The second is fairly translucent and a greenish color. The cream color is probably characteristic of the early part of the period. There is a letter written by Dr. Pococke, dated 1750, in which he refers to sauceboats produced by Lund's factory having a yellow cast, in both the ware and the glazing. In those days this was regarded as undesirable, the aim being to produce a porcelain that looked as nearly as possible like China Trade hard paste. The fact that there is also a group of pieces which are consistently and characteristically greenish seems to indicate the correctness of the claim sometimes made that around 1750 the factory tried to rectify the yellow color by the addition of cobalt.

*First period.* Throughout this rather long period the paste is fairly translucent and shades in many variations from palish yellow to green. In the latter part of the period the paste seems to have been modified: it tends to be almost white by transmitted light. This is frequently the case with the square-marked pieces. There is a popular theory that any piece of eighteenth-century porcelain which shows a greenish color can be attributed to Worcester of this period, but this is, of course, quite unreliable. Fortunately it is seldom necessary to resort to transmitted-light tests to recognize Worcester, which generally can easily be distinguished by other means.

Caughley

Transmitted light is useful in differentiating Caughley products from those of the Worcester factory which were copied, as the Caughley specimens show a satisfactorily consistent color and translucence. They are fairly translucent and have a yellowish tint. It seems probable that Caughley made more types than is generally supposed. Attribution based on decoration is complicated by the fact that at the time many pieces were decorated by outside decorators. A London decorator, James Giles, well known for his work on Bow and Worcester porcelains, recorded in his ledger having dealings with Thomas Turner. There is also a record, dated 1773, of payment of carriage on a box from Salop. Turner became proprietor of the Caughley works in 1772 and it is possible that he continued to supply Giles with Caughley porcelain, as he had formerly done with Worcester.

Liverpool

The Liverpool factories are a special study. The Richard Chaffers porcelain was directly derived from Worcester. We would expect, therefore, and we do find, among the Liverpool groups, pieces scarcely distinguishable from Worcester by transmitted light. Pennington's "China Body" formula, published by Sadler in 1769, shows that it contained thirty-three per cent of bone ash. This paste is green and only slightly translucent, corresponding to the fourth group in the schedule. The same transmitted-light color is shown by a well-known group of Liverpool pieces, the glaze of which has a distinctly bluish color by reflected light.

Another type of Liverpool porcelain, usually attributed to Zachariah Barnes, shows a yellow color not unlike khaki.

## HARD PORCELAINS

Plymouth, Bristol, and New Hall

Very little need be said about the English hard-paste porcelains, which are consistently very translucent and which all show rather similar shades of gray. Plymouth is distinguished from the others by being warmer in tint. Bristol tends to be more highly translucent than either Plymouth or New Hall, except in the later period of the New Hall factory when we get the characteristic brilliant translucence of English bone porcelain.

*Eighteenth-century English porcelain seen by transmitted light*

| Factory | Period | Translucence | | Color |
|---|---|---|---|---|
| **GLASSY PORCELAINS** | | | | |
| Chelsea | Triangle | H.T. | C. | Pale misty ivory |
| | Raised anchor | H.T. | C. | Almost white, sometimes with small bright specks |
| | Red anchor | | | |
| | (1) | F.T. | V. | Slightly greenish yellow, sometimes with moons |
| | (2) | H.T. | C. | White with pale greenish tinge |
| | Gold anchor | | | |
| | (1) | H.T. | V. | Pale slightly pinkish ivory |
| | (2) | H.T. | C. | Smooth white |
| Chelsea-Derby | | V.T. | V. | Pale cream or greenish |
| Derby | (1) | V.T. | C. | Rather misty pale grayish green |
| | (2) | S.T. | V. | Brownish |
| Longton Hall | (1) | H.T. | C. | Almost white, thicker parts cold icy blue |
| | (2) | V.T. | C. | Duck-egg-bluish green, sometimes with moons |
| | (3) | S.T.-A.O. | | Brownish |
| **BONE PORCELAINS** | | | | |
| Bow | (1) | V.T. | V. | Slightly greenish yellow |
| | (2) | S.T. | V. | Brownish |
| Lowestoft | (1) | H.T. | V. | Cold white to pale creamy white |
| | (2) | V.T. | V. | Streaky misty yellow |
| | (3) | S.T. | V. | Brownish yellow |
| **STEATITE PORCELAINS** | | | | |
| Worcester-Lund's Bristol Period | (1) | V.T. | V. | Almost white to cream |
| | (2) | F.T. | V. | Greenish cream to green |
| 1st Period | | F.T. | V. | Greenish yellow to green |
| Caughley | | F.T. | C. | Golden ocher |
| Liverpool | (1) | V.T. | V. | Greenish yellow to yellowish green |
| | (2) | F.T. | V. | Yellow |
| | (3) | F.T. | V. | Warm gray, sometimes with moons or bright spots |
| | (4) | S.T. | V. | Green, sometimes with moons |
| | (5) | A.O. | V. | Brownish |
| **HARD PORCELAINS** | | | | |
| Plymouth | | F.T. | C. | Warm pale gray |
| Bristol | | V.T. | C. | Cool misty gray, lighter than Plymouth and more uniform |
| New Hall | | V.T. | C. | Pale misty gray |

Key to symbols used: H.T., highly translucent; V.T., very translucent; F.T., fairly translucent; S.T., slightly translucent; A.O., almost opaque; C., consistent; V., variable.

# III Wedgwood

The role played by Josiah Wedgwood in the creation of the English ceramic industry is well known, for he represents the only truly household name in the world of pottery and porcelain. That Wedgwood was far more than a successful potter is also well known, but these less obvious aspects of his life still warrant further study. Above all, he was a successful businessman, and this success was based primarily on his taste and judgement. It has often been stated that he turned a peasant craft into a modern industry, but this is unjust to both Wedgwood and the industry in which he worked. By 1760, the Staffordshire pottery industry was already established as one of national significance. By his acumen and foresight, however, Wedgwood enabled it to follow its already determined path of development more rapidly. His contribution was that of the entrepreneur who was able to recognize an opportunity and exploit it to the fullest. He masterminded many technical advances, which affected both the preparation and firing of the wares, and the organization of the factory. Realizing that imperfect firing meant a potentially disastrous loss of revenue, he worked for years to perfect his pyrometer, which made it possible to control precisely the temperature of the oven. He also realized that a satisfied work force and a thriving export market were both essential requirements in the industry. Most important of all, he well understood the financial risks inherent in the manufacture of porcelain and so was able to steer well clear of any such temptation. He knew that he could rely on the far more predictable creamwares, earthenwares, jasper, and stonewares to bring in all the revenue he required. In some ways this was his greatest contribution to the English industry, for by his example he encouraged potters throughout England, and in Staffordshire in particular, to leave porcelain-making well alone, at least until an adequate material (i.e., bone china) had been developed.

The other side of Wedgwood's contribution was reflected in his sense of style. By ensuring that his products and designs were up to the minute in fashion, in a way that no potter before or since has really been able to match, he was able to exploit an international, style-conscious market. By the same token, he elevated the ceramic industry from its previous, essentially domestic status into one of considerable artistic significance. He played his part in establishing the neo-classical style in England, partly by his friendship with leaders of fashion such as Sir William Hamilton and Matthew Boulton, partly by his interest in the archaeology of the Egyptian and Classical civilizations, and partly by his use of avant-garde designers such as Flaxman. He was able to match his jasper wares to the so-called Etruscan colors of the Adam style, and so made them vital and compatible parts of interior design schemes. In order to see Wedgwood products at their best, it is necessary to see them in context as complementary parts of a total design scheme.

The popularity of Wedgwood in America is one of the curiosities of art and design history. Although its reputation in the 18th century was second to none, the company was totally eclipsed during the 19th century by other great names, such as Minton, Copeland and Doulton. As a result, Wedgwood was not able to develop its export trade so effectively as its rivals. Nor was it able to compete with the vast displays put on by the great names of the Victorian period at exhibitions such as the Philadelphia Centennial of 1876 or the Chicago International of 1893. Yet, the name and personal significance of Josiah Wedgwood was such that this alone was sufficient to carry his company through the lean years. As a result, Wedgwood wares have been continuously studied and researched to such an extent that only the merest details remain uncovered. The great majority of this work has been carried out in America, which has its own Wedgwood Society, its own Wedgwood Museum, and an annual Wedgwood seminar for collectors all over the world. Even the many other users of the Wedgwood name have been studied who, though in no way connected, have been able to bask in the reflected glory of the reputation that Josiah Wedgwood launched on the world.

# Josiah Wedgwood, Industrialist

*By* Joseph H. Park

*Except as noted, illustrations from the author's collection*

*Fig. 1 (above)* — Marbled Vase (*c. 1768*)
One of a pair. Impressed mark *Wedgwood & Bentley*. During his early working years Wedgwood devoted his attention to improving green-glazed, agate, marbled, and tortoise-shell wares with which the name of his partner Whieldon is usually associated.
Height, 7 ¾ inches.
From the Art Institute of Chicago

*Fig. 2 (right)* — Cream or "Queen's Ware" Plate
Wedgwood did not invent cream ware; but he improved it. Furthermore, upon his appointment as potter to Queen Charlotte, he glorified his everyday domestic crockery by changing its name to Queen's ware. Thus distinguished, the product conquered the markets of Europe and America

JOSIAH WEDGWOOD, to quote his epitaph, was responsible for the conversion of "a rude and inconsiderable manufacture into an elegant art, and an important branch of national commerce." Likewise, in the opinion of William E. Gladstone, spoken at the foundation of the Wedgwood Institute at Burslem, he appears as a potter whose most signal and characteristic merit lay in the application of the higher arts to industry. But probably neither Wedgwood's contemporaries nor Gladstone — whatever the latter's clairvoyant powers — fully realized the vast scope of the interests and activities that occupied this Englishman whose bicentennial has recently been celebrated.

Whatever may be the ultimate judgment regarding Wedgwood's place in the history of art, there may be no question of his dominance as a business man during that part of the eighteenth century that is frequently known as the period of industrial revolution. Though fond of discussing philosophy and science, he was, nevertheless, constantly experimenting with the most practical of the potter's problems. Liberal, even radical, in his view of home and foreign affairs, he was, notwithstanding, apparently the most effective political lobbyist that his locality could send forth to represent its interests. Though he pretended to be uncertain as to whether he should pose as a landed gentleman, an engineer, or a potter, his fellow craftsmen knew that his heart was in the last of these vocations.

If it be true, indeed, that Wedgwood made the manufacture of pottery an important branch of national commerce, he immediately becomes an outstanding figure both in the history of ceramics and in the history of industry. What part, then, did he play in the developments of his generation?

In the first place, he accomplished much in improving various wares already in common use. The story of his labors in this direction is fully described in the manuals. He was justly proud of his progress. His rosso antico interested him but little; for it could be made, he complained, at first trial by anyone. On the other hand, the jasper ware with which his name is intimately connected gave him opportunity to exercise his originality to the full. Clays for experimentation were sought for him not only throughout England, but even in the regions of South Carolina and Florida. This jasper — he was not above suggesting — was costly and consequently desirable because the essential Cherokee clay was extremely difficult to obtain. In such a suggestion we perceive the keen advertiser's play to the gallery of popular credulity.

With the story of his improvement of different wares is associated his handling of such problems as the organization of workmen, the emigration question, and the difficulties involved in outwitting spies. Order and regulation, whatever their spiritual effect upon the workmen, made for factory efficiency. The emigration of trained workmen and the activity of spies disturbed more than one industrial leader. James Watt and other friends, for example, informed Wedgwood of three sets of spies, from three different nations, who were attempting to learn the secrets of English machines and manufactures.

*Fig. 3* — Teapot in Rosso Antico
Such pieces, if they bear the irregular old Wedgwood mark, are highly prized, even though the ware was not greatly esteemed by Wedgwood himself. The design is of Oriental inspiration

August, 1934

And among Wedgwood's papers we find a document entitled *Proposed as part of a plan to prevent emigration*, which includes provisions for counteracting attempts of foreign manufacturers to lure English craftsmen from allegiance to their native employers. So far as the home market was concerned, however, Wedgwood strove to put the dread of rivalry behind him.

But the production of better wares and the efficient ordering of workers did not necessarily imply increased sales of merchandise. Wedgwood was cognizant of the need for advertising. His business acumen is apparent in a letter dated *18 July 1766*:

"What do you think of sending Mr. Pitt [perhaps the most outstanding Englishman then living] upon Crockery ware to America. A Quantity might certainly be sold there now and some advantage made of the American prejudice in favor of that great man."

That, however, was an insignificant incident. Wedgwood's large-scale advertising consisted in part of establishing Continental agencies and of widely distributing sheets of engravings portraying various articles of his manufacture. He did not hesitate to act personally as a salesman, urging England's ambassador to Russia to introduce Wedgwood ware to the Russian court — with well-known results. He was pleased to write to his partner, Bentley, that Lord Shelbourne had "recommended it strongly to our Envoy at Lisbon to endeavour to introduce such of our manufactures at that Court as were not there already, and to inquire what alterations would be acceptable in such as are now bought of us." Wedgwood believed devoutly in foreign markets, and was sensitive to foreign feelings and foreign prejudices.

But whether the demand for their products came from home or from abroad, Wedgwood and his fellow potters were constantly hampered by difficulties of transport. The eighteenth century stands forth as a great period of road and canal construction. In such projects Wedgwood actively participated. His task was not only that of sending far and wide from Staffordshire a most fragile product, but likewise that of obtaining the raw materials necessary for its manufacture. James Brindley, famous engineer, was an authority on canal building. Between him and Wedgwood an intimate relationship was maintained for a number of years. Brindley did much of the technical work for the Grand Trunk Canal from the Mersey to the Trent. Bentley saw to the distribution of pamphlets on the general advantages of inland navigation, and Wedgwood attempted to organize the local potters to the point of influencing Parliament to pass desired legislation "without mentioning too much about our manufacture, lest our Governors should think it worth taxing."

The result of his efforts in behalf of canal building was satisfactory. The cost per ton for earthenware transport for a given distance dropped from $12.50 to $3.33. And if some of Wedgwood's neighbors looked askance at the favorable location of his factory upon the new canal, the general judgment was in his favor.

*Fig. 4 (above)* — APOTHEOSIS OF HOMER (*c. 1780*)
This and a companion urn represent the triumphal coronation of the two chief poets — Homer and Virgil — of the ancient world. The designs were prepared by John Flaxman. Light blue jasper with white reliefs.
*From the Art Institute of Chicago*

*Fig. 5 (left)* — "BASALT" BUST OF ROUSSEAU
Wedgwood's basalt, an improvement upon a black material much used before his time, lent itself to the finest and most delicate of ornamental work, including portrait statuary. In the eighteenth century it was the fashion for gentlemen to adorn their libraries with the busts of notables

*Fig. 6* — TEAPOT IN BAMBOO COLOR (*c. 1780*)
Experiments with cane and bamboo colors were emphasized between 1776 and 1786. The teapot here pictured was found by the author in a peasant home in Normandy, where apparently it had been for several generations

Since Wedgwood believed in the importance of the export trade, it was natural that movements of world consequence should stir him to comment. "To political knowledge I have no pretensions," he wrote, "but every manufacturer can judge whether particular measures are likely to promote, or to ruin, his manufactury, and will accordingly do his endeavors, by all the legal means in his power, to promote the one and oppose the other."

In 1783 he petitioned Fox, Secretary of State in the Coalition Ministry, urging that statesman to negotiate commercial treaties that would facilitate the exportation of ceramic wares to various foreign markets. Eventually he was summoned before a committee of the Board of Trade, which was gathering data preliminary to the famous Eden treaty with France — an arrangement which has recently been considered one of the causes of the French Revolution, in so far as it permitted importation of English goods to the detriment of certain portions of the French working population.

But Wedgwood was unperturbed by the political catastrophe across the Channel. Instead he wrote: "The politicians tell me that as a manufacturer I shall be ruined if France has her liberty, but I am willing to take my chance in that respect, nor do I yet see that the happiness of one nation includes in it the misery of its next neighbor."

When, on the other hand, questions of Irish trade arose, Wedgwood worked for restriction of such trade, and the Irish were correspondingly bitter against him.

More characteristic of the man and his policies was his attitude toward the American colonies. He believed that the English government was determined "to *Conquer England in America*" and that Townshend's proposals for taxing America would tend "to render the Americans independent a century sooner than they would be in the common order of events." He never had faith "in reports for which bells had rung and rung again," of the overthrow of Washington. He subscribed to the fund that was being raised to alleviate the misery of American prisoners in England, and was so delighted with America's progress toward freedom that he made the statement: "The pleasing ideas of a refuge being provided for those who chuse rather to flee from than to submit to the iron hand of tyrany has raised so much hilarity in my mind that I do not at present feel for our own situation as I may do the next rainy day." And in addition he was much disturbed over the way commerce had suffered by this "most wicked and preposterous war with our brethren and best friends."

His strong desire for abolishing the slave trade showed itself in a number of ways, one of which, the production of the famous slave cameos and intaglios which were both given away and sold, has been largely advertised. His sympathy for the oppressed, indeed, appears to have been deep. On the one hand, he subscribed $500 to aid the Poles against Russia, notwithstanding the interest of the Russian court in his work; and, on the other, he stood for Parliamentary reform and a wide extension of the franchise in England even though he maintained special display rooms "for those who had wealth and taste."

Space forbids a discussion of his work on the pyrometer, his association with other industrial leaders like Boulton and Arkwright, his friendship with philosophers and experimenters like Erasmus Darwin and Priestley. Suffice it to say that the quality of his wares, his ability as an organizer, and his business acumen in affairs both domestic and foreign enabled him to accumulate a fortune of $2,500,000, and to create a commerce so active and universal that a French contemporary wrote:

"In travelling from Paris to St. Petersburg, from Amsterdam to the furthest point of Sweden, from Dunkirk to the southern extremity of France, one is served at every inn from English earthenware. The same fine article adorns the tables of Spain, Portugal, and Italy: it provides the cargoes of ships to the East Indies, the West Indies, and America."

One might naturally ask: Would not Josiah Wedgwood, were he living a hundred and fifty years later, have produced something entirely different from the fine wares which collectors now prize so highly? The answer is, probably, Yes. Wedgwood was fortunate: his products could represent a nice balance between manual skill of an older era and efficiency of an industrial age, as Beethoven's music may represent a perfect balance between harmony and dissonance. It may even be that, in the field of his accomplishment, the world can scarcely hope ever again to see the like of either man.

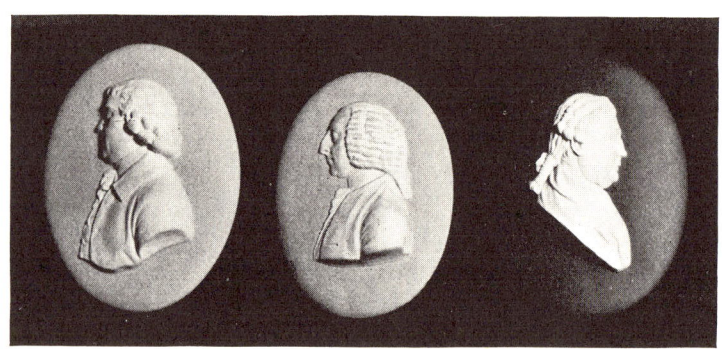

*Fig. 7* — CAMEO PORTRAITS OF WEDGWOOD, CHATHAM, AND KEPPEL
Wedgwood was quick to seize upon any subject for portraiture that stood high in popular esteem. The profile of a national hero like Admiral Keppel might sell by the thousands

*Fig. 8 (above and left)* — SMALL ARTICLES OF JASPER WARE AND BASALT
Wedgwood turned out an immense quantity of small objects in the various hard fine-bodied earthenware to whose perfecting he devoted endless time and patience. Such articles include scent bottles, watch backs, ink pots, decorative insets for furniture, and seal cameos and intaglios for rings, brooches, and other forms of jewelry

*Fig. 9 (right)* — "AM I NOT A MAN AND A BROTHER" (*c. 1785*)
Black relief on white jasper ground. Modeled by William Hackwood. Thousands of similar intaglios and cameos were issued by Wedgwood in furtherance of Wilberforce's movement to abolish the slave trade.
Size: 1 3/4 by 1 5/8 inches.
*From the Art Institute of Chicago*

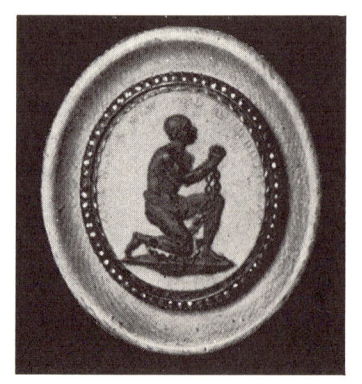

*Self-portrait* by John Flaxman (1755-1826); wax; 1779; diameter 7½ inches. *Victoria and Albert Museum.*

# Flaxman's work for Wedgwood

## BY JEAN GORELY

THE TWO-HUNDREDTH ANNIVERSARY of the birth of the English sculptor, John Flaxman, R.A., seems an appropriate time to clear away some of the confusion which exists about the work he did for Josiah Wedgwood between 1775 and 1794. Flaxman has been credited with many designs he did not do, and one is constantly offered specimens of Wedgwood with designs after the antique, or by one of Flaxman's contemporaries, as original works of this noted English artist. As Flaxman's advent in Wedgwood's life happened to coincide with the potter's trials with his new jasper body, this study is mainly concerned with designs in white relief on black and colored ground on small medallions and objects after 1775, on large plaques and tablets after 1778, and on vases after 1780.

Flaxman, the son of a molder of figures for sculptors, was born on July 6, 1755. In his early years the boy was often seen modeling and copying medals in his father's shop. According to the records of the Royal Society of Arts and the Royal Academy, he won several medals and honors before he was fifteen.

In January 1775 Wedgwood wrote to Bentley, his partner: "I am glad that you have met with a Modeler, & that Flaxman is so valuable an artist"; and in July of the same year: "Suppose you were to employ Mr. Flaxman to model some figures." Thereafter Wedgwood suggested the design he wanted, Flaxman would make a sketch, and when it was approved, prepare a wax model conforming to the potter's specifications. In short, Flaxman's work consisted of translating into low relief or figure a desired subject from a marble, a gem, a print, a vase painting, or a miniature on a snuffbox, adapting it in size and thickness to a form which could be used by the potter and which would permit the inevitable shrinkage in the firing.

The sculptor continued to live and work in London; Wedgwood sent dimensions and instructions "by the coach," and the sketches and models were sent back to Etruria the same way—in many instances to be remodeled by Hackwood, the chief artist at the works. Although this long-distance communication must have been difficult, apparently both found it profitable. Wedgwood was not unaware of Flaxman's growing reputation in the art world; on February 14, 1776, he wrote to Bentley: "I wish you would give Flaxman a head or two to Model as it may excite our Modelers' emulation."

The difficulty of attribution is increased by the fact that Flaxman's father sometimes furnished Wedgwood with casts. Some bills are receipted by the father, while one at least, that for 1775, is receipted "for my father" by "John Flaxman, Junr." This bill is of particular interest because it mentions objects which have been assigned to the

*Linnaeus*, after Inlander's portrait done from life in 1774; blue and white jasper, marked *Wedgwood & Bentley*; c. 1779. Cast and mold furnished to Wedgwood by Flaxman Sr. in 1775. *Metropolitan Museum of Art.*

*Dr. Boerhaave* (1668-1738); white on pink-washed jasper, marked WEDGWOOD; c. 1786. Modeled by Flaxman after relief by Pesez. *Emily Winthrop Miles collection, Brooklyn Museum.*

Right. *Sir Joshua Reynolds, R.A.* (1733-1792); white on pink-washed jasper marked WEDGWOOD; c. 1790. Modeled by Flaxman from print of painting by Pierre Etienne Falconet. *Emily Winthrop Miles collection, Brooklyn Museum.*

Left. *The Apotheosis of Homer*; white relief on black jasper, called the Homeric Vase; marked WEDGWOOD; c. 1786. Wedgwood considered this vase his own greatest work. Modeled in 1778 from a design on a painted vase in Sir William Hamilton's collection. *Lady Lever Art Gallery, Port Sunlight, England.*

Print of the vase in the British Museum which was the source for the *Apotheosis of Homer.*

*Height 18 Inches.*

*From a Vase in the British Museum.*

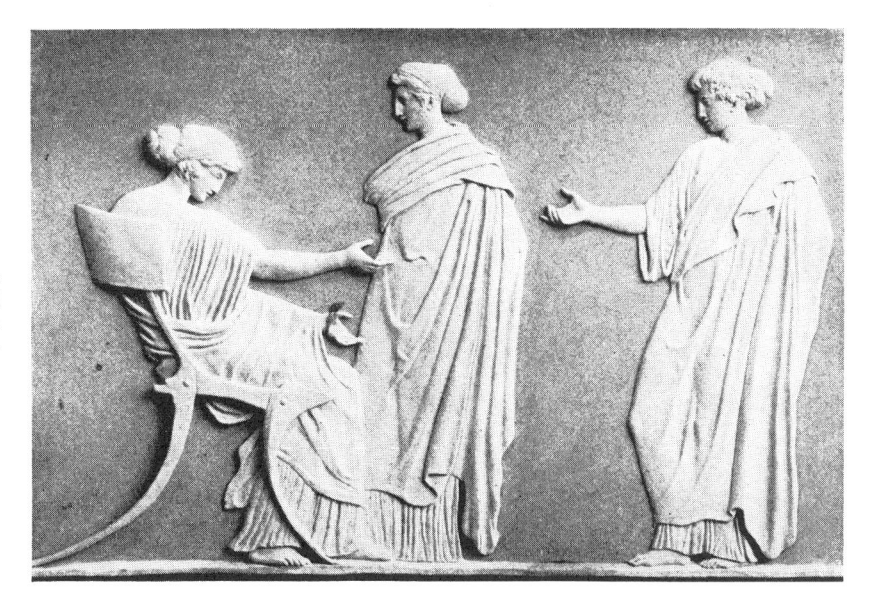

*Veturia and Volumnia Entreating Coriolanus to Return to Rome;* blue and white jasper, marked WEDGWOOD; c. 1790. Modeled in 1785 from a print of a painted vase in Sir William Hamilton's collection.

## Portrait medallions

(None of the portraits listed here was done from life—medals, gems, miniatures, or prints were used as models in every instance.)

**Mr. Banks, Dr. Solander.** Wedgwood's letter to Bentley, July 1775.
**Lord Chatham.** Wedgwood to Bentley, July 1, 1778. (Not to be confused with the portrait of William Pitt the younger.)
**Mr. Banks.** Flaxman's bill, August 21, 1779. (Classic type without wig, for 10¼-inch plaque.)
**King and Queen of Sicily.** Flaxman's bill, June 21, 1781. ("Received Five Guineas for the Portraits of their Sicilian Majesties in wax, of Mr. Hilditch in full . . ." "Mr. Hilditch" has been listed, erroneously, as one of Flaxman's subjects.)
**Harpocrates.** Flaxman to Wedgwood, February 1782. (Not Hippocrates.)
**Duke of Russia.** Flaxman to Wedgwood, February 1782. (Modeled from a print of an engraved stone.)
**De Ruyter.** Flaxman to Wedgwood, February 1782.
**Dr. Herman Boerhaave, Temmink** (Wedgwood's spelling), **Captain Peter Hein, Hogerboots, Admiral Kortenaar.** Flaxman to Wedgwood, July 8, 1782. (Admiral de Ruyter and the above group of five were the six additional Dutch portraits in the Catalogue of 1787. Wedgwood gives Pesez of Amsterdam as the artist Flaxman copied.)
**Mr. Herschel, Dr. Buchan.** Flaxman's bill, July 11, 1783.
**Captain Cook.** Flaxman's bill, January 24, 1784. (From the Copley gold medal awarded to Cook by the Royal Society in 1776; not previously recorded.)
**Dr. Johnson.** Flaxman's bill, February 3, 1784. (This was evidently done from a print by Trotter showing the wisp of hair at the top of the head which appears on the eighteenth-century Wedgwood portraits and does not appear in the modern casts made for Professor Tinker's study, published in 1926.)
**C. Jenkinson, Esq.** Flaxman's bill, March 21, 1784. (Mr. Jenkinson became Earl of Liverpool in 1796.)
**Warren Hastings.** Flaxman's bill, January 14, 1785.
**King of Sweden** (Gustavus III). Flaxman's bill, November 23, 1785.
**Mr. and Mrs. Meerman.** Flaxman's bill, December, 1785. (These were art patrons at The Hague.)
**Queen of Portugal** (Maria I). Flaxman's bill, June 1, 1787.
**Sir Joshua Reynolds.** Testimony of Raspé, 1791. (From a print of a painting by Pierre Etienne Falconet, found by the author.)
**Prince of Piedmont** (Victor Amadeus II). Flaxman to Byerley, November 15, 1788. (From a miniature on a snuff box.)

## Busts and Figures

**Dr. Fothergill, Rousseau, Sterne.** Usually assigned to Flaxman on the strength of his bill of March 7, 1781, which mentions "Moulding a bust of Dr. Fothergale" and "Two busts of Rosseau & Sterne." (On this same bill are **A Shell Venus, A Bacchante, Cupid & Psyche,** and **A Sitting Flora.** As the **Cupid & Psyche** are evidently the pair Wedgwood listed as "Cupid Sitting Pensive and Psyche to match," which I have found were after the famous *Cupid Menaçant* and *Psyché* by Falconet. The rest were after famous statues and cannot be regarded as Flaxman originals, although he may have adapted them to the potter's requirements.)
**Mercury.** Flaxman to Wedgwood, August 22, 1782. (Perhaps the bust Flaxman exhibited at the Royal Academy in 1782. There are at least three known models marked WEDGWOOD—one reminiscent of the head of Mercury by Pigalle, another with some likeness to the bust by Thorwaldsen, and a third which may be the one by Flaxman referred to in this letter.)
**Mrs. Siddons.** Flaxman's bill, April 28, 1782. (Also Flaxman to Wedgwood, February 5, 1784: "Since I repaired the bust of Mrs. Siddons after moulding, a friend of mine . . . has been desirous . . . to set it with the model of Mercury and several other models he has of mine. As you have the mould of the Model, I think it [the model] cannot be of much use. If I have your permission to sell it to him, I shall take off half my charge for it from your bill." Wedgwood agreed [February 20, 1784] that the mold would serve his purpose.)
**Chessman.** Wegwood to Flaxman, February 20, 1784.

## Designs in relief

**Six Muses.** Wedgwood to Bentley, October 29, 1777. (Many versions, some by other artists, are known; sources vary.)
**The Apotheosis of Homer.** Wedgwood to Bentley, April 6 and August 9, 1778. (From a painted Greek vase in Sir William Hamilton's collection in the British Museum; *not* from a relief in the Colonna Palace. The "Apotheosis of Hesiod" is not a separate work; the seated figure here is Hesiod.)
**Blind Man's Buff, Game of Marbles,** two **Triumphs of Cupid.** Flaxman to Wedgwood, July 8, 1782, and October 28, 1782.
**Psyche on a Flower Pot, A Companion to Venus Adolescens.** Flaxman to Wedgwood, July 8, 1782.
**Jupiter, Mercury.** Flaxman to Wedgwood, August 22, 1782.
**Veturia and Volumnia Entreating Coriolanus to Return to Rome.** Flaxman to Wedgwood, August 20, 1785; and Flaxman's bill, December 12, 1785. (Erroneously called **Penelope and Her Maidens;** for my discovery of source see *Old Wedgwood,* 1941, and ANTIQUES, February 1942.)
**Peace Preventing Mars from Bursting Open the Gates of the Temple of Janus.** Flaxman's bill, January 16, 1787.
**Mercury Uniting the Hands of England and France.** Flaxman's bill, March 26, 1787.
**Hercules in the Garden of the Hesperides.** Flaxman's bill, August 10, 1787. (From a design on a vase in Sir William Hamilton's collection.)
**Birth of Bacchus.** Flaxman to Byerley, December 24, 1788. ("Restored from the Antique.")
**Apotheosis of Virgil.** Flaxman to Wedgwood, December 13, 1785.

Print of design on vase in Sir William Hamilton's collection from which Flaxman modeled *Veturia and Volumnia Entreating Coriolanus to Return to Rome.*

younger Flaxman, but which are in no way original works. These include the famous *Wine* and *Water,* or *Satyr and Triton,* vases, which many years ago I traced to designs by the great French sculptor Clodion; "Basso Relievos" of four of the Muses (Thalia, Melpomene, Terpsichore, Euterpe), Sappho, and Apollo; three of Hercules, and one each of Bacchus and Ariadne; four of the Seasons; one each of Jupiter, Juno, Minerva, Justice, and Hope; an "Antique Vase sculptured with figures"; and molding and making a cast from "a Medall of Lennaeus."

The portrait of Linnaeus is one of Wedgwood & Bentley's "Illustrious Moderns." It shows the botanist with the twinflower *(Linnaea borealis)* in his buttonhole, as the Swedish sculptor Inlander modeled him in 1774. According to Linnaeus himself this was done from life by Inlander, and the original wax is now at Hammarby, the home of Linnaeus at Upsala, Sweden. It was issued in Sweden as a medal and was used on a memorial medal after the death of the botanist in 1778. No writer on Wedgwood or on Flaxman to my knowledge has commented on this entry about the portrait. Evidently the spelling "Lennaeus" has been misleading.

The portraits of Mr. Banks and Dr. Solander, who had accompanied Captain Cook to the South Pacific, and that of Linnaeus were listed for the first time in the Wedgwood Catalogue of 1779. After Banks was made President of the Royal Society in 1778 Wedgwood issued a large portrait of Banks of classic type without wig, and after Banks became a baronet his name was entered in the 1787 Catalogue as "Sir Joseph Banks." Other existing large portrait plaques in the Illustrious Moderns series include Dr. Solander, Franklin, Cook, Boyle, Priestley, and Sir William Hamilton, all without wigs, but there is no evidence to connect Flaxman's name with these.

Most of the Wedgwood portraits of Flaxman himself date from long after the death of the first Josiah Wedgwood, although the originals were done in the eighteenth century by Flaxman independently of Wedgwood. No Wedgwood medallion of the self-portrait shown here is known. There is, however, a small jasper portrait of the artist inscribed on the back *J Flaxman when 14 years old*. An oval bronze gilt portrait to correspond is in the Lady Lever Gallery, and there is a three-and-a-quarter-inch pattern model in the Wedgwood archives. The profile portraits of the mature Flaxman and his wife were done in Rome, but were not made by the Wedgwood firm in the eighteenth century. These companion portraits, which are frequently seen in collections of Wedgwood, are quite modern.

During the period from 1775 to 1794 Flaxman did not confine his work to sketches and models for Wedgwood, but executed many private commissions for sculpture and ornaments for other patrons, monuments to the dead, and illustrations for the works of Homer and Aeschylus. However, in 1787 when Flaxman went to Rome so that he might study on the actual sites of antiquity, Wedgwood in great part financed the journey and gave letters of introduction, and his agents handled the luggage. In Rome Flaxman executed only one or two commissions for Wedgwood, but he supervised the work of Devaere, a young sculptor whom Wedgwood employed.

When Flaxman returned to England in 1794, his illustrations of Homer and his monuments and sculptures had established his reputation throughout Europe. Wedgwood had retired from active work, and in January of 1795 he died. Many designs Flaxman had modeled continued to be used, and some of his outline drawings for the *Iliad* and the *Odyssey* including *Diomedes and Minerva Wounding Mars,* were rendered by other artists in encaustic painting on basalt vases. Flaxman had also done other types of work for the potter: the bills list drawings of crests and arms, and in 1782 he had given instruction to Wedgwood's sons. After the potter's death, he designed the marble monument to Wedgwood in St. Peter's church at Stoke.

The fact that Flaxman's name is not found on Wedgwood pieces has puzzled many collectors and critics, but the reason seems plain. The designs were not Flaxman's own. Wedgwood knew, and the modelers knew, that the patrons and buyers would in many cases recognize the origins of the portraits and other subjects, and Wedgwood had promised in his catalogues that the creators of the originals would have nothing to fear from the multiplication of copies; indeed, he frequently cited the original and gave the name of the artist. The Wedgwood medallion or vase, even the *Apotheosis* vase in its final form, was a product of the art of Josiah Wedgwood. A thousand experiments had produced the body and more had overcome the difficulties of luting a relief design to a curved surface to withstand the shrinkage and other effects of

*Hercules in the Garden of the Hesperides;* green and white jasper, marked WEDGWOOD; c. 1860. Modeled by Flaxman in 1787 from a painted vase in the British museum. *Private collection.*

Design on vase, c. 440 B.C., from which Flaxman modeled his *Hercules* tablet. *British Museum.*

*Hercules in the Garden of the Hesperides,* original watercolor drawing done by Flaxman for Thomas Hope of Amsterdam. *Collection of Captain and Mrs. Edward H. Holdstock.*

fire. The relief design was only one of many elements in the over-all production; the artistic conception was Wedgwood's own.

Besides the lack of signature, there are other handicaps in identification: the potter's use of figures and details from different designs in new combinations, and the loss of documentary material. The disappearance of Bentley's letters to Wedgwood and the sale to a junk shop in 1846 of the records of the firm, were major disasters. The accidental discovery and the purchase of the remaining papers in 1848 by Joseph Mayer, a private collector, their preservation in Liverpool, and their transfer in 1924 to the Wedgwood archives in Staffordshire where they escaped being destroyed by bombs during the war, is a story in itself. Among the items retrieved were the list of contents of the box Flaxman took to Rome and some of his letters and bills. Unfortunately there remain many gaps in the records between 1775 and 1795.

# FROM THE NILE TO THE TRENT

## Wedgwood "Egyptian" Wares

### By ELIZABETH CHELLIS

*Mrs. Chellis, well known in Wedgwood circles, shares with us here some researches on a rather neglected aspect of the subject.*

FIG. 1—FIRED CLAY IMPRESSIONS of Egyptian designs from the early Wedgwood working molds at Etruria, England. Each clay intaglio has its catalogue number impressed. (*Reading down*): *Top*, Isis with sistrum; *left*, Egyptian figure; *right*, headdress (see Figure 2); *center*, Isis; *left*, sphinx with wheel; *right*, Jupiter and Isis; *center*, canopus; *left*, Horus standing in a bark; *right*, a sphinx. *Author's collection.*

FIG. 2—BASALT INTAGLIOS. *Left*, Isis with budding horns, listed in Wedgwood catalogues (no. 261) from 1774 on. Note horns, symbol of heaven, in lower left. Mark, impressed *261*. Size ⅝ by ½ inch, beveled edge. *Author's collection. Right*, listed in Wedgwood catalogues (no. 256) under intaglios as *the flower, lotus*, but probably rather the headdress of an Egyptian deity with the sun disk in center surmounted by two plumes and the uraeus—a snake, symbol of royalty—on either side. See also Figure 1, top right. Mark, impressed *Wedgwood and Bentley* and *256*. Size, ¾ by ⅝ inch, beveled edge. *Mr. and Mrs. Louis H. Henkels.*

JOSIAH WEDGWOOD'S FERVOR for all ancient arts brought the Egyptian influence as well as the classic into his work.

The first and second Wedgwood catalogues (*1773-1774*) begin with Wedgwood cameos and intaglios from Egyptian mythology—designs of the deities, the sphinx, the lotus, and hieroglyphs deriving from the Egypt of the Pharaohs. From 1773 on Wedgwood made cameos of many of the fourteen Ptolemies, and one of Cleopatra, and from 1774, cameos, intaglios, and busts of Cleopatra and of Antony as well as a double portrait medallion of them both.

The early cameos were made in black basalt, a body Wedgwood also called "Egyptian black," and in a pure white fine biscuit ware, forerunner of his jasper body perfected in 1775.

From then on jasper was used extensively. A letter written late in 1775 by Wedgwood to his partner Bentley mentioned the Antonies and Cleopatras, of the perfected jasper, as the finest things imaginable: "It really hurts me to think of parting with these gems, the fruit of twenty years toil, for the trifle I fear we must do to make a business worth our notice of it." In the collection of Doctor Henry G. Smith is the original wax portrait of the dying Cleopatra made by Flaxman for the Wedgwood medallions. Gatty's catalogue lists an oval medallion of this dying Cleopatra in pale blue and white jasper body, marked *Wedgwood and Bentley*.

A widespread interest in all things Egyptian flourished in England after the success of Napoleon's campaign in Egypt

FIG. 3—WEDGWOOD TABLET, *Isis Procession*, of heavy earthenware thickly coated with black glaze and figures painted in brown, flesh, and gray, the paint so thick as to be partially in relief. Possibly a trial piece in encaustic painting. Length, 16½ inches; height, 9½ inches. From *Memorials of Wedgwood* (Plate XX).

FIG. 4—SOURCE ENGRAVING for Wedgwood's tablet, *Isis Procession*, from Pietro Santi Bartoli's *Admiranda Romanarum Antiquitatum* (1693). Roman-Egyptian design of archaic, stiff figures carrying attributes symbolical of the rites of Isis—a sistrum, a vase for sacred water, a scroll, and a dipper.

in 1798. The discovery of the Rosetta stone by one of Napoleon's officers in Egypt in 1799 gave the longed-for tool for deciphering the hieroglyphs, and the interest in things pertaining to the land of the Nile grew to a popular enthusiasm. Wedgwood's sources for his Egyptian designs were varied. He never traveled out of Britain, but he had sent to him the best illustrated books that could be had. First relying only on these books and on such casts as those supplied by James Tassie, Wedgwood soon turned directly to the cabinets of his best patrons—such famous collectors as Sir Watkins Williams Wynee, Sir Roger Newdigate, and the Duke of Marlborough.

Josiah Wedgwood II, carrying on the business after his father's death in 1795, made Egyptian wares far more extensively from 1805 to 1815 than were ever made in the eighteenth century. The order books at Etruria from 1801 to 1812 show many requests for Egyptian wares from patrons, such as that by Lord Viscount Petersham for an incense vase with lotus on the pedestal and Egyptian figures on the band between the sphinx heads; candlesticks of Egyptian form and decoration; six pairs of sphinx candlesticks, and two canopic vases.

At the exhibition of over 600 Wedgwood objects at the Brooklyn Museum in 1948, only three items showed Egyptian influence. However, there are examples with Egyptian motifs in most of the classes of Wedgwood wares—cameos, intaglios, tablets, busts, candelabra, lamps, tea sets, vases, paterae, and ink vessels. Some of the finest Wedgwood, in fact, is in this category. Though Egyptian design never attained the popularity of the classic, it made its impress to a much greater extent than is generally known by Wedgwood collectors.

Osiris, Horus, and Isis form the most popular triad of Egyptian deities. Osiris was the highest of all powers, judge of the dead, distinguished by a tall cap and hooked staff. His son Horus (called by the Greeks Harpocrates) is depicted with the leaves of the sacred Persea tree on his head, standing on a bark, or sitting upon the lotus. Isis, wife of Osiris, is shown with the lotus on her forehead; or with the sistrum, an Egyptian musical instrument used in solemn religious services; or with horns, since she is often identified with the heavenly cow, Hat-hôr. Additional designs not included in Wedgwood's catalogues but noted in private collections are: Horus and Apis (sacred bull) on a sacred Nile boat; Apis with winged disk and the emblem of the soul; Anubis (god who presided over embalming of the dead) holding palm branch and caduceus. These designs were often taken from amulets. *See Figures 1-5*

FIG. 5—CAMEO of *Isis with Sistrum* (c. 1780), in solid medium-blue jasper and white relief, with lotus on forehead and sistrum at left. 2⅜ inches by 2 inches. Mark, *Wedgwood and Bentley*. This design from a carnelian gem was first noted in Wedgwood's second catalogue of 1774 under cameos (no. 7) and intaglios (no. 258). *Collection of Mr. and Mrs. S. B. Oster.*

FIG. 7—CANOPIC VASES with relief bands of Egyptian hieroglyphs and signs of the zodiac Each is one of a pair. *Left*, in redware (rosso antico) with black relief; meander on square plinth (c. 1805). Height, 11 inches. Mark, *Wedgwood*. Oster collection. *Right*, in white and blue jasper; stylized lotus prominent in lower part of body (c. 1805). Mark, *Wedgwood*. Height, 9½ inches. *From the collection of Dr. H. G. Smith.*

FIG. 6—EGYPTIAN AMPHORA, tetrapod of redware with black Egyptian hieroglyphs in relief, modified pointed base (c. 1810). Height, 8½ inches. Mark, impressed *Wedgwood*. Oster collection.

Josiah Wedgwood was the first English potter to study antique vase forms. Three forms he used were popular in Egypt—the canopus, the ewer, and the amphora. The last, equally well known through Greek examples, was Egypt's most useful vase. It was Wedgwood's most widely adapted shape in basalt, encaustic-painted, redware, and—after 1782—jasper. The Wedgwood amphorae were made in medium sizes, often in sets of five and seven for chimneypieces.

The canopus was the vase form most peculiarly Egyptian—mummy-like in shape and surmounted by a cover in the shape of a head. In Egypt it was made first of alabaster and later of faience. The jars, containing the embalmed internal organs of the deceased, were often placed in chests in the tomb. Wedgwood made great numbers of these canopi, as decorative objects, in variegated bodies, in redware, in cane-color with redware relief, and later with jasper body. They were usually in pairs, from about 6 to 11 inches high.

The Egyptain "meander" pattern—also called the door pattern, because used on false doors of Egyptian tombs—was a forerunner of the Greek key pattern. Wedgwood used both the Egyptian and the Greek meander on plinths, on shoulders of vases, and as a border for plates.

The signs of the zodiac came to Egypt late, from Greek art. They were modeled for Wedgwood in 1774 by Mary Landre.

*See Figures 6-9*

Fig. 8—INKWELL in canopic form, cane-color body with redware relief of hieroglyphs and other designs (*c. 1805*). One of a pair. The covers and square plinths are gilded. Height, 5¼ inches. Mark, impressed *Wedgwood*. *Oster collection.*

Fig. 9—*Left and right*, BASALT BUSTS OF ANTONY AND CLEOPATRA, modeled by Homer and Hackwood (1775). Height, 6¾ inches. Mark, impressed *Wedgwood*. From the Burslem Museum. *Center*, BASALT INKSTAND in impressed design of Egyptian hieroglyphs and symbols, with ink pot of canopic form. Length of inkstand, 12 inches. Mark, impressed *Wedgwood*. Reproduced from Grant's *The Makers of Black Basaltes*, William Blackwood & Sons, Ltd., publishers.

The sphinx is one of the oldest sculptured monuments of Egypt. A Wedgwood bill in 1770 records modeling sphinxes in various sizes to be shipped to the Hague for use as ornaments on balustrades, furniture, and candlesticks. The upright sphinx was often used in triple supports for candlesticks, tripods, pastile burners, and as a figure for niches and recesses. The reclining sphinx, with or without wings, was used on paper weights, as a holder for the nozzles of candlesticks, and as a decorative figure. The sphinx head was used as a finial on canopic vases, pen trays, inkstands, teapot covers, and as vase handles.

*See Figures 10-12 and Frontispiece*

Fig. 10—BASALT CANDLESTICK with triple upright-sphinx support holding single nozzle, redware petals and redware geometrical border in relief (*c. 1806*). Height, 6¾ inches. Mark, *Wedgwood*. *Author's collection.*

Fig. 11—OVOID PASTILE BURNER (perforated lid missing) of redware on tripod of basalt upright sphinxes, bands of Egyptian hieroglyphs in red relief on black ground (*c. 1805*). Height, 6¼ inches. Mark, impressed *Wedgwood Z*. *Oster collection.*

Fig. 12—*Left*, BASALT PAPER WEIGHT with reclining sphinx on plinth (*c. 1805*). One of a pair. Mark, *Wedgwood*. From the collection of Mr. and Mrs. Frank H. Dillaby. *Above*, BASALT PEN TRAY (*c. 1775*), with sphinx head supporting a single nozzle for the taper used in sealing letters. Mark, *Wedgwood and Bentley*, in script, unique example of this mark. *Etruria Museum, Staffordshire.*

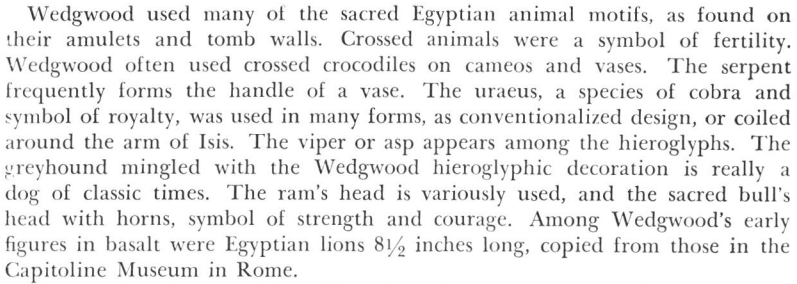

Wedgwood used many of the sacred Egyptian animal motifs, as found on their amulets and tomb walls. Crossed animals were a symbol of fertility. Wedgwood often used crossed crocodiles on cameos and vases. The serpent frequently forms the handle of a vase. The uraeus, a species of cobra and symbol of royalty, was used in many forms, as conventionalized design, or coiled around the arm of Isis. The viper or asp appears among the hieroglyphs. The greyhound mingled with the Wedgwood hieroglyphic decoration is really a dog of classic times. The ram's head is variously used, and the sacred bull's head with horns, symbol of strength and courage. Among Wedgwood's early figures in basalt were Egyptian lions 8½ inches long, copied from those in the Capitoline Museum in Rome.

Hieroglyphs—the pictorial writing of the Egyptians—were used extensively in relief patterns from 1805 on, though they had been impressed on black basalt vases since the 1770's. After 1805 hieroglyph borders in relief were used to decorate canopic vases, redware plates, and the shoulders of teapots. The hieroglyphs most frequently used by Wedgwood were the ankh, symbol of life; the feather, symbol of truth; the winged scarab, symbol of fertility; Apis, sacred bull worshipped by Egyptians from earliest times, emblem of strength and courage; the winged disk, placed over gates and doors to give protection; the crocodile, symbol of darkness. Wedgwood's use of all these motifs was decorative, however, rather than symbolic.

From the lotus, both flower and bud, Wedgwood found inspiration for much decorative use and as a shape for teapots and vases. In Egypt the lotus was a sacred flower and symbol of immortality.

*See Figures 13-18*

FIG. 13—BLOCK MOLDS, clay-fired (hard biscuit), used for making ornaments in relief at the Wedgwood pottery since about 1805, of importance in dating the Egyptian borders in relief. *From Josiah Wedgwood & Sons, Etruria.*

FIG. 14—REDWARE PATERA (saucer-like vessel) with cream biscuit reliefs of Egyptian subjects—ram's head, bull's head, sphinx, sacrificial table, and the crossed crocodiles, symbol of fertility. Diameter, 8 inches. In the Trevor Lawrence collection is a similar dish, slightly deeper, with the reliefs in black. *Lady Lever Gallery, Port Sunlight, England.*

FIG. 15—REDWARE PATERA with black relief border of Egyptian hieroglyphs and symbols (*early nineteenth century*). One of a pair. Diameter, 5⅞ inches. Mark, *Wedgwood*. *Grenville Winthrop Collection, Fogg Museum of Art.*

FIG. 16—TEA SET, redware with black Egyptian hieroglyphs and meander in relief, and crocodile finials (*c. 1810*). The inside of the teapot and creamer are glazed. Height of teapot, 3¾ inches. Mark, impressed *Wedgwood*. *Oster collection.*

FIG. 17—LOTUS VASE in redware with black relief; stylized lotus motifs on body of vase; bud alternating with flower on foot; lotus finial. Egyptian meander on square plinth; variant of Egyptian scarab on border below sphinx heads. Mark, *Wedgwood*. *Bragg Collection, Birmingham*. Reproduced from Meteyard's "*Wedgwood and His Works,*" plate XXII.

FIG. 18—REDWARE cup and saucer, with border of black Egyptian hieroglyphs in relief (*c. 1805*). The inside of the cup is not glazed. Mark, impressed *Wedgwood* on both cup and saucer. *Author's collection.*

# CREAM COLOR, ALIAS QUEEN'S WARE

By JEAN GORELY

ALL QUEEN'S WARE is cream color, but not all cream color is Queen's ware, and not all Queen's ware is Wedgwood. In 1767 Wedgwood wrote: "The demand for the said Cream Colour, alias Queen's ware, alias Ivory, still increases. It is amazing how rapidly the use has spread allmost over the whole globe and how universally it is liked." In 1774, about ten years after its introduction, a document prepared for a committee in Parliament stated:

... when Mr. Wedgwood discovered the art of making Queen's ware, which employs ten times more people than all the china works in the kingdom, he did not ask for a patent for this important discovery. A patent would have greatly limited its public utility. Instead of one hundred manufactories of Queen's ware there would have been one, and instead of an exportation to all parts of the World, a few pretty things would have been made for the amusement of the people of fashion in England.

By 1799 Queen's ware had become a generic name for perfected creamware, applied to the fashionable Wedgwood and also to similar ware from Leeds, Castleford, Liverpool, Ferrybridge, Longport, Glasgow, or from any of the many potteries which were making it in the British Isles and on the Continent.

This perfected cream or Queen's ware was very different from the experimental cream color of the mid-eighteenth century. The beginnings of both lay in Staffordshire in the discovery about 1720 of the whitening of the clay body by the introduction of calcined flint. This lighter body was then glazed with dry lead ore, which was dusted over the ware, and then fired once. This was cream color in its infancy. When, about 1750, Enoch Booth of Tunstall fired a piece, then dipped it into a fluid lead glaze and fired it again, cream color had reached its adolescence. This was the sort of cream color that was made in Staffordshire, Liverpool, and other places, and by Wedgwood himself when he was in partnership with Whieldon and later in 1759 when he set up in business independently at Burslem.

This second stage of cream color was a great improvement over the earlier one. The ware lent itself to painted decoration, and, by the application of uncolored and colored fluid glazes, to the simulation of rare and costly materials like tortoise-shell and agate, and of exotic fruits and vegetables like melons, pineapples, and cauliflowers. Nevertheless, it was still in an experimental state. It chipped readily and the glaze was apt to flake off if cracked by sudden changes of temperature. In addition, there was danger of lead poisoning from the action of acids in the food.

This danger loomed large in the eighteenth-century world and lead-glazed utensils were held to be unsafe. Housewives were warned by the cook at the London Tavern to beware of pottery glazed with lead as "it was corroded with anything with vinegar or acid in it . . . on evaporating the liquor a quantity of salts of lead will be found at the bottom, the acids having dissolved the glazing." He also warned against using fruit juices on delft plates. Chinese porcelain, he said, was the safest material, but too costly. Next came salt-glazed stoneware "which was not injured by acids, salts, or alkalies" but "was apt to crack with any change of temperature or sudden heat," according to the cook.

The Society for the Encouragement of Arts, Sciences, and Manufactures likewise declared:

The objections to a glaze wholly or in part composed of lead, are first that it cracks when raised rapidly to the temperature of boiling water, on account of the different ratio of expansibility between the glaze and the clay, and then admits the liquor into the body of the ware; secondly, the glass of lead by itself, or even mixed in small proportion with earthy substances, is very soluble in vinegar, in acid juices of the common fruits, and in animal fats when boiling. When such substances, therefore, are cooked in vessels of common earthenware, a quantity of salts of lead is found, which mixing with the food, produces violent colics, and all the serious and often fatal effects that attend the internal administration of the salts of lead.

And in America the *Pennsylvania Mercury* for February 4, 1785, warned:

The mischievous effects of it [lead glaze] fall chiefly on the country people and the poor everywhere even when it is firm enough not to scale off, it is yet imperceptibly eaten away by every acid matter; and mixing with the drinks and meats of the people, becomes a slow but sure poison, chiefly affecting the nerves, that enfeebles the constitution, and produces paleness, tremors, grippes, palsies, etc., sometimes to whole families.

The need of a safe and durable ware for use at the table and in the kitchen was great, and naturally Wedgwood turned his attention to this problem. He had already invented the green glaze and applied it to cauliflower, melon, pineapple, and other forms in tea and dessert ware of the ordinary cream-color body. For several years he experimented with cream color, working on every detail of the potting from the preparation of the ingredients of body and glaze, to the tools, the temperature, and the kiln itself. Of his "Cream Colour table services" Lord Gower said in 1765 "nothing of the sort could exceed them for a fine glaze."

In the same year Wedgwood came to the Queen's attention because he made a set of tea things in green and gold on the cream color body in imitation of Dresden china, a set which was ordered by the Queen from some Staffordshire potter but which no potter except Wedgwood was willing to undertake. This set lead to an order for a plainer cream color service which came to be known as the *Queen's Pattern*; the design for the set of the same ware ordered by the King was henceforth known as the *Royal Pattern*. The ware was still called "Cream Colour" in the invoices and could be had plain, printed by Sadler & Green in Liverpool (*Fig. 2*), painted by the Widow Warburton in Hot Lane (*Fig. 4*), or pierced in the manner of silver and Oriental porcelain. By 1767, the Queen had permitted Wedgwood to call the improved ware *Queen's ware,* and honored him by making him Her Majesty's Potter. Cream color ware had definitely come of age. Orders flowed in from many parts of the world.

The superiority of Wedgwood's product to earlier cream-colored ware lay in the fact that, besides fineness of potting and design, it had "several of the properties of porcelain," as he stated to Parliament in 1774, and a so-called "China Glaze". It would not crack and chip readily and it would withstand acids and changes of temperature. Thus it was adapted to many uses in kitchen, dairy, sickroom, nursery,

August, 1943

wine cellar, chemical laboratory, and apothecary's shop. It was also fine enough for ornamental pieces for the drawing room and for use on the grand banquet tables of the period.

The date of Wedgwood's improvement of cream color is given by Doctor Aiken in his *History of Manchester* as 1763. The book was written while Wedgwood was alive and the author knew the potter. The part referring to the potteries was probably written for Doctor Aiken by Alexander Chisholm, Wedgwood's secretary, who was a chemist in charge of Wedgwood's laboratory. The passage reads:

In 1763, Mr. Josiah Wedgwood . . . invented a species of earthenware for the table, of a firm and durable body, covered with a rich and brilliant glaze, and bearing sudden vicissitudes of cold and heat without injury.

This ware is composed of the whitest clays from Devonshire, Dorsetshire, and other places, mixed with a due proportion of ground flint. The pieces are fired twice, and the glaze applied after the first firing, in the same manner as on porcelain. The glaze is a vitreous composition of flint and other white earthly bodies, with an addition of white lead for the flux analagous to common flint glass, so that when prepared in perfection, the ware may be considered as coated over with real flint glass; this compound being mixed with water to the proper consistence, the pieces, after the first firing, are separately dipt into it; being somewhat bibulous, they drink a quantity of the mere water, and the glaze that was united with that portion of the water remains adherent, uniformly all over the surface so as to become, by the second firing a coat of perfect glass.

Wedgwood's early pattern books of Queen's ware show 105 classes of articles for the table with 57 different shapes of vegetable dishes, 27 fruit baskets, 40 salts, 28 tea cups and saucers, 40 teapots, and such miscellaneous articles as spoons, ladles, monteiths, argyles, fish trowels, punch strainers, and épergnes. Many of these pieces were designed after silver models which they were intended to replace.

The color of Wedgwood's creamware varied from a deep straw color to almost white. Some of the early ware was quite yellow. Often it had a greenish or bluish cast due to the pinch of cobalt which was added to whiten the ware as bluing whitens clothes. Customers were demanding whiteness, often to the despair of the potter. This variation in color within one factory shows that a particular color cannot be taken as a characteristic of a particular factory.

Lightness in weight was a more constant quality. Wedgwood's Queen's ware was extremely light for economic as well as esthetic reasons. Transportation costs were high, and France imposed a tax by weight on imported ware. Weight was so important to the potter that Wedgwood wrote to Bentley, April 9, 1769, "I am giving my people lessons upon the loss of clay, & with it loss of credit in making heavy ware, but all will not do. I have bot them half a doz. pair of scales but there seems one thing wanting still, which I propose to have soon, a Clerk of Weights and Measures, whose constant business shall be to weigh the goods as they are got up."

Some of the ware was plain, but all sorts of treatments were possible with printing, embossing, painting, fluting, and piercing. In Wedgwood's lifetime, this piercing was all done by hand and not *en bloc*. His punches included the oval, the heart, the circle, the rice grain, the triangle, the diamond, the club, and the leaf. (*Fig. 5*). Twisted and crossed handles with leafage ends (*Fig. 3*), flower knobs (*Fig. 8*), the shell edge (*Fig. 3*), "twig" (*Fig. 7*), and interlaced work (*Fig. 8*), were favorite decorative devices. Cabbage-leaf spouts (*Fig. 4*) and scrolled handles were other typical Wedgwood treatments, and these treatments do not seem to have been used at Leeds.

In 1774 Wedgwood issued a catalogue of his Queen's ware which was without doubt the first illustrated catalogue of

FIG. 1 — QUEEN CHARLOTTE, WIFE OF GEORGE III. For her Wedgwood named his perfected cream color "Queen's ware". Wax portrait by Isaac Gosset. *From the collection of Rev. Glenn Tilley Morse.*

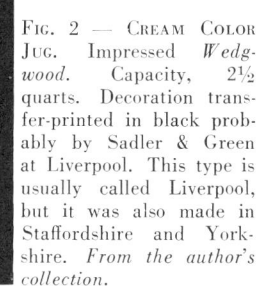

FIG. 2 — CREAM COLOR JUG. Impressed *Wedgwood*. Capacity, 2½ quarts. Decoration transfer-printed in black probably by Sadler & Green at Liverpool. This type is usually called Liverpool, but it was also made in Staffordshire and Yorkshire. *From the author's collection.*

FIG. 3 — CREAM COLOR CUP AND SAUCER. Impressed *Wedgwood*. The design, known as the *Liverpool Birds*, was transfer-printed or "jet enamell'd," as printing in black was called. Note shell edge and twisted handle with leafage end. *From the Museum of Fine Arts, Boston.*

FIG. 4 — CREAM COLOR TEAPOT. Impressed *Wedgwood*. With fruit and flowers painted in enameled colors. This sort of painting was done by the Widow Warburton in Hot Lane for Wedgwood until 1770 and then by Wedgwood's own painters at Chelsea. Note the cabbage-leaf spout. *From the Museum of Fine Arts, Boston.*

cream color ever issued by a potter. Nine years later, in 1783, the Leeds Pottery issued its first catalogue of the ware, taking many of the shapes and decorations as well as the name, "Queen's" ware, from Wedgwood. Later editions of the Leeds catalogue followed in 1785, 1786, 1794, and 1815. In 1796 David Dunderdale at Castleford published his Queen's ware catalogue and in 1808 the Don Pottery issued one. Hundreds of other potters made so-called Queen's ware, achieving different results according to their skill and the materials used. In 1787 twenty-six potters were listed in Tunicliff's *Survey* as making it in Staffordshire. On January 18 of the same year, Ring announced in the *Bristol Gazette* the establishment of "a manufactory of the Queen's and other earthenware" at Bristol. In 1791, 450 dozen pieces of Queen's ware were shipped from Port Glasgow to America, and in 1795, 21,000 pounds came from that port to Virginia and Carolina. Potters in Italy, France, Holland, Germany, Bohemia (*Fig. 7, right*), and other countries on the Continent made the same kind of ware after Wedgwood models. In Sweden it was called *flintporslin* and in 1810, according to Emil Hannover, a pottery in Ulfsunda openly called itself *Wedgwood-Fabriken paa Ulfsunda*. In Germany it was *steingut*; in France, *faience-fine*.

As early as 1766, one John Bartlam, a Staffordshire potter, came to this country bringing with him a number of Wedgwood's skilled workmen who were familiar with the method of making the improved cream color (letter from Josiah Wedgwood to Sir William Meredith). He opened a pottery and advertised in the *South Carolina Gazette* of January 31, 1771, that he "already makes what is called Queen's ware equal to any imported and if he meets with suitable encouragement makes no doubt of being able to supply the demands of the whole province". "Suitable encouragement" was evidently not given, for the enterprise was abandoned. (Full details are given in a pamphlet published by Wedgwood in 1783). In 1792 the Philadelphia Society for the Encouragement of Manufactures and the Useful Arts offered as a prize "a plate of the value of fifty dollars, or an equivalent in money" to the person exhibiting the "best specimens of Earthenware or Pottery, approaching nearest to Queen's ware."

Much cream color and Queen's ware is marked. But study of marked pieces of early ware, such as *Wedgwood, Leeds Pottery, Wedgwood & Co.* (Yorkshire), *Davenport, Herculaneum, Spode, Nowonty* (Bohemia), *Leigh & Cie* (France), *Creil* (France), and *Treviso* (Italy), shows how difficult it is for the collector to assign unmarked pieces of cream color and the perfected ware to a given maker on the strength of color or design. Some potters left their ware unmarked, perhaps in the hope of having it mistaken for Wedgwood's work. Others marked their pieces with the name *Wedgewood*, spelled with a second *e*, or with *Wedgwood & Co.*, while the firm of *W. Smith & Co.* of Stockton in the middle of the nineteenth century used the mark *W. S. & Co.'s. Wedgewood*, or *W. S. & Co.'s Queen's Ware, Stockton*. This is good evidence that Wedgwood's Queen's ware was the standard. That the improved ware was not easy to make is evidenced by the ditty sung at Bristol in 1788:

Then let us all strive, my Brave Lads, to excell
That when we are Gone, our Children may Tell
What Labour we had for to Bring it to Bear
Before we could make *good* Cream Colour ware.

These facts show how complicated are the problems for the collector of cream color Queen's ware. You may have the ordinary cream color or the perfected Queen's ware. Moreover, if you have an unmarked early cream color "twig" basket of fine quality, you may have Wedgwood or Leeds or Castleford, but also you may have Spode, or Davenport, or Nowonty, or any of the numerous potters who were making "twig" baskets in "ye most fashionable kind of Queen's ware" after Wedgwood's models at the end of the eighteenth century.

FIG. 5 — QUEEN'S WARE DISH FOR STRAWBERRIES. With enamel-painted border and pierced bottom. Impressed *Wedgwood*. Note the variety of punch marks. *Photograph from the author's collection.*

FIG. 6 — QUEEN'S WARE CRUET STAND. Each piece impressed *Wedgwood*. Pierced and embossed design reminiscent of the patterns found on silver dish rings. Note shell edge with traces of oil gilding. *From the collection of Mrs. Marcus A. Coolidge.*

FIG. 7 — "TWIG" BASKETS. *Left*, impressed *Wedgwood*. Made to replace baskets of osier twigs which held bread and cakes on English tables. "Twig" baskets in cream color were made by many different potters, up to the outbreak of the war. *Right*, impressed *Nowonty*, the name of a Bohemian maker in the late eighteenth century. *Both from the author's collection.*

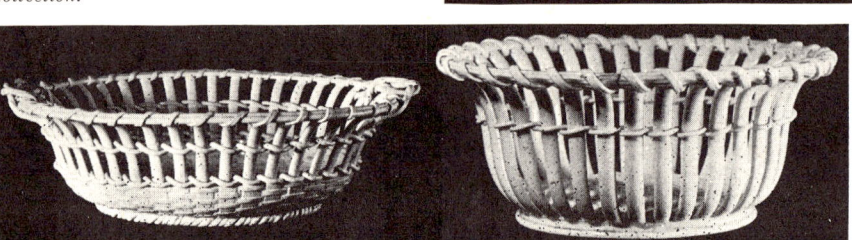

FIG. 8 — QUEEN'S WARE HORS D'OEUVRES DISH. With pierced and embossed cover and flower knob. Impressed *Wedgwood*. *From the author's collection.*

# JASPERWARE AND SOME OF ITS CONTEMPORARIES

## By ALICE WINCHESTER

WRITERS ON ENGLISH CERAMICS agree in hailing Josiah Wedgwood as a great innovator, and in singling out jasperware as his greatest innovation. It is the ware most commonly associated with his name among collectors, and its fame has spread so far that the veriest tyro recognizes the familar light blue as "Wedgwood blue" and has the name "Wedgwood ware" on the tip of his tongue ready to apply to any and all ceramic objects with white cameo designs on a colored ground. But not all such objects are jasper, and not all jasper is Wedgwood.

The story of potting in Staffordshire during most of the eighteenth century is the story of a long succession of trials and errors to achieve wares that could compete with porcelain. The porcelain introduced from China and imitated with considerable success at Meissen had the desirable qualities of being white, hard, non-porous, and light in weight. The aim of the Staffordshire potters seems to have been not so much to achieve a true porcelain as to produce wares, earthen or stone, that had those desirable qualities.

The salt-glaze stonewares were a step in this direction — light-weight, non-porous, and not far from white. The cream-colored earthenwares were equally light and impervious and had a richer surface and tone. These had both been perfected by the time Josiah Wedgwood *(1730-1795)* got to experimenting with his more novel inventions — black basalt, *rosso antico* which was really a dressed-up version of the old unglazed red stoneware, buff or cane-colored ware, and finally jasperware. These were all worked out primarily for ornamental uses, not for practical tablewares. In developing jasper Wedgwood was still seeking a hard, white material but wanted it also to have a certain versatility: it was to be modeled in fine relief designs. He experimented with stonewares and others and by 1773 had "a fine white terra-cotta, of great beauty and delicacy, proper for cameos, portraits, and bas-reliefs." A year or two later he discovered the ingredient that gave him what he wanted. It was barite, or sulphate of barium, which has a very high specific gravity. By using more than 50% of this in his mixture with clay and flint he obtained a ware that he called jasper because it was so hard and dense that, like the

BULB POT IN ALL-WHITE JASPER. One of a pair, unmarked. In two pieces, with molded decoration and applied vignettes in high relief, very well modeled and undercut. Wedgwood produced some fine pieces in all-white jasper in his early days of experimentation with the ware and was particularly pleased with them.

stone of the same name, it could be polished on a lapidary's wheel. Strictly speaking, jasper is, it would seem, a stoneware, in that it is hard and needs no glaze to make it non-porous; but it is vitrified and in thin enough pieces it has a certain translucence, a quality that characterizes porcelain. In fact, it has often been called a porcelain or semi-porcelain. Actually jasper is jasper, for its essential ingredient makes it different from any other ware.

After achieving the ware itself, Wedgwood exploited it to the full. The details of its development from the first simple candlesticks and inkstands to such creations as the copies of the Portland vase, from the use of solid color to the dip or surface color, the gradations of the seven basic colors and the combinations in three-color effects, the extensive use of antique models for the designs and also of portraits of "illustrious moderns," and Wedgwood's vast production of imposing ornamental pieces, vases, plaques, tea and coffee services, medallions, as well as trinkets and jewelry in jasper, are amply recorded in most writings on English ceramics. Jasper became popularly recognized as the typical Wedgwood ware and has

MARKED JASPERWARE. All with white relief decoration, all with ground color of slightly different shades of light blue. *Left to right:* HANDLED CUP, cupid motifs in high relief, marked *Turner* on rim of base. VASE in two pieces, leaf decoration, marked *Adams;* the border of interlaced circles in white relief between raised bands in ground color is typical of Adams' jasper. TEAPOT, classic decoration, swan finial, silver tip, finely modeled, marked *Adams* on base. COVERED VASE in three pieces, same shape and decoration as Adams vase but much heavier in weight and coarser in modeling, marked *Adams & Bromley;* this firm in 1873 succeeded John Adams & Co. of Shelton—no relation of William Adams of Tunstall—and till 1880 produced majolica and a jasper of middling quality, chiefly imitations of late eighteenth-century pieces. COVERED BOWL, playing children motifs, marked *Turner* on base.

continued to be made by the firm up to the present time.

But the secret of jasper did not long remain a secret. By 1785 the recipes had leaked out and other Staffordshire potters were following them. John Turner (*working c. 1756-1786*), one of the ablest of the time, has been credited with inventing the jasper formula quite independently of Wedgwood. He produced pieces of various types, including the small seals, cameos, and the like, also portrait busts, and many jugs with a rather distinctive brown-glazed neck and handle. However, his earlier production of this kind lacked barite and so was not true jasper but a fine white semi-vitreous ware that was something between stoneware and true porcelain. After 1790 apparently Turner made real jasper, using the essential ingredient.

But the "secret" formula for jasper had been pirated by other potters by 1785. Perhaps one of the first to adopt it was William Adams (*c. 1745-1805*) of Tunstall, "Wedgwood's favorite pupil." He, at any rate, was one of Wedgwood's most faithful imitators and serious competitors. His jasper was of fine quality, both the ware itself and the relief ornaments. It was of the two kinds, solid color and dip, and was made in various colors, especially a light violet-blue that appears to be a little different from that of any other potter. Adams' jasper, like Turner's, is often, though not always, marked with the maker's surname, impressed. Its manufacture ceased within a few years of William Adams' death in 1805 but was resumed by the firm, which still exists, in the late 1800's, when jasperware enjoyed a sort of revival of favor.

Among the Staffordshire potters who are recorded as having made jasper in competition with Wedgwood are Palmer and Neale, Elijah Mayer, Josiah Spode II, Enoch Wood, Samuel Hollins. At the same time they and their contemporaries were putting out quantities of wares that were not an attempt to reproduce jasper but were designed merely to appeal to popular taste. The public was no more concerned then than it is now with the composition of its tablewares, and it probably gave relatively little thought to the particular pottery from which they had emanated. It bought what looked attractive and reasonably durable. A considerable variety of stonewares and earthenwares met these requirements.

Many of these had decoration in relief. Some were fashioned as jasper was: the ornament was formed in a plaster mold which carried the intaglio design, then it was "sprigged" on—that is, applied to the body with water. Other kinds were made by forming the entire body of the piece in a mold so that the raised decoration was an integral part of it. Sometimes the two techniques were combined on a single piece. Then, too, color was an important element of the decoration. In jasper and the closely similar wares, color was either mixed throughout the body or applied as an even layer all over the surface. In others it was provided by means of colored glazes. In others it was painted on, often in several hues.

A potter who produced so much ware with relief decora-

THREE STONEWARE TEAPOTS. *Left*, white body trimmed with narrow blue bands, brown medallions with raised classic figures in white on sides, all-white medallions with designs of prunus blossoms in relief around spout and handle; reticulated cover with lion finial; marked *Turner*. Similar in size, shape, cover, and prunus-blossom decoration to a marked Turner teapot in black basalt from Mr. Morris' collection (see ANTIQUES, July 1946, p. 45). *Center*, white body with white relief touched up with blue lines, classic motifs all in white; marked *Heath & Son*. Heath was an old Staffordshire name and several potters carrying it are recorded, including one Lewis Heath working in Burslem in 1802—about the time this pot was probably made—but references list no Heath & Son. *Right*, white body with white relief, trimmed with lines of rose and blue; very light in weight; classic figures on either side; on base of pedestal on side shown the name *Clulow & Co. Fenton* is impressed. (All other marks noted are impressed on bases of pieces.) Robert Clulow & Co. are recorded as working in Staffordshire in 1802, though their location is variously given as Etruria and Lower Lane, not Fenton. Without the mark this pot might have been called "typical Castleford."

MARKED JASPER-LIKE WARES. *Left*, CANDLESTICK, white with blue bands and red and green vine, raised and colored, marked *Chetham & Woolley*; this firm worked at Lane End, Staffordshire, about 1795, producing a dry-bodied ware without glaze or smear called pearlware. *Center*, BASKET, one of a pair, white with raised blue decoration molded with the body, marked *Hackwood & Co.* This mark, and the name *Hackwood* alone, were used by W. Hackwood & Son who operated the works at New Hall from 1842 to 1856. *Right*, SUGAR BOWL, marked *D. D. & Co Castleford Pottery*.

CREAMWARE PLATE. Dull red border, floral center in red and green. Marked *D. D. & Co. Castleford*. Creamware, comparable to that made at Leeds and in Staffordshire, was really quite as typical of Castleford's production as were the stoneware tea services.

STONEWARE BOWLS. White body with molded relief decoration, blue bandings, and medallions in enamel colors, one with a landscape, the other a chinoiserie scene. Though unmarked, these are unusually fine examples of their type.

tion of a certain type that his name has come to be applied generically to it was Felix Pratt (*c. 1775-1810*) of Fenton. He also used transfer printing and polychrome painting for decoration, but the name Prattware usually refers to jugs of light-weight, creamy earthenware with a bluish glaze which have molded relief decoration, distinctively colored — scenes, flowers, stripes or other conventional motifs — covering much of their surface. The colors, often brownish orange and dull blue and green, were applied under the glaze and appear rather blurred. Pratt sometimes marked his production with his name, but not always, and some other potters in Staffordshire as well as in Sunderland and elsewhere also produced similar wares.

The stonewares of roughly analogous type are also fairly light in weight, hard and smooth, and often with a surface that has almost the mat, waxy quality of jasper. The decoration, both molded and painted, is usually rather more distinct and clean-cut than in Prattware, and the body is usually not glazed, though jugs and other hollow vessels sometimes have a glaze inside or around the neck or handle.

The name perhaps most commonly associated with such wares is Castleford. A pottery was established at Castleford, near Leeds, about 1790 by David Dunderdale. In 1803 it became D. Dunderdale & Co. Its output included queensware and a black ware like basalt, but more widely familiar are its little stoneware teapots, patterned after a contemporary octagonal silver model, with relief decoration and blue borders. Marked examples have been found, but again comparable pieces were produced by other potteries.

Despite their obvious differences, these wares may logically be grouped together in one category. It would probably be stretching a point to suggest that the earthen- and stonewares here considered were intentional adaptations of the more exacting jasperware, a cheaper and more easily produced substitute for the lower-priced market. Rather, all these wares, including the jasper, expressed a certain taste of the period just before and just after the turn of the nineteenth century in England. They were undoubtedly exported in some quantity to this country and are found here today, but are rarely considered as a single category by collectors. Admirers of jasper are inclined to overlook the other types which are really quite closely related to it and to each other in source, period, technique and taste. John B. Morris of Saugatuck, Connecticut, has recognized this collecting category and has assembled a remarkable group of examples — remarkable not only for its size but for the opportunity it affords for study and comparison. His numerous marked pieces offer unsuspected revelations regarding the makers of these wares, and the entire group shows some surprising similarities as well as differences. The items here illustrated are a small sampling from Mr. Morris' collection, selected with the hope of indicating the scope of the whole and of suggesting the interest that this field of ceramics offers collectors.

*Left.* STONEWARE PITCHERS. White body, molded relief decoration; unmarked. *Left,* with raised figures on the sides and underglaze coloring on figures and around neck. *Right,* enamel-painted scene under spout; neck and handle coated with colored glaze. These two jugs, though strongly similar, show interesting variations in treatment.

*Right.* PRATTWARE. *Left,* LIGHT-WEIGHT EARTHENWARE JUG with raised decoration and underglaze colors: blue bands, green leaf borders, polychrome figures on sides, and *IB 1796* in dull red under spout. Though unmarked, this jug can safely be ascribed to Felix Pratt; the acanthus-leaf borders top and bottom are characteristic of his work, as is the whole piece, for that matter. *Right,* COVERED BOWL, white body with figures and leaves in relief, underglaze polychrome coloring; unmarked; probably of somewhat later date than the Pratt jug.

*Fig. 1* — BASALT INTAGLIOS (*enlarged*)
 *Left*, likeness of King Alfred. Marked WEDGWOOD. *Width:* 3/4 inch; *height:* 7/8 inch. *Centre*, Eros group. Marked 'Wedgwood & Bentley.' *Width:* 1 3/16 inch; *height:* 7/8 inch. *Right*, head of woman. Marked 'Wedgwood & Bentley.' *Width:* 5/8 inch; *height:* 3/4 inch

# Some Age Tests for Wedgwood

*By* JOSEPH H. PARK

THE antiquary is like the historian in finding himself constantly confronted by the queries *what? when? why?* But the historian, if he thinks in other terms than those of mere facts, is perhaps most perplexed by the ever-recurring *why;* whereas the collector of old pottery, at any rate while he is still a novice, must ever face the question *when.* *What* need not trouble him unduly — for a period.

Marked examples of wares such as those of Wedgwood may still be found in such quantity that there is no necessity for the inexperienced person to purchase unmarked items. But the task of determining the approximate date of even marked examples is difficult. Wedgwood ware, it must be recalled, has been made in Etruria from the days of Josiah Wedgwood (*c. 1760*) to the present; furthermore, it has been manufactured from a bewildering diversity of materials. The connoisseur of one type of this ware may, therefore, easily be at a loss in attempting to judge another variety.

Nevertheless, certain tests for age may be applied to this English product. In the first place, we have some fairly helpful marks. Any piece bearing the printed or impressed inscription *Made in England* may immediately be assigned to the twentieth century. On the other hand, the single word *England* has been applied since 1891 on articles manufactured for the American trade.

The presence of combinations of three letters — as, for instance, NHP — indicates a date not earlier than 1860. The last letter of the three represents the year of

*Fig. 2* — CAMEOS, WHITE ON BLUE JASPER
 *Left*, Apollo, by Wedgwood and Bentley. *Width:* 1 3/4 inches; *height:* 2 1/8 inches. *Right*, Portia — of a later period. *Diameter:* 1 3/8 inches. Enlarged to show inferior workmanship of later item

*Fig. 3* — LAMPS IN ROMAN STYLE
 One in biscuit, the other in black with red ornament

August, 1931

manufacture, with o beginning the series. Thus o stands for 1860; P, for 1861; Q, for 1862, and so on. I have proved this rule by the examination of many Wedgwood pieces whose date could be fixed by their recorded bestowal as wedding gifts.

The British registry mark (*Fig. 6.* See also my article in ANTIQUES for March, 1931) places the ware on which it appears somewhere in the period 1842-1882. The Portland vase design was registered as a trademark, July 4, 1876, and, according to records in the Patent Office, had been used for twelve months before that date.

There remain to be considered the pieces marked WEDGWOOD and *Wedgwood* in different sizes of type and accompanied by various letters, commas, and other workmen's devices. Tradition has it that the

*Fig. 4* — PITCHERS WITH SAME DESIGN
Black figures on terra cotta, and white figures on blue ground

*Fig. 5* — PITCHERS WITH DESIGN SHOWN IN FIGURE 4
Red figures on black, and red figures on yellow, ground

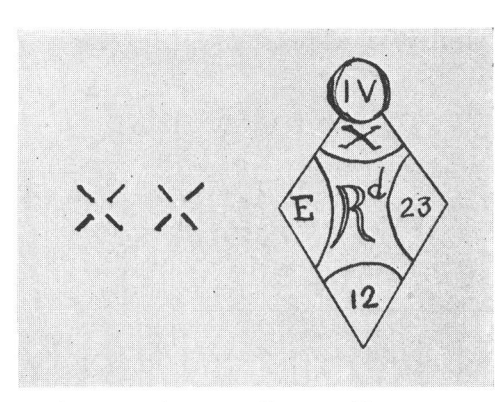

*Fig. 6* — MARKS SOMETIMES FOUND ON WEDGWOOD
*Left*, marks said to place piece in nineteenth century. *Right*, the British registry mark. See ANTIQUES for March, 1931, p. 204

*Fig. 7* — GAME PIE DISH
Known technically as cane ware, but likewise by the more popular designation of pie-crust ware, these unglazed biscuit pieces are, in both color and texture, quite suggestive of perfectly baked pastry. They were nicely calculated to lend an appetizing aspect to the most commonplace of stews, and thus to compensate in appeal to the eye for whatsoever their contents might lack in subtlety of flavor. In the illustration note that the shape of the dish is that of a well-constructed crust and that the crimping around top and bottom precisely accords with that even yet to be encountered in the more magnificent creations of the skilled pastry cook. The decoration of such pieces, though exquisitely modeled, is usually more vigorous than the cameolike appliqués on jasper. In many respects its technique foreshadows the less meticulous but more flamboyant treatment accorded to parian

very irregular lettering sometimes encountered denotes an early specimen made when the mark was still stamped with types instead of with a single die. It is likewise maintained that the starlike mark shown at the left in Figure 6 places an article in the nineteenth century. However, additional tests are a help in doubtful cases.

General workmanship, finish, and the undercutting of relief figures frequently provide safe guidance in determining the age of Wedgwood wares. There were times during the nineteenth century when Wedgwood workmanship showed signs of deterioration. The earlier cameo ware has a subtle clarity and exquisiteness of outline, and some kinds of ware have a lightness of weight and refinement of potting that are perceptible even to the ordinary observer. Excellent Wedgwood is made today, but it will usually carry a mark indicating its country of origin.

Again, the sense of touch may be called upon for assistance. Modern pieces of basalt and jasperware are so much coarser in texture than their older prototypes that sometimes the eye as well as the touch will detect their inferiority. (Compare the cameos illustrated in Figure 2.) Especially does this statement apply to jasperware. Perhaps time itself has added something of the velvety smoothness to products of the earlier generations; but it is safe to believe that the old methods of selecting, mixing, and grinding the materials were more painstaking than those latterly employed.

The tests enumerated vary in usefulness according to the type of ware. Jasper has made the name of Wedgwood so famous that any unglazed blue material showing relief figures in white is popularly accepted as a creation of the Wedgwood factory, without regard to the fact that similar products were turned out not only by a number of English potters but by Continental concerns as well. It is well to remember, also, that jasper objects were made in a great variety of colors, although, in so far as I know, never in an extremely bright hue by the first Josiah. Lilac and mauve he made. In blues and greens he found great delight. But bright pink and bright red, except in terra cotta, are recent ventures. The lack of a good red in jasper seems especially strange since both Samuel Hollins and Wilson made a beautiful red stoneware that approached jasper in texture. Personally, I find the very light blue solid jasper the most difficult color upon whose relative age to pass judgment.

The basalt or black body has been utilized for a large number of objects — intaglios, cameos, busts,

*Fig. 8* — PITCHER
Enameled decoration in colors on a terra cotta body

figures, vases, and tea services. I have found it rather easy to pick up intaglios, all of them old; many, indeed, have the Wedgwood and Bentley impression. Busts and figures in the basalt made today are frequently so excellent in material and modeling that it is impossible for anyone but an expert to determine their age without reference to their marks. Black body with encaustic painting is old; black body decorated with enameled designs was also made at an early period — but many examples bear the telltale three letters of the 1860's.

Red ware, terra cotta, or rosso antico, was never a favorite material with Wedgwood. When he employed it alone, he seems hardly to have competed successfully with the potters of the Elers school. But using it in combination with other colors and materials, he and his son developed many interesting and artistic objects. The terra cotta was used also as a base for enameled ornament. Much of this enameled red ware now offered to collectors, however, is impressed with the three letters. Likewise frequent are pieces of a rather unlovely brick-red body with black designs, apparently made *c.* 1850.

Wedgwood's agate and granite wares were usually unmarked, although specimens marked *Wedgwood*, as well as *Wedgwood & Bentley*, are occasionally encountered. Little of the biscuit ware seems to have survived; and the queen's ware, because of its glaze, is rather difficult to test for age. Porcelain was made at Etruria for a few years during the early part of the nineteenth century, and then again from the decade of the 1870's.

Cane ware, I believe, can be relied upon for its age. A rather heavy, glazed pottery now turned out by the Wedgwood firm under the same name is quite unlike the old cane ware, examples of which are to be found in almost all of the English museums. In these, the Wedgwood basic material differs somewhat from that used by Turner and Elijah Mayer, both of whom are famous for this product. Strange to say, the old cane ware is out of favor with English collectors, and in consequence only a small amount of it is offered in the antique shops.

The old cane ware, also called buff, was not glazed, and hence preserves a sharpness and clarity — often an exquisiteness — in the modeling of its ornament that is possible only to wares whose finishing does not proceed beyond the biscuit stage. It is one of those fine clay products whose development begins with the red wares of the Elers and reaches its climax in the jaspers of Wedgwood.

*Fig. 9* — VASE
Encaustic painting in white on a black body

130

# Wedgwood: what's in a mark?

BY GEOFFREY A. GODDEN, F.R.S.A.

CERAMIC MAKER'S MARKS are applied in three basic ways: they may be impressed into the soft clay before firing, printed during the process of decoration, or painted by hand during, or after, decoration. Some marks include the maker's name in full, others incorporate initials (which often apply to more than one manufacturer), a crest, or a similar trade sign.

It might be thought that an impressed name would be the most certain guarantee of genuineness, as this type of mark is applied during the process of manufacture and can not be added later by persons hoping to enhance the value of specimens. For instance, the standard impressed WEDGWOOD mark, used from about 1759 to the present day, would appear to be a good example of a foolproof impressed name mark, and some reference books do little to warn the collector that this is far from the case.

In forming a collection of documentary marked specimens, and in connection with the preparation of my two works on English ceramic marks (*Encyclopaedia of British Pottery and Porcelain Marks* [1964] and *Handbook of British Pottery and Porcelain Marks* [1968]), I have found several examples bearing marks which have been mistaken for those of the main Wedgwood firm. In some cases these were produced by other potters named Wedgwood, who could use the name with a clear conscience, but some who used it should at least have had a few restless nights!

In the case of the potters who used the simple true WEDGWOOD name mark employed by Josiah Wedgwood from 1759 (the Wedgwood & Bentley marks of the 1768-1780 period were placed on ornamental wares only) the question is complicated by the fact that Wedgwood was in the habit of farming out orders for types of ware that he did not himself make. These items made especially to his order may well have had his name impressed with his consent, since they were probably originally sold as being made by him. One example out of many that may be quoted is of William Greatbatch of Lane Delph, Staffordshire, who may have used this mark when he supplied to Wedgwood in 1760 teapots of six different patterns, large leaves, large fluted candlesticks, melon sauceboats and stands, leaf candlesticks, and five dozen "large Toys" (figures?).

This last item leads to a consideration of a class of creamware figures bearing the impressed mark WEDGWOOD. The example illustrated in Figure 1 has this mark, yet factory records do not mention creamware figures, and the general standard of workmanship is not up to the high standard set

Fig. 1. Enameled creamware group *Charity* with the impressed mark WEDGWOOD, but lacking the quality of Josiah Wedgwood's own productions; possibly a legitimate use of the mark by a firm to which Wedgwood farmed out orders. *Except as noted, photographs are by courtesy of the author.*

Fig. 2. Enameled creamware harvest jug and beaker dated 1796 and bearing the impressed mark WEDGWOOD & CO. Probably by Ralph Wedgwood, who used this mark on his own wares between c. 1790 and 1797 and again on the products of the Knottingley Pottery between 1797 and c. 1800, while he was a partner in that firm.

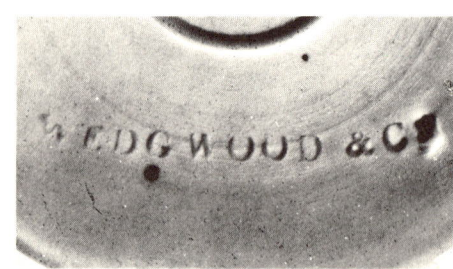

by Wedgwood, so that this may represent a line farmed out by Wedgwood to other potters. The approximate period of such figures is from 1780 to 1800 and it has been suggested that they were made by Ralph or Enoch Wood of Burslem, but my own theory is that at least some were made by Ralph Wedgwood, who potted at Burslem from 1785 to 1796. Whoever did make the marked WEDGWOOD creamware figures it was certainly not Josiah Wedgwood, who is sometimes credited with them.

This Ralph Wedgwood (1766-1837) was an extremely capable potter. His early wares of the 1780's probably bore the impressed WEDGWOOD and so may be mistaken for true Wedgwood wares; after about 1790, he employed the impressed mark WEDGWOOD & CO, but in some instances the & CO was indistinctly stamped. His wares may have been too good and hence too expensive for the market: in April 1793 Josiah Wedgwood wrote, "I believe too that Ralph Wedgwood is tottering he has parted with many of his men." By 1797 Ralph Wedgwood had left Burslem for the Knottingley (Ferrybridge) Pottery in Yorkshire. Here he was a partner in the firm of Tomlinson, Foster, Wedgwood & Co., which found it expedient to mark its wares with the short title WEDGWOOD & CO. The harvest jug and beaker

Fig. 3. Mark registered in the Patent Office Design Registration by Podmore, Walker & Co. in April 1849. Enoch Wedgwood was a partner in this firm.

illustrated in Figure 2, which bear this mark, are dated 1796. When Ralph Wedgwood left Yorkshire for London in 1800 (or 1801) the WEDGWOOD & CO mark was no longer employed.

Another firm that used the name Wedgwood legitimately in its marks was Podmore, Walker & Co. of Tunstall, Staffordshire (1834-1859): the "& Co." here was Enoch Wedgwood (1813-1879), who became a partner about 1835. The mark reproduced in Figure 3 occurs in the Patent Office Design Registration files and on a printed design called *California,* recorded in the name of Podmore, Walker & Co. in April 1849.

From 1860 the successor to this firm, at the Unicorn and Pinnox Works, used WEDGWOOD & CO both impressed and incorporated in printed marks. The blue-printed plate shown in Figure 4 bears both forms of mark. The company continued trading at Tunstall as Wedgwood & Co. Ltd. until 1965, when it was retitled Enoch Wedgwood (Tunstall) Ltd., in an effort to avoid confusion with the principal Wedgwood firm. Their early products are, however, often taken for those of Josiah Wedgwood of Etruria.

Besides these firms which had some right to the use of the famous name, there were others more unscrupulous. For example, a rare form of mock Wedgwood mark occurs on the brown-printed plate in Figure 5. The name at the right of the globe appears to read "J. Wedgwood," but it is, in fact, a mark employed by John Wood of Burslem and Tunstall (w. 1841-1860). John Wood had, or took, "Wedg" as a middle name, and so used the name mark J. WEDG. WOOD. If one looks closely at the mark, a dot and *slight* space can be seen between the two words, and, although other marks employed by this potter do not show any stop or gap between the two words, the initial J, which is not found on true Wedgwood examples, should warn the knowledgeable collector.

Away from the Staffordshire potteries, William Smith & Co. of the Stafford Pottery at Stockton-on-Tees used the name Wedgwood from 1826 until it was restrained by an injunction in 1848. Most of its wares have printed decoration, but some have patterns in silver luster. The most common impressed mark here is W.S. & CO'S/ WEDGWOOD/ WARE, but several variations occur, both impressed and printed; in some cases a middle E is inserted in the word WEDGWOOD (Fig. 7). Several marks incorporate William Smith & Co.'s initials, with the words QUEEN'S WARE replacing WEDGWOOD. The term Queen's Ware (associated with Josiah Wedgwood's refined cream-color earthenware) may have been used by William Smith & Co. after the 1848 action which restrained the company from using the name Wedgwood. The Smith firm deliberately attempted to palm its wares off as true Wedgwood examples and, as will be seen below, in many cases it was successful.

There are in the Victoria and Albert Museum two earthenware plates decorated with colored prints (one similar in type of print and in form to that shown on the right in Fig. 6). For many years the display card stated that these bore the impressed mark WEDGWOOD and attributed them to Josiah Wedgwood's factory at Etruria. In fact, the impressed mark is VEDGWOOD—an obvious effort to pass off these wares as Wedgwood by the use of a mark which is just different enough to prevent action for wrongful use of the name. The purpose was clearly achieved if examples could be displayed in a premier British museum as true Wedgwood! The error, needless to say, has now been rectified. I have a plate, similar both in form and in decoration, with the impressed mark W. S. & CO'S/ WEDGEWOOD (Fig. 7), a mark known to have been used by William Smith & Co. Furthermore, I have another such plate with a very clear impression of the VEDGWOOD mark, leaving no doubt that the first letter is V, not a faulty W. It occurred to me that this VEDGWOOD mark might have been used by William Smith & Co. after the injunction of 1848 and before the firm became George Skinner & Co., about 1856. The problem is, however, confused by the existence of a fine, blue-printed earthenware platter (Fig. 8) which bears the printed initial mark of Carr & Patton (or Patten) of the Low Lights Pottery, North Shields, Newcastle-on-Tyne, which was in operation from about 1838 to 1847, and the impressed mark VEDGWOOD. Thus it appears that at least two potteries in the North of England used this impressed mark and that the device was employed before the 1848 injunction designed to prevent the use of the Wedgwood mark by other potters. Subsequent research may well allow that other firms, on the Tyne and Tees, also employed the VEDGWOOD mark.

Another mark which is so close to the true Wedgwood mark that it can be mistaken for it by the casual observer is WIEGWOOD, again just sufficiently dissimilar to avoid

Fig. 4. Blue-printed plate bearing the impressed and printed marks WEDGWOOD & CO used after 1860 by the Tunstall firm in which Enoch Wedgwood was a partner.

Fig. 5. Printed earthenware plate bearing the misleading mark J. WEDG. WOOD.

Fig. 6. Two small plates by William Smith & Co. of Stockton-on-Tees, bearing the impressed VEDGWOOD mark.

legal action. It is occasionally found on Wedgwood-type creamwares and also on black basalt wares. A superb covered tureen with this mark is shown in Figure 9; both its shape and its enameled pattern are copied from a Wedgwood original (a true Wedgwood tureen of this design is shown in No. 607 of my *Illustrated Encyclopedia of British Pottery and Porcelain* [1966]). On comparison it can be seen that the molded finial and the relief-molded flowers at the sides of the handles differ somewhat from the original, but seen alone the WIEGWOOD tureen can easily be mistaken for the standard and true Wedgwood model.

To establish the identity of the maker of these marked WIEGWOOD pieces presents difficulties, but it could well have been the Ralph Wedgwood mentioned earlier in connection with his use of the WEDGWOOD & CO mark. Josiah Wedgwood complained in a letter dated December 1790 of the way his models were copied by others: "We have had several potters, particularly Rph. Wedgwood, send to our works for pieces, apparently intended to take moulds from to supply our customers" (Finer and Savage, *The Selected Letters of Josiah Wedgwood*, New York, 1965). But Ralph Wedgwood was obviously not the only one of Josiah Wedgwood's contemporaries who copied the master's shapes. This problem would be solved if we could discover a service bearing two forms of marks, one the WIEGWOOD version, the other an identifiable name mark such as WEDGWOOD & CO.

Incidentally, it should be noted that in recent years the well-known and desirable circular, raised WEDGWOOD & BENTLEY mark has been copied and applied to unmarked (and sometimes non-Wedgwood) articles. These frauds can be discovered by pricking the mark with a pin or other sharp-pointed instrument, for the applied marks are relatively soft in contrast to the fired originals.

It should not be thought, however, that all Wedgwood marks are open to suspicion. The true marks greatly outnumber the dubious, and the purpose of this article is simply to show that marks should be closely examined, for they are not always what they seem at first glance. Remember that no *true* Wedgwood mark has a middle E or the initial J or & Co added, so any mark with these features is that of one or more of the British potters mentioned above—or perhaps of some copyists on the Continent.

Fig. 7. Impressed mark W. S. & CO'S/WEDGWOOD from a William Smith & Co. color-printed scenic plate similar to that in Fig. 6 (*right*).

Fig. 8. Blue-printed platter bearing the impressed VEDGWOOD mark and also the printed mark of Carr & Patton, c. 1838-1847.

Fig. 9. A fine creamware imitation of a standard Wedgwood shape and pattern, with the rare mark WIEGWOOD.
*Collection of W. E. Wiltshire III.*

135

# IV  Ceramic Figures and Portraits

Despite the industrial and artistic revolution provoked by Josiah Wedgwood, there were some aspects of Staffordshire production that remained true to the crude but powerful dynamism of the 17th century. The true descendants of the Toft slipwares were not really the orientally inspired white stonewares and creamwares, but were rather the animal and figure models that are an expression of a tradition that has flourished in England since the Middle Ages.

The first flowering of this tradition in Staffordshire occurred in the familiar pew and arbor groups whose simplified modeling and naive sense of humor and caricature reveal them to be directly descended from medieval stone carvings. In the 18th century, guided by the hands of potters such as Astbury, Whieldon, and the Woods, these flat, almost two-dimensional groups were developed into a range of mounted and seated figures, and semi-realistic animals, whose stylized modeling and casually splashed glazes seem to suggest a line of descent from the Chinese figures produced during the T'ang dynasty. Later, at the end of the century, the Staffordshire potters were able to adapt their products to match the sophistication of contemporary European porcelain figures without losing sight of their essentially rustic qualities.

Perhaps the best known of these late 18th-century models is the Toby jug, that popular anthropomorphic form whose background is a curious blend of medieval, pre-Columbian, and other primitive forms with the grotesque satire of the period of Hogarth and Rowlandson. The actual origin of the Toby jug is as confused as that of the willow pattern, but the production of these wares has been a mainstay of the English industry until the present day. The continuing popularity of the form is reflected by the success among collectors of the Character jug range produced by Royal Doulton since 1932.

The possibilities for satire and direct cartoon-style portraiture inherent in simple figure models have been steadily exploited and developed. From the pew groups and Astbury-Whieldon figures are descended the vast range of portrait figures produced in Staffordshire during the 19th century. These simple, flat-back models with their crude features, casual indifference to rules of proportion, and childish decoration were designed to be produced as cheaply as possible by unskilled labor in a great number of small back-street potteries. When they were new, their popularity was assured by the immediacy of the subjects and personalities they depicted. Although essentially ephemeral, however, their popularity (and indeed, their production) continued, and so early examples sell today for prices that would amaze the original manufacturers.

In their extraordinary simplicity these figures often achieve an ikon-like quality and clearly played their part in reporting vividly the people and events of the Victorian scene. Soldiers and politicians, Royalty and preachers, and personalities from literature, the theater and the music hall find their place alongside murderers, sporting and folk heroes (and heroines) and other characters of more temporary fame. Ranged among them can also be found the many animals, from the simple, toy-like spaniels made in many sizes to decorate the mantlepiece, to models of specific animal heroes, such as Jumbo the elephant, whose untimely death in a railway accident in America provoked paroxisms of commercialized grief from the Staffordshire potters.

As one of the articles in this section suggests, the possibilities of ceramic sculpture are endless. They can range from the sophisticated to the primitive, and so can span popular interest more effectively than any other ceramic form. By being essentially useless, they also enable the collector to consider the potential of ceramics as a sculptural medium. Though but rarely practiced or studied, ceramic sculpture is actually of far greater interest and artistic value than the endlessly repetitive tablewares and ornaments that form the bulk of the potters' production.

# Staffordshire Pew Groups

*By* John E. Lerch

ALTHOUGH English clay workers of the eighteenth century were bound by business considerations to produce relatively humble earthenware, they did not cramp their creative genius by copying Continental originals as did their rivals in the china factories. Hence their unfettered originality achieved some minor sculptures that were both strong and humorous in their appeal and, because of their homely veracity, as delightful to the average public as were the tales of Fielding and of Smollett.

A multitude of figurines ranging from representations of dogs and gamecocks to those of contemporary folk, portrayed singly or in groups, demonstrates this versatility in fictile production. Supreme among such *genre* creations were certain groups in which the constantly recurring employment of a pew or settle as background for compositions involving two or more human figures is observable. Today all items thus distinguished pass under the general name of "pew groups."

Pew groups have acquired special merit in the eyes of veteran earthenware collectors, who, indeed, usually reach a state where the acquisition of at least one example seems to be the *sine qua non* of a contented life. This almost passionate yearning is easily explained. The majority of statuettes made during the course of English ceramic history were, in whole or in parts, pressed, or cast, in molds. Each pew group, on the contrary, was individually modeled by the potter's hand. The average statuette could be indefinitely duplicated by methods largely mechanical. Each pew group was a unique creation, full of spontaneity and exuberant vitality.

Authorities on English pottery, though generous in their praise of these fascinating sculptures, have been content to stress the scarcity of surviving examples, perhaps as an excuse for illustrating no more than two or three of the more familiar ones. No doubt the compilation of a fully inclusive list of extant works of the kind is beyond hope of accomplishment. Pew groups are elusive. Examples not securely anchored in museums have a way of changing hands with incalculable suddenness, and are quite likely to be whisked away from private cabinet or dealer's shelf by some ardent collector who declines to permit his name to be revealed. Yet, whatever the difficulties involved, pursuit of every discoverable group should be undertaken, and the quarry, once traced to its lair, duly recorded. The appended tabulation is the outcome of several years of search, in which a number of students have cordially participated. The accompanying illustrations are, in many instances, from specially taken photographs of hitherto unpublished pieces. Only where the securing of photographs has proved quite impossible has effort in that direction been abandoned. Even though one or two titles may have been overlooked, and a few subjects have escaped the camera's eye, we nevertheless believe that we have, at length, produced a check list likely to prove helpful to collectors and students in England, where the pew groups originated, as well as to members of the antiquarian fraternity in the United States, where, of late years, the accumulation of groups has reached increasingly significant proportions.

*Fig. 1* — Biblical

Contrary to what might be expected, the theme of the pew group is almost never associated with religion. In fact, the articles of furniture from which these compositions derive their name are obviously not pews at all, but settles, whose connotations are of the convivial tavern and the hospitable warmth of the domestic fireside, quite unrelated to ecclesiastical doings. With these connotations the behavior of the little sculptured figures is in complete harmony. Love, or music, or love with music, appears to be their chief concern, though the personages portrayed manage to keep their emotions well in hand, and never permit themselves to be surprised in the frankly languishing attitudes of the court beauties and gallants depicted by Watteau and his compeers.

Whatever their particular subject, all of these groups are permeated with humor. In some instances this attribute verges on caricature — whose symbolism, alas, usually defies accurate interpretation. What, for example, is the meaning of the huge, thrice repeated countenance with distorted mouth and goggling eyes that overshadows the discreetly separated, but mutually interested, couple in the group from the Glaisher collection pictured in Figure 10? May we infer that the woman is thinking regretfully of a corpulent husband at home, or, on the contrary, that the swain is inopportunely recalling the fact that his fair companion has already been thrice wed? Perhaps indeed, the great face may be that of a minor female divinity — a prospective mother-in-law. Quite horrific black masks of more nearly normal proportions grin from the back of another settle (*Fig. 11*). But even their threatening import, coupled with the forbidding presence of a bulldog, cannot deter the hand of the lover from reaching slyly to close upon the fingers of his lass.

With slight variations, all pew groups wear virtually the same attire. The stiffly posed female of the species is garbed in a ruffled cap, tight bodice, and widely

*Fig. 2* — Musical

September, 1936

138

*Fig. 3* — MUSICAL

*Fig. 4* — MUSICAL

flowing skirt, partly covered with a long apron. The man displays a portentous wig whose manifold curls are twisted like snail shells or bakery rolls. He is clad in a frock coat worn over a frogged and buttoned waistcoat. His feet are encased in long, tapering shoes.

The pew group in the collection of Mr. and Mrs. Frank P. Burnap of Kansas City is less artlessly amorous than the two previously mentioned, but only because its subtle purport is the eternal triangle — to outward seeming conventionally subdued (*Fig. 5*). A woman, comely and well groomed, sits between two musicians, one perhaps her husband, who is absorbed in aiding his bagpipes to give tongue; the other ogling the fair one, as he fiddles his way to her heart. Only the dog upon his mistress' lap seems really displeased with the situation. He is yowling dismally.

Pew groups of three figures constitute an exceedingly rare class. Our list records only five — and of these three are in America. That in the Burnap collection is probably the most important because of its unrestored and almost perfect state of preservation, and because of the suavity of its unusually complex compositional design.

### Technique

Having had the fortunate opportunity to examine and personally to handle the last-named group, I think it well to describe the technique of its making, particularly since the methods revealed in this instance are the same that were employed in all the others.

The group is rendered in two colors, white and a brownish black, which are so disposed as to achieve brilliantly sparkling contrasts. The black portions are produced not by painting or glazing on the white body, but by the use of separate batches of dark clay. Thus a rolled strip of white clay and a similar strip of black were twisted together to form the arms of the settle, as well as the shoes, buttons, and other dark elements of costume. The eyes and the dots of black in the settle are of slip. Quite evidently the figures and their setting were swiftly and dexterously modeled by hand with the aid of the simplest of tools. First, no doubt, the

*Fig. 5* — MUSICAL

settle was formed. Then the cylindrical bodies of the characters were squeezed into shape and appropriately clothed. Arms, mere strings of clay, rolled perhaps in the palm of the potter's hand, were applied to the bodies and draped, at will. Their ends flattened with a tool were incised to represent fingers. A ball of clay transformed into a head was adorned with ringlets on whose topmost crest was perched a hat.

When fully dry, the clay masterpiece thus constructed was ready for the furnace. After it had been exposed to the heat of the kiln until it had reached the ultimate point of endurance, it was suddenly subjected to a bath of vapor produced by shoveling table salt upon the roaring fires of the kiln. As this vapor enwrapped and settled upon the surface of the clay, it slowly condensed, and, in cooling, assumed the aspect of a finely pebbled, brilliant, and singularly enduring transparent glaze. This process of salt glazing did not originate in England, but was borrowed from Germany. Nevertheless, credit for its development to a high pitch of perfection belongs to the English potters, who, furthermore, evolved a clay body whose whiteness and delicacy vied with that of porcelain, and whose strength was such that it could be used for articles of astonishing lightness and delicacy. (While the majority of pew groups exhibit a salt-glazed surface, it is to be remembered that a small minority of them are cream glazed.)

Further examination of the Burnap group leads to additional findings. The settle is 6 ½ inches high, 8 ⅞ inches long, and 2 ½ inches wide (the woman's skirt extending slightly beyond the flooring). It is composed of six parts: base, back, sides, seat, and a molding 7/16 of an inch wide, which gives added thickness along the top. The major slabs are but 3/16 of an inch thick. The sides of the settle below the seat are cut with a knife into irregular arches. A similar treatment is more clearly observable in the Macy group of two lovers, where the maker wielded his knife still more decoratively to achieve a medallion of spades, circles, and a heart in the settle's back (*Fig. 11*). Solon, in his *Art of the Old English Potter*, remarks that such deep cuttings imitate a type of decoration

*Fig. 6 — Conversation Piece: Two Figures*

*Fig. 7 — Conversation Piece: Two Figures*

found on German wares and that it was very popular for decorating English pottery during the first half of the eighteenth century.

Jointures, carefully smoothed, are still further concealed by the glaze. Dots of brown slip decorate the revetment of the settle, while around the head of the woman a pattern of seven arrangements of dots creates a kind of halo. An identical motive of seven dots, haphazardly applied, occurs on the apron of the woman in the Macy pew group.

The brilliant effectiveness achieved by the skilful use of two contrasting biscuits is well exemplified in the Burnap group. The garments of the figures are cut from a crust 1/16 of an inch in thickness, while the various anatomical members are rolled, pinched, and deftly modeled to make torsos, arms, and legs. From the waist up the woman is a solid core, with carefully modeled breasts, neck, and head; but the arms are of rolled clay and attached. Black cuffs wrapped around them create the illusion of sleeves. The ribbed bodice of dark biscuit is superimposed, and fits between two white strips imitating ruffles. No legs are concealed by the widespread skirt, which is composed of alternate strips of black and white clay — the latter milled. Thus we have the semblance of an elaborately pleated creation fronted by a capacious white apron. The costume is completed by a cap of folded clay and a necklace of slip dots.

The men are fashioned more completely than their companion, since their costume permits less disguise. Their similarly styled clothing fits over skeleton cores. Dark biscuit constitutes the tricorn hats, the throat ribands, cuffs, and boots, but the edges of the hat brims are of white biscuit. So likewise are the shoe buckles.

*Fig. 8 — Conversation Piece: Two Figures*

*Fig. 9 — Conversation Piece: Two Figures*

Since in so far as concerns technique, what is true of the Burnap group is true of all, we need burden the reader with no more descriptive details, leaving our illustrations to reveal, as they may, the sequence of little dramas and the manner of their making.

*The Question of Date*

Solon has written, "The costumes of the figures refer it [the pew group] to the period of slip dishes and it suggests to us the idea of Thomas Toft trying his hand at sculpture." Apparently a misunderstanding of these words led the author of the preface to the catalogue of the Burlington Fine Arts Club exhibition of English earthenware in 1914 to regard the pew group as a product of the third quarter of the seventeenth century. From the standpoint of ceramic technique it is now generally acknowledged that such groups could not have appeared until fifty years later, that is, not until after 1720.

Nevertheless, we observe a definite continuity in English ceramic technique from 1650 until, after the lapse of nearly a century, the potters began the regular employment of molds for the easy multiplication of figures. The demand for ornaments in relief, applicable to engine turned tableware and produced separately by means of metal stamps or by pressing clay into a mold, or by hardening slip poured into a mold, about 1745 revolutionized the processes of pottery sculpture, which, from then on, was assembled from units shaped in molds, thus paralleling the porcelain method. The tradition of English free-modeling, most glorious in the work of seventeenth-century John Dwight of Fulham, seems to have reached its illustrious termination in the pew-group series.

One reason for dating these groups between 1720 and 1740

lies in the use of much incised or scratch decoration whose pattern is emphasized by fillings of dark slip. From the latter end of this period we encounter inscribed and dated salt-glaze vessels ornamented in "scratched blue," that is, showing an incised pattern filled with powdered cobalt and fused. Thus both pew groups and scratched-blue vessels exemplify technical steps slightly antedating the decorating of salt-glaze objects with colored enamels. Only one of the two extant pew groups in cream glaze, *as distinguished from the usual salt glaze*, betrays the mingling of pigment with the glaze. A slightly greenish tint is the result.

Perhaps, however, the most convincing evidence as to the date of pew groups is that afforded by the costumes of the figures. These indicate a shorter period of production than might be calculated on purely technical grounds, namely some part of the decade between 1730 and 1740.

*Authorship*

The honor of making most of the pew groups is by some authorities conferred upon Aaron Wood. This member of a famous family was apprenticed, in 1731, to Doctor Thomas Wedgwood, the principal potter of Burslem. Later he achieved the distinction of being the finest block cutter and moldmaker of the period. Pew groups, however, were not made in that fashion. Furthermore, the precision and meticulous care necessary to the production of dies and molds seem hardly to comport with the free, creative spirit that radiates from every pew group of our acquaintance.

John Astbury (*1688–1743*) is the potter who seems most likely to have had a hand in the fashioning of pew groups. He is credited with a series of figures representing men playing bagpipes or other instruments. These musicians bear a distinct resemblance to some of the pew-group figures. A three-figure cream-glaze pew group formerly in the H. Davis collection is ascribed to Astbury. Further worth noting is the circumstance that the date of this potter's death closely coincides with that which marks the conclusion of the pew-group series.

Probably of slightly later date, when the factory system invoked the businesslike method of stamping the maker's name on his wares, is an unusual pew group portraying two seated youths, one reading a book, the other holding a scroll. It is marked WEDGWOOD, and exhibits the Astbury-Whieldon style in its slightly green-tinted cream glaze touched with manganese and brown.

In closing let it be said that another type of figurine has at times been placed in the pew category. This comprises the arbor specimens, depicting people seated or standing beneath a vine-covered garden trellis. Yet another type uses a flourishing tree for background. Needless to say, such compositions are not pew groups.

*Check List of Salt-Glazed Pew Groups*

The classification and numbering employed in this list are of course purely arbitrary, but have been adopted as probably affording the readiest means of reference identification. All items credited to the Glaisher collection now permanently repose in the Fitzwilliam Museum, Cambridge, England. Where the location of specimens is unknown, the fact is indicated.

*Fig. 10* — CONVERSATION PIECE: TWO FIGURES

*Fig. 11 (above)* — CONVERSATION PIECE: TWO FIGURES

*Figs. 12 (left) and 13 (right)* — CONVERSATION PIECES: THREE FIGURES

*Fig. 14* — CONVERSATION PIECE: THREE FIGURES

*Fig. 15* — CONVERSATION PIECE: THREE FIGURES

The numbers correspond to those of the illustrations. Few if any of the surviving pew groups have escaped at least slight damage. Some badly broken items have undergone considerable restoration. Only in one or two instances does the list call attention to imperfections or to the extent of repairs. In order to avoid confusion, cream-glazed pew groups have been omitted from the list, though one is pictured for comparison. Mention should be made of a remarkable single pew figure pictured in Honey's *English Pottery and Porcelain*, Plate VI (*b*). Whether it is salt glaze or creamware is not indicated.

*Biblical*

1. ADAM AND EVE. (Two figures standing before settle which supports an espalier apple tree. Serpent broken.) *Location*, Dr. J. W. L. Glaisher collection, Fitzwilliam Museum, Cambridge, England. *References*, Burlington Fine Arts Club, London, *Illustrated Catalogue of Exhibition of Early English Earthenware*, 1914, Pl. XXXIII, Case F39; Rackham and Read, *English Pottery*, Fig. 169; Read, *Staffordshire Pottery Figures*, Pl. 4.

*Musical*

2. BAGPIPER AND FIDDLER. (Horse and dog on pierced settle back. Damaged.) *Location*, Glaisher collection. *References*, Burlington Fine Arts Club, Pl. XXXIV, F55.

3. WOMAN AND BAGPIPER. *Precise location unknown*; private collection in England. Formerly Captain Frank Price collection; sold by Sotheby & Company. *References*, Rhead, *The Earthenware Collector*, p. 112, where it is erroneously credited to the Glaisher collection. Subsequently much restored.

4. WOMAN AND BAGPIPER. (Incised leafage decoration on settle back.) *Location*, Glaisher collection. *References*, Read, *Pl. 5*.

5. WOMAN BETWEEN FIDDLER AND BAGPIPER. *Location*, Harriet and Frank Burnap collection, Kansas City. Formerly M. Dent collection.

*Conversation Pieces: Two Figures*

6. MAN AND WOMAN ON TWO-BACKED SETTLE. *Location*, William B. Goodwin collection, New York City.

7. MAN AND WOMAN ON TWO-BACKED SETTLE. (Damaged. Apparently allied with No. 6.) *Location*, uncertain. Said to have been purchased at sale of Solon collection in 1911 for a Captain Luxmore, who soon after sailed for Auckland, New Zealand. Enquiry has elicited no further information concerning its fate. *References*, Burlington Fine Arts Club, Pl. XXXIV, F83; Blacker, *ABC of English Salt-Glaze Stoneware*, p. 89; Solon, *Art of the Old English Potter*, p. 171.

8. MAN AND WOMAN. (Dog on floor between figures. Scrolls on settle back.) *Location*, Kathleen Mason (Mrs. Frank Tilley) collection, England. (Photograph by courtesy of *The Antique Collector*.)

9. MAN AND WOMAN. (Settle back pierced and die-impressed.) *Location*, Glaisher collection. *Reference*, Rackham and Read, Fig. 165.

10. MAN AND WOMAN. (Three masks on settle back.) *Location*, Glaisher collection. Prior ownerships: Mrs. Hamilton Clements; Frank Falkner and Dr. E. J. Sidebotham collection, Peel Park, Salford, England. *References*, Burlington Fine Arts Club, Pl. XXXIII, F34; Read, Pl. 6B; Rhead, *Staffordshire Pots and Potters*, p. 170; Blacker, p. 106.

11. MAN HOLDING WOMAN'S HAND. (Dog between the pair. Masks and die-impressed figures on pierced settle back.) *Location*, Helen and Carleton Macy collection, Metropolitan Museum of Art, New York. Formerly Lord Revelstoke collection. *References*, Read, Pl. 6A; Metropolitan Museum Bulletin, Vol. XXX, No. 3, March 1935.

*Conversation Pieces: Three Figures*

12. WOMAN BETWEEN TWO SNUFF-TAKING MEN. *Precise location unknown*. Recently sold by Sotheby to Cyril Andrade, London; formerly John Henry Taylor collection.

13. WOMAN BETWEEN TWO YOUNG MEN. (Woman holding dog; one man wearing a hat.) *Location*, Morgan collection, Wadsworth Atheneum, Hartford, Connecticut. Formerly Frank Stoner collection, London.

14. WOMAN BETWEEN TWO HATLESS YOUNG MEN. *Location*, Willett collection, British Museum, London. *References*, Rhead, p. 170; Blacker, p. 72.

15. WOMAN BETWEEN TWO HATLESS YOUNG MEN. (Ape's heads on settle arms. Damaged.) *Location*, Macy collection, Metropolitan Museum. Previous ownerships: Dr. J. W. L. Glaisher; Colonel and Mrs. Dickson.

CREAM-GLAZED PEW GROUP: IMPRESSED MARK "WEDGWOOD"
Two youths, one reading a book, the other holding a scroll in his left hand, an ale glass in his right. Slightly green-tinted cream glaze touched with manganese and brown.
*Formerly in the Frank Stoner collection*

*Fig. 1 (center)* — HUDIBRAS ON HORSEBACK (*Astbury*); *(sides)* — PUTTI ON LIONS (*Ralph Wood*)
An interesting contrast between early eighteenth century honest rusticity and late eighteenth century artificial urbanity.

# Staffordshire Figures of the Eighteenth Century

## By Mrs. Gordon-Stables

THE fact that very little of real critical value has thus far been published on the subject of Staffordshire figures is, perhaps, a matter for rejoicing rather than for regret, since it leaves the field open to individual and unbiased judgment of a branch of artistic output of which a modern craze tends to confuse the issues. There have, indeed, been a great unearthing of records and documents, a great sifting of evidence concerning methods of glazing and firing, a great effort to assign definite pieces to specific modelers, and so on; but the result of all this industry, when finally boiled down, gives comparatively little, and still leaves opportunity for independent speculation and the exercise of originality and taste on the part of the potential collector.

For the sake of convenience, certain figures of archaic type, such as *The Lady Holding a Fan, The Pair of Lovers Seated on a Rock* (Figs. *4* and *2*), and others of similar aspect, are now comprehensively referred to as by Astbury, that master-potter who trained under the Brothers Elers, Dutchmen, who settled in England toward the close of the seventeenth century and introduced into their new abode the use of salt in the production of glazes.* The Brothers Elers were technicians; Astbury was the artist who made use of their technique to enhance his own work as modeler and designer. It is customary to describe his figures as crude, or even coarse; but those to whom primitive art makes a real appeal discover in them the directness and force of the truly archaic.

These vigorous small sculptures appear to have emanated from a man who had been spared contact with a more highly evolved art, and who could, in consequence, approach his task with mind unconfused and undominated. And yet, in spite of this, there would seem to abide in Astbury's unsophisticated renderings of man and beast something of the virility and beauty of early Chinese art, so that, now and again, one is tempted to believe that, in some way or other, he must have been touched by that fondness for Oriental modes which, following the rise of the East India Company, manifested itself in so many branches of art during the entire eighteenth century in England.

*Fig. 2* — TWO LOVERS ON A ROCK (*Astbury*)
This example is lead-glazed with yellow, bright green, blue-green and purple-brown. The group usually occurs in white salt-glaze.

*John Astbury is said to have been born about 1678, and to have died in 1743. To his son Thomas some writers incline to give chief credit for developing figure work and for improving methods of treating pottery clay.

143

January, 1927

On the whole, however, one is inclined to the view that, in the main, this haunting similarity is to be accounted for not by conscious or unconscious imitation, but by that inherent dynamic impulse which is part and parcel of primitive art, no matter among what races or in what period it manifests itself.

So archaic in type are many of the Astbury figures that, when shown to those ignorant of their history, they are usually attributed to a period antecedent to their own by at least two centuries, a fact which tends to corroborate the theory that, in England, art progresses at a slower rate than obtains in many European countries. Compare Astbury's output with the eighteenth century potting in Germany and France, and the validity of the contention becomes immediately obvious.

Now, although the figures produced by the Wood family of Burslem loom largest of all in the eyes of the *average* collector of Staffordshire, the *careful* student is disposed to dwell at great length upon Astbury and upon his pupil Thomas Whieldon; because in their comparatively rude modeling, exist both imaginative force and creative lifelikeness, whereas in the more advanced work of later masters, technique, by its own advancement, tends to lose in respect of eloquence.

Astbury's *Musicians* playing their various instruments, his *Hudibras* astride his nag (*Figs. 4 and 5*), may be possessed of limbs which appear strangely rudimentary in structure; their features may recall the contours of halfpenny buns with currants for eyes; yet, the more one studies them, the more one reacts to the life in these little objects. They *do* move and have their being, they *do* invoke music from their pipes and flageolets, they *do* make love and enter into conversation one with another.

In the greater number of works by later potters, the figures, academic in comparison, appear posed; they belong to the realm of the stage; and though, in point of the purely decorative, they may surpass the others, they are less appealing, less near to us.

As an example of this, regard Ralph Wood's *Strephon and Phyllis*, a group also known as *The Birdcage* (*Fig. 3*), which offers us a charming couple, unlike any real shepherd and shepherdess that ever truly existed, and who, one feels sure, must have deliberately ordered their costumes from a theatrical costumier, and studied their poses well before they sat for their portraits. Here they are, wondering very much what effect they are producing upon their audience.* Note, too, the imperfect fashion in which heads are set on necks, and necks on shoulders — details in which the Woods seldom excelled. They had arrived at the stage when impeccability in such matters might reasonably be expected; but the expectation is not always satisfied.

*Fig. 3* — STREPHON AND PHYLLIS (*Ralph Wood*)
An attempt to interpret in cottage statuary the bucolic romanticism of the French school of painting.

---

*Thomas Whieldon died in 1798. The chief members of the Wood family were Ralph the elder (1715–1772); his son Ralph (1748–1795); Aaron Wood (1717–1785), a mold cutter, brother of the elder Ralph; and Aaron's son Enoch (1759–1840).

*Fig. 4* — FIGURES (*Astbury*)
An extraordinary series, displaying powers of expressive delineation, with rare economy of effort, on the modeler's part. The bust of a man, and the figures of a woman (perhaps a Madonna) and child particularly deserve to be termed great little sculptures. In both pieces the artist has, all unconsciously, achieved those qualities of spontaneity and naïve directness for which modern sophistication labors in vain.

The work of Thomas Whieldon is by no means easy to identify, any more than that of the various members of the Wood family. Much that goes by Whieldon's name must actually have been made by Wedgwood; while Whieldon's fellow pupil, the elder Ralph Wood, was doubtless responsible for a good deal more. Whieldon specialized in animals rather than in men, and experimented freely in manganese splashed effects, and in tortoise-shell glazes — often with small regard to their appropriate use. His *Virgin and Child*, for instance, though an interesting piece of modeling, may hardly be said to look its most attractive as a bit of tortoise-shell ware.

It is fairly safe to assert that *no* figures which display the beady use of manganese for eyeballs may be correctly attributed to either Whieldon or the Woods, for, toward the end of his career Astbury himself discarded this device and adopted that of slightly tooling the eyes, without the addition of any local color at all. He left it for those who followed after him to adopt the method of bestowing a slight color wash and of developing elaborations of tooling. Of the latter, perhaps the finest example of all is to be found in the Wesley bust, (by Enoch Wood), in which the eyes are quite extraordinarily expressive (*Fig. 6*).

Under the Woods, both flesh tints and plain white are used during the same period, for faces; but of these two processes, the former, as a rule, creates the more pleasant effect. With the larger portion of the Woods' best pieces, John Voyez — one of those a-moral geniuses to whom everything, save so much as a stable code of ethics, comes easy — is almost certainly to be credited. Voyez, having left the employ of the Wedgwood firm under

*Fig. 5* — HUDIBRAS ON HIS HORSE (*Ralph Wood, Jr.*)
Notable for its broad humor, its forceful modeling, and its lusciousness of glaze.

145

somewhat shady circumstances (and here it may be remarked that some of his best modeling was done while in prison) entered the service of the Woods; and his name appears on a number of pieces, notably plaques, medallions, and other articles obviously glazed and potted by Ralph Wood, Jr., with whom Voyez seems to have worked in close and constant collaboration.* In all, there were four successive generations of Ralph Woods; but, in the development of the potter's craft, *there were only two that count;* namely, the second Ralph Wood and his son.† It is these two, who, in conjunction with Enoch Wood, known affectionately as the "father of the potters", and Aaron Wood, brother of Ralph II, uncle of Ralph III, and father of Enoch, who left their impress on their craft.

When one considers the modest prices at which the majority of these Staffordshire figures were offered for sale, their quality is more than ever to be marvelled at. Even on examples that were to be vended at little more than a shilling apiece, the glaze amazes one by its translucency and brilliance.

Now that the market is being flooded with imitations of the original work, it is this quality in the glaze that establishes itself as the most reliable means of distinguishing the spurious from the genuine. The glaze employed at this period is so exquisite that it conveys to the surface of the clay a texture that, to the touch, seems almost like velvet. It is so rich in quality that there is no contradiction in describing it as, at the same time, soft and brilliant. And yet, strange to relate, it is only comparatively recently that this quality has been duly appreciated. Even those entrusted with the responsibility of buying for museums failed at one time to understand the merits of these early figures as compared with those dull, lifeless, enamel decorations that chip so horribly and give such a cheap effect to the whole.

It is often claimed that one can tell the genuine Wood figure by the fact that such a one invariably displays, in some portion or another of its anatomy, a space where the glaze has missed, and where, in consequence, one may make a mark with a lead pencil. But this is by no means a certain test, since there exist indubitable Wood figures on which no such area is to be discovered.

In the same way, the dictum that authentic examples must prove unglazed at the base is not to be regarded as infallible, since specimens are by no means infrequent where the base is at least lightly brushed over with glaze. Apart from intrinsic evidence as to characteristics of modeling and of color, the glaze and the weight perhaps offer the most trustworthy guide to authenticity. The weight in the genuine figures is found to be distinctly slight in proportion to size, owing to the composition of the clays employed at the time. When a piece is heavy in the hand, it may be rejected with reasonable certainty.

*Fig. 6* — JOHN WESLEY (*Enoch Wood*)
Face uncolored, robes green. A fine bit of portraiture.

Though the Wood family were the first to adopt the plan of stamping their figures with their name or their rebus (four trees side by side) they, nevertheless, frequently omitted their mark, so that a specimen without such a stamp may still be perfectly genuine. Ralph Wood, Sr. used a stamp in which his name appears in capital letters; thus, R. WOOD, while that of his son was RA WOOD. A series of mold numbers was also employed, but of these a considerable proportion still remains untraced. Hence, the collector of Staffordshire figures may hope to enjoy the triumph of discovering some hitherto unknown example.

Marked RA WOOD, BURSLEM, and bearing the mold number, *42*, is the group, *Hudibras on His Horse*, a piece, which, in common with many another, has in it much of that sturdy humor which the novelist of the Five Towns, Arnold Bennett, has succeeded in bringing home to his readers. Indeed, in studying this Staffordshire pottery, one is conscious, over and over again, of that spirit of shrewd kindliness, of self-reliant doggedness, of wit, of insight that are distinguishing characteristics of the folk of this part of the country.

When it comes to the portrayal of some popular divine, there is brought to the task a profound sense of reverence and respect. The different versions of the preachers Whitefield and Wesley are eloquent of the aspiration which both succeeded in arousing in their hearers, men only too ready to lend ear to those whom they believed capable of leading them into the straight and narrow path.

Of Wesley, Enoch Wood modeled from life the magnificent portrait bust which, though it was executed when the artist was but twenty-two years of age, yet is a superlative achievement in potting. It shows us Wesley at the age of seventy-eight, and is generally accepted as the classic presentment of the great divine in this, the closing stage of his career. In every line of the subtle modeling there is evidence of a keen realization of the arresting individuality of the sitter. The face is uncolored (with the exception of the slightest tinge to the eyes) and the gown is tinted to the same delicate shade of green as that

---

*C.f. Rackham and Read: *English Pottery*, New York, 1924, p. 102.
†Ralph and Aaron Wood were brothers, sons of a Ralph Wood, known as "the honest miller of Burslem" (b. 1676).— ED.

employed in the Whitefield bust, at one time in the Stoner collection.

Frank Falkner in his volume *The Wood Family of Burslem*, which was published in 1912 — prior to the discovery of this particular version of Wesley — throws out the suggestion that some day a Wesley bust corresponding to the Whitefield might possibly come to light. It was not, however, until 1920 that he was proved in the wrong by the discovery of the bust here pictured. This, the only known specimen in existence, was one day brought in unexpectedly to the collector and author, Edward Sheldon, from whose keeping it later passed on to that of Mr. Andrade, its present owner.

I find the quality of humor conspicuously present both in the Whieldon bust of the Duke of Cumberland, a very debonair bit of work (*Fig. 7*), and in the Astbury group of King George II on horseback (*Cover*). In neither is there the slightest hint of that submissive state of mind which is so apt to overtake the portraitist, whether in paint or in pottery, at the thought of a royal sitter. There is an irrepressible jollity, a suggestion of the hail-fellow-well-met about both pieces that engages one's affections straightway. Were it not for the initials *G.R.* on the holsters of the mounted figure, one would hardly have suspected this to be a portrait of His Majesty, himself, as he appeared at the Battle of Dettingen, in 1743. The color of the group is particularly gay and jolly. The cocked hat is touched with green and brown; there are yellow buttonholes to the white tunic, and the tail of the jacket is green. Horse and trappings are in brown, with a touch of yellow in the holsters.

The earlier Staffordshire pieces keep to cream and brown, and it is believed that Astbury's first essays were made in red clay. From the two-color experiments he passed on to three tints, introducing at the same time the manganese eyeballs, later abandoned. The George II figure belongs to the three-color era and was probably produced by the artist quite toward the end of his career.

Ralph Wood, in his companion pair of *Cupids* on their respective lion and lioness, was catering to the well-to-do townsman, the successful shopkeeper, or, possibly, a more aristocratic patron still. We feel the touch of Voyez in such pieces, as we do in the many *Venuses*, *Neptunes*, *Seasons*, and *Sphinxes* that emanated from the Wood factory. In these *Cupid* groups, the animals are, to my mind, finer than the little figures astride them; and suggest that an even more interesting and profitable hobby than the collecting of Staffordshire figures might be discovered in the collecting of Staffordshire animals. Horses and dogs, squirrels and goats, deer and rams, elephants and hippopotami, boars and bulls, all figure among the virile animal studies of the day and possess a spirited quality which marks them as works of art well deserving of specialization on the part of the collector.

The output of the Staffordshire factories during the eighteenth century was so varied that it would be impossible, even within the scope of a far more exhaustive review than this, to consider each and every type of figure produced during this epoch. It is by familiarity with the general work, by the constant handling of specimens, and patient concentration upon the various points of modeling, color and glazes, that the potential collector will eventually come to discern, as if by second nature, the true from the false, the good from the indifferent, the old from the new.

*Fig. 7* — THE DUKE OF CUMBERLAND (*Whieldon*)

THE OSTEND GATE AT BRUGES
  Blue Staffordshire plate by an unknown maker.

# TOBY JUGS

## By EDWARD WENHAM

MANY BYGONE ARTISTS and craftsmen live on in the work they left to later generations; the names of many writers of the past survive in their contributions to literature; some divines are remembered for their spiritual, others for their sporting qualities, and the memory of one divine is perpetuated in the beer jug popularly known as Toby.

During his lifetime, Francis Fawkes who was born in 1720 at Warmsworth, Yorkshire, held various church offices, eventually becoming one of the chaplains to the Princess of Wales. He achieved a certain literary fame from several volumes of original poems and translations, but those poems have long since passed to things forgotten with the exception of his ballad *Toby Fillpot,* published in 1761. And it is generally thought this song was indirectly the origin of the Toby jug.

Indirectly, because the actual form of the Toby jug was most probably taken from the engraved portrait of Toby Fillpot. This pictures Toby as a happy, laughing, bald-headed fellow of immense girth with his three-cornered hat set none too securely on the back of his large head. He is seated in a low chair with turned legs in a beautiful arborlike setting, smoking a long clay "churchwarden" pipe and holding a huge jug of foaming ale in his right hand. There is a small table with plain square legs of the Chippendale type at Toby's side and on this a small beaker.

This picture was doubtless inspired by Francis Fawkes' song which appears under Toby Fillpot's portrait and reads:

Dear Tom this brown Jug that now foams with mild Ale,
(In which I will drink to sweet Nan of the Vale)
Was once Toby Fillpot a thirsty old Soul
As e're drank a Bottle or fathom'd a Bowl,
In boozing about 'twas his praise to excell,
And among Jolly Topers he bore off the Bell.
It chanc'd as in Dog-days he sat at his ease,
In his Flow'r woven Arbour as gay as you please,
With a Friend and a Pipe, puffing Sorrow away,
And with honest old Stingo was soaking his Clay
His breath Doors of Life on a sudden were shut
And he died full as big as a Dorchester Butt

His Body when long in the Ground it had lain
And time into Clay had resolv'd it again
A Potter found out in its Covert so snug
And with part of fat Toby he form'd this brown Jug
Now sacred to Friendship and Mirth and mild Ale
So here's to my lovely sweet Nan of the Vale

FIG. 1—SMALL TOBY JUG by Ralph Wood. Height, 6½ inches. *From J. R. Cookson.*

The word *stingo* is old slang for strong liquor, more especially ale.

Another early rural ballad having a similar theme also tells of a potter who, having seen on a tombstone the inscription,*The wife of old Toby, fair Agnes, lies here,* decided:

That Toby and Agnes should never be parted.
So he took her fair clay which was whiter than milk
And tempered with brandy till softer than silk;
Then formed into pipes he advised, sly and snug
That we kiss her fair clay and shake hands with his jug.

It has also been suggested that the Toby jug is a representation of that delightful character, Uncle Toby, in Laurence Sterne's *Tristram Shandy,* the first two volumes of which were published in 1759. But the likeness between the form of the Toby jug and the portrait of Toby Fillpot seems to support the contention that the latter was the source of the model adopted by the eighteenth-century potters.

Only a keen enthusiast can fully appreciate a large collection of Toby jugs—and there are several such collections. To others it is merely a number of similar specimens of colorful pottery. Admittedly, this similarity does exist, but the specialist recognizes many and discovers more distinct features with individual jugs. Possibly it is only a difference in the height of the base, but far more interesting variations occur in the facial expressions, the style of the hair, the dress, the shapes of the jug and goblet which Toby holds, and numerous other details, in addition to the coloring.

Happy-looking as most of the rotund fellows are, none expresses quite the cheery inviting smile of Toby Fillpot's portrait; the nearest approach to it is an impish-looking fellow with a naughty twinkle, not inappropriately called the *Sinner.* This figure, which is thought to have been modeled by the Staffordshire potter Walton, has a black coat and striped vest, the drinking goblet in the left hand and an unusually small jug in the right. Another carefree, jovial Toby is a well-upholstered figure in a full wig, wearing a blue and orange coat, tasseled breeches, and black shoes with large buckles; this is thought by some collectors to represent Doctor Johnson, though the same model is also known as the *Unfrocked Parson* (Fig. 2).

A good many Tobies are long of face with wrinkled brow and a noticeably worried expression; some are clearly modeled from characters who, like Toby Fillpot himself, belonged among the jolly topers. Occasionally you come on one of censorious or patronizing mien as, for example, one known as the *Squire.* He is a dignified, rotund, but by no means fat figure with long hair, wearing a green (sometimes blue) coat,

May, 1947

Fig. 2 — DOCTOR JOHNSON, also known as *Unfrocked Parson*. Ascribed to Enoch Wood. *Private collection*.

Fig. 3 — MAN ON THE BARREL, also called the *Lord Vernon* jug. By Ralph Wood. *Delomosne & Son Ltd*.

a black vest, and an unusually large hat; he also wears a white neckerchief or, as it was formerly called, berdash — from which we get out modern word haberdasher. Another characteristic of this model is the chair which, in place of the usual square seat, is a three-legged writing chair with cabriole legs.

One lean Toby, generally ascribed to Whieldon, is often called the *Thin Man*. This is an austere individual with unusually long hair wearing a small hat; the color of the coat varies with different specimens, though it is most often green. He is smoking a somewhat clumsy short clay pipe and his left hand holds a large jug of foaming ale, the bottom of the jug resting on his knee. Both this and the *Squire* jug are noticeable for the clear-cut facial features and other details indicating the hand of a skilled modeler.

Obviously, the principal coloring is in the coats of Toby jugs and this covers a very wide range even with ordinary models, although certain colors are rarer than others. The finest colored glazes are found with the Ralph Wood Tobies (*Fig. 1*), but it has to be remembered that specimens by either of the Woods are not plentiful, nor are they cheap. One of the characteristics of Ralph Wood jugs, yet one seldom noticed except by experienced collectors, is the frequent occurrence of the Roman nose. This feature is also found in Tobies by other potters and both are among the several variations which add much to the interest of assembling these popular jugs.

Very few Toby jugs carry a maker's mark. Potters whose wares have been thus identified include Neale & Co., Walton, Enoch Wood, and Wood & Caldwell, all working not far from 1800. Most of the earlier, unmarked Tobies are attributed to the elder Ralph Wood, Whieldon, or Astbury. These have the robust modeling and the rich colored glazes that are particularly prized by collectors. Some time in the latter part of the eighteenth century on-glaze enamel colors began to be used, at first in conjunction with colored glazes, later in place of them.

Apart from the known few, it is not possible to identify the character which any given early Toby jug is supposed to portray; and it has to be admitted that the names applied to some are inspired by wishful thinking as in the case of the model that has more than once been paraded as *Benjamin Franklin*. Actually this is an attractive modern jug, but one does not need very close observation to realize that the modeler of the chubby little figure in white pants and gaiters was more familiar with Dickens' portrait of Mr. Pickwick than he was with the facial characteristics and carriage of Doctor Franklin.

Then there are the Tobies — many of them by Ralph Wood — which because of some particular detail are regarded as specialties. One, usually known as the *Shield* Toby, has a shaped shield on the left side of the seat inscribed with the advice, *It is all out. Then fill him again*. The *Night Watchman* is another in the same category; this model is a bewildered man dressed in black, holding a large lanthorn in his right hand while his left hand holds the big round hat which rests on his knee.

Others, well worth seeking, are the *Convict*, distinguishable by the broad arrows on the vest and by the striped stockings (a "broad arrow" is an arrowhead used in Britain to mark government stores); the *One-armed Toby*, whose right arm is amputated; the *Man on the Barrel*, also called the *Lord Vernon* jug (*Fig. 3*); the model with a firkin between the legs (a firkin was a small barrel holding about a gallon, formerly carried by farm workers (*Fig. 4*); and the Tobies with a small beaker-shaped cup which, inverted, forms the crown of the hat.

Besides these many variants of the squat Toby modeled on the seated figure of Toby Fillpot, there are a number of attractive jugs which vary from the original model. As a rule, these are slightly taller, some of them being over twelve inches high. Most Tobies are about nine to ten inches high. One of the finest is a Ralph Wood jug known as *Rodney's Sailor* which usually has an olive-green coat, white trousers, and buckled shoes. The hat is round instead of the usual tricorn shape and the figure holds a white, pear-shaped pitcher in his right hand, a goblet in his left, and there is an anchor on the ground at his feet.

A similar model by Ralph

Fig. 4 — TOBY with small barrel, or firkin. Whieldon. *From Delomosne & Son, Ltd*.

Fig. 5 — THE PLANTER, with striped trousers and white vest. *From a private collection*.

Fig. 6—One of Several variants of *Martha Gunn. From a private collection.*

Fig. 7—Pair of Bristol Delft polychrome Toby jugs attributed to Joseph Flower of Redcliffe. *J. R. Cookson.*

pline and strident voice of "Old Tom."

While the portrait Toby jugs made in more recent times differ from the earlier specimens, they none the less carry on the same tradition and many excellent models have been produced by both English and American potteries. Toward the end of the last century, one of the Staffordshire potteries issued an attractive *Gladstone* Toby showing the famous statesman with his axe resting against a tree—a kindly reminder of the Grand Old Man's favorite pastime of felling trees.

Wood is also sometimes known as *Rodney's Sailor,* though it is often called the *Planter.* The facial expression resembles closely that of the *Rodney's Sailor* jug mentioned above; but this second model has the tricorn hat, and the shapes of both jug and goblet are different. Furthermore, instead of holding the handle of the jug, he has a plug of tobacco in his left hand which rests against the jug. Another model called the *Planter* has striped trousers and white vest, but this, too, is a Toby which seldom comes on offer (*Fig. 5*).

If you are fortunate, you may meet up with a jug figure of *Martha Gunn,* the famous Brighton bathing attendant who used to dip George IV, when an infant, in the sea (*Fig. 6*). In 1919, a *Martha Gunn* Toby by Ralph Wood the elder brought well over $3,000 at a London auction; this huge price, it may be added, established a level which has not even been approached.

Probably the rarest are delft Tobies. Both of the two examples illustrated (*Fig. 7*), which recently came to light, depart from the squat type and both are Bristol delft, possibly from the pottery of Joseph Flower. This potter started in business at Redcliffe about 1743 and much of the work bearing his signature still survives, including pieces decorated in both blue and white and polychrome and others painted with flowers and miniature oriental scenes.

Some few Tobies are standing instead of seated figures. Of these the best known is the type referred to as *Hearty Good Fellow* (*Fig. 8*). Some examples are in knee breeches and some in trousers; others hold a goblet in the left hand, or a pipe; otherwise they differ little except in the colorings.

Now and then you come upon a jug of the Toby type which suggests a caricature of an unkindly character, as the *Cat Toby* shown here (*Fig. 9*). From the style of the coat and the fact that the hat is of the old-mortar-board type, we may assume that the jug was a caricature of a not-too-popular pedagogue and that it was one of a number made to the order of a group of students to commemorate their release from the disci-

A considerable number of fine Tobies appeared after the war of 1914-1918, including among their subjects King George V, President Wilson, Lord Kitchener, Earl Haig, and other eminent men of that time. So far, few men connected with the more recent World War have been perpetuated in Toby jugs. Doulton & Co. issued a particularly fine model of Winston Churchill, and Spode produced a Franklin Roosevelt and Winston Churchill.

Of American Toby jugs, the earliest that is known, of brown-glazed stoneware, was made and marked by D. & J. Henderson at the Jersey City Pottery in 1830 (see ANTIQUES, January 1933, p. 4, and December 1946, p. 390). Other early examples are the small brown tavern jugs made about 1850 at Bennington. The finer examples date from the 1890's and after, many of them being of porcelain made at Trenton, New Jersey. Their subjects include George Washington, Theodore Roosevelt, and William Penn. Presidents McKinley and Hoover, Al Smith, and other prominent Americans have also joined the host whose effigies carry on the Toby tradition.

Fig. 8—The Hearty Good Fellow, with pipe in left hand. Ascribed to Neale & Co. *From a private collection.*

Fig. 9—Cat Toby with mortar-board hat. *From the collection of Mr. L. Percy Allen of Westbury-on-Trym, Bristol.*

BY BRYAN LATHAM

# Victorian Staffordshire portrait figures

COLLECTORS IN AMERICA AND GREAT BRITAIN are taking an increasing interest in Victorian Staffordshire portrait figures, that remarkable array of nineteenth-century personalities in pottery that has no counterpart in the field of ceramics. Emperors and kings, queens and princesses, poets and preachers, actors and singers, soldiers and sportsmen provide ample scope for most collectors; for those who must have something more recherché there are figures and groups showing murderers and their victims, their homes and their haunts. In this manifestation of a true popular art, aimed at the taste of the humble folk of town and country alike, there is something for everyone.

Mr. Latham is the author of *Victorian Staffordshire Portrait Figures for the Small Collector* (London, 1953).

*Victoria–Albert.* Victoria's accession to the throne really started the cavalcade of Victorian portrait figures. The enthronement of a pretty young queen who promptly made a romantic marriage and then proceeded to fill the nursery with dimpled royal babies provided the Staffordshire potters with ideal subjects—and how they rose to the occasion! Representations of the royal family alone would fill a large cabinet, and the figures of Victoria and Albert together are numbered by the dozen.

The portrait figures vary in height from a twenty-four-inch model of Garibaldi to dainty little six-inch figurines; this group is 8 inches high. *Illustrations are by courtesy of Alec Tiranti, Ltd; except as noted, photographs are by Stanley Way.*

*Napier* and *Garibaldi.* These figurines of the British military hero and the Italian patriot were obviously modeled as a pair. Garibaldi is wearing his famous red shirt, and Lord Napier of Magdala is dressed in red uniform jacket, white breeches, and jack boots. Each is 8 inches high.

*Empress of France.* Small mounted figures are quite common. This portrait of the beautiful and charming wife of Napoleon III is frequently found in a pair with the emperor. Eugénie's Parisian wardrobe created a sensation in Victorian London and aroused a great deal of envy; here she is wearing a fashionably cut yellow-sprigged riding habit and her hat is encircled by a gay scarf. Height 8 inches.

*Sankey.* Quite a number of the figures are connected with the American scene. These include Benjamin Franklin (whose likeness is frequently labeled "General Washington"), Abraham Lincoln, John Brown, the heavyweight boxing champion Heenan, and several characters from *Uncle Tom's Cabin. Sankey,* of course, represents Ira David Sankey, who with Dwight L. Moody came to London in 1873 to hold revival meetings. These forerunners of Billy Graham were joint authors of the famous hymnbook (Sankey's left hand rests on a copy). This figure and a companion figure of Moody belong to a group of late nineteenth-century characters in what may be called the black-and-white class: they all wear black frock coats and white trousers, a costume that permitted the potter to economize on colors. Height 12 inches.

*Shakespeare.* This one of many representations of Britain's great playwright shows him in pink cloak, yellow sprigged surcoat, yellow breeches, and blue stockings; height 12 inches. Most other versions are based on the monument in Poet's Corner in Westminster Abbey. *Photograph by Runham.*

*King John signing Magna Charta.* When Victorian actor-managers considered the pace of a play too slow they interpolated a scene or two to brighten things up; hence this Staffordshire group represents a Shakespearian scene, although you will not find it in *King John.* It exists in a white and gold version (a popular combination), as well as gaily colored. Height 12 inches.

In theatrical groups the players can often be identified from contemporary prints, since the potters worked from these. *Photograph by Runham.*

*Md. Lind* and *Jullien.* Figures of singers and dancers form a picturesque assembly. There are at least half a dozen pottery portraits of the Swedish Nightingale, who sang in London in 1848, and most of them are charming, colorful, and well modeled. Here she is wearing the costume of Maria, heroine of Donizetti's *Daughter of the Regiment;* the cobalt blue of her jacket is one of the few colors that will endure the heat of the glazing kiln and so could be applied under the glaze.

The companion figure is that of the impresario Louis Jullien, who boasted no less than thirty-six Christian names and was known, not surprisingly, as "the Mons." His coat is of the same blue as Jenny Lind's jacket, and he wears black striped pants. Height of each, 6 inches.

*Departure* and *Return.* These two groups showing the sailor's departure and his return are not strictly Victorian, since the popular contemporary prints from which they were copied date from the days of Nelson and Trafalgar. On the one labeled *Departure* the bedraggled sailor has his few poor belongings in a little bundle, and his sweetheart has a woebegone look; on *Return* he looks much more spruce, her face is rosy and lit up with pleasure, and there is a box at his feet labeled *Dollars*—Spanish, not American, judging from the date.

# A peaceable kingdom of Staffordshire animals

BY JEROME IRVING SMITH

JUST AS THE American Quaker Edward Hicks (1780-1849) was inspired by Isaiah 11:6-9 to paint more than one hundred primitives entitled *The Peaceable Kingdom,* so perhaps were the potters of Staffordshire, when as early as the mid-seventeenth century they began to decorate slipware plates, bowls, mugs, and posset pots with representations of animals.

The earliest known dated piece of Staffordshire salt-glaze ware is a mug of 1701, now in the Stoke-on-Trent Museum, which is decorated with a duck in high relief. From about 1725 to 1775 birds, lions, dogs, rabbits, squirrels, and other creatures became finials on covered creamers, sugar bowls, teapots, coffeepots, and punch pots (Figs. 1, 2). Jaunty lions with upright tails were applied to the sides of teapots along with leaves and berries; rampant lions faced rampant unicorns; dogs sauntered between flowers; impish monkeys climbed tree branches—all in relief. Scratch-blue mugs had exotic birds swooping among acorns, while fish swam between dancing lions and flowers on sgraffito-ware bowls. Around 1740 teapots were molded ludicrously into the shapes of animals, such as a seated camel with its head the spout, or an elephant with its upright trunk the spout and a mischievous monkey the knop on the lid. Still another teapot represents an ornate mansion with a haughty looking dog settled on its roof acting as the knop of the cover. Frequently the spouts of the tea and coffeepots were made to resemble the long necks and heads of ridiculously amiable monsters (Fig. 3), while handles often were dragons, dolphins, or other animals. Lion's heads were impressed on the knees of footed containers (Fig. 2).

The first Staffordshire animal figures were covered jugs, tobacco jars, salt containers, mustard pots, and other utilitarian receptacles. Owls decorated with combed slip and dating from the last quarter of the seventeenth century were in reality jugs with detachable heads which also served as cups. Later, owls were fabricated in salt-glaze but disappeared from the Staffordshire market with the discontinuance of salt-glaze about 1775. About 1690 vases in the form of seated cats were made of redware decorated with white slip in dotted and striped bands. From the late seventeenth to the mid-eighteenth century tobacco jars were often molded in the shape of bears with detachable heads and with or without pottery chains dangling from their noses and cubs or even men clasped in their forepaws (Fig. 4).

Staffordshire kilns produced equally useful sauceboats in the shape of ducks, swans, and even fish. Standing cows first appeared as creamers, their curled tail the handle, their open mouth the spout, and a small cap on their back to cover the hole used to fill them. Pitchers in the shape of cows were introduced late in the seventeenth century and continued to be made well into the Victorian period.

Fig. 1. Salt-glaze teapot, c. 1740. Height 5 inches. *Greenfield Village and Henry Ford Museum; photograph by Charles T. Miller.*

Fig. 2. Whieldon-type teapot, c. 1760. Height 3¾ inches. The pot is supported by three legs which terminate in lion's-paw feet and have lion's masks impressed on the knees. *Greenfield Village and Henry Ford Museum, Miller photograph.*

Whieldon-type pitchers of this kind added a maid on a milking stool, while nineteenth-century ones did away with the cap on the back, and added a tree trunk to be used as a spill holder, at which point they served not as pitchers but as containers for the thin wax tapers, or spills, used to light candles or oil lamps.

Candlesticks and flower holders further illustrate the Staffordshire potters' fondness for animals (Figs. 5, 6). A vividly enameled salt-glaze candlestick of about 1740[1] shows two feathered cranes facing in opposite directions standing on a flowered base and buttressing a flowered tree trunk into which the candle was set. An uncolored candlestick of the same date with a single crane can be seen in the Glaisher collection at the Fitzwilliam Museum in Cambridge. Rhytons for wine were cast as the heads of foxes (Fig. 7), dogs, deer, cows, sheep, and other animals. Perhaps the quaintest of all the useful animal figures to appear from the Staffordshire kilns were the hedgehog flower holders made between about 1760 and 1825 (Fig. 8).

Domestic animals such as cats and dogs were the first Staffordshire figures to be created without any utilitarian purpose. First offered for sale about 1680, they were sometimes made of buff-color clay decorated either with cream-color slip and brown streaked tortoise-shell glazes or trailed slip markings. Sometimes they had red clay

Fig. 3. Redware coffeepot, c. 1750. Height 9¾ inches. *Greenfield Village and Henry Ford Museum, Miller photograph.*

Fig. 4. Salt-glaze tobacco jar in the form of a bear and its cub, c. 1725. Height 8 inches. The grayish-white body is made hairy with clay frit. The glazed collar of the adult bear is white with purplish-brown decoration. *Greenfield Village and Henry Ford Museum, Miller photograph.*

Fig. 5. Vase attributed to Ralph Wood the elder (1715-1772), c. 1765. Height 7 inches. The birds are yellow, the trunk of the tree pale brown with green leaves, and the base green. *Collection of Helen McGehee.*

Fig. 6. Stag candlestick by Thomas Whieldon (1719-1795), c. 1760. Height 10½ inches. The stag has purplish-brown markings. The back of the *bocage* shows pale-green leaves in an artichokelike arrangement. *Except as noted, illustrations are from the author's collection; photograph by Carl Malotka.*

Fig. 7. Rhyton, or drinking horn, in the form of a fox head, c. 1825. Length 5 inches. *Malotka photograph.*

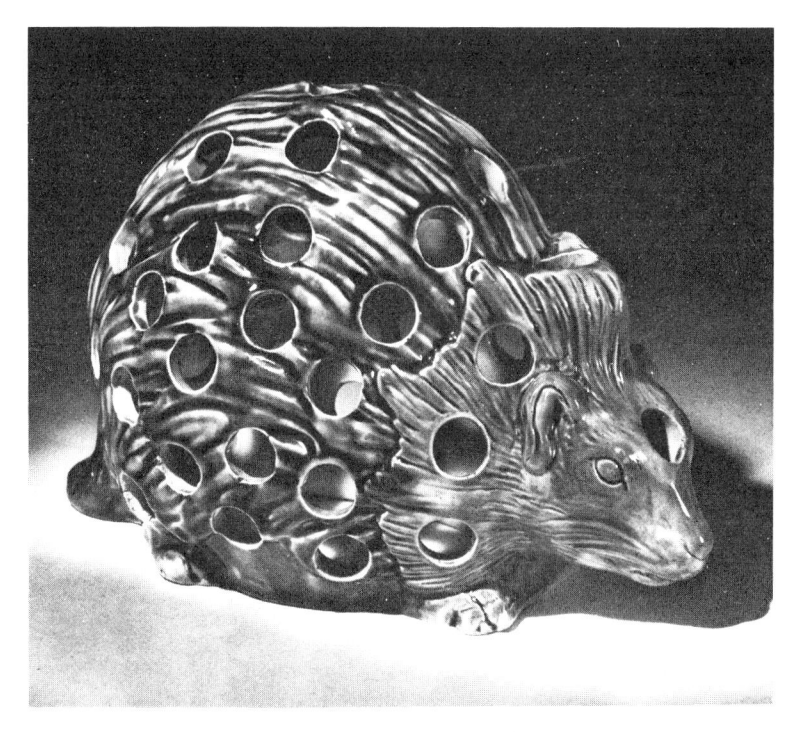

Fig. 8. Whieldon-type flower holder in the form of a hedgehog, c. 1775. The hedgehog is tortoise-shell splashed with greens and yellows. Length 9⅝, height 9 inches. *Greenfield Village and Henry Ford Museum, Miller photograph.*

bodies dotted with cream-color slip. It is possible that the delftware owls and cats created at Lambeth a decade or more earlier prompted the Staffordshire potters to issue pottery domestic animals that soon came to include roosters, hens, rams, lambs alone or with ewes, and horses, most of which had riders.

Many early Staffordshire animal figures were made to resemble natural stone or wood. This striated effect was obtained by blending narrow strips of different colored clays, some of which had been tinted with manganese or cobalt. A pair of hawks in the Burnap collection at the William Rockhill Nelson Gallery and Atkins Museum of Fine Arts in Kansas City, Missouri, are veined in this fashion in blue and dark gray. In the same collection a lion and two cats of about 1745 to 1750 are veined in orange, brown, and cream. These figures bear a striking resemblance to Chinese examples of the T'ang dynasty.

Little by little the Staffordshire potters began to copy the Chinese ceramic wares imported into England in the late seventeenth and early eighteenth centuries. About 1750, for example, Thomas Whieldon made tortoise-shell glaze water buffaloes which in the Oriental manner were surmounted by herdsmen or boys, and were even occasionally flanked by peach trees.[2]

155

Fig. 9. Whieldon-type lion, c. 1775. Length 8½, height 7 inches. *Greenfield Village and Henry Ford Museum, Miller photograph.*

Fig. 10. Whieldon-type lion, c. 1770. Length 4⅜, height 2¾ inches. The lion's face is said to be that of the statesman William Pitt the elder (1708-1778). The sponged glazes are predominantly blue-gray with touches of mustard yellow. *Malotka photograph.*

Fig. 11. Whieldon-type pipe in the form of a snake, c. 1775. Length 9 inches. The body of the snake is green, the tail and head light brown underglaze. *Malotka photograph.*

From the standpoint of craftsmanship, fineness of design and modeling, imagination, and the use of lovely soft glazes, Thomas Whieldon (see Figs. 2, 8-11) and his contemporaries Ralph Wood the elder (see Figs. 5, 12, 13) and his son, known as Ralph Wood the younger (see Fig. 14), were without peers. Each of these men produced examples of a wide variety of animals. Two figure groups by the Ralph Woods strongly suggest the inspiration of Isaiah 11:6, "The wolf shall also dwell with the lamb, and the leopard shall lie down with the kid; and the calf and the young lion and the fatling together; and a little child shall lead them." One of these groups is a pair—a lion and a lioness with a playful cupid on the back of each. The other is a relief-modeled plaque of a child riding a lion and nursing a lamb. Whieldon's great achievement was a tortoise-shell glaze splashed with colors obtained from oxides of cobalt, iron, and copper. He even produced black ware decorated with gold on a red clay body. The

Fig. 12. Stag by Ralph Wood the elder, c. 1760. Height 5 inches. The horns are deep brown, the sponging on the body yellow and tan, and the base deep-green underglaze. *Malotka photograph.*

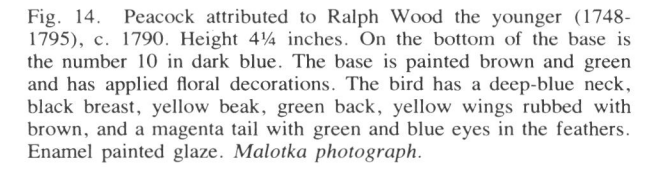

Fig. 13. Pair of dogs by Ralph Wood the elder, c. 1760. Height 2¾ inches. They are covered with a deep-green underglaze. *Miller photograph.*

Fig. 14. Peacock attributed to Ralph Wood the younger (1748-1795), c. 1790. Height 4¼ inches. On the bottom of the base is the number 10 in dark blue. The base is painted brown and green and has applied floral decorations. The bird has a deep-blue neck, black breast, yellow beak, green back, yellow wings rubbed with brown, and a magenta tail with green and blue eyes in the feathers. Enamel painted glaze. *Malotka photograph.*

Fig. 15. Pratt-type cat, c. 1790. Height 4½ inches.

157

Fig. 16. Lamb with ewe by Ralph Salt (1782-1846), c. 1825. Height 6 inches. On the back is the impressed mark SALT. *Malotka photograph.*

Woods' animals owe their attractiveness to their harmonious tones of metallic colors such as manganese purple, copper green, iron yellow, and cobalt blue. All three potters possessed the subtlety and ingenuity of their Chinese predecessors which no Staffordshire potters before or since have quite been able to capture.

Later Staffordshire potters also created animals of great appeal. Although their creatures were crude and often garishly colored, they had in many cases an innocent, childlike charm which reminds one of the quaint simplicity of the early Staffordshire slipware. Felix Pratt (for whom a type of ware was named; see Fig. 15) painted his creatures from a distinctive palette of high-temperature colors often spotted and splashed with various yellows, mustard browns, greens, and blues. John Walton and Ralph Salt (see Fig. 16) sheltered their rather thickly modeled sheep and other animals under a flowered, leafy *bocage*. Obadiah Sherratt, whose animal groups were mostly bull-baiting groups, provided four and sometimes six-legged platforms for them. Sampson Smith was one of the developers of the flat-backed mantel ornaments which were introduced in the 1840's (see Fig. 17). These were often fashioned in the form of zebras, the ever-popular lion, goats, and especially spaniels and poodles.

A collection of Staffordshire animals, whether domestic or wild, offers an Edenlike peaceable kingdom verifying Isaiah's prophecy.

Fig. 17. Pair of birds, c. 1840. Height 10⅛ inches. These flat-backed mantel ornaments are in the style of Sampson Smith (1813-1878). *Malotka photograph.*

Fig. 18. Bank in the form of a spaniel's head, c. 1860. Height 4¼ inches. *Malotka photograph.*

---

[1] Illustrated in Herbert Read, *Staffordshire Pottery Figures* (Boston, 1929), Pl. 3.
[2] The manifest for an English ship sailing from China to England in 1704 lists miniature parrots, boys on water buffaloes, pug dogs, Chinese hound dogs, and other toy ceramic figures. (The manuscript manifest is in the collection of Mrs. Lammot Copeland).

KING CHARLES II
After the battle of Worcester, 1651, Charles fled, and, it is reported, disguised as a servant, he concealed himself for twenty-four hours in an oak tree at Boscobel

This plate, made at Lambeth (*1660*), pictures the oak and the royal fugitive, whose initials are added as an aid to identification. *From the Willett Collection, Brighton*

## Possibilities in Ceramic Portraiture

*By* ALBERT LEE, *author of "Portraits in Pottery"*

EVEN in earliest times, pottery was employed as a vehicle for honoring individuals or commemorating events. Upon their vases the ancient Greeks portrayed their gods and heroes; the Roman amphoræ often glorified war; and when men began to fashion platters and plates of clay, they decorated their choicest wares, crude as they may then have been, with effigies of their rulers. Thus was prepared the way for a delightful phase of ceramic collecting. Assembling portraits in pottery has become a pursuit which is enlisting enthusiasts so rapidly that good specimens are steadily increasing in value.

The collector in this field is not trammeled by the restrictions that often confine the efforts and hamper the ambitions of other china-seekers. He is not limited to any one period, or type, or make, or even quality, in the ware of his choosing. Any ceramic material, molded to portraiture or imprinted with the likeness of any character in history or fiction, comes within the sphere of his acquisitive scheme. He will, quite naturally, prefer and seek out items of eighteenth and nineteenth-century

VOLTAIRE (*left*)
Black basaltes bust by Wedgwood, modeled after the original by Rosset. Produced at Etruria in *1775*. *Height: 4¾ inches.*
*From the Victoria and Albert Museum*

ADMIRAL LORD RODNEY (*right*)
A mug representing the British victor over the French Admiral de Grasse in the West Indies. Inscribed about the rim: *Success to Lord Rodney*. Produced in Staffordshire about *1782*. *Height: 4¼ inches.*
*From the Victoria and Albert Museum*

159

November, 1931

HENRI DE LA ROCHEJACQUELEIN
Perhaps a genuine plate of the period of the Revolution. This young man, an ardent royalist, led the peasants of the Vendée against the republican forces. He thus met his death in 1794. The inscription reads, "If I advance, follow me; if I retreat, kill me; if I die, avenge me." The majority of such plates are quite new, though "antiqued"

QUEEN CAROLINE
Transfer-print portrait of the wife of George IV. Staffordshire, 1820. A great variety of portrait pieces was made at the time of the Queen's divorce in 1820.
Diameter: 6 inches.
From the Metropolitan Museum of Art

manufacture, and, indeed, earlier examples if he can find them; but a portrait made even day before yesterday fits perfectly into his considered plan. And, let me say, some very excellent portrait jugs have been produced in England within the last fifteen years, notably those designed by Owen Hale, R. A., Sir F. Carruthers Gould, and Percy Metcalfe.

Not only do faces of the great appear modeled in the round, as on Toby jugs, mask jugs, and stoneware flasks, but they are encountered as transfer prints on pitchers, plates, mugs, teapots, bowls, cups, plaques — indeed, on practically every form of ware. In addition, the potters of Staffordshire, Rockingham, and Chelsea, as well as French and German makers, produced hundreds of portrait statuettes, figures, busts, and groups. All in all the variety in ceramic portraiture is infinite, and, furthermore, historically illuminating. I am afraid that before I became actively engaged in collecting portrait pieces, I knew very little, definitely or specifically, about English history or French history. But the minute I began collecting English and French, and even American, portrait pieces, I found myself compelled to absorb a great amount of very real knowledge concerning relative periods of art and the succession of historic events.

For instance, I surmise that we all of us think of George III of England as a crabbed old gentleman in periwig and breeches who lived in a remote age; while we look upon Queen Victoria's reign as an era closely associated with our own. As a matter of fact, however, Victoria was born before the death of George III, and she ascended the throne only a brief seventeen years after the latter event. The portrait collector must be aware of such chronological conjunctions. Gradually he finds himself on intimate terms with George III, George IV, and William IV, as he acquires specimens bearing their portraits or those of other notable figures of their day.

The best English ceramic period began in the late eighteenth century under George III, with Ralph and Enoch Wood, Josiah Wedgwood, Felix Pratt, and other potters as its leaders. It closed with the decadence that set in during the first half of Victoria's reign. Thus, generally speaking, the best portrait pieces were made between 1790 and 1850, though amid the great variety and quantity produced, both good and bad occur. The earliest English efforts, designs in slip decoration on plates and platters, were followed by crude attempts at modeling by Astbury and his contemporaries. John Dwight of Fulham is probably the first of the English potters deserving recognition as a first-class sculptor. His busts of James II and of Prince Rupert, judged even by modern standards, are master works.

But it was the Wood family — the two Ralphs, Aaron, and Enoch — who developed the potting of clay figures into a

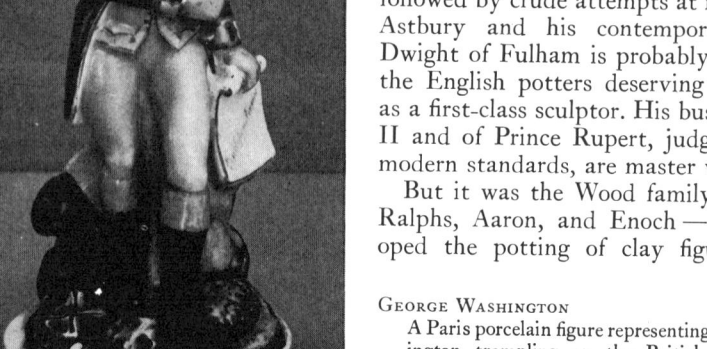

GEORGE WASHINGTON
A Paris porcelain figure representing George Washington trampling on the British flag and the British lion, and holding in his hand a scroll inscribed *Independence*. Marked *Badin Frères à Paris* (c. 1810).
From the Metropolitan Museum of Art

160

typical English art. Many of their earlier pieces represent mythological characters, but Enoch, whose producing life covered a period of nearly sixty years, made countless portraits of contemporary characters during one of the most important eras of the world's history — the last quarter of the 1700's, and the first quarter of the 1800's.

Wedgwood, too, was accomplishing his best work in these late eighteenth-century years, and made portrait pieces, both figures and busts, almost too numerous to mention; while his jasperware medallions may be counted in the thousands. Both Wood and Wedgwood were imitated and plagiarized by their contemporaries, until figuremaking (much of it original after the impetus had been given) became one of the principal industries of Staffordshire.

Throughout the first half of the nineteenth century Staffordshire figures, generally known as cottage ornaments, enjoyed a great demand. They were sold freely at provincial fairs, and the contemporary plenitude of naval and military heroes encouraged the potters to cater to hero worship by making a wide variety of figures, busts, and groups, representing Nelson, Duncan, Wellington, and Rodney, in addition to more fanciful subjects.

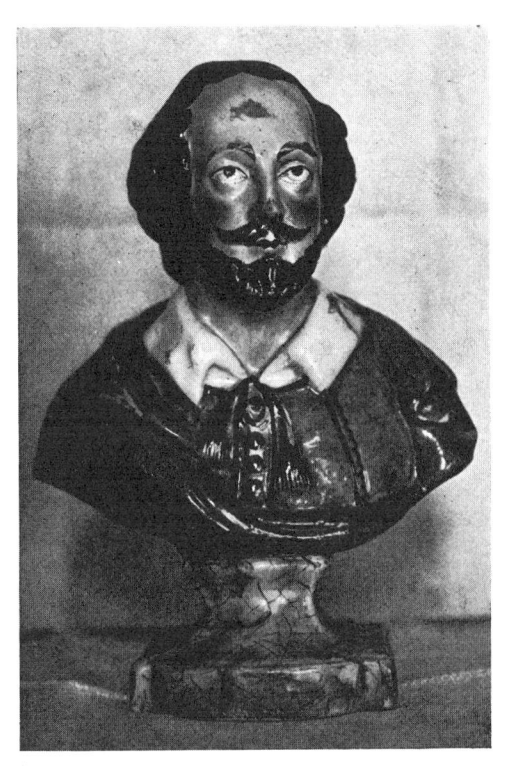

Nor was the Reverend John Wesley neglected. That great Methodist revivalist twice visited the Staffordshire district, where he created a profound impression among the potters. It is perhaps no exaggeration to state that every Staffordshireman possessed of any skill as a modeler tried his hand at a bust or a figure of Wesley. No wonder that a single collection of Wesleyana in England includes more than four hundred different pottery portraits of the preacher. On the occasion of Wesley's second visit to the potteries, he stayed at the house of Enoch Wood, who seized the opportunity to model the bust that is now considered one of his greatest artistic achievements. At the time, Wood was only twenty-two years of age.

After transfer printing on china had become a thoroughly established, inexpensive process, a vast number of portraits in this technique was produced on tableware, such as jugs, cups, bowls, teapots, and the like, and to a lesser degree on plates. The British potters never made many portraits on plates, preferring to adorn such inviting surfaces with scenic illustrations, for which they developed a vast market both at home and in the United States. The French and the Dutch, on the contrary, used plates extensively for portraiture.

During the Napoleonic wars, and under George IV and William IV, transfer-printed jugs were a favorite vehicle for portraits, both in cartoon form and as memorial souvenirs. Particularly at the beginning of George IV's reign, when the unregenerate monarch divorced Queen Caroline, such jugs, bowls, and other pieces were made in considerable quantity. A collection of Queen Caroline pottery alone would fill many cabinets.

A decline in the art of figuremaking became apparent in the early part of Victoria's reign, despite a lively production of portrait figures and groups of the Queen and her family. Mass production was already beginning to take its toll of quality. Nevertheless, the works of this period afford a presentation of folk pottery, and it is to be regretted that up to the present so little care has been taken for their preservation.

SHAKESPEARE
Staffordshire earthenware bust, c. *1820*, decorated with brilliant enamel colorings. *Height: 8 inches*

NAPOLEON AND HIS NEMESES, WELLINGTON AND NELSON (*above*)
The Napoleon and Nelson jugs are of Lambeth salt-glaze stoneware. Uniform brown coloring. The Napoleon jug was produced by Stephen Green (*1820*); the Nelson by Doulton and Watts (*1820*); both pieces marked. Wellington is of colored and glazed Staffordshire ware, c. *1815*

KING WILLIAM IV (*left*)
Brown, salt-glazed stoneware flask with ochre-dip top, cartooning the King at the time of the Parliamentary debates over the Reform Laws. Flasks of this type were also made portraying Lord Grey, Lord Brougham, and Daniel O'Connell, the Irish patriot. Doulton and Watts, Lambeth, *1832*. *Height: 7 ½ inches*

LORD BROUGHAM (*right*)
Brown stoneware spirit flask, Lambeth, *1832*, portraying Lord Brougham, one of the principal figures in Parliament during the Reform Law debates. He was also chief defender of Queen Caroline during her trial for divorce

WELLINGTON JUG
Staffordshire decorated in colors

WELLINGTON
In 1828 Wellington became Prime Minister, under George IV. He held high office under William IV and under Victoria, and fought as many battles in Parliament as in the field. This figure represents him as he appeared in the early days of Victoria's reign, *c. 1840*

WELLINGTON JUG
With Rockingham's rich brown glaze

Several important collections of Staffordshire pottery are to be found in English museums, notably — to mention but a few — at Hanley, Etruria, Cambridge, South Kensington, and Brighton. But these collections, although they include many important portrait pieces, are based rather on types of ware than upon what the specimens may pictorially represent or historically imply. The Willett Collection at Brighton comes near to being an exception to this rule, since it exemplifies its donor's belief that national history may, to a large extent, be traced in the homely pottery of a country. Mr. Willett maintained that, while a piece of English pottery may derive interest from its place of manufacture, its design, its maker, its date, its form, or its color, yet all these features are of secondary importance. His own intention was to demonstrate how the incidents of English life, both public and domestic, have found an expression in pottery. The resulting Brighton Museum collection consists of over seventeen hundred pieces, mostly figures, groups, and transfer prints on jugs and other vessels. It is one of the most interesting collections of pottery known to me.

Within the space at my disposal it is impossible to discuss the topic of ceramic portraiture in any detail; but it is perhaps well to remark that, after the late war, a revival of portrait wares occurred, and that today the collector may acquire many excellent modern pieces of genuine merit,

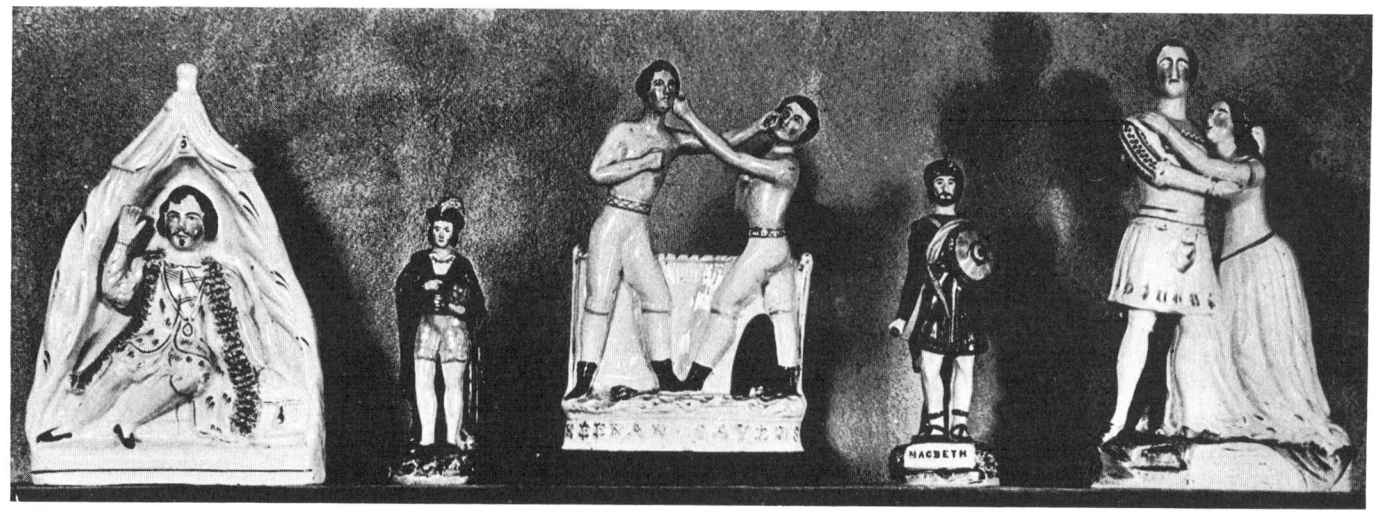

SPORT AND THE DRAMA
Edmund Kean, the noted Shakespearean actor of the early nineteenth century, is here shown in his greatest rôle, that of King Richard III. Kean acted, as a boy, before George III, and, in his later years, in New York, in November, 1820. Beside him stands Hamlet. The central group pictures an international prize fight — John Heenan, the American champion, *vs.* Tom Sayers, champion of England. The battle took place at Farnborough, in April, 1860, lasted two hours and twenty minutes, and was officially called a draw when stopped by the referee because neither fighter was in condition to continue. Next stands Macbeth, and beside him are Romeo and Juliet. These pieces are all of Staffordshire ware. Kean dates *c. 1830*; the others *c. 1860*

162

FULL-LENGTH FIGURES
The central group portrays King John signing *Magna Charta*, in his tent on the field at Runnymede. The two horsemen are Dick Turpin and Tom King, noted eighteenth-century highwaymen. All are Staffordshire cottage ornaments of the Victorian period

which in time will rank with some of the best produced in the past.

The field of French ceramic portraiture is almost as broad as that of the English type, although the variety is perhaps less extraordinary. In the early nineteenth century several series of French dishes were produced with portraits of Louis XVI and members of his court, and about 1840 a number of well-executed transfer-printed plates picturing incidents in the career of Napoleon. Of the genuineness of the innumerable faïence plates decorated with the named portraits of various heroes and heroines of the French Revolution I have serious doubts.

It was at Sèvres that the largest quantity of portrait pieces was made, from the mid-eighteenth century onward, even until today. These are almost always in bisque porcelain, the majority being busts, and many are exquisite works of art.

The French potters were less inclined to the making of popular figures than were their over-channel neighbors, and, being a wine-drinking rather than an ale-drinking people, they produced comparatively few jugs of the Toby type. Nevertheless, in the potteries of Paris and the neighborhood, figuremaking was quite extensively practiced from the early nineteenth century on. The figures were of porcelain, usually quite elaborately colored, and are now known under the general and somewhat misleading term of "Old Paris" ware. Porcelain statuettes of the Louis Philippe era modeled by Jacob Petit are today quite highly esteemed. And, again, in recent years the demand for so-called historic figures has stimulated such competent firms as Sampson to considerable activity in manufacturing the figures of Francis I, Henry IV, Napoleon, and George Washington, some reproducing early models and some, virtually new conceptions. Elaborately colored and well-modeled busts of early French kings in enameled earthenware are another recent product.

Many portrait pieces were also made in Saxony, of the

JUGS OF THE TOBY TYPE
The standing figure of Nelson is one of the most popular representations of the British naval hero, made in many different Staffordshire potteries and still being produced. The Wellington jug is another favorite, and may be found in various sizes and colorings. Napoleon was produced at the Columbian Art Pottery, in Trenton, in 1876, for the Philadelphia Centennial. Washington and Roosevelt were modeled by Isaac Broome and produced by Lenox in Trenton, in 1896 and 1909 respectively

#### AN INTERESTING GROUP
The portrait jugs of Pope Leo XIII and George Washington were modeled by S. W. Starkey in 1892 and produced in East Liverpool, Ohio. The McKinley jug was made in Baltimore, in 1896, when the employees of the Bennett Pottery Company visited Canton, Ohio, and marched in a political parade, each carrying one of these jugs. The other two pieces are Staffordshire about 1880, one representing Mr. Gladstone and his ax, with which he chopped down a tree every morning before breakfast, and the other representing Mr. Pickwick

exquisite and daintily decorated porcelain for which Meissen is famous. The British copied and adapted many of these figures. From Italy too we may obtain portrait pieces. But my feeling is that Americans will always find their greatest enjoyment and greatest success in collecting English specimens, many of which, during the past hundred years, have been brought to the United States.

American portraiture of American manufacture is, apparently, up to the present, a more or less unexplored field. No patient investigator has as yet recorded the performance of our native potters in this direction. But I fear that it has been insignificant.

S. W. Starkey of East Liverpool, Ohio, modeled portrait jugs of Washington, William Penn, and Pope Leo XIII, in the last decade of the nineteenth century. Isaac Broome and W. W. Gallimore, two able modelers of Trenton, New Jersey, produced excellent figure jugs of Napoleon, Washington, William Penn, and Theodore Roosevelt. During the last presidential campaign, face jugs of Herbert Hoover and Governor Smith, the candidates, were made at Syracuse. This short list pretty nearly covers American-made ceramic portraiture of this type. At Bennington, about 1857, a few Toby jugs were produced, one being a copy of an English Rockingham face-jug of Wellington; another, having a booted leg for a handle, is frequently but incorrectly listed as a portrait of Benjamin Franklin.

What our potteries have made in the way of transfer prints in connection with our national history is a story still unwritten.

#### VARIOUS PERSONAGES
The large bust is one of the many Wesley portraits popular in the early nineteenth century. Next is George Washington. Both pieces are after models by Enoch Wood. In the centre are Bishop Laval of Quebec, and Champlain. These were made in France, in 1908, on the occasion of the tercentenary celebration of the foundation of Quebec. The bust of John Locke is Staffordshire, about 1820. King Edward VII is a match box, of hard paste porcelain, probably made in Germany at the time of his accession in 1901, as indicated by the mourning brassard on his left sleeve

# V  Blue Printed Wares

The technique of transfer printing on ceramics was developed in the early 1750s. It was probably first used on small enamel boxes and other similar wares made at Battersea and Bilston and then spread rapidly into other fields. The success of the Worcester porcelain factory was based in part on its early exploitation of this cheap and practical method of decoration, while the popularity of creamware was greatly helped by its extensive use of transfer printing.

Printing, or the transferring of an image from an engraved copper plate to the surface of the biscuit-fired ceramic body by means of tissue paper, was clearly an example of the application of the technology of one field to that of another. All the early experiments were undertaken by printers rather than potters, and many famous potters, for example Minton and Turner, started life as engravers. Although different colors were used from the early days, the blue achieved from cobalt rapidly became dominant. The reasons for this have never really been adequately explained, for the obvious influence of Chinese blue and white porcelain is only a part of the story. Perhaps the preference for blue was actually established by the color of food, blue being the one color that never occurs.

The Chinese influence was more significant in the choice of patterns, for throughout the latter years of the 18th century the majority of the engraved patterns were based on a curious European interpretation of oriental themes, a quite fanciful style commonly known as *chinoiserie*. Because of its continual popularity, the willow pattern is the most obvious example. Despite the many attempts that have been made to prove otherwise, the pattern is totally English, having first appeared during the 1790s. Similarly, all the legends popularly associated with the pattern were developed only after it had been in common use for some years.

By the end of the 18th century, blue-printed wares were being made at every British center of ceramic manufacture. They were cheap, simple to produce, and so could be made in vast quantities by relatively unskilled labor. Patterns were copied, adapted, and then copied again from one factory to another. Such prodigious output forced the potters to develop new markets, the most significant of which was North America. Although English potters had been sending their wares across the Atlantic since the 17th century, it was only during the 1830s and 1840s that this trade achieved the levels associated with it today. To the manufacturers in Staffordshire and elsewhere of cheap printed earthenwares, North America represented a market of unbelievable size, able to absorb all their over-production, and still come back for more. Many British companies established complex networks of agents across North America, while some, such as Andrew Stevenson and J & R Clews, devoted themselves so extensively to the North American trade that their products were virtually unknown in their home town. As a result, items considered extremely rare by English collectors of blue-printed wares can still survive in thousands, if not millions in North America.

The demands of this new market affected dramatically the patterns used. Broadly, the pseudo-Chinese designs did not appeal in America, and so these were replaced by series of historical and topographical views, some realistic, and some as fanciful as the early oriental designs. These simple wares reflect all contemporary artistic styles, such as the gothic and rococo revivals, as well as the popular interest in naturalism and natural phenomena. Many designs were borrowed directly from contemporary books and prints, and indeed many retailers actually supplied the originals that the potters' engravers were to follow. In this way, many wares were decorated with American views, or scenes from American history that would have been quite incomprehensible to the English engravers. These many designs made especially for the North American market are among the most interesting aspects of mid-19th-century Staffordshire production. The whole subject of blue printed wares, however, has been extensively researched and studied in North America, with the result that English collectors and scholars lag far behind in the appreciation of their own products. Ironically, for many years the only way for English collectors to find out about 19th-century transfer printed wares was for them to subscribe to American and Canadian antiques magazines.

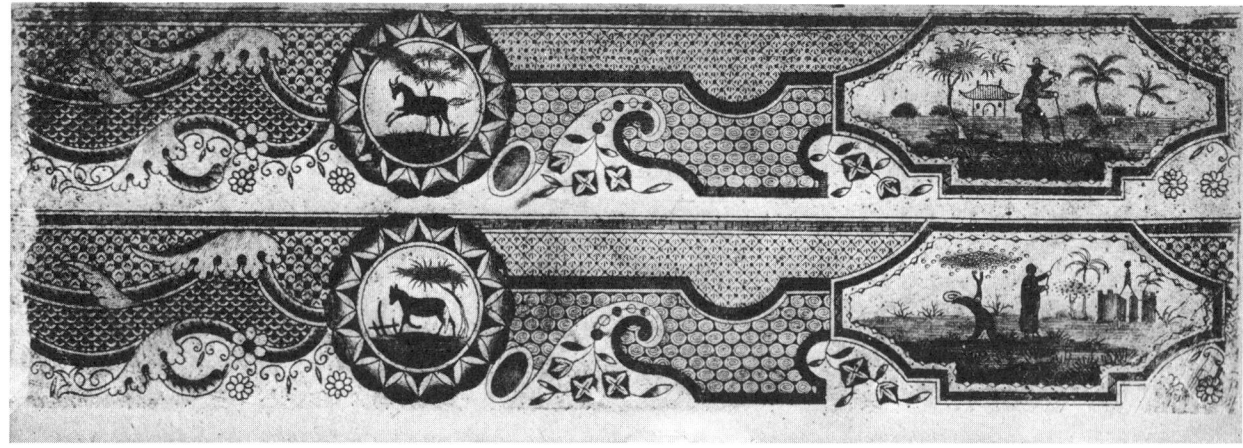

*Fig. 1* — PAPER PRINT FOR TRANSFER
Spode border design for platters. The printed strips would be cut apart with scissors just before application to the ware. The motives are characteristically oriental. Though transfer printing on porcelain made great progress at Caughley under Turner, Josiah Spode introduced into Staffordshire the process of underglaze-blue transfer on earthenware. The border illustrated is one of his earliest, about 1784

# Staffordshire Ware in a Nutshell

*By* GREGOR NORMAN-WILCOX

*Note.* Awareness of the widespread uncertainty among owners and beginning collectors regarding the factors of desirability in the Staffordshire goods of the first half of the 1800's prompted the preparation of these notes. Study of both text and illustrations should help the reader to perceive why some examples of the wares discussed bring fairly high prices in the market, while others are considered virtually worthless. At the same time, the author's hints as to the acquisition of worthy but hitherto neglected patterns should not be slighted. — *The Editor.*

"STAFFORDSHIRE?" The antiques addict in his rounds among the innumerable American shops and shoppes dedicated to the preservation of more or less venerable household gear will be shown a baffling variety of wares, all called by that one name. The articles offered may range from a blurred blue sauce dish marked *Chusan, J. Clementson,* at fifty cents, to a busily panoramic blue platter marked *New York from Brooklyn Heights, A. Stevenson,* at several hundred times the sum asked for the *Chusan.*

Why, asks the marveling neophyte, this amazing difference in valuations? Is the dealer suffering from delirium, or does he really know what he is about? Perhaps some element of rarity, apparent only to the initiate, accounts for the widely separated price levels; or is there Staffordshire and *Staffordshire?* And how does one discover which is which?

The answer is to be learned only by a consideration of certain dry facts, and facts are not fun. But we shall deliver the necessary points as briefly and painlessly as possible.

*The Body*

To begin with, *Staffordshire* is a general term designating common earthenware of many types, made in the English district of Staffordshire, where for centuries potteries and potters have flourished. In these notes, however, we confine ourselves exclusively to those various Staffordshire wares made during the first half of the nineteenth century, and decorated with scenes, flowers, or portraits, printed on the ware in color, sometimes in black.

It is necessary to understand that pottery of this kind was quantity-production merchandise, made for wide sale at popular prices, and intended to appeal to markets not in England alone but on the European Continent, and in the United States. Staffordshire found such favor in this country as soon to supersede the pewter and woodenware which had been in general use in average American homes. Potters prominent in the history of the Staffordshire industry devoted their best efforts to making ware of this kind. Spode II, Enoch Wood, Adams, and the Stevensons were conspicuous in the earlier period, while later work bears such names as Mayer, Jackson, the Ridgways, and Clementson. It was the aggressive enterprise of these men, applied to developing a satisfactory "body" (as the ware itself, exclusive of glaze or decoration, is called) better and cheaper than that of Continental faïence, which eventually won them a vast market. Spode II, before 1800, had perfected his "new fayence"; Chetham & Wooley's "pearl ware" appeared in 1795; about 1805 Spode II introduced his "stone china," which became the model for other potters. Charles Mason secured a patent on his celebrated "ironstone china" in 1813 or 1814. And the subsequent years found most of the

*Fig. 2* — TRANSFER-PRINTED TEAPOT (*probably before 1825*)
By Hilditch & Sons of Longton. Here the still popular Chinese motives recur. Imitation of Spode is fairly obvious. In this instance the design was transfer printed under the glaze and after firing was colored by hand with bright enamels. This method was first employed by Spode

March, 1936

166

Staffordshire factories experimenting with "patent" and "improved" bodies of one kind or another.

The less desirable bodies were light, porous, and likely to show surface imperfections. In the 1830's we find a more solid, smoother body in general use. By the 1840's the market was quite given over to such heavy, thick wares as Mason's "granite china," Minton's "new stone," Ridgway's "stone ware," and the "opaque china" that was made by almost everyone. Earthenware glazes in general, during this period of development (if hardly of progress), gradually lost their earlier softness and depth (juiciness, some have called this rich quality of the older glazes). The latest productions display a glassy coldness of surface quite in sympathy with the spirit of contemporary arts in general. In short, as tableware became harder and less fragile in body, and less permeable in glaze, and thus approached mechanical perfection, it steadily declined in æsthetic appeal.

*The Decoration*

The story of nineteenth-century color-printed Staffordshire is the story of the rise and decline of transfer printing. It was transfer printing, a facile and inexpensive process of pottery decoration, that made possible the large-scale output of Staffordshire. And it was, in part, the abandonment of this process in favor of still cheaper modes that brought the industry to an unhappy era of uninspired mechanized production. The name "transfer printing" describes the principle involved. The required pattern is first engraved by hand on a copperplate, from which a tissue-paper print, called a "pull" or "proof" is taken. Then, by pressing this tissue against a piece of undecorated ware, the design is deposited or "transferred" to the surface of the article. Glazing and baking complete the process. (This is fully demonstrated by a picture sequence published in ANTIQUES for January 1930, *p. 49*.)

*Fig. 3* — EARLY NOVELTIES IN BLUE STAFFORDSHIRE (*probably first quarter of 1800's*)
During the first quarter of the 1800's English potters sought new decorative themes for their earthenware. The three platters illustrated exemplify departures in several directions. *The Game Keeper* (maker unknown) portrays an English sporting scene, and would therefore be considered more desirable than the more romantic *Locarno* (by Spode) at the left, or the romantically exotic *Absalom's Tomb* in Petra, Transjordania (by Wedgwood), at the right below. Nevertheless, since all these scenes are representative rather than merely fantastic, they qualify as collectibles

As it was necessary to use separate "proofs" for each step of the printing — one for the centre view, another for the border, and others for handles, spouts, and feet — transfer-printed wares invariably reveal evidences of their hand production. Breaks may be found in the running motives of the border, where the design at start and finish of the printed "proof" will not neatly join. Small printed areas on spout and handle will not be complete in themselves, but are obviously sections taken at random from the border design.

Transfer printing, perfected in England by Sadler and Green about 1756, was developed for wider commercial use by Thomas Turner (working at Caughley 1772–1799), who in 1780 introduced the underglaze-blue willow pattern which has even to this day been repeated by other manufacturers.

Spode I, Minton, Wedgwood, and other potters were not slow, however, to adopt a style which swept so quickly into demand; and by the turn of the century, deep-blue transfer-printed wares in the Oriental taste were widely offered. But in due course (roughly, 1800–1820), purely oriental themes were replaced by naïve anglicized versions, in which the customary mandarins inhabit Gothic ruins, huge and improbable Eastern flowers enliven representations of the familiar English countryside, and border designs betray an unblushing indebtedness to oriental precedent.

Shortly before 1820, when transfer printing itself had ceased to be a novelty, someone, today unidentified, conceived the idea of using views of actual places instead of the imaginary landscapes hitherto employed. An immediate impetus was afforded the industry. Views of English cities, manors, and cathedrals, scenes in France and Italy, pictures of naval engagements and portraits of their heroes, followed. What is more, the American market was courted with a series of subjects depicting American

167

*Fig. 4* — "Ostend Gate at Bruges" (*probably first quarter, 1800's*) Maker unknown. An excellent example of the pleasing foreign views to be found on old Staffordshire. Less costly than American scenes, but, aside from national preferences, quite as well worth having and often more decorative

buildings, picturesque views, and notable events. Deep blue was the color used. Sales boomed; the potters throve. This last is the type of pictorial ware known today as "American-historical Staffordshire." Literally tons of it were sold at prices expressed in pennies, and not, as today, in dollars.

deep blue purposely applied while the pottery was still moist in order to produce the smudgy uncertainty from which its name derives. Equally regrettable was the advent of an unpleasant faded brown-purple shade known, for some obscure reason, as "mulberry" — a perpetration destined to delight the 1850's but to distress the 1930's. At times, in a desperate excess of ornamentive zeal, color prints were touched up by hand in colored enamels, over the glaze. Doubtless intended to lend an effect of variegated richness, the treatment seldom succeeded

*Fig. 5* — "New York from Heights near Brooklyn" (*c. 1825*)
By A. Stevenson after W. G. Wall. The latter, an Irish artist, came to the United States in 1818 and in subsequent years for lengthy visits, during which he painted many landscapes. Not a few of these views were produced on earthenware by the Staffordshire potters. A platter like that illustrated recently brought $240 at the American Art Association Anderson Galleries, New York. Size, rarity, perfect condition, age, and the delineation of a local scene were all factors in this valuation. A still scarcer platter by R. Stevenson & Williams, *Esplanade & Castle Garden, New York*, brought $350 at the same sale

*Fig. 6* — A Doctor Syntax Platter (*c. 1825*)
Oddly enough, American and English collectors are alike partial to the earthenware issued by James Clews of Cobridge and adorned with scenes after Rowlandson's portrayals of the adventures of Doctor Syntax. The *Pat in the Pond* platter illustrated brought $200 at the Hudnut sale of 1926 at the American Art Association, Inc. (See Antiques for December 1927)

By 1828, when the public had wearied of the invariable deep-blue prints, the Staffordshire potters responded by announcing transfer prints in light colors — pink, green, light blue, brown, lavender, and so on. Sales again boomed. But light-color transfer prints had arrived only to be eclipsed. For presently, not long after 1830, color printing came under the baneful influence of lithography. Lo! said the potters — if the same effects can be produced by the cheaper lithographic method, why continue the old-fashioned transfer printing? And so, developed in the light colors, began the deadly accuracy, the awful perfection, of the final period of color printing.

Views of actual places continued to be made, occasionally, through the 1850's. But a far greater proportion of the output of the 1840's and 1850's was merely decorative. Pastoral scenes, views of imaginary pseudo-classic gardens with torrential fountains, strange perversions of the earlier *chinoiserie* prevailed.

The popular "flow blue" now came into being, an ill-advised

in being other than crudely gaudy. It has little appeal today.

Finally, after about 1830, it became customary to name all views of subjects, whatever their character. Nondescript floral patterns, incongruous Asiatic confections, and sentimental barnyard fantasies bore such elegant titles as *Doric*, *Scinde*, *Oriental*, and *Medici*. And thus did color-printed Staffordshire pass into oblivion, pleading a proud, boiled front of respectability.

*Collecting Range*

It must be apparent, even to the most casual reader, that no class of Staffordshire is "collectible" in the same sense or to the same degree as, let us say, soft-paste Vincennes or Sèvres, early Worcester, or the fragile Chelsea. These latter represent the highest form of Western ceramic art; they are desirable partly because of intrinsic excellence, and partly because first-grade specimens are today exceedingly rare.

Staffordshire, on the other hand, with few and notable exceptions, offers no comparable claim to present-day rarity. The ware was turned out in enormous quantities, and many thousands of examples have survived the rigors of a century of household use and adornment. No one will be disposed to crow over-noisily about a possession that may be duplicated at the next street crossing. Nor can it be held that Staffordshire, even in its earlier and worthier estate, is or ever was of the ceramic nobility. It is frankly and always plebeian. It is cottage pottery, most at home with cherry furniture, homely chintzes, and hooked rugs.

The sole point of interest in Staffordshire, then, and the measure of its desirability lie in its surface decoration. The "body" is unimportant to collectors, save as its character serves to confirm the date indicated by the decoration. "Granite" wares, for example, will always be recognized as late; light, porous earthenware as earlier. It is only the color-printed subject, whether scenic or floral, historical or imaginary, transfer printed or lithographic, with which the collector deeply concerns himself.

In this country today, obviously the most eminently collectible of Staffordshire color prints are the American historical views. For the collector, no ambitious pictorial combination of Swiss chalets, lagoons, pagodas, and Italian gardens, however artistically disposed, can have a fraction of the interest that resides in a new collector, has long been recognized. And competitive buying, more than any other one factor, has sent their prices skyward. But there are other pleasant fields. Half-brothers to the group described are the English-historical views of like period. Patriotism, obstinately abiding, has scorned these foreign portrayals, with the result that they are obtainable at a fraction of the price asked for the more highly favored American-historicals. In richness of deep blue, in authenticity of subject, in transfer-printed technique, English- and American-historicals are identical.

Scarcely less desirable, though we shall be criticized for so saying, are the American-historical prints in other colors than deep blue. They lack the rich charm of the dark cobalt views, and they are later in date. Devotees of the "old blue" pretend to despise them. Hence few of the paler prints reach the price level occupied by their dusky progenitors. Nevertheless, their subject appeal is no different, and their execution at least is marked by greater (at times, almost photographic) pictorial verisimilitude. The rose-bordered Jackson series, the *Catskill Moss* series by

*Fig. 7 (above, left and right)* — THE BOSTON STATE HOUSE: EARLY VIEW AND LATE
That at the left by Rogers of Longport, about 1825, printed in medium blue, is fairly common, but more desirable as a collector's item than the more accurate but rather ironclad pink delineation by J. & J. Jackson, about 1835, at the right. A discussion of variants of this view appeared in ANTIQUES for December 1931

*Fig. 8 (left)* — "CATSKILL MOSS" SERIES: "TOMB OF WASHINGTON"
The *Catskill Moss* series was first issued in 1844 by William Ridgway Son & Co., of Hanley. It was discussed in ANTIQUES for September 1930. One of sundry American patterns produced in diverse colors during the 1830's and 1840's by English potters. Not so highly valued by collectors as the early blue, but significant because of the subject

realistic view of the New York City waterfront in 1820. No idyllic representation of Hannibal jogging grandly across the Alps with his cortège of elephants can stir such covetous enthusiasm as will be awakened by views of those American buildings wherein was enacted the drama of our early national life.

The importance of these American-historical views, alas for the

William Ridgway, the Godwin views with morning-glory border, and the *American Cities* group by Mellor Venables & Company are examples of good American views whose color has prevented them from equality of representation in the more notable collections. Whether transfer printed or lithographic, they definitely merit more considerate notice than they have hitherto received.

169

Non-historical subjects of the late period, including the *Chapoos* and *Circassias* and other fanciful designs bearing meaningless names, are scarcely to be considered collectible save for utilitarian purposes. Having scant subject interest and no subject significance, they qualify only as decorative. Though useful and even charming on the breakfast table, they are without value for the collector's cabinet.

It is possible, however, to modify this statement. The fancifully printed wares may be regarded from another angle, and judged not merely as cheap pottery, but as examples of border patterns. Simeon Shaw, by the way, writing of the Staffordshire industry in 1828, states that the borders employed on color-printed Staffordshire were derived from "paper hangings for rooms." Surely, then, it is feasible and proper to collect such pieces of the 1840's and 1850's for what they are — albums of ceramic motives. Many of them display really well-conceived borders, offering a variety of running designs, medallion effects, and geometric mazes that would do credit to many of the present-day designers who fretfully seek, often with grievous result, for something new under the sun.

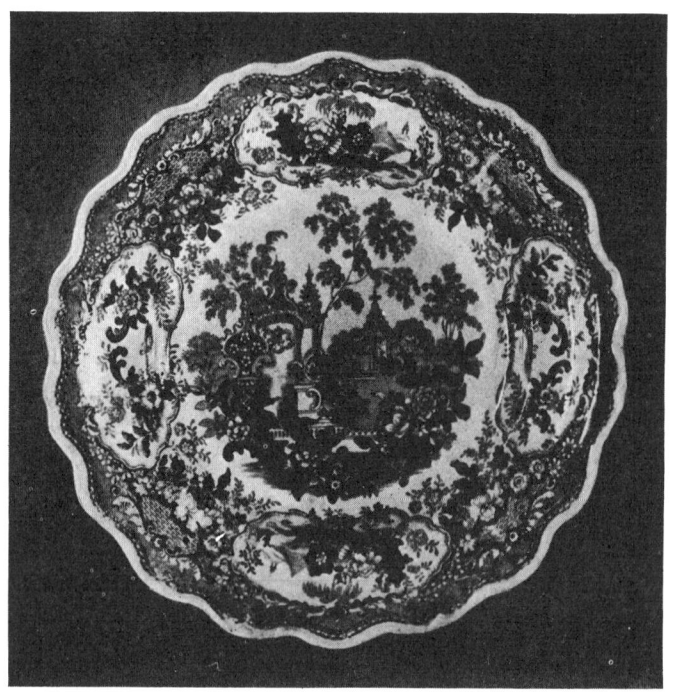

*Fig. 9* — "ADELAIDE'S BOWER" (*c. 1835*)
Maker unknown. A pattern whose purely fantastical design conveys no meaning to the collector of specimen pieces, and hence is of very small value. (See ANTIQUES for November 1935, *p. 188*.) Such nondescript plates are, however, sufficiently common to be quite easily accumulated for table use. Matched dozens in a momentarily popular color may, therefore, command a fairly high price

More than this on the topic of collecting range it is unnecessary to add. Given the yardstick of "subject interest" to govern his measurement, the collector is quite adequately equipped to discover new collecting possibilities for himself. Generally ignored opportunities among the later wares will reveal themselves; the actual importance of the early-century *chinoiserie* designs, now commonly languishing unhailed, will become perceptible. Indeed, what the collector does not work out for himself contributes very little to his permanent satisfaction. The true enjoyment of collecting lies in experiment and discovery, not in following directions at second hand.

### Advice That Will Not Be Heeded

First (and let this be shouted), the new collector will travel more happily, as well as more profitably, if he charts his course in advance. It is not well to rush ecstatically into market, scattering dollars for whatever strikes the moment's fancy. The woods are full of Staffordshire "collectors" who, lacking the collecting instinct, are suffering only from accretion fever. Their purpose is simply to acquire as many different specimens as possible. With avidity and funds, this end may be only too completely accomplished. Eventually, having grown and been outgrown, the resultant aggregations of earthenware will languish as a frozen, unheeded memorial to random ardor.

Secondly, it is not unnecessary to remark that seriously defective specimens fail to improve the appearance of the collector's cabinet. Missing handles, yawning cracks, blighting chips add neither to the market value of a piece nor to its possessor's satisfaction or reputation. It is admittedly impossible to find, at all times, absolutely proof (perfect) items, since we are dealing with fractile ware a century in age. Still, the collector should set himself a reasonably high standard in this respect. A few of the rarest views may be acceptable despite casualties; but rarity seldom compensates for decrepitude.

Thirdly, a simple card index of the collection will be invaluable. This suggestion may draw protests. Nevertheless, we insist that an uncomplicated card index requires but little attention and constitutes an important record. If the items are worth collecting, their individual history and collective meaning deserve permanent registration. Such an index, numerically arranged, should show where and when each piece was secured and at what price. Brief descriptions may be placed on each card; but at least, the names of potter and subject should appear. From time to time, such further notes and bibliographical references as occur to the collector may be added. The system will require that each specimen be numbered, for identification in the card index. This may be accomplished by the use of small gummed stickers, which will almost immediately drop off and become lost. In time the exasperated collector will learn to number his pieces with labels made from adhesive tape; or he may print tiny numbers, in black paint, on the back of each specimen.

And lastly, the ideal collector (who probably has not yet come upon the scene, and probably never will) may not limit his concern to the purely visual aspects of his examples. He will acquaint himself with their historical antecedents, that is, with the social, industrial, and economic conditions under which the wares constituting his collection were produced. He will thus discover the why and how of their development. Differences in composition, technique, and style will be observed and explained. The whole process of collecting will become a completely rounded experience.

However, no amount of prating about ideal collectors is worth the actuality of one hopeful convert setting purposeful foot upon the road. Let him collect intelligently, yet travel, so to speak, under his own power. That he will make mistakes is certain; that he will keep happily on is inevitable — since collecting, as we have implied by our use of the word addict, is a one-way road of infinitely alluring prospect.

# DESIGNS IN OLD BLUE

*The Development of Staffordshire Transfer-Printed Wares as Seen by an English Potter and Collector*

## By GRESHAM COPELAND

THE FAMILIAR blue-printed Staffordshire earthenware carrying pictures of American scenery is but a small part of the English potters' production of transfer-printed wares. Its interest to American collectors lies primarily in the subject matter of its decoration. As an English potter and collector, however, I have found it and the related early pictorial wares well worth studying from the point of view of potting technique and design.

All these early works form a history of their own, the charm of which grows on the collector as he becomes aware of the difficulties and anxieties of the potter making his first attempt at the new art of transfer printing. We can picture him feverishly awaiting the results of his experiments as his ovens were fired up and he had to wait for them to cool before he could see whether or no his efforts had been successful. From our perspective of over a century we may follow his progress. First he experimented with the various materials with which he was making his "body," some of which were only newly discovered; some had to be ground to a fine

FIG. 1 — DESIGN FOR WILLOW PATTERN. Taken from one of the original Caughley copper-plate engravings which came to the Coalport works when it absorbed the Caughley factory and now in the author's collection. The S mark above the design was transferred to the back of the item, and may stand for Salopian. The initials *T. T.* are those of Thomas Turner and register his ownership. The *C* and crescent marks stand for Caughley.

*Illustrations from the author's collection*

FIG. 2 (*above, left*) — WILLOW PLATE. Impressed *Spode* on back. An early production, believed to be the identical pattern engraved for Spode by Minton, and first produced in 1784. Thomas Minton, engraver and printer, who had been trained by Turner, came to Spode from the Caughley works. This and Figure 1 offer interesting comparison. Both are crowded with detail, and in this respect are quite different from ware imported from China about this time. The latter, though showing pictures of pagodas, trees, bridges, and people, was far freer in design. It is in Spode's pattern that the willow tree first makes its appearance.

FIG. 3 (*above right*) — DISH OR BASKET STAND, WILLOW PATTERN. Impressed with Spode's name. The design is entirely line engraved, and the color, while paler than earlier forms, is an attractive shade of blue.

FIG. 4 (*right, corner*) — LEEDS PLATE, VARIANT OF WILLOW PATTERN. Impressed mark *Leeds Pottery*. Similar to a design produced at Swansea. Willow-type patterns were also produced by Davenport, D. Dunderdale of Castleford, and others.

Fig. 5 (*left*) — Spode's "Rock," Variant of Willow Pattern. Impressed Spode. Diameter, 8 inches. Pattern closely resembles a Chinese porcelain decoration in the author's possession.

Fig. 6 (*right*) — Plate with Sino-European Decoration. Impressed mark *Davenport*. Diameter, 10 inches.

Fig. 7 (*below*) — Copper Engraving. Sino-European type. Spode's *Gothic Castle* pattern.

powder by means of the mill driven by the water of a small stream, and later by some of the first "fire-engines" (we call them steam engines now). Then he tried new tricks with glazes, which were just emerging from an era when only one method, salt glazing, was used.

And all the different elements would have a different effect on the tones of the cobalt he was experimenting with to produce the color required for his prints. The earliest engravings were cut with deep, broad lines. Some of the dark-blue prints made from them are rather "flown," that is, with a blurred effect and a glaze often showing an "orange peel" surface. The body has a grayish tone. The plates are without a foot, following, one surmises, the line of the silverware used in the great houses, the pewter, or the simple wooden platter of more humble dwellings. Later, the finer lines of engraving appear on a whiter body covered by a more even glaze. Gradually the tone of color changes to a grayish blue of delightful hue, and finally to the paler but brilliant blue which showed, clearly and concisely, the delicacy of the engraving upon ware which had now become beautifully made and glazed. In its degree of excellence, the final product gives little hint of the many experimental stages through which it had passed in so short a number of years.

Transfer printing on ceramics was introduced almost simultaneously between 1753 and 1756 in London and Liverpool. From Battersea (London) the method was taken in 1756 by an engraver, Robert Hancock, to Worcester. Thence it spread to Caughley, a Shropshire village farther up the River Severn, where it was practiced by Thomas Turner, a pupil of Hancock. Although the secrets of this new process were carefully guarded, William Adams of Cobridge obtained an engraver from Worcester and commenced printing ware in 1775. Few examples of the work of the Baddeleys and John Yates seem to be available. John Turner of Lane End (both these places are now incorporated within the city of Stoke-on-Trent) was one of the early potters to use printing. It was, however, Josiah Spode who took a firm hold on this new method of decoration and carried it to successful and extensive production. To him is generally given the credit for introducing *underglaze* printing as differentiated from the

Fig. 8 — Copper Engraving, European Historical Scene. Spode's *Tiber*. A composite picture showing the Basilica of St. Peter's, the Castle of St. Angelo, and Trajan's Column with the river Tiber in the foreground.

that circumstance is not the whole conclusion of the matter.

The most universally known design used in this type of transfer-printed decoration is the willow pattern. Showing strong Chinese influence, it has numerous variations, but its original interpretation is attributed to the potter Thomas Turner of Caughley and to the year 1780 (*Fig. 1*). It was later continuously used by many of the Staffordshire potters. This *type* of pattern, a center picture framed by a surrounding border, was later adapted to the American views.

Ware from China was being imported in considerable quantities in the late 1700's, and in decoration much of the Staffordshire ware resembles, or imitates, Chinese porcelain, hand-decorated in blue (*Fig. 5*). The reason was chiefly, no doubt, an attempt to meet competition with the popular Chinese wares by producing a less expensive substitute. We may infer also that English potters were occasionally asked by owners of ware imported from China to replace breakages or deficiencies. About 1805, Spode produced a body called "stone china," a gray-tinted body of great hardness which was made specially to compare with the Chinese imports. By this time, the technique of his engravers had reached the highest standards of meticulous skill, the lines being so finely cut as almost to resemble the work of the miniature artist.

About this time the designers, while consciously working in their own interpretation of the Chinese manner, nevertheless used their imaginations and introduced original designs. The resulting patterns, of a Sino-European character, were produced by many of the Staffordshire potters (*Figs. 6, 7*). It is impossible to give dates to these productions; conclusions can only be reached by observing that the body has become whiter, the potting lighter and better, the color of the blue paler and more "still," and the engravings show a wider use of stipple-work for grounds and cloud effects.

FIG. 9 (*above*) — COPPER ENGRAVING, EUROPEAN HISTORICAL SCENE. Spode's *Tower*, which achieved wide popularity and today is still being reproduced as a great favorite.

FIG. 10 (*right*) — ENGRAVING FOR 6-INCH PLATE, INDIAN SPORTING SUBJECT. Design entitled *Grooms leading out*, from an aquatint published in *Oriental Field Sports* (1807).

FIG. 11 (*below*) — ENGRAVING, HISTORICAL SCENE, For 18-inch dish, with center design of classic ruins, *Scenes near Corinth*, and the border in the style of the *Indian Sporting* scenes.

*overglaze* type of work, often loosely called Liverpool.

Examples of the earliest transfer-printed wares are hard to find today. Revealing the potter's pioneering effort to overcome many technical difficulties, they have a special appeal for the collector. Their decoration shows how the first engravers followed woodcut technique; the lines are cut deeply and wide apart and produce a picture of deep blue effect. Whereas the Worcester and Salopian factories were printing upon porcelain, the Staffordshire potters were producing earthenware. Their earliest forms, though somewhat gray of body, were covered with a glaze slightly stained with blue, which helped to give a whiter effect. As their experience grew, the body became whiter and their engraving finer, with less crowded detail (compare Figures 1 and 3).

With the finer engraved lines comes a finer and slightly paler color. Various potters produced designs revealing a similar technique, but as few of them are marked, it is impossible to attribute them to any particular factory. There is little doubt that designers and engravers moved about the country from one pottery to another, taking their ideas with them. This has probably led to the belief that some potters copied the work of their competitors; while partly true,

173

It may be assumed that the first of them were made at the very end of the eighteenth and the beginning of the nineteenth centuries.

Following these types of design there seems to have been a demand for ware decorated with pictures of actual scenes. That was the beginning of the vast crop of "historical" china. Apparently the first had European scenes, views of ancient Rome, Greece, and other parts of the Mediterranean and Near East. Then came scenes of the English countryside. Following these beginnings came the demand for pictures of American scenes and subjects on china, which had been admirably illustrated and described by writers of that country. There are pictures, too, of such things as game hunting in Asia. Spode in particular made use of a publication in which *Oriental Field Sports* were described and illustrated with aquatints (see ANTIQUES, September 1938, p. 142). One of the charms of this series, and of another illustrating ancient ruins in the Levant, is that each piece of ware had a different picture. The borders of both these series are taken from the same book, which was published in London in 1807. This gives an approximate idea of the time when these picture subjects were in transition from the oriental and European-Continental to those of the English countryside, and subsequently to the American views.

In considering these various pictorial productions, it is a temptation to concentrate on the subject of the picture itself and overlook the other aspects of the china which contribute to or detract from its quality. In this type of ware, as in other ceramics, quality depends on the character of the body, the potting, the glaze, and the decoration. Excellence of decoration implies not merely a rare or interesting view, but one which is well designed and clearly printed. Figure 12, for example, is not only carefully engraved and printed, but thoughtfully designed, so that the combined work of potting, decorating, and glazing has contributed to produce an article of great charm and delicacy.

However, since technical developments went hand in hand with changing tastes in pictorial decoration, it is possible to classify these Staffordshire wares largely on the basis of their designs. I have found that they fall into four major types, as follows: (1) *a*, willow patterns (*Figs. 1, 2, 3*), and *b*, willow-type patterns (*Figs. 4, 5*); (2) Sino-European designs and the historical scenes of Continental Europe and the Near East, actual and fanciful, including Spode's *Indian Sporting* subjects (*Figs. 6-12*); (3) scenes of the English countryside, both actual and fanciful (*Figs. 13, 14, 15*); (4) American views, and such literary subjects as *Dr. Syntax*. The accompanying reproductions illustrate all but the last of these types.

FIG. 12 (*left*) — ROGERS PLATE, HISTORICAL SCENE. Impressed mark. Diameter, 10 inches.

FIG. 13 (*below, left*) — DISH, ENGLISH COUNTRYSIDE SCENE. A picture beautifully designed and executed. Marked with the name of Yorkshire potters, *Brameld*.

FIG. 14 (*below, right*) — PLATTER, ENGLISH COUNTRYSIDE SCENE. View of Ripon Cathedral. Printed on back *Rippon Yorkshire*. Diameter, 17 inches. Compare the fanciful rustic scene of Figure 13 with this actual, or historical, view.

FIG. 15 (*above*) — BELVOIR CASTLE. Scene on a plate with same border as that of Figure 14.

# A Chronology of Spode Patterns

To determine the approximate date of a piece of late eighteenth or early nineteenth century English porcelain or earthenware on the basis of its shape or its mode of ornamentation is an almost impossible task. Once the English potters had freed themselves from the traditional thralldom of salt glaze, tortoise-shell glaze, and primitive creamware, and had begun to compete among themselves, as large manufacturers, in devising novelties, not only in the fabric of their wares but in their decorative treatment, new ideas and new methods crowded one upon another with bewildering speed. The best of sculptors were engaged to model figures and reliefs for reproduction in porcelain and earthenware; the cleverest of flower painters did not disdain to turn their talents to tracing dainty bouquets and wreaths upon dinner services; while the most versatile of engravers often cut the copperplates from which transfer prints were drawn.

Even the really scholarly treatises on the subject of the English potters and potteries hesitate to offer a style chronology more exact than the broad generalizations derivable from a tabulation of marks, some of which remained almost unaltered for a long period of years. ANTIQUES, therefore, is happy to present, herewith, a dated series of Spode designs, which, though it includes but a few among a great multitude of patterns, may be looked upon as probably accurate in so far as it goes. The reproductions are taken from drawings and direct transcripts of engraved plates, for whose use ANTIQUES is indebted to the courtesy of Ronald Copeland, present head of the firm which today is conducting the works founded in the eighteenth century by Josiah Spode.

It should, of course, be borne in mind, that, since their first appearance, all, or nearly all, of these designs have been frequently reissued, and that many are in course of production today. Hence the date assigned to any one of them may not invariably be accepted as indicating the year of manufacture for the piece upon which the design appears.

The history of the Spode factory — for the purposes of these notes — may be compressed into a paragraph or two. Josiah Spode the first, born in 1733, was apprenticed to Thomas Whieldon in 1749. In 1754 he is said to have left his master and set up in business for himself. In 1776 he established, in London, a wareroom and sales office, which gave him a large outlet for his products and accelerated the prosperity of his enterprises. On the death of the elder Spode, in 1797, Josiah Spode the second dominated the business, and succeeded in still further improving the firm's products. Josiah Spode the second died in 1827, when a third Josiah undertook the headship of the concern. On the latter's death, six years after, control passed to Spode's London representative, William Taylor Copeland, who, in partnership with Thomas Garrett, took over the factory and continued operations under the name of *Copeland and Garrett late Spode*. When this partnership was dissolved, in 1847, the firm name became *Copeland late Spode*, and so continued until 1867, when the present entitlement of *Copeland and Sons* was assumed.

The Spode factory has produced every variety of ware, including stoneware, creamware, ironstone china, highly glazed earthenware, jasper ware, and basaltes in imitation of Wedgwood, together with great quantities of useful and decorative porcelain. To the approximate period of some thousands of recorded patterns, the dates of the few designs here reproduced may serve as a helpful, if not universal, key.

For convenient reference these designs are classified as:
Transfer Designs in One Color, Figures 1–8.
Transfer Designs Colored by Hand, Figures 9–14.
Hand-Decorated Porcelain, Figures 15–24.

*Fig. 1 (left)* — CHINESE PATTERN (c. 1776)
Engraved transfer design, printed from the copperplate. An elaboration of the simple, blue-painted Chinese designs common to English creamware from the time when the invasion of blue and white porcelain from the Orient threatened destruction to the English potteries.

*Fig. 2 (right)* — "ITALIAN" PATTERN (1780)
This ancient Italian scene exemplifies the Classic revival which was beginning to offer competition to the previous Chinese taste.

*Fig. 3 (left)* — THE FAMOUS "WILLOW" PATTERN *(1782).* Engraved for Spode by Thomas Minton, but probably originated by Turner of Caughley.
*Fig. 4 (centre)* — ANOTHER VERSION OF THE "WILLOW" PATTERN. Specially engraved for printing on stone china. *From the engraver's plate.*
*Fig. 5 (right)* — SPODE'S "TOWER" *(c. 1800).* Perhaps another concession to the Classic taste, though more rusticly romantic in its implications. *From the engraver's plate.*

*Fig. 6 (left)* — "BLUE HERON" PATTERN *(1784).* Chinese influence. Produced first in blue, and later, about 1810, in underglaze colors. *From the engraver's plate.*
*Fig. 7 (centre)* — "GREEK" PATTERN *(1784).* A Classic design. Another Greek pattern, produced 1860–1870, is illustrated in ANTIQUES, Vol. XIII, p. 233.
*Fig. 8 (right)* — "GRASSHOPPER" PATTERN *(produced 1804).* One of the Chinese designs gathered by William Copeland before his association with Spode.

*Fig. 9 (left)* — "BANG-UP" PATTERN *(1804).* Produced by printing the outline, and filling in by hand with red, blue, and gold. The resemblance of this Japanese Imari adaptation to similar adaptations by the Derby factory will be observed. The origination of these designs, while usually credited to Derby, is claimed by Spode.
*Fig. 10 (centre)* — "BANG-UP" PATTERN *(1806).* Fundamentally identical with Figure 9, but altered in effect by the Chinese *famille rose* coloring under the glaze.
*Fig. 11 (right)* — "PEACOCK" PATTERN *(1805).* An engraved outline filled with color by hand. Used on stone china.

176

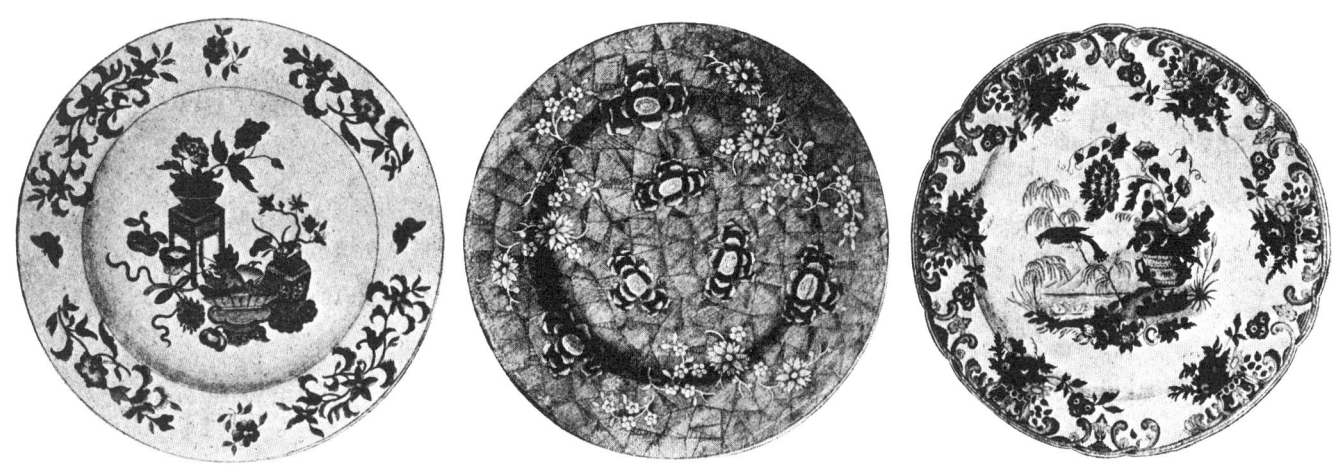

*Fig. 12 (left)* — "Bow-Pot" Pattern (*1805*). Produced on stone china. Printed in outline under the glaze, and enameled over the glaze.
*Fig. 13 (centre)* — Chinese Crackle (*c. 1806*). Adapted from the Chinese "cracked ice" design. Used in hand-colored transfers on stone china.
*Fig. 14 (right)* — Flower Vase (*1817*). For stone china. Printed brown outline filled with underglaze color by hand. Remnants of Chinese influence are apparent.

*Fig. 15* — Pattern Number 664 (*c. 1792*)
Floral wreaths hand-painted on a gold ground, thoroughly English in feeling. Spode is credited with being among the first of the potters to break away from the influence of foreign designs, and to adopt familiar motives from the English countryside.

*Fig. 16* — Pattern Number 967 (*1794*)
The form of the cup is familiar in late eighteenth- and early nineteenth-century porcelain and earthenware. Here we have the so-called Japanese Imari pattern as applied to porcelain. Similar designs were produced at Derby and, to some extent, at Worcester.

*Fig. 17* — Pattern Number 1166 (*1797*)
A porcelain pattern in which English flower bouquets imposed on a fish-scale ground are interspaced with Japanese medallions.

*Fig. 18* — Pattern Number 1619 (*1804*)
Porcelain vase with a quiet English landscape painted in a rich magenta monochrome which was widely popular at the time.

177

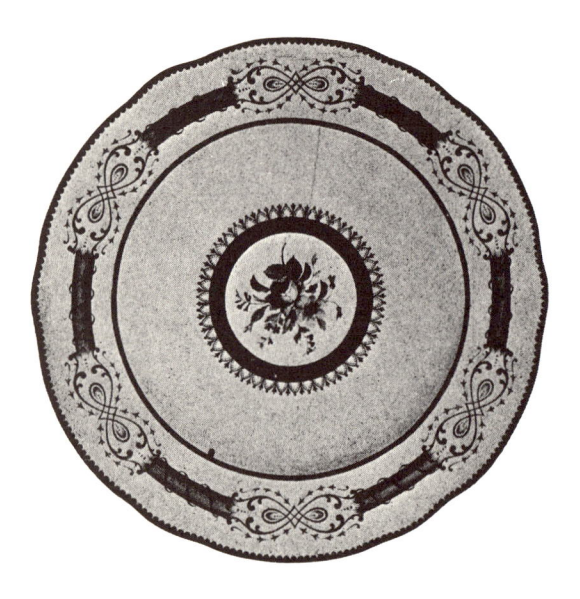

*Fig. 19 (left)* — Pattern Number 1745 (*1804*) The beginning of the nineteenth century witnessed a diminution in the use of Chinese and Classic motives for the decoration of porcelain, though they were retained for the printed and enameled stone china. On porcelain we find the adoption of frankly naturalistic flower, bird, and landscape designs, carefully painted by hand and enriched with gold lines and borders.

*Fig. 20 (right)* — Pattern Number 2114 (*1807–1808*) Another example of naturalistic painting.

*Fig. 21* — Pattern Number 2009 (*1808*)
The same form of cup as that bearing a design of 1794. The background of gold *picotage* and the scattered flowers suggest chintzes of the period.

*Fig. 22* — Pattern Number 3503 (*c. 1808*)
Roses against golden seaweed; a cheerful and typically English design, which would not be mistaken for that of any other country.

*Fig. 23 (left)* — Pattern Number 2330 (*1810*) A porcelain design, hand-painted in the exact and miniature-like technique of the period.

*Fig. 24 (right)* — Pattern Number 2329 (*1810*) Another porcelain decoration which attained wide popularity. Discussed in Antiques, Vol. VI, pp. 76, 77.

*Check list No. 1* — HARVARD COLLEGE (*dark blue*)
BY R. S. W.
*Ellouise Baker Larsen collection*

*Check list No. 2* — HARVARD COLLEGE (*red*) MAKER
UNKNOWN
*From the Pennsylvania Museum of Art*

*Check list No. 8* — HARVARD COLLEGE (*light blue*)
BY E. W. & S.
*Ellouise Baker Larsen collection*

# Staffordshire Views of American Universities

## By ARTHUR H. MERRITT

AMERICAN universities prominent in the early 1800's seem to have been a shining mark for the Staffordshire potters, since more than forty different views of such institutions are still to be found on various items of tableware. Five universities and one military academy supplied the subjects thus diversely represented. Harvard heads the list with fifteen views to its credit. It is followed by Yale with nine; Columbia with eight; West Point Military Academy with seven; Transylvania, two; and the University of Maryland with but one.

Among the potters R. Stevenson & Williams supply ten different views; Wood, nine; Jackson, seven; Ridgway, two; whereas Andrew Stevenson, Clews, Adams, Meigh, and Godwin each contribute only one. Nine views are by unknown potters. Of the entire lot, no less than eighteen occur in dark blue, Yale being the only institution depicted solely in the lighter colors.

As might be expected, specimens of old college Staffordshire are at present widely scattered, no collection having as many as half the views now known to exist. The Morse collection in the American Antiquarian Society in Worcester, Massachusetts, probably the most representative collection in existence, boasts but eighteen. *Old China* (*Vol. I, p. 115*), which in 1902 undertook an inventory of college views on old Staffordshire, lists twenty different portrayals, including West Point Military Academy. Halsey, in *Early New York on Dark Blue Staffordshire Pottery*, lists ten. But he omits mention of Yale, doubtless because no views of that institution in dark blue are known to exist.

In spite of patient search, it is not at all improbable that college items exist that have never been identified or listed. In the present discussion I shall materially expand any previous catalogues; but I shall be surprised if omissions are not soon called to my attention.

### Harvard University

Harvard has the greatest number of Staffordshire views to its credit. It also leads in the comprehensiveness of its picturing, and the variety of colors employed.

*Note.* In the preparation of this monograph and its appended check list the author has had the assistance and cordial coöperation of the following persons and institutions: American Antiquarian Society, Otis M. Bigelow, Mrs. Carolyn H. Curtis, Mrs. Louis Derr, Mrs. Ellouise Baker Larsen, Henry Leworthy, Mrs. Nina Little, Pennsylvania Museum of Art, Gregor Norman-Wilcox, and Yale University. To all these sources of helpfulness he desires to express his sincere appreciation. Accompanying illustrations are numbered to correspond to numbers in the check list. These illustrations and the items referred to in the list cover the entire university series in so far as actual examples are known. — *A. H. M.*

Five imposing halls — Harvard, Hollis, Holworthy, University, and Stoughton — may be identified. One dinner plate (*No. 1*) pictures all except University Hall in a single group. On this plate may also be descried the distant spire of Christ Church, where, tradition has it, Martha Washington attended divine services during the siege of Boston. This view was probably copied, as are other Harvard scenes by R. Stevenson & Williams, from paintings made by Alvin Fisher in 1821, and still hanging in University Hall. Indeed, it is not improbable that Fisher himself furnished the sketches from which the engravings were made.

One of the rarest items in the Harvard group is Number 2. This is a red, transfer-printed, saucer-shaped dish, about seven and a half to eight inches in diameter. The example illustrated has, for many years, been in the possession of the Pennsylvania Museum in Philadelphia.

A very rare platter also by an unknown potter is the light-blue specimen (*No. 11*). The border is unlike that on any other piece of Harvard College ware known to me. Platters in light blue, brown, and red, and also a soup tureen, with the same border are occasionally seen with views of Yale.

Number 13, described as a "large saucer" in the Hudnut sale, may well be identical with Number 2, referred to above. The similarity in size (7 ¾ *inches*) lends color to this supposition. Has any one ever seen a Harvard view on a cup with this border? The only Harvard view cup known to me is Number 15; and this has a floral border. It does not follow, of course, that a cup with a view of Harvard was accompanied by a saucer bearing a like portrayal, or *vice versa*. A case in point is the University of Maryland cup, whose saucer presents a view of the Baltimore Hospital.

### Columbia University

Columbia University has to its credit eight views on old Staffordshire. Of this number six are printed in dark blue on plates of relatively small size, the largest being but eight and five eighths inches in diameter. Of the remaining items, one is a gravy tureen tray, also in dark blue (*No. 23*); and the other a cup, which appears in red and black. In striking contrast to Harvard, with its spacious campus and stately halls, Columbia, until 1856, was housed in a single building. It was located on Barclay Street just west of Broadway in what is now downtown New York, but at that time touched the northern limits of the city. This structure, with the wings added in 1820, is repeated with slight variations on eight different Staffordshire items.

Except for the cup above mentioned, all the Columbia views were made by Andrew Stevenson, and R. Stevenson & Williams. Among these, the rarest are the six-and-a-half-inch dark-blue plates, each with a single portrait medallion and an insert of the Erie Canal. Three of these medallion designs are known, one portraying Washington, another Jefferson, another Lafayette. As these plates were probably issued to celebrate the opening of the Erie Canal, it seems logical to assume the existence of a plate bearing the portrait of De Witt Clinton, who, more than any other individual, was responsible for the digging of the canal. However, I have never seen such a plate or heard of anyone who has. All these medallion pieces are exceedingly rare. I have seen or heard of only one each of the Jefferson and Lafayette type. The Washington is more common. The Jefferson plate is listed by Moore (*No. 675*).

Also very rare are the teacups presenting views of Columbia College, in red and black (*No. 22*). These cups were part of a teaset consisting of teapot, sugar bowl, creamer, cups and saucers, each cup showing two different views and the saucers one each. Among these views, which were not confined to Columbia College, were Scudder's Museum, Boston Court House, Stoughton's Church, New York Alms House, Octagon Church, Boston State House, and the New York Hospital. There may have been others.

In referring to these pieces, *Old China* (*Vol. I, p. 66*) says: "The ware is Staffordshire although of a somewhat different paste from the dark blue, the glaze being white with creamy tint instead of the bluish glaze found on the dark blue."

### Yale University

Of all the universities appearing on old Staffordshire, Yale is most poorly represented. None of the views, not even those marked *Yale College*, give an adequate idea of college buildings or campus. The most prominent building is always the old State House, though two or three churches are also usually to be seen. Yale is conspicuous by its absence.

The plate by Meigh (*No. 24*), clearly marked *Yale College, New Haven*, shows the old State House and churches, while only an indistinct outline of one of the Yale buildings is seen at the extreme left. This is also true of the cup and saucer by Godwin marked *Yale College*. The best Yale view appears on a large platter by an unknown potter (*No. 25*). In addition to the old State House and the New Haven Green at the right, we have at the left a glimpse of the college buildings with their three towers. One of these platters, light blue in color, is the property of Yale College. Another in brown may be seen in the Morse collection. They are marked respectively *State House N. H.* and *State House New Haven*, and each bears the impressed figure *16*. The maker's name does not appear on either specimen. The platter in the Morse collection is listed as by Jackson, though a letter from the librarian of the American Antiquarian Society states that he has "no idea what proof the cataloguer had for this attribution."

The only other pieces of Staffordshire showing this border known to me are the Harvard College platter (*No. 11*) and the Yale soup tureen (*No. 29*), from which, again, the potter's name is missing.

The cup and saucer by Godwin are another rare Yale item. The only specimen of which I have knowledge belongs to Yale College. I have seen it listed only in Mrs. Larsen's article on Godwin in the March 1933 number of ANTIQUES.

### University of Maryland

The University of Maryland dates from 1807, and is, therefore, the youngest of the colleges portrayed by the Staffordshire potters, and the only one organized later than the eighteenth century. It was located in Baltimore. It is perhaps natural that the youngest of the American universities should have been represented by but a single item of ware made by an unknown potter. This view of the University of Maryland was placed on a teacup of which few seem ever to have been produced. And yet, through the operation of that law by which the stone rejected of the builders sometimes becomes the head of the corner, this insignificant blue teacup without a handle leads all the university pieces in point of rarity. During the years that I have been studying and collecting old Staffordshire I have seen or heard of fewer than half a dozen specimens.

### Transylvania University

Transylvania University, organized in 1783 at Lexington, Kentucky, was the first institution of learning west of the Alleghenies. It was at one time in a flourishing condition, maintaining among its other activities excellent schools of law and medicine. The substantial building that appears on Staffordshire dinner plates of various colors was built in 1817. At the time when these plates were made, the university was at the height of its career, and doubtless seemed to the enterprising potter quite as important as almost any other American educational institution. But two views of it ever appeared on old Staffordshire. Both are by Wood. One is in dark blue with shell border; the other appears in various colors under the general designation of *Celtic China*.

### West Point Military Academy

West Point Military Academy, organized in 1802, is to be found on old Staffordshire in seven different views. Of these, the most comprehensive appears on the large platter by Adams (*No. 36*), which, for this reason, is the piece most sought by the collector, though its color may be less attractive than the dark blue. The dark-blue platters, vegetable dishes, and so on, by Wood, are seldom good prints, and afford but a faint and indefinite idea of the Academy buildings.

Of these the most satisfactory is Number 37, though it affords a better view of the Hudson River and the Highlands than of the Academy itself. Curiously enough, few plates with views of the Academy were ever made, and these in the lighter colors only. Clews is represented by one in his "Picturesque Views" series.

In the last twenty-five years more than a score of hitherto unlisted college views have come to light; there are probably others.

*Check list No. 10 (above) —* HARVARD HALL *(brown)* BY JACKSON
*Ellouise Baker Larsen collection*

*Check list No. 11 (left) —* HARVARD UNIVERSITY *(light blue)* MAKER UNKNOWN
*Otis M. Bigelow collection*

*Check list No. 12 (right) —* HARVARD UNIVERSITY *(brown)* BY JACKSON
*Ellouise Baker Larsen collection*

*Check list No. 17* — COLUMBIA COLLEGE (*dark blue*) BY R. S. W.
Without portrait medallion.
*Ellouise Baker Larsen collection*

*Check list No. 19* — COLUMBIA COLLEGE (*dark blue*) BY R. STEVENSON
With Jefferson medallion.
*Author's collection*

*Check list No. 20* — COLUMBIA COLLEGE (*dark blue*) BY R. STEVENSON
With Washington medallion.
*Carolyn H. Curtis collection*

## Check List of American Colleges Represented on Old Staffordshire

*Note.* It is probable that this list is not complete. Any amplifying information will be appreciated. An asterisk indicates items of exceptional rarity.

### Harvard University

1. Plate and soup plate. *Color:* dark blue. *Border:* acorn. *Mark:* stencil either HARVARD COLLEGE or HARVARD COLLEGE RSW. *Description:* view of Hollis, Harvard, Holworthy, and Stoughton Halls; six human figures in three groups; large tree at right. *Size:* 10 inches. *Maker:* R.S.W. (R. Stevenson & Williams). Example in collection of Henry Leworthy, Fredonia, N. Y., has impressed stamp *Clews Warranted Staffordshire*. Here illustrated.

2.* Soup plate or saucer-shaped dish. *Color:* red. *Border:* roses at seven equidistant points joined by a conventional motive along edge. *Mark:* stencil HARVARD COLLEGE. *Description:* large hall (probably Harvard) in centre flanked on either side by smaller buildings and trees; two groups of figures in foreground; equestrian figure fronting hall. *Size:* 7 ½–8 inches. *Maker:* unknown. Here illustrated.

3. Plate. *Color:* dark blue. *Border:* acorn. *Mark:* none. *Description:* view of University Hall; equestrian figure in foreground; low fence, behind which is shrubbery. *Size:* 8 ¼–8 ¾ inches. *Maker:* R.S.W. *Ill.:* Camehl *Blue China Book*, p. 31; *Old China*, Vol. I, p. 116.

4.* Plate. *Color:* dark blue. *Border:* acorn. *Mark:* stencil HARVARD COLLEGE, sometimes mismarked SCUDDER'S MUSEUM. *Description:* another view of University Hall; flanked on either side by tall trees; two figures in foreground. *Size:* 5 ¾–6–6 ¾ inches. *Maker:* R.S.W. *Ill. in color:* Camehl *Blue China Book*, p. 22.

5. Doubtful. *Color:* dark blue. *Border:* floral with roses. *Description:* Harvard University. *Size:*? *Maker:* unknown. *Reference:* listed, Barber *Anglo-American Pottery*, p. 132, No. 430; referred to, *Old China*, Vol. I, p. 116, "No. 5." No other information available. May be non-existent.

6. Cover of a soup tureen. *Color:* dark blue. *Border:* rose medallion. *Mark:* stencil CAMBRIDGE COLLEGE MASSACHUSETTS. *Description:* group of three buildings with chapel at left; four-story building in centre, with gables and tower at right. *Size:* 9 x 12 ½ inches *Maker:* Ridgway. *Ill.: Old China*, Volume II, page 176.

7. Cup plate. *Color:* various. *Border:* flowers with beaded edge. (Only the outer half of the regular floral border by Jackson is shown in this and Nos. 12 and 15, probably due to small size.) *Mark:* usually none. *Description:* view of University Hall, same as No. 3. The same view is also found on cups with handles. *Size:* 4–4 ½ inches. *Maker:* Jackson. *Ill.: Old China*, Vol. I, p. 116; ANTIQUES, November 1930, p. 394.

8. Plate. *Color:* various. *Border:* flower and fruit. *Mark:* stencil HARVARD COLLEGE. E. W. & S. CELTIC CHINA. *Description:* large central hall (probably Harvard) flanked on either side by lower buildings; equestrian and two groups of figures much the same as check list Nos. 2, 10, 11. *Size:* 10–10 ½–11 ¾ inches. *Maker:* Wood. *Ill.:* Camehl *Blue China Book*, p. 31; and here.

9. Platter. *Color:* various. *Border:* flower and fruit. *Mark:* stencil HARVARD COLLEGE. E. W. & S. CELTIC CHINA. *Description:* view of Harvard campus and several buildings; trees at either side; equestrian figure at left. *Size:* 14 x 16 ½ inches; 13 ½ x 15 ½ inches. *Maker:* Wood. *Ill.:* Camehl *Blue China Book*, p. 25; *Old China*, Vol. I, p. 117.

10. Plate. *Color:* various. *Border:* floral with beaded band inside white edge. *Mark:* stencil HARVARD HALL, MASS. JACKSON'S WARRANTED. *Description:* view of Harvard Hall with lower buildings on either side; three figures in foreground and equestrian figure at right. *Size:* 6–6 ¼–6 ½–7 inches. *Maker:* Jackson. *Ill.: Old China*, Vol. III, back cover for June opposite p. 184; and here.

11.* Platter. *Color:* various (light blue, red, brown). *Border:* elaborate filigree background and floral vignettes at either side and end with floral and leaf ornamentation. (Same border on Yale platter and soup tureen, Nos. 25 and 29 of list.) *Mark:* HARVARD UNIVERSITY. *Description:* two-story building with cupola in centre flanked by lower buildings and trees on either side; in foreground four groups of figures and one equestrian. Much like Nos. 2 and 8. *Size:* 12 x 15 inches. *Maker:* unknown. Here illustrated.

12. Gravy tureen cover. *Color:* various. *Border:* same as No. 7, see comment. *Mark:* none. *Description:* view of University Hall on either side of cover; equestrian figure in foreground. *Size:* 5 x 6 inches. *Maker:* Jackson. Listed, *Old China*, Vol. II, advertising page V of March number, as 555. Here illustrated.

*Check list No. 21* — COLUMBIA COLLEGE (*dark blue*) BY R. STEVENSON
With Lafayette medallion.
*Carolyn H. Curtis collection*

*Check list No. 22* — COLUMBIA COLLEGE AND SCUDDER'S AMERICAN MUSEUM (*black and red*) MAKER UNKNOWN
*Author's collection*

181

13. Saucer. *Color:?* *Border:?* *Size:* 7 ¾ inches. Only listing as No. 80 in Hudnut sale (American Art Association) November 1926. No other information at present available; may be identical with No. 2.

14. Cup plate. *Color:* dark blue. *Border:* acorn. *Mark:* R.S.W. *Maker:* No. 64 of Gregor Norman-Wilcox's list of cup plates, ANTIQUES, November 1930, p. 397. By him said to be the same view as No. 24, Morse Collection.

15. Cups with handles. *Color:* various. *Border:* floral. *Mark:* none. *Description:* view of University Hall; same elements as in Nos. 3 and 7. *Maker:* probably Jackson.

### Columbia College

16. Plate. *Color:* dark blue. *Border:* vine leaf. *Mark:* impressed STEVENSON, sometimes stenciled COLUMBIA COLLEGE. *Description:* three-story building with cupola; fence with gate open; two figures in foreground, two seen through gate. *Size:* 8–8 ⅝ inches. *Maker:* Stevenson. *Ill.:* Halsey *Early New York on Old Staffordshire*, p. 81.

17. Plate. *Color:* dark blue. *Border:* acorn. *Mark:* stencil COLUMBIA COLLEGE, N.Y., R.S.W. (sometimes marked CLEWS, see *Anglo-American Pottery*, p. 47, No. 101). *Description:* three-story building; fence with gate open; two groups of figures in foreground; pump at left; two stiff poplar trees at right. *Size:* 6 ½–7 ½ inches. *Maker:* Stevenson. *Ill.:* Camehl *Blue China Book*, p. 53; *Old China*, Vol. I, p. 120; and here.

18.* Plate. *Color:* dark blue. *Border:* flower and scroll. *Mark:* stencil COLUMBIA COLLEGE; impressed A. STEVENSON WARRANTED STAFFORDSHIRE. *Description:* three-story building with cupola; group of three figures in foreground; two seen through open gate; pump at left; trees both right and left. *Size:* 7 ½ inches. *Maker:* A. Stevenson. *Ill.:* Halsey *Early New York on Old Staffordshire*, p. 85; *Old China*, Vol. I, p. 119.

19.* Plate. *Color:* dark blue. *Border:* acorn. *Mark:* none. *Description:* same as No. 17 of check list and with insert in lower foreground showing VIEW OF THE AQUEDUCT BRIDGE AT LITTLE FALLS; on upper border is a medallion (2 ⅝ inches high) of Jefferson, marked JEFFERSON. *Size:* 6 ½ inches. (Moore *Old China Book*, p. 282, lists one as 7 ½ inches; also Halsey, p. 310.) *Maker:* Stevenson. *Here illustrated.*

20.* Plate. *Color:* dark blue. *Border:* acorn. *Mark:* none. *Description:* same as No. 18 with following changes: insert lower foreground ENTRANCE OF THE CANAL INTO THE HUDSON AT ALBANY; above, medallion of Washington marked PRESIDENT WASHINGTON. *Size:* 6 ½ inches. *Maker:* Stevenson. *Here illustrated.*

21.* Plate. *Color:* dark blue. *Border:* acorn. *Mark:* none. *Description:* same as Nos. 18 and 19 except following: insert at bottom with legend VIEW OF THE AQUEDUCT BRIDGE AT LITTLE FALLS; above, a medallion of Lafayette marked WELCOME LA FAYETTE. THE NATIONS GUEST. *Size:* 6 ½ inches. *Maker:* Stevenson.

*Check list No. 25* — STATE HOUSE, NEW HAVEN *(light blue)* MAKER UNKNOWN

*Check list No. 26* — YALE COLLEGE *(pale blue)* BY GODWIN

*Here illustrated.*

22.* Cup with handle. *Color:* red and black. *Border:* plain narrow band around edge, same color as print. *Mark:* COLUMBIA COLLEGE, N.Y. outside of cup below print. *Description:* three-story building with cupola; fence across entire front; gate open showing two figures; view much like No. 16 but less foreground and large figures missing. *Size:* height, 2 ⅛ inches; diameter, 3 ⅞ inches. *Maker:* unknown. *Ill.:* *Old China*, Vol. I, p. 64; *Antiquarian*, July 1930, p. 34; and here.

23. Gravy tureen tray. *Color:* dark blue. *Border:* vine leaf. *Mark:* stencil COLUMBIA COLLEGE, N.Y. *Description:* same as check list No. 15. *Size:* 6 x 8 ½ inches. *Maker:* Stevenson. *Ill.:* *Old China*, Vol. II, p. 177.

### Yale University

24. Plate. *Color:* various. *Border:* chickweed. *Mark:* stencil AMERICAN CITIES AND SCENERY: YALE COLLEGE, NEW HAVEN, C.M.; impressed stamp IMPROVED STONE CHINA. HANLEY. *Description:* view of Old State House in centre, at right North Church; at left and across the road a building with tower, presumably one of college buildings; in foreground a group of five figures, at left two; two tall trees in centre with one on either side. *Size:* 9 ⅜ inches. *Maker:* Charles Meigh. Examples in possession of Yale University.

25.* Platter. *Color:* various (light blue, red, brown). *Border:* floral vignette at either side and end as in check list No. 11. *Mark:* stencil STATE HOUSE NEW HAVEN or STATE HOUSE N.H. (*16* impressed). *Description:* view looking up College Street; at left Yale College with three towers showing; at right old State House with North Church beyond; trees with heavy foliage in centre; several groups of figures in foreground. *Size:* 14 x 16 inches and 13 ½ x 17 inches. *Maker:* unknown. *Ill.:* Camehl *Blue China Book*, p. 10; *Old China*, Vol. I, p. 118. Example in possession of Yale University. Another in Morse Collection, Worcester, Massachusetts, catalogued as by Jackson, but not so marked; attribution doubtful. *Here illustrated.*

26.* Cup and saucer. *Color:* pale blue. *Border:* morning-glory and nasturtium. *Mark:* stencil YALE COLLEGE T. GODWIN WHARF; also the number *150* with British coat of arms and words AMERICAN VIEWS. OPAQUE CHINA. *Description:* view of New Haven Green showing State House in centre flanked on either side by a church. *Size:* saucer, 5 ¾ inches; cup, 2 ¼ inches high, 3 ⅞ inches in diameter. *Maker:* Godwin. Example in possession of Yale University. *Here illustrated.*

27.* Deep dish. *Color:* red. *Border:* floral with beaded band. *Mark:* stencil YALE COLLEGE AND STATE HOUSE: NEW HAVEN. JACKSON'S WARRANTED. *Description:* view of old State House in centre; North Church at right; college buildings at left and across the road; two figures and dog in central foreground; also groups

*Check list No. 28* — YALE COLLEGE *(gray)* BY JACKSON

*Check list No. 29* — YALE COLLEGE *(light blue)* MAKER UNKNOWN

*Nos. 25 and 28 from the Gallery of Fine Arts, Yale University; No. 26 from the Mabel Brady Garvan Collections, Yale University; and No. 29 from the Library of Yale University*

182

of two at right and left; equestrian figure in background; two similar views on outside of dish. *Size:* 10 x 6 inches. *Maker:* Jackson. Example in possession of Yale University.

28. Vegetable dish. *Color:* various. *Border:* floral with beaded edge as No. 27. *Mark:* stencil YALE COLLEGE, AND STATE HOUSE: NEW HAVEN. JACKSON'S WARRANTED. *Description:* same as No. 27; outside undecorated. Uncolored handles either end. *Size:* 9 ½ x 12 inches. *Maker:* Jackson. Example in the possession of Yale University. *Here illustrated.*

29.* Soup tureen. *Color:* light blue (probably various). *Border:* same as Nos. 11 and 25. *Mark:* STATE HOUSE NEW HAVEN. *Description:* blue handles, each end; on either side, view of State House and North Church; College across treelined road at left; two figures at right; three at left; three central foreground; equestrian in background. *Maker:* unknown. *Size:* 8 x 10 x 6 inches. Example in the possession of Yale University. *Here illustrated.*

30.* Saucer-shaped dish. *Color:* brown. *Border:* flowers enclosed in solid border. *Mark:* stencil YALE COLLEGE, AND STATE HOUSE; NEW HAVEN. JACKSON WARRANTED. *Description:* same as No. 27. *Maker:* Jackson. Example in the possession of Yale University.

31. Deep plate. *Color:* light blue. *Size:* 10 ¼ inches. *Maker:* Ridgway. Listed in Cuthbertson sale (Anderson Galleries, April 8, 1927) as YALE UNIVERSITY. No other information available.

32. Cup plate. Listed by Gregor Norman-Wilcox as YALE COLLEGE AND STATE HOUSE, NEW HAVEN. *Description:* said by Mr. Norman-Wilcox to be about same view as No. 24. *Maker:* Jackson. *Reference:* ANTIQUES, November 1930, p. 398, list No. 173; *Old China*, Vol. I, p. 118, No. 1; *Anglo-American Pottery*, p. 97, No. 277.

*Check list No. 33* — UNIVERSITY OF MARYLAND (*dark blue*) MAKER UNKNOWN

*Check list No. 34* — TRANSYLVANIA UNIVERSITY (*dark blue*) BY WOOD

VERSITY, LEXINGTON, E. W. & S. CELTIC CHINA. *Description:* large building; two cows right foreground. *Size:* 10 ½ inches. *Maker:* Wood. *Reference:* *Old China*, Vol. I, p. 122.

*West Point Military Academy*

36.* Platter. *Color:* various. *Border:* roses, medallions, and scrolls. *Mark:* none; sometimes marked MILITARY SCHOOL, WEST POINT, N.Y.U.S. *Description:* in foreground two deer view of Hudson River on which may be seen five small sailboats; in centre and on elevation several large buildings; large tree at right. *Size:* 14 ⅝ x 17 ¾ inches. *Maker:* Adams. *Here illustrated.*

37. Platter. *Color:* dark blue. *Border:* shell. *Mark:* ? *Description:* view of Hudson River with Highlands beyond; on an elevated plateau several white buildings; in foreground two figures, one holding a pole; large tree at right. *Size:* 9 ½ x 12 inches. *Maker:* Wood. *Ill.:* *Old China*, Vol. I, p. 121.

38. Fruit dish with handles and perforated sides. *Color:* dark blue. *Size:* 10 inches. *Maker:* Wood. No. 105 in the Kellogg collection, where listed as WEST POINT MILITARY ACADEMY. No other information available. Probably same view as Nos. 37, 39, and 40. (Sold at American Art Galleries November 6, 1925.)

39. Vegetable dish with scalloped edge. *Color:* dark blue. *Border:* shell. *Mark:* impressed E. WOOD & SONS, BURSLEM WARRANTED SEMI-CHINA. *Description:* view of Hudson River and Highlands; same as No. 37. *Size:* 10 inches. *Maker:* Wood. No. 108 in Kellogg collection; listed as WEST POINT MILITARY ACADEMY.

40. Vegetable dish without scalloped border. *Color:* dark blue. *Border:* shell. *Mark:* impressed E. WOOD & SONS BURSLEM WARRANTED SEMI-CHINA. *Description:*

*Check list No. 36 (left)* — MILITARY SCHOOL, WEST POINT (*pink*) BY ADAMS

*Check list No. 40 (right)* — WEST POINT MILITARY ACADEMY (*dark blue*) BY WOOD

*Check list No. 41 (below)* — WEST POINT, HUDSON RIVER (*brown*) BY CLEWS

*Illustrations on this page from the Ellouise Baker Larsen collection*

*University of Maryland*

33.* Cup. *Color:* dark blue. *Border:* conventional white chain; on inside rim same chain with wreath of flowers and leaves extending to middle of cup. *Mark:* none. *Description:* view of two-story building with large dome; shown on each side of cup, with the legend UNIVERSITY OF MARY LAND forming a semicircle above. *Size:* height, 2 ⅜ inches; diameter, 3 ⅞ inches. *Maker:* unknown. *Here illustrated.*

*Transylvania University*

34. Plate. *Color:* dark blue. *Border:* shell. *Mark:* stencil TRANSYLVANIA UNIVERSITY, LEXINGTON; impressed WOOD. *Description:* three-story building with cupola in centre; two figures in foreground; three trees on left side, four on right. *Size:* 8 ½–9 ¼ inches. *Maker:* Wood. *Ill.:* *Old China*, Vol. I, p. 121; *Anglo-American Pottery*, p. 33; and here.

35. Plate and soup plate. *Color:* various. *Border:* flower and fruit. *Mark:* stencil TRANSYLVANIA UNI-

same as No. 37. *Size:* 10 ½ x 7 ¾ inches. *Maker:* Wood. *Here illustrated.*

41. Plate. *Color:* various. *Border:* birds, flowers, and scrolls. *Mark:* stencil PICTURESQUE VIEWS, WEST POINT, HUDSON RIVER; impressed WARRANTED CLEWS STAFFORDSHIRE. *Description:* view of West Point and Hudson River, steamer and rowboat in foreground. *Size:* 7 ½–7 ¾ inches. *Maker:* Clews. *References:* Earle, *China Collecting in America*, p. 375, No. 266. *Ill.:* ANTIQUES, December 1929, p. 485; and here.

42. Vegetable dish. *Color:* various. *Border:* flower and fruit with white beaded edge. *Description:* view of the Hudson River, Highlands, and Military Academy; two groups of figures (two each) in foreground; tall trees at either side; much like No. 37. *Size:* 12 inches. *Maker:* Wood. *References:* *Old China*, Vol. I, May cover, and p. 126, for description and illustration.

*Fig. 1 —* HIGHLANDS, HUDSON RIVER
Vegetable dish, 11 ½ by 8 ¾ inches

*Fig. 2 —* LAKE GEORGE
Platter, 16 ¼ by 12 ¾ inches

# Some Idiosyncrasies of the Staffordshire Potters

*By* ELLOUISE BAKER LARSEN

*Illustrations from the author's collection*

SO INCOMPLETE and fragmentary is the information handed down to us during the hundred years since the Staffordshire potters of England were in the midst of producing our historical Old Blue pottery, that we are obliged to build up our knowledge, both of the men and of their methods of achievement, from bits of scattered evidence.

Commerce was modest in those days. The English potters courted popularity for their wares by producing them in quantities sufficiently large to permit selling at low prices. If they could have looked far enough into the future to see that single pieces of the pictorial types that they sold for seven, twelve, twenty-five, or fifty cents each would, a century later, bring hundreds of dollars from collectors in the United States, they would have placed their trade-mark on every specimen of American views, thereby providing helpful records for posterity. Their neglect in this respect will doubtless forever prevent the identification of many of their finest works.

Some of the major potters were inaccurate in the labeling of their views. The geography of this country meant little to those Englishmen who did not cross the Atlantic. In their day travel was slow and costly, but since they were denied the aid of the camera — which was yet to be invented — the potters occasionally sent their artists overseas to paint or draw pictures of American cities, scenery, and inventions. The accuracy of the result was dependent upon the skill of these artists; yet today it is the potter who receives praise or criticism for his product.

Confusion in the labeling of views may have been due either to the carelessness of the artists themselves, or to the ignorance of the workmen in the potteries. However that may be, while most of the specimens in deep blue are correctly labeled, several discrepancies have been found. Enoch Wood, the father of pottery, who (among the major potters) seems to be the greatest offender in this respect, has been known, among other mistakes, to interchange *Highlands, Hudson River (Fig. 1)*, and *Lake George (Fig. 2)*. He has identified the thundering cataract *Niagara Falls from the American Side (Fig. 3)* as *Castle Garden, Battery, New York (Fig. 4)*, and has placed his Niagara label on the placid lineaments of New York harbor and its pill-box fortification.

The most astounding instance of Wood's mismarking occurs in an eighteen-and-a-half-inch platter with medium blue and white border of fruit and flowers. This I discovered recently among several freak pieces in a Staffordshire collection that I acquired in the northern hills of Massachusetts. The item is a platter labeled *Harvard College*, though it will readily be observed that the view really represents *New York from Staten Island (Fig. 5)*. Wood's correctly labeled *Harvard College* portrays Harvard Hall with figures disporting themselves on the long lawn in the foreground *(Fig. 6)*. Compare with this old view the close-up of the same building, still standing, which appears today on the Harvard dinner plates ordered by President Lowell two or three years ago *(Fig. 7)*. At the office of the company in Boston through which the order for the four thousand dozen plates of the new edition was sent to the Wedgwood Potteries in England, I have seen the drawings of the

*Fig. 3 —* NIAGARA FALLS FROM THE AMERICAN SIDE
Platter, 14 by 11 ½ inches

July, 1931

184

*Fig. 4* — CASTLE GARDEN, BATTERY, NEW YORK, MISMARKED NIAGARA FALLS
Platter, 18 ¾ by 14 ¾ inches

*Fig. 5* — NEW YORK FROM STATEN ISLAND, LABELED HARVARD COLLEGE
Platter, 18 ½ by 15 ½ inches

*Fig. 6* — HARVARD COLLEGE
Compare with Figure 7.
Plate, 10 ½ inches

*Fig. 7* — HARVARD HALL
A recent Wedgwood plate, 10 ¼ inches

*Fig. 8* — ARMS OF SOUTH CAROLINA, BY MAYER
Plate, 5 ¾ inches

*Fig. 9* — NEW YORK (JACKSON'S SELECT VIEWS)
Platter, 17 by 13 ¾ inches

*Fig. 10* — BALTIMORE, BY MEIGH
Platter, 15 ¾ by 12 inches

185

border taken from an original Wood specimen. The twelve views of this modern series, of which *Harvard Hall* is one, are from photographs of university halls, chapels, and dormitories, taken by Professor Conant. The fact that Wood's plate was printed in medium blue made the task of duplicating his border less difficult than it would have been were the original in dark blue. It has been said by authorities that the rich, deep blue used in printing the earlier historic Staffordshire cannot be matched today. Its peculiar richness and depth of color seem to elude contemporary potters.

So well known are Stevenson's change of titles in the case of *Octagon Church, Boston* and *Staughton's Church, Philadelphia*, and his confusing of *Scudder's American Museum* with *University Hall, Harvard College*, as not to need illustration.

Another oddity in old Staffordshire produced for the American market is a matter of color. In their earlier printed ware of this kind, the Staffordshire potters never used anything except dark blue, the color now most prized by collectors. Yet later, from the 1830's on, two hues were occasionally combined. I have an example in a thirteen-inch platter by Jackson. It is marked *New York, Select Views*. For years I have owned this view printed in brown, but the newly acquired specimen has a green centre and blue border — not an altogether enticing color scheme.

Another unusual combination of colors appears on a platter of *Baltimore* by Charles Meigh with that maker's moss and chickweed border. The central picture is brown, and the border is in brown, green, and pink, the last-named colors evidently applied by hand.

The majority of the important potters seem to have followed some fairly definite plan as to the color and sizes of their product and the character of the views depicted. Some made whole sets of dishes devoted to a single scene; for example, Enoch Wood in his dinner set of *Landing of the Pilgrims* and Clews in his set of *Landing of Lafayette*. They also repeated uniform sizes in plates and platters for various unrelated views.

An exception to this is found in the products of Thomas Mayer.

*Fig. 11* — ARMS OF PENNSYLVANIA, BY MAYER
Platter, 21 by 16 inches

*Fig. 12* — CADMUS (*so-called*)
Border of sea shells.
Plate, 10 inches

*Fig. 13* — CADMUS UNDER FULL SAIL (*so-called*)
Plate, 5 ½ inches

*Fig. 14* — CADMUS AT ANCHOR (*so-called*)
Cup plate, 3 ¾ inches

*Fig. 15* — CADMUS (*so-called*). TREFOIL BORDER. Cup plate, 3 ½ inches

*Fig. 16* — PLATE
8 ½ inches; design in pink

*Fig. 17* — CUP PLATE, DOUBLE PRINT. 3 ½ inches

His was an original mind. He produced what is now one of the most highly prized series of historic Staffordshire, the arms or seals of twelve of the thirteen original states. Apparently no specimen with the arms of New Hampshire has ever been discovered. Except for a ten-inch plate of New York and one of South Carolina, no two views in Mayer's series are alike in size.

The following statements of dimensions for the series agree, in the main, with those confirmed by the Morse collection of Staffordshire in the Museum of the American Antiquarian Society, Worcester, Massachusetts; and with listings in the October, 1903, issue of *Old China* magazine; R. T. Haines Halsey's *Pictures of Early New York on Dark Blue Staffordshire Pottery;* the catalogue of the Kellogg Sale of Blue Staffordshire, 1925, at the American Art Galleries, New York, when prices of Historic Blue reached their highest peak; Mabel Woods Smith's *Anglo-American Historical China*, in which sizes and prices are given of pieces "sold at the New York Auction Art Galleries during the years 1920, 1921, 1922, 1923"; and, lastly, my own collection of three hundred and forty pieces.

The slight differences in dimensions of a few platters are evidently due to errors either in measuring or in recording the measurements taken. I have found, in every instance of Old Blue, that the Morse figures more nearly coincide with those of my own collection than do any others. Three years ago I checked the Morse list at the Museum of the Antiquarian Society and analyzed its catalogue for the librarian, Clarence S. Brigham.

Ada Walker Camehl in *The Blue China Book* records no sizes for the series of Arms of the States; neither does N. Hudson Moore in *The Old China Book*, nor Alice Morse Earle in *China Collecting in America*.

In the following list, wherever a difference of two inches or more is found, I have mentioned the fact. There are eight platters varying in length: *Arms of Pennsylvania*, 21 inches; *New Jersey*, 19 inches (Halsey records one of 16 ½ inches.); *Maryland*, 16 inches (This platter is also called a tray. The design is repeated on a bowl, 13 ½ inches in diameter; a dish, 11 ½ inches; a pitcher, 10 inches high; and a tureen.); *Delaware*, 17 inches; *North Carolina*, 14 ½ inches; *Georgia*, 12 inches; *Massachusetts*, 9 ½ inches (also a fruit dish, 10 ½ inches); *Connecticut*, 8 ½ inches (gravy tureen, 6 inches high).

In plates there are three of these armorial designs: *Arms of New York* (also soup plate), 10 inches; *Rhode Island*, 8 ½ inches; *South Carolina*, 10, 7 ½, 5 ¾ inches — and a 4-inch cup plate.

*Arms of Virginia* appears on a vegetable dish 12 inches long, and on a small platter.

It will be readily observed that Mayer greatly varied the dimensions of his pieces. The illustrations show the largest specimen of this series, a platter of *Pennsylvania (Fig. 11)*, and the smallest, a *South Carolina* plate *(Fig. 8)*. The latter is the only one of this group made in cup-plate size.

The seal of Maryland as depicted by Mayer was used by that state for only a short period. Some of the other states have changed their seals at various times, and the Mayer designs, though accurate in general, do not in every instance coincide with present-day usage.

When a Staffordshire potter produced a cup plate, he generally diminished one of his own views that he had used on a larger piece. In departing from this custom, Enoch Wood was again the chief transgressor. In the check list of American-historical cup plates compiled by Gregor Norman-Wilcox (ANTIQUES, November, 1930) nine views of the so-called *Cadmus* cup plates are listed. Seven of these credited to Wood differ so widely in the details of their central view that they are described in the list, "sails down," "full sail," "half sail," and so on. The author states that "some, at least, of this marine series of cup plates are neither pictures of the *Cadmus*, nor part of any known *Cadmus* view."

The second edition of Barber's *Anglo-American Pottery*, 1901, lists three larger views of the so-called *Cadmus (Figs. 12-14)*. They belong in the well-known series by Enoch Wood in which the views are irregularly framed within a border of sea shells. One characteristic of the series is that most of its views are labeled on the face of the plate. Only in the marine items is this identification omitted. The assumption that the latter represent the *Cadmus* is therefore a matter of pure guesswork. One view with trefoil border is illustrated in Figure 15. The *Cadmus*, the vessel that brought Lafayette to America in 1824, had three masts. Perhaps that circumstance accounts for the easy belief that her portrait is intended in any ceramic version of a three-masted craft. One author, however, states his opinion that there is no *Cadmus* in Staffordshire.

Halsey, on the contrary, holds that still another marine view represents the *Cadmus*. It occurs on a plate with a floral border by an unidentified maker; but in its recognition as the *Cadmus* Halsey seems to hold the field without support.

It is worth while to remember that some of the early nineteenth-century English potters occasionally printed on the back of their wares the name of the American distributor, a custom frequently observed today when a dealer prefers to advertise himself rather than his source of supply.

Enoch Wood produced thirteen French scenes, in the main associated with Lafayette, and, for that reason, interesting to American collectors. Their border consists of grapes, iris, and hollyhocks. One unknown scene is marked on the back *Peter Morton, Hartford*. From a directory of that city, printed in 1828 by Ariel Ensign, we learn that Peter Morton was a local dealer in earthenware and glass. A view of *Castle Garden, New York* with trefoil border is also marked *Peter Morton, Hartford*.

Clews produced one view of the *Landing of Lafayette* with the inscription on the back, *J. Greenfield's China Store, No. 77 Pearl St., New York*.

I have always considered the inscription *Thorpe and Sprague, Albany*, on the face of the plate illustrated in Figure 16 as an advertisement of a distributor, but could find no reference to it anywhere. I have now discovered one authority who calls the building *Albany Theatre*. This seems to justify the assumption that the inscription refers to the firm distributing the product. The maker is unknown.

Another unusual feature sometimes encountered in Staffordshire cup plates is the double print. Half of the plate shows part of a certain view, while the other half is printed with quite another scene. Some years ago, in the hope of analyzing this peculiarity, I acquired the cup plate here illustrated *(Fig. 17)*. Since then I have discovered several other similar freak pieces. All except two, however, are pastoral English scenes. But beyond the fact that students of Staffordshire admit that these peculiarities exist, there seems to be no explanation for them unless that they represent trade samples sent out by the potter to introduce new patterns as compactly as possible.

It is a matter of constant wonder that the Staffordshire potters, during a period when travel was as new and difficult as it was a century ago, could produce such a number and variety of views of a distant country as they managed to turn out. Their wise choice of the most important subjects, their faithfulness to detail, which preserves for us the aspect of many minor points, and the general excellence of their work in color and design, have all earned the lasting gratitude of those who are collectors of American Old Blue.

FIG. 1 (*left*) — HUNTING SCENE IN INDIA: "CHASE AFTER A WOLF"

By Spode. The picture is derived from an engraving by Samuel Howitt (1807)

FIG. 2 (*right*) — "DEATH OF THE BEAR"

Spode's ceramic interpretation of Howitt's design. Part of a large dinner service employing the same border throughout, but showing a diversity of adventures as originally depicted by Howitt

# SOURCES OF STAFFORDSHIRE DESIGNS

## By SYDNEY B. WILLIAMS

*Illustrations from the author's collection*

*Introductory Note.* Collectors of Staffordshire wares depicting American views have of late become increasingly interested in discovering the pictorial sources from which the English potters derived their designs. In so far as we are aware, neither in this country nor in England has anyone been similarly concerned with finding the prototypes of the innumerable Staffordshire portrayals of Near and Far Eastern scenes, of hunting adventures at home and abroad, and of domestic and Continental architecture and landscapes. The following notes afford clear evidence that not only for their American designs but for those of quite different import the English potters were alert to employ whatever material they considered worth copying or adapting. It has long been known that certain of Spode's border designs were quite faithful transcripts of those found on Chinese porcelain. But the writer of the present notes is, we believe, the first to prove the great potter's readiness to copy a piece of Chinese porcelain virtually *in toto*, with only minor alterations. The ground thus broken by Mr. Williams deserves a more comprehensive tilling by English students. —*H. E. K.*

TWENTY years ago I purchased a Spode soup plate (*Fig. 1*) and, because of its colorful picturesqueness and alluring subject, decided to acquire additional examples of similar design. An unusual feature of my plate was the explanatory title inscribed on the back, *Chase after a Wolf*, in addition to the impressed mark SPODE.

Nineteen years later the story of this plate was curiously revealed. Passing a print shop in London, I noticed a familiar picture (*Fig. 3*). This, on investigation, I found to be one of a series of forty published in 1807 to illustrate the work of Captain Thomas Williamson titled *Oriental Field Sports*.

At that period India was little known to English people, though interest in that mysterious land was stirring, and information pertaining to it was eagerly sought. The manufacture of my Spode plate and its mates is evidence of the potter's alertness in capitalizing a public demand. The original prints were aquatints, produced when this kind of engraving was at the height of its perfection. Hence it is not surprising that their wealth of detail was repeated in the copperplates from which Spode's earthenware transfers were taken.

In adapting to ceramic use the print *Death of the Bear* (*Fig. 2*), some parts of the original had to be omitted for lack of space. The original shows two bears, the Spode version only one.

In all of the illustrations for Captain Williamson's volume the hunters are in the main safely mounted, some on elephants, others on horseback. Only the native beaters precede the hunt on foot.

The next illustration (*Fig. 4*) shows a 14 ½-inch dish whose ample area has permitted the ceramic engraver to include most of the original picture, *Hunting at the Edge of the Jungle*. Here we observe a diversity of sports. Hare coursing occupies the foreground. Bird shooting engages the middle distance. In the background an elephant and a saddled horse suggest that a more ambitious hunt may soon be undertaken.

This Spode collection, which comprises six different views from the original series of illustrations, is, I have learned, part of a complete dinner service. The artist who made the drawings to accompany Williamson's account was Samuel Howitt (sometimes spelled Howett) (1765–1822), who was distinguished for his skill in portraying wild animals and hunting scenes.

Our next two illustrations (*Figs. 5 and 6*) acquaint us with Spode's immediate indebtedness to Chinese porcelain, whose influence has been and, it seems, always will be evident in the work of English potters. Figure 5 shows a printed Spode plate which I acquired for its own sweet sake as a charming English *chinoiserie*. Probably made between 1800 and 1815, it was, like its Indian-hunt brother, aimed to satisfy a public demand. But my own interest in this particular pattern was greatly increased when I discovered and purchased one of the original Chinese plates

FIG. 3 — "DEATH OF THE BEAR" (1807)
Photographed from an aquatint engraving by Howitt

September, 1938

188

from which Spode must quite literally have drawn his inspiration (*Fig. 6*). On comparison it will be noted that Spode did not make an exact copy of the oriental design. His engraver must have been puzzled by such details as the bridge, which in the original might be a bit of fence, but in the copy becomes a bridge without doubt. Observe, too, that the Chinese artist has made a bush or tree grow apparently from the unfertile fence top. This evidently scandalized the logical English copyist, who carefully transplanted the vagrant bush to real soil at the edge of the bridge.

The Chinese porcelain plate from which the decorative Spode example was borrowed is probably of the Ch'ien Lung period (*1736–1795*). But the resemblance between the two should not permit us to jump to the conclusion that all Chinese ceramic artists were invariably originators and their occidental contemporaries no more than copyists and adapters. For example, compare the plate of Figure 7 with that of Figure 6. The former may be ascribed to the K'ang Hsi period (*1662–1722*) and is certainly far earlier in date than the latter. The one portrays warriors in action, the other peaceful domestic scenes. Nevertheless, the arrangement of the border panels and their intervening fretwork is very similar in both designs. It will also be observed that in both instances the border panels show alternating figure and floral motives. Perhaps there is no such thing as complete originality in design, but only a process of adaptation and alteration.

Our last illustration portrays yet another plate of Chinese implications, though obviously of English manufacture. It is unmarked except for the pattern name, *New Canton*, inscribed on the back. In *The Old China Book* by N. Hudson Moore (*p. 159*) we find *New Japan* (*1815*) and *New Nankin* (*1815*) in a list of Spode patterns; but no mention of *New Canton*. Whether this last-named pattern should be credited to Spode or to some other firm that was seeking profit by imitating a well-established competitor is anybody's guess. Somehow the border of the plate in question hardly suggests Spode's style. Its mixture of *chinoiserie* medallions with a kind of Frenchified rococo ornament seems out of accord with the great potter's sense of the proprieties. However, only the discovery of a marked example will completely solve the problem of authorship.

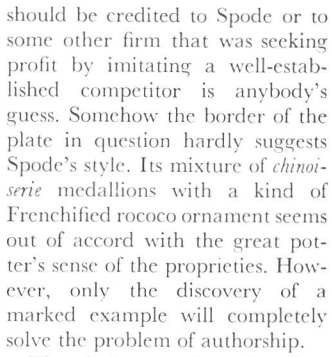

The piecing together of evidential fragments pertaining to the why, wherefore, and whence of appealing ceramic patterns is one of the most fascinating aspects of collecting. It serves to vitalize what might otherwise become a dull process of mere accumulation.

FIG. 4 — "HUNTING AT THE EDGE OF THE JUNGLE"
Spode platter from the previously cited dinner service

FIG. 5 — SPODE PLATE (*c. 1800–1815*)
A slightly altered copy of an eighteenth-century Chinese plate

FIG. 7 (*below*) — CHINESE PLATE (*1662–1722*)
An early plate such as this inspired the oriental decorator of the item pictured in Figure 6

FIG. 6 — CHINESE PLATE (*1736–1795*)
From this or a like example, painted by hand, engraved transfer for plate of Figure 5 was derived

FIG. 8 (*below*) — ENGLISH PLATE (*c. 1820*)
Marked only with the pattern name, *New Canton*. The potter remains unidentified

# HISTORY ON STAFFORDSHIRE

## By ELLOUISE BAKER LARSEN

EDITOR'S NOTE: *When Mrs. Larsen's book,* American Historical Views on Staffordshire China, *was published in 1939, it listed all views known to her on that ware and the items on which they occur. An item, as Mrs. Larsen defines it in this connection, is a specific shape on which a given view or combination of views in a specified color appears. She recorded previously published views and many unestablished views on china unearthed by her during twenty years of intensive collecting. Since publication of her compendium the collector-author has made note of a few unrecorded items that have come to light. Some of these were reported in* ANTIQUES *for June 1942. Others are added here, and are given numbers to indicate their place in the list in the author's book.*

SOME OF THE most common scenes of America as transferred to china a century ago by the potters in the Staffordshire district of western England are still to be found in antique shops today. Serious china collectors are more or less familiar with approximately seven hundred views that have been recorded over the past fifty years. The general reading public knows that the English potters after the War of 1812 made a very successful effort to win back the dwindling trade with the United States by producing this tableware. At that time it was inexpensive, and, decorated with familiar paintings and engravings of our country, it was attractive and popular. Though much has been written on the subject there is still much to be learned. Research continues in the effort to discover new views on the china which, however, are seldom found today on dark blue, and also to unearth and reconcile data about unusual source pictures of transfers which provide valuable historical contacts with the past.

In Enoch Wood's *Celtic China* series of American views in various colors with the fruit-and-flower border, a new view has been found. This raises the number in this series to twenty-one. The creamer on which the view appears and the source picture for the transfer are shown in Figures 1 and 2.

In 1827 and 1828, when this view was drawn from first-hand observation by Captain Basil Hall, the steamboats on the Mississippi used only wood as fuel, and it was essential that frequent landings be made to restore the supply. At a station the boat was tied to a tree nearest the bank and deck passengers carried the wood on their backs to the steamer, in return for a rebate of their fare. The deck passengers were men on their way home from trips on hundreds of "arks," rough, flat-bottomed boats used to carry produce down the stream from the interior of the country to New Orleans.

FIG. 1. WOODING STATION ON THE MISSISSIPPI (Larsen, 69½). Light blue creamer. 7½ over handle by 5¾ inches high.

FIG. 2. WOODING STATION ON THE MISSISSIPPI. Artist of sketch, Captain Basil Hall, R. N. Engraver, W. H. Lizars. Published by Cadell & Co., Edinburgh; Simpkin & Marshall & Moon, Boys & Graves, London, 1829 in *Forty Etchings from Sketches Made by the Camera Lucida in North America in 1827–1828*, by Capt. B. Hall, R. N.

FIG. 3. CALDWELL, LAKE GEORGE (Larsen, 379½). Light blue gravy tureen. 8 over handles by 4½ inches high.

FIG. 4. CALDWELL (LAKE GEORGE). Artist, William Henry Bartlett. Engraver, C. Cousen. Published in London for the Proprietors by George Virtue, 26 Ivy Lane, 1838. Illustrated in *American Scenery* by N. F. Willis, 1840.

FIG. 5. OUTLET OF LAKE MEMPHREMAGOG (Larsen, 381½). Cover of tureen, 6½ by 4¾ inches. The potter made a few changes in his transfer, replacing the cattle on the bridge with people.

Another heretofore unlisted item is a gravy tureen by Thomas Godwin, potter at Burslem Wharf, after 1829. The border is a design of morning glory and nasturtium for a series of twelve American views in blue, brown, maroon, and pink. The view on the tureen itself is *Caldwell, Lake George* (*Figs. 3, 4*); that on the tureen cover, also unlisted, is *Outlet of Lake Memphremagog* (*Figs. 5, 6*). Caldwell, noted for its fine hotels, was situated at the head of Lake George which as early as 1642 was known for its pure, blue water. Lake Memphremagog extends for thirty miles through northern Vermont and the southern section of the Province of Quebec.

Two of the naval views on china I have been investigating for several years. These are recorded in my book as #334, platter, *Chesapeake and Shannon* (*Fig. 8*), and #335, plate, *Shannon* (*Fig. 9*), but since it appeared identification of the views and their source has been questioned. The view on the platter, with the unusual border of shells, flowers, and vines which surrounds the views on both platter and plate, has also been found on a pitcher (*Fig. 10*).

These two views were illustrated in the *Antiquarian* magazine in July 1930 in an article, *New Notes on American Historical Staffordshire*, by Doctor Arthur H. Merritt. He quoted from Arthur Hayden's *Chats on English Earthenware* where the potter was named as Rogers and the platter given the title *Chesapeake and Shannon*. The source picture of the view of the frigate *Shannon* is seen here in the woodcut of Figure 11, where the left half of the picture shows the same ship. Few items of china with this view have been found.

The naval engagement between these two frigates, the British *Shannon* under Captain Broke and the United States *Chesapeake* under Captain Lawrence, took place on June 1, 1813, outside Boston Harbor. The two ships were about equal in number of guns and of men, but the *Chesapeake* had an untrained crew and had recently had a change of captains. At about half past five in the afternoon the two frigates drew near each other and soon began firing heavy cannon. Fifteen minutes after the beginning of hostilities, the fighting had ceased. The *Chesapeake* had been forced to surrender. Captain Lawrence had been killed.

FIG. 6. OUTLET OF LAKE MEMPHREMAGOG. Artist, W. H. Bartlett. Engraver, H. Allard. Published in London by George Virtue. Illustrated in *Canadian Scenery* by N. P. Willis (*1842*).

FIG. 7. CHESAPEAKE AND SHANNON. Artist, Michele Felice Corné. Engraver, Wightman. Published by Abel Bowen in the *Naval Monument*, Boston, 1816. *Photographs of engraved views, courtesy New York Public Library.*

FIG. 8. CHESAPEAKE AND SHANNON (Larsen, 334). Platter, 20¾ by 15¼ inches. Medium blue.

FIG. 9. SHANNON (Larsen, 335). Plate, 10 inches. Medium blue. *Collection of Dr. Arthur H. Merritt.*

One naval print student, on seeing the picture of the platter (*Fig. 8*), advanced the opinion that the view was not the *Chesapeake* and the *Shannon*, but the *Bon Homme Richard* and the *Serapis*, whose battle was fought on September 23, 1779, near the English coast. He reasoned that the latter was one of few battles fought at night (the disk in the sky he called the moon, though it may quite as well be the sun), and that the small boat in the rear at the right was the *Countess Scarborough*, which took part in the engagement.

I have examined many rare naval print collections, public and private, and have consulted curators of print departments in libraries and museums. I have been directed from one expert to another, and many have agreed that the platter view was the *Bon Homme Richard* and the *Serapis*, but none could find the source picture. Finally Harry Shaw Newman has given me his solution of the problem: "The *Bon Homme Richard* and the *Serapis* were ships with two-gun decks such as were used in the Revolutionary War. They were of the 1776 era. The boats shown on the platter are frigates of the 1812 period, with single-gun decks. The picture cannot be the *Bon Homme Richard* and the *Serapis*."

Many of the paintings by Michele Felice Corné, the Italian artist, living in Massachusetts from 1799 to 1822, were published in the *Naval Monument* and were transferred by the Staffordshire potters to American historical china. In Corné's painting of the *Chesapeake and Shannon* (*Fig. 7*), the position of the hulls and other essential points seem to coincide with the view on the platter (*Fig. 8*). It is understood that allowance must always be made for changes in minor details by the potters of the American views.

*Items of china from author's collection unless otherwise noted.*

FIG. 10. CHESAPEAKE AND SHANNON. Pitcher. *Collection of Mrs. Marcus A. Coolidge.*

FIG. 11. THE SHANNON FRIGATE. Woodcut. *Collection of Dr. J. Clarence Webster, New Brunswick Museum, St. John, Canada. Published by Simms & McIntyre, Belfast.*

# Staffordshire and steam

BY RANDALL J. LeBOEUF JR.

FOLLOWING THE WAR of 1812, the potters of Burslem, Stoke-on-Trent, Hanley, and the other towns which had access to the rich clay of the Staffordshire district were alert to employ the new art of transfer printing on pottery with subjects appealing to American tastes. Washington, Jefferson, John Paul Jones, and other heroes of the War of Independence and the War of 1812 were featured. Scenes of British defeats were printed on the new ware—the battle of Bunker Hill, Commodore Macdonough's victory on Lake Champlain, the surrender of Cornwallis. The American eagle was permitted to scream triumphantly on plates, cups, bowls, and pitchers.

As a student and collector of manuscripts, books, prints, and paintings related to Robert Fulton, I hoped that among these Staffordshire views there might be some based on accurate contemporary but long-lost prints of early steamboats, including those of Fulton. I soon learned that when Robert Fulton's so-called *Clermont* inaugurated the steamboat age with its successful trip from New York to Albany in 1807, the Staffordshire potters had been quick to capitalize on American pride in the achievement. Scenes which, if destined for the British market, would have been of rivers, harbors, and cities—and no more—when designed for export to this country often included the little huffing and puffing and fire-belching craft which were multiplying on the rivers of America.

As a student, I pored over the pictures on the china in the hope that there might be shown some early, historic boats of which no other record had survived and which might prove to be the missing links in my research. It must be admitted that side by side with Dr. Jekyll, the discriminating researcher who sought accurate representations of early American steamboats, Mr. Hyde, of the beady acquisitive eye, yielded to an uncontrollable compulsion to collect the plates, platters (with and without lacy borders), pepper pots, and pitchers.

The student's starting tools included Ellouise Baker Larsen's valuable book *American Historical Views on Staffordshire China*, Sam Laidacker's two-volume *Anglo-American China*, and Ada Walker Camehl's *Blue-China Book*. Mrs. Larsen had often tracked down the print or painting which might be the source of the potter's

Fig. 1. *Tappan Zee from Greensburg*, now Dobbs Ferry (Larsen 22; Laidacker W.42). The early Staffordshire potters under Enoch Wood who made this vegetable dish probably had never seen a steamboat. They believed the Americans would be satisfied with a symbolic craft, if it had a tall stack emitting a smoke plume—even if the stack apparently rose out of the paddle wheels. *Except as noted, illustrations are from the author's collection; photographs by Taylor and Dull.*

Fig. 2. *Philadelphia Dam and Water Works* (Larsen 535, 536; Laidacker U.32, U.33). The unknown potter here copied Thomas Birch's drawing, but gave his customers a choice by issuing a companion plate showing a sailing ship equipped with side paddle wheels and a smokestack amidships.

Fig. 3. *View of York Minster* (Laidacker U.37; Part II UD 11). Highest award for imagination goes to the unknown potter who combined in this plate the historic English cathedral and a primitive steamboat flying the American flag.

design; and Sam Laidacker's and Mrs. Camehl's books gave additional information. Among books on steam those found particularly useful were Samuel Ward Stanton's *American Steam Vessels*, 1895; H. Parker and F. C. Bowen's *Mail and Passenger Steamboats of the Nineteenth Century*, undated; Erik Heyl's *Early American Steamers*, 1953, 1956; William M. Lytle's *Merchant Steam Vessels of the United States 1807-1868* (the "Lytle List"), 1952; and Seymour Dunbar's *A History of Travel in America*, 1915.

The trade customs and the uncertain ethics of the Staffordshire potters did not help the quest. One would copy another's design, with modifications either for artistic effect or to mitigate a piracy charge. But if two plates bore different representations of the same steamboat, which was authentic? The potters, moreover, considered themselves artists, with all the poetic license that that implies. If they had a definite print as a model, they chose the portion to be used and might add to or remove some salient part of the original drawing. Stevenson's plate *View of Governor's Island* (Larsen 106; Laidacker S.27) and Stubbs' *New York Bay* (Larsen 244; Laidacker S.113) are both patently based on W. G. Wall's painting bearing the former title. Stubbs, however, added a steamboat which some erroneously call the *Clermont*; and Enoch Wood's potters, who may never have seen a steamboat, created in *Tappan Zee from Greensburg* (Fig. 1) a beautiful vegetable dish which also ignored the fact that in real life the stacks of early American steamboats were either forward or aft of the wheels.

Nor was freedom of fancy in portraying steamboats on the "historic blue" the exclusive privilege of the potter. When John Hill engraved W. G. Wall's water color of *New York from Weehawk*, he added a steamboat of uncertain lineage which was carried over onto the Staffordshire platter (R. J. Koke, *A Checklist of the American Engravings of John Hill 1770-1850*, 1961; Larsen 98; Laidacker S.14). This steamboat is nearer to reality than many of the efforts of the Staffordshire potters, who probably felt the Americans would be content with a symbolic boat as long as it had a smokestack emitting a smudge plume and something circular amidships to represent paddle wheels. The unknown potter of the two *Philadelphia Dam and Water Works* plates tried to satisfy all customers by showing a stern-wheeler on one plate (Fig. 2) and a side-wheeler on the other. Another imaginative potter reached the heights with his *View of York Minster* (England) (Fig. 3), depicting a primitive steamboat plying the river below the cathedral and flying the American flag.

A new confusion appeared when as reliable a potter

as Enoch Wood portrayed in detail the *Chief Justice Marshall* (Fig. 4) and then made another plate with the identical steamboat, foreground, and border, but changed the name of the vessel to the *Union Line*.

Mrs. Larsen, referring to Stubbs' plate *Highlands, North River* (Fig. 5), mentions its fine steamboat "spoken of as the *Fulton*, launched in 1813-14 . . ." but concludes her account on a wistful note: "The *Fulton* had one funnel . . ." which all research supports. One regrets that Mr. Stubbs' steamboat is drawn with such clarity that the two stacks cannot be ignored. In the Diorama series discussed by Laidacker there are two steamboats, often called *Fulton's Steamboat*, each with one stack and a choice of cows (Laidacker UD 9; Larsen 639) or men (Laidacker UD 10) in the foreground. Either may be English or mythical, but the boat is not Fulton's. So the quest is on again.

Enoch Wood's beautiful *Highlands, Hudson River* platter (Larsen 23; Laidacker W.27), shows a three-masted steamboat carrying full sail which is widely accepted as the *Chancellor Livingston*. One notes with satisfaction that the teapot and sugar bowl (Fig. 6) in another series by Wood illustrate unmistakably the same vessel. But—did not Mrs. Larsen say in connection with the *Fulton* (Larsen 239) that the *Chancellor Livingston* had three funnels? All of these pieces show only one. Here, for a change, the researcher finds comfort in the authoritative works by Stanton and Parker and Bowen (see references above), which show her both ways and report her rebuilding prior to being placed on the New Haven run. With this support, the student resolutely closes his eyes to Heyl's representations of her "original appearance" as a two-stacker. The china must depict the authentic *Chancellor Livingston*.

Fig. 4. *Chief Justice Marshall* (Larsen 5; Laidacker W.1). The master craftsman Enoch Wood, who made this plate, later produced an exact duplicate but complimented another group by changing the boat's name to *Union Line* (Larsen 9; Laidacker W.6).

Fig. 5. *Highlands, North River* (Larsen 239; Laidacker S.105). This fine plate produced by Joseph Stubbs is commonly called the *Fulton*, for the ship with a single smokestack launched in 1813. It may well, however, be a rare instance of an authentic representation of the *James Kent*, an 1823 steamboat honoring the New York chancellor who had upheld the Fulton-Livingston Hudson River monopoly.

Fig. 6. *Chancellor Livingston* (Larsen 47; Laidacker W.66). The steamer under full sail in this tea set by Wood is probably an authentic representation of Fulton's last boat, completed in 1816, and named in honor of the partner who had helped finance his plans ever since the launching of their experimental steamboat on the Seine in Paris in 1803. The sails were still deemed a wise precaution. The *Chancellor Livingston* was later converted to a three-stacker and put on the New York to Providence run.

Fig. 7. *Pittsburgh* (Larsen 159; Laidacker C.47). In spite of her explicit lettering *Pennsylvania*, it is impossible to identify the steamship in this view of Pittsburgh, particularly as the background seems to be modeled on drawings of the scene made in the 1790's long before Fulton had brought steam to the area.

6

When it came to crockery with steamships bearing legible names on their sides, it seemed to the student that at last he would find accuracy—and perhaps the end of the collector's fun. Not so. *Pennsylvania* (Fig. 7), *Allegheny, Home, Nile,* and *Lark* are drawn so precisely that one can feel the engines throb as the engineer tightens up the safety valve another notch. Here are ships he could really study. Unfortunately, when the authoritative "Lytle List" is consulted, none is satisfactorily authenticated—so the field for research is again wide open.

On the application of steam to land carriage or railroads, the story is shorter, but even more discouraging. America had no inventor of locomotives comparable to Fulton, to appeal to national pride and thereby stimulate the sale of crockery. In consequence Staffordshire seems to have sent us only three purportedly American railroad items: *Baltimore & Ohio Railroad*, inclined plane (Larsen 13; Laidacker W.16), *Baltimore & Ohio Railroad*, level (Fig. 8), and *Little Falls, N. Y.* (Fig. 9), which purports to show a train of the Mohawk & Hudson River Railroad. The inclined plane *Baltimore & Ohio* must be eliminated, as it is only a stationary engine pulling coal cars up a hill by cable; and the *Baltimore & Ohio Railroad*, level, as Dunbar points out, is actually an illustration of the English Hetton Railway.

That leaves only the Mohawk & Hudson train platter, which is an exact replica of a drawing by W. H. Bartlett in *American Scenery*, by N. P. Willis (1840). Bartlett's drawings, made on his American tours commencing in 1836, are regarded as accurate contemporary portrayals of our American cities and scenes. Nevertheless it is

7

196

impossible to ignore the clear resemblance of the Little Falls locomotive to the original English design of George Stephenson, and the obvious difference of the Little Falls locomotive from the famous DeWitt Clinton engine of the Mohawk & Hudson River Railroad as Dunbar shows it. Dunbar, moreover, completely upsets us when he publishes the identical locomotive we find in Bartlett and on dishes of the Ridgway *Catskill Moss* series, with the disturbing caption "Published in Cincinnati about 1838. The locomotive shown is fictitious." He further suggests that the artist may never have seen a locomotive.

Collectors everywhere who prize Bartlett's charming scenes of home towns or other favorite spots would be shocked if his reliability were in any way questioned. Yet someone has to be wrong. The collector would rather throw the excellent Dunbar to the wolves than be ashamed of the Bartlett print that hangs on his wall. The student, however, sadly notes that the volumes from which Bartlett's prints have been taken were published in London in 1840, and he has to admit that the locomotive could have been copied from the Cincinnati print. So he ends his railroad trip with no reasonably authenticated American locomotive.

Having thus steamed around full circle, the student and the collector finally face each other over that beautiful *rouge-de-fer* tea service with copper luster borders known as *Fulton's Steamboat on the Hudson, Flying United States Flag* (Fig. 10). The source is probably Saint-Mémin's rare lithograph *A View of West-Point on the River Hudson, with the Steam-boat, invented by M. Fulton, going up from New-York to Albany* (cover of this issue), since this is the only known contemporary view of the Clermont. But the student, holding the teapot in one hand and the print in the other, indignantly demands: "How could anyone believe that the design for this china was taken from the Saint-Mémin print?" The collector beams happily on both and does not care.

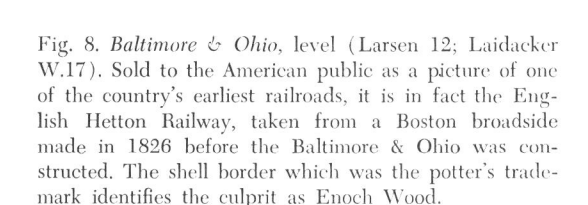

Fig. 8. *Baltimore & Ohio*, level (Larsen 12; Laidacker W.17). Sold to the American public as a picture of one of the country's earliest railroads, it is in fact the English Hetton Railway, taken from a Boston broadside made in 1826 before the Baltimore & Ohio was constructed. The shell border which was the potter's trademark identifies the culprit as Enoch Wood.

Fig. 9. *Little Falls, N. Y.* (Larsen 220; Laidacker R.62), one of the 14 *Catskill Moss* views by William Ridgway, Son & Co.; 1844. Instead of being an early train on the Mohawk & Hudson River Railroad, it was surely published in Cincinnati about 1838 and shows a wholly fictitious locomotive. *Collection of Ellouise Baker Larsen, Smithsonian Institution.*

Fig. 10. *Fulton's Steamboat on the Hudson, Flying United States Flag* (Larsen 743, 728). In addition to the steamboat there is a frigate on this tea service in *rouge-de-fer* with purple luster bands; it is called the *Cadmus*, for the ship in which Lafayette made his triumphant return visit to America in 1824. The covers are called La Grange, the name of Lafayette's home in France. The pottery compliment is not diminished by the steamboat's bearing no resemblance to Fulton's *Clermont*, the frigate's probably being the *Constitution*, and the château scenes looking little like La Grange.

197

# The Truth about Andrew Stevenson

*By* Ellouise Baker Larsen

AN EDITORIAL in the Magazine Antiques, November 1930, debated a seemingly unanswerable question. A medium-blue, ten-inch Staffordshire plate owned by Doctor Henry Leworthy of Fredonia, New York, presented the enigma. Its central view is surrounded by the well-known Ralph Stevenson and Williams border of the oak leaf and acorn. On the back of the plate the name *Harvard College* appears in the scroll common to this series; but the impressed mark discloses the words *Clews Warranted Staffordshire* accompanied by the customary Clews crown.

The unwritten ethics of the pottery world a hundred years ago, when this plate was produced in England, apparently precluded the possibility that one firm should trespass upon the border of another firm. Each potter developed his own distinctive design, which thereupon became the exclusive property of its creator. How the above breach of etiquette occurred became a matter of speculation in the Magazine.

The editorial stated that Gregor Norman-Wilcox, now of Los Angeles, who had brought the plate to the attention of the Editor, remarked "that Ralph Stevenson or R. S. W. (R. Stevenson & Williams) should not be confused with Andrew Stevenson, whose Cobridge works were purchased by the brothers Clews in 1818. This Harvard College plate, he thinks, therefore, is hardly to be viewed as a reissue of engravings thrown in with the sale of Andrew's factory. Such a conclusion, though unsatisfactory, is unavoidable if we accept the statements concerning the Stevensons that Barber offers in his *Anglo-American Pottery*. Yet it may be that Barber is in error. Rhead's *British Pottery Marks* observes that the accounts of the Stevensons 'are somewhat conflicting.'"

The point raised about Doctor Leworthy's plate with the oak leaf and acorn border of Ralph Stevenson and the Clews mark (which I have seen at the owner's home) revives a similar question discussed in 1899 by Halsey in his *Pictures of Early New York on Dark Blue Staffordshire Pottery*; by Barber in *Anglo-American Pottery (1901)*; by Robineau, editor of *The Old China Magazine (1902)*; all of which we shall consider later. But the agitation originally grew out of the confusion of dates caused by the medallion plates.

The editorial continued: "Chaffers, in reproducing the circular mark, *A. Stevenson Warranted, Staffordshir*, attributes it to Ralph Stevenson, and specifically states that the *A* before the surname is a mistake on the part of the die cutter, who should have formed the letter *E* to complete his truncated *Staffordshir.*" In this Chaffers must have erred, for the accompanying pictures marked *A. Stevenson*, taken from pieces in my own collection, show the word *Staffordshire* complete; the *A* is clear and unquestionably intended to be where it is. No indication that the die cutter has made a mistake can be discovered.

The editorial further mentions Chaffers as the source of the information that "the firm listed in 1802 as Stevenson & Dale of Cobridge became Ralph Stevenson, alone, in 1815; Ralph Stevenson and Sons, in 1834; and that it gave up business about 1840. On the other hand, Rhead tells us that the works established by Stevenson and Dale were taken over by R. & J. Clews in 1818, and continued under the new management until 1829, when the firm's failure led to seven years' shut-down. In 1836 Robinson, Wood, and Brownfield became the proprietors and resumed operations. By making a judicious selection from this decidedly jumbled testimony, it would seem quite possible to argue that the long-cherished A. Stevenson is a purely mythical character; that to Ralph of the same surname is properly to be credited the long and fine line of American views on Staffordshire ware; and that it was Ralph's factory, or one of his factories, that was bought by the brothers

*Note.* A purely tentative balloon of paper and hot air, designated *An Academic Problem* and launched from the Attic in November 1930, has accomplished its purpose, which was that of arousing some really constructive curiosity concerning the identity of A. Stevenson, early nineteenth-century potter, of Cobridge, Staffordshire. In the following article, Ellouise Baker Larsen responds to the Attic's challenge with a discussion that is commended to the attention of collectors of "old blue," not alone for its informational value but likewise as a praiseworthy example of careful and pertinacious digging in an ungracious soil.

It is probably enough that Mrs. Larsen has established beyond dispute by means of documentary evidence, which no preceding writer has troubled to cite, that Andrew Stevenson was an actual person. She might, however, have gone slightly further without fear of serious contradiction. One reason for the confusion as to the Stevensons, R. and A., has been the assumption that when — and if — Andrew Stevenson sold out to Clews in 1819, or thereabouts, he at once and forever eliminated himself from the potting business. Evidently nothing of the kind occurred, since Andrew is listed in Pigot's *Commercial Directory* at the late date of 1828–1829 as an independent manufacturer. — *The Editor.*

Clews in 1818. Such an hypothesis, at any rate, would account for the Clews mark on Doctor Leworthy's plate."

Because of my long and ardent admiration for the careful, artistic, and unique type of historical American Staffordshire always attributed to Andrew Stevenson, I *wanted* to believe that a potter of that name had lived and worked in Cobridge in 1818. I, therefore, searched every source available to me in this country for possible evidence favoring, or denying, the existence of such a man, or capable of throwing light on the mystery.

It is interesting to note that apparently American writers on our historical Staffordshire, during the past forty years, have extracted their information concerning the above points from just two sources. The first of these is Chaffers' *Marks & Monograms on Pottery and Porcelain*, published in 1876 (page 676), republished in the *New Chaffers* of 1912 (page 695), with virtually the same data. Both editions ignore A. Stevenson. The other source is Llewellynn Jewitt's *Ceramic Art of Great Britain (1878)* (Vol. II, page 290), which credits A. Stevenson with ownership of the Cobridge Works before they were closed in 1819 and sold to Clews.

Wherever possible, I shall quote opinion about the Stevensons verbatim. Several writers whose authority was obviously one of the two above-mentioned books, I shall omit.

(1). *Histories of the Staffordshire Potteries and Rise and Progress of the Manufacture of Pottery and Porcelain*, by Simeon Shaw. Printed for the author by G. Jackson, Hanley *(1829)*.

"At Cobridge are the Manufactories of R. Stevenson, J. & R. Clews, N. Dillon, Mansfield & Hackney, S. Godwin, S. Alcock and some others not at present in operation. The various kinds of Pottery and Porcelain are here manufactured in great perfection." [Nothing about A. Stevenson, although the words "some others" indicate that not all of the Cobridge potters are mentioned. At this time, Clews was operating the A. Stevenson Pottery.]

(2). *Staffordshire Pots and Potters*, by the Brothers G. Woolliscroft Rhead, R. E., and Frederick Alfred Rhead. Hutchinson and Co., London *(1906)*.

[The authors say nothing pertinent to this question. They quote Simeon Shaw constantly, though they apologize for the sources of his information, as Shaw states it came from persons "living near the spot" or "very aged persons" or "of unimpaired memory." But of course it was news gathered at this period (one hundred years ago) when the historic American pottery was made. Simeon Shaw, L. L. D., is spoken of as Master of the Grammar School, Burslem, in a magazine named *Pottery Mercury (1824)*, at the William Salt Library, Stafford, England. William Shaw's book, *When I Was a Child*, gives very interesting information: "Jewitt states that they [Cobridge Works] were erected in 1808 by Bucknall & Stevenson who were succeeded by A. Stevenson and afterwards by Ralph & James Clews in 1818. Stevenson either took a new works or his stamp was combined by Clews; otherwise Jewitt is wrong in his dates as designs relating to the year 1824 bear the stamp *A. Stevenson*"!]

(3). *History of Ceramic Art in Great Britain*, by Llewellynn Jewitt. [As this reference has been used by Mr. Rackham of London, in a letter which I will quote later, I shall omit it here.]

(4). *Old China Magazine*, S. Robineau, editor.

*Vol. I, No. 4, January 1902 (p. 57)*: "Each firm had its special bord-

November, 1934

198

ers, and these were not copied. . . . The use of the same border by two different potters is exceptional."

*Vol. II, No. 2, November 1902 (p. 32)*: "In every case in which borders are exceptionally found with two names of makers, it may safely be assumed that the border was not copied, but was disposed of by the firm who originated it and acquired by another firm. . . . Mr. Percy W. L. Adams, of Wolstanton, Staffordshire, wrote to us [that] he found in an old ledger of the Adams firm the proof that at the time the firm of Ralph & James Clews failed, they were considerably indebted to the Adams Potteries, for materials furnished, and that the Adams had to take what they could in payment, among other things, engravings. This explanation may also apply to the Clews-Stevenson exceptions."

*January 1902 (p. 54)*: "Some collectors are inclined to consider Enoch Wood as the maker of the acorn."

*January 1902 (p. 53)*: "Pieces of that series never bear any other mark than the initials *R. S. W.* Both Mr. Barber and Mr. Halsey, the best authorities on these questions, agree that these initials are a variation of the *R. S. & W.* initials found on the flower and scroll series, and standing for Ralph Stevenson & Williams."

*January 1902 (p. 58)*: "It may be interesting to notice that on American views an exception of this kind [Clews-Stevenson] is found in the well known rose and scroll border of Stevenson. Mr. Barber will mention in his second edition of *Anglo-American Pottery* four views which are found with this border and the Clews mark: *Columbia College, New York from Brooklyn Heights, New York Almshouse* and *Temple of Fame (Memorial to Perry)* and explains this exceptional case by the fact that Clews succeeded A. Stevenson in 1818. But the rose and scroll border is by Ralph and not by A. Stevenson, if we are not mistaken, and the Ralph Stevenson factory went out of existence only in 1840. Is it not possible and even probable that Ralph Stevenson and Adams bought some of the Clews engravings?" [On the back of some views by Clews have been found Adams' stamp. Why deprive A. Stevenson of his rose and scroll border and give it to Ralph when it is marked *A. Stevenson*? Pictures showing A. Stevenson marks on rose and scroll border accompany this article.]

(5). *Anglo-American Pottery*, by Edwin Atlee Barber. Patterson & White Co., Philadelphia (*1901*).

*Preface (p. 4)*: "Not the least important feature of the present work is the separation and rearrangement of the designs of A. Stevenson and R. Stevenson, which have occasioned so much confusion in the minds of collectors."

(P. 39): "A pottery was established at Cobridge, Staffordshire, England, in 1808, by Messrs. Bucknall & Stevenson, which, a few years later, was operated by Mr. Andrew Stevenson alone. The latter was among the first to make blue printed china decorated with American views."

(P. 40): "Very little is known of Stevenson himself, save that he was a prominent and careful potter. . . . His border designs were handsome and varied in character, that most frequently used being a well-executed design of flowers and scroll-work. . . . Mr. A. Stevenson was succeeded at the Cobridge works by Ralph and James Clews, as shown by the Staffordshire directory for 1818."

(6). *Pictures of Early New York on Dark Blue Staffordshire Pottery*, by R. T. Haines Halsey. Dodd, Mead & Co., New York (*1899*).

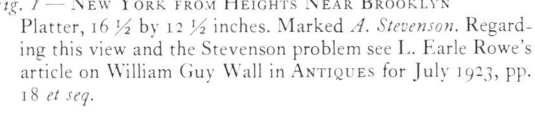

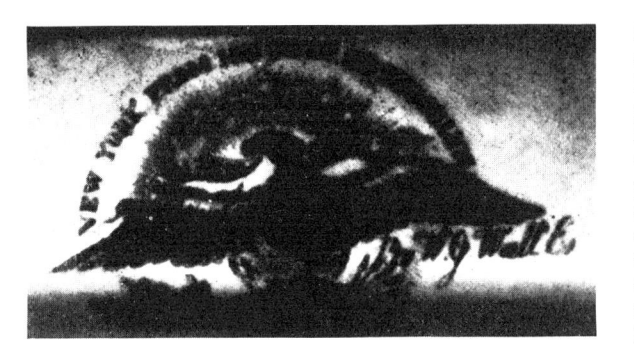

(*P. 153*): Of the Medallion Portraits Halsey says: "The importance of these plates is very great for they certainly prove conclusively that the plates impressed with the familiar mark *A. Stevenson* are not, as universally considered, the work of the potter who lived at Cobridge and who succeeded to the pottery of Messrs. Bucknall & Stevenson in 1808, but of Ralph Stevenson. A. Stevenson was succeeded in 1818 by the firm of J. & R. Clews. The absurdity of this error is plainly seen from the fact that the stamp *A. Stevenson* appears on plates showing views of the Erie Canal and portraits of Lafayette 'The Nation's Guest,' which were not printed until six years after the Messrs. Clews succeeded A. Stevenson. The events which they recall, did not occur until 1824 and 1825. That the Stevenson was Ralph is certain, for the identical portraits and scenes appear on the characteristic acorn border plates of Ralph Stevenson. This proof is strengthened by the fact that in 1828 Stevenson combined his forces with those of S. Alcock, a neighboring potter, better known for his ingenuity and taste than for his success in making a market for his wares. Undoubtedly the trade mark *A. Stevenson* was adopted with the view of retaining the prestige which the former products of R. Stevenson's pottery had secured in the American market." [The fact that "identical portraits and scenes (A. Stevenson in the Medallion Series) appear on the characteristic acorn border plates of Ralph Stevenson" is not proof that they belong only to the latter, for Barber gives, as quoted above, four pictures with A. Stevenson's rose and scroll border and the mark of Clews. Therefore in certain rare cases pictures *were* copied or used by two potters.]

*Fig. 1* — NEW YORK FROM HEIGHTS NEAR BROOKLYN
Platter, 16½ by 12½ inches. Marked *A. Stevenson*. Regarding this view and the Stevenson problem see L. Earle Rowe's article on William Guy Wall in ANTIQUES for July 1923, pp. 18 *et seq*.

(*P. 285*): "His [R. Stevenson's] earliest efforts, the crockery bearing the vine leaf border chiefly decorated with views of New York are impressed with the mark *Stevenson*. In some cases they have also the blue printed letters, *R. S.* or *R. S. W.* His next series is decorated with the oak leaf border and bears on the back the title printed in blue in a scroll accompanied by the initials, *R. S. W.* These are known to be the work of Stevenson, for on the back of the small *Scudder's Museum* plate with the white edge is found the impressed mark, *Stevenson*, as well as that of *R. S. W.* Another of Stevenson's plates bears an elaborate mark" [*R. Stevenson & Williams, Cobridge, Staffordshire*]. [All authors agree in giving R. Stevenson and R. S. W. credit for these two borders.]

(P. 287): "Working with Alcock, Ralph produced his most artistic series of three designs in border.
1. Roses and other flowers.
2. Large roses and rose buds.
3. Scrolls, skillfully intermingled with various flowers among which are roses, field daisies and clover.

The names of the views in these three series as a rule, are printed in blue upon a ribbon looped across an urn, though in some cases special designs were made for the title, as shown on the back of the plate, as well as the platter bearing a view of *New York From Heights near Brooklyn.*" [I shall discuss this point later.]

(7). *The Old China Book*, by N. Hudson Moore. Frederick A. Stokes Co., New York (*1903*).

(*P. 27*): "The potter who immediately preceded them [Clews] at Cobridge Works [was] Andrew Stevenson. As early in the last century as 1808, pottery works were established at Cobridge, Staffordshire, England, by the firm of Bucknall & Stevenson. . . . After a few years Bucknall withdrew, and Stevenson carried on the works alone."

(*P. 28*): "Ralph Stevenson, who also potted at Cobridge, but some years later. . . ."

(*P. 29*): "It was Andrew Stevenson who was succeeded by James and Ralph Clews."

(*P. 92*): "After it had been comfortably settled for years that A. Stevenson sold his business to James Clews in 1819, the discovery of these portrait plates with his stamp on them has set the collector adrift once more. Of course, these plates, made to celebrate an event which occurred in 1825 (opening of the Erie Canal), must have been made after that date. . . . It is thought by some collectors that Ralph Stevenson used the stamp *A. Stevenson* at his own works, which were operated till 1834. From this date until 1840 they were worked under the firm name of Ralph Stevenson & Sons. But why should R. Stevenson have got possession of A. Stevenson's stamps and designs when the works were sold to James Clews, probably with the dies and stamps? To my mind it seems more likely that Clews used these properties, for Clews did not part with the Cobridge works until 1829, and all the events commemorated by these pieces took place some years before that." [This sounds logical.]

Halsey apparently took his dates from Chaffers. In his *Marks & Monograms*, Chaffers states: "In a directory of 1802 we find the names of Stevenson and Dale as earthenware manufacturers at Cobridge, and in 1815 it was Ralph Stevenson alone, so also it is described in Shaw in 1828." Then Jewitt says: "Bucknall and Stevenson who operated for a few years from 1808 were succeeded in Cobridge by A. Stevenson."

I believe both Chaffers and Jewitt were right, and the confusion has arisen because each was speaking of a different firm. There is authority for saying there was more than one potter named Stevenson in Cobridge (Jewitt's *Ceramic Art etc.*).

Unsatisfied because of my inability to locate a Staffordshire Directory of 1818 and because of the meagreness of the information about Andrew, I wrote to the Curators of the British Museum and of the Victoria and Albert Museum. I quoted Barber in his *Anglo-American Pottery* about Andrew Stevenson, with its reference to the Staffordshire Directory. I asked each Curator if he would kindly quote for me all that was given in the Directory or any other authority about the Cobridge potter, Andrew Stevenson. I told them that Mr. Barber died in 1916 and therefore could not tell me the source of his information. I said I wanted to establish the truth as to whether Andrew Stevenson as a Staffordshire potter at Cobridge ever existed or whether *A. Stevenson* was merely a convenient mark adopted by Ralph.

Very promptly I received the following gracious answers:

Department of Printed Books, British Museum
March 18th, 1931

DEAR MADAM,

In reply to your enquiry of March 9th, I write to inform you that this library does not possess a directory of Staffordshire so early as 1818.

However, in "Pigot and Co.'s London and Provincial New Commercial Directory, 1822-3," in the section *Staffordshire*, and the subsection I looked to the district known as *The Potteries*, page 477, I find in the list of *Earthenware Manufacturers*, the name "Stevenson, Andrew, Cobridge," immediately following that of "Stevenson, Ralph, Cobridge."

This seems to be proof that "Ralph" and "Andrew" were distinct individuals.

W. W. MARSDEN, *Keeper of the Department of Printed Books.*

Department of Ceramics, Victoria & Albert Museum
24th March, 1931

DEAR MADAM,

In reply to your letter of the 9th March, I beg to inform you that the source of Mr. Barber's information was probably Llewellynn Jewitt, *Ceramic Art of Great Britain*, 2 vols. (*1878*). Jewitt states (*Vol. II, p. 290*): "*Cobridge Works.* The manufactory of Messrs. W. Brownfield & Son was erected in 1808, and from that time for a few years was worked by Messrs. Bucknall and Stevenson, and afterwards by Mr. A. Stevenson alone. In 1819 the works were closed, and afterwards passed into the hands of Mr. James Clews."

On page 297 Mr. Jewitt writes: "Other potters at one time or other at Cobridge are N. Dillon, R. Stevenson, etc."

*P. 431:* "*Stevenson.* There was more than one firm of potters named Stevenson in Staffordshire. Some were of Cobridge. One potter of that name used a vesica-shaped mark bearing a three-masted ship with the name *Stevenson* above it impressed in the ware. Another used the mark of a crown within a circle, bearing the words *A. Stevenson, Warranted, Staffordshire,* impressed in the ware. Another mark was simply the name *Stevenson,* also impressed."

Jewitt's work was based on contemporary directories, local researches, etc., and it is not likely that any further information would be forthcoming without additional research. I think it may be accepted that Andrew Stevenson (of Bucknall and Stevenson) and Ralph Stevenson (sometime Stevenson and Williams) were different persons. G. Woolliscroft Rhead, *British Pottery Marks* (*1910*), substantiates this view.

BERNARD RACKHAM, *Keeper of the Department of Ceramics.*

During the past six months I have had an especially equipped research worker make additional investigation for this article in the Staffordshire District in England, the "Black Country, where the minarets are chimneys, where the towers are potters' ovens, where the plastic clay is fashioned into forms of use and beauty." The pottery towns of Hanley, Burslem, Stafford, Cobridge, and Stoke-upon-Trent were combed for news of Andrew. Commercial and ecclesiastical directories from 1802 to 1850, old files of newspapers, manuscripts, magazines and pamphlets, wills, parish records, histories civic and personal, in public and private libraries, church libraries and town halls, were examined.

Much was found about Ralph, but Andrew was more elusive. Yet he is recorded in many places. Here are some of the most interesting items revealed by the search. We are concerned with Cobridge because it was the scene of the pottery of Andrew, *before* 1818. Cobridge was never a post town, but was part of Burslem. It is not to be found on any ordnance survey map, nor in a postal guide, but in the ecclesiastical directory. The Parish Church of St. John the Baptist, Burslem, included Cobridge, which had no parish of its own until about 1844.

Parish Registers printed up to 1812 revealed nothing about

*Fig. 2* — ALMSHOUSE, NEW YORK
10-inch plate. Marked *A. Stevenson*

Andrew Stevenson. Under *Baptisms*, from 1819 (*January*) to 1823 (*August*), no children were born to any Andrew Stevenson. *Burials*, 1818-1823, 1823-1831, 1831-1840, 1840-1850: no Andrew Stevenson is recorded as buried except a year-and-a-half-old child buried October 20, 1833. *Marriages*, 1812-1833: no Andrew Stevenson was married or appeared in a printed register.

There seems to be no discoverable record of the Stevenson-Clews transfer of the pottery in Cobridge in 1818 or 1819. In the *Staffordshire Advertiser* for April 4, 1818, under *Sundries to Let*, "two sets of Potworks, situate at Cobridge" are mentioned, and two other entries during that year announce potworks to be let and to be auctioned off, but nothing indicates that Stevenson was connected with these transactions. The next year, in May, certain potworks in Cobridge were sold. In July a firm of potters decided to retire and offered its works for sale, and in November still another retired. (Andrew sold his pottery at a popular time.)

The Staffordshire Directories appear to have been published at intervals of four, five, or six years. In London, only three Directories (Pigot's) are available, 1822-1823, 1828-1829, and 1835-1842. Mr. Marsden, Keeper in the Department of Printed Books, in the British Museum, has quoted from the first (*1822-1823*). In that of 1828-1829 we find the following (*p. 726*):

*Staffordshire*          *The Potteries*
    *Earthenware Manufacturers*
    Stevenson, Andrew      Cobridge
    Stevenson, Ralph        Cobridge

From *Pigot and Co.'s National Commercial Directory*, London (*1835*), pages 430 and 431:

*Staffordshire*          *The Potteries*
    *Earthenware Manufacturers*
    Clews, Ralph & James    Cobridge
    Stevenson, Ralph & Son   Cobridge

No Stevensons are listed under *Coal Masters*, and Andrew has fallen out of the list of *Earthenware Manufacturers*. Andrew is likewise missing from the 1834 list shown below.

From *William White's History Gazetteer and Directory of Stafford*, Sheffield (*1834*), page 584:

*Burslem*
    *Earthenware Manufacturers*
Stevenson, Ralph & Son              Cobridge
Clews, Ralph & James               Cobridge
    *Coal Masters*
Clews, Ralph & James            Jackfield Colliery

From *History of the Borough of Stoke-upon-Trent*, by John Ward, London (*1843*), page 286:

*Burslem*
A List of Manufacturing Firms engaged in Earthenware or China Business at Cobridge.                                    (*1839*)
Wood & Brownfield (at the large works formerly Stevenson & Bucknall, afterward R. & J. Clews). [This is the one accredited to A. Stevenson by Jewitt.]
John & George Alcock (late R. Stevenson's works).

From the *Stafford General and Commercial Directory*, compiled by W. Parson & T. Bradshaw, Manchester (*1818*) — bound with the copy of Simeon Shaw at the William Salt Library, Stafford:

*Burslem*
(*p. 47*) Stevenson, Ralph, earthenware manufacturer.     Cobridge
(*p. 47*) Stevenson, Andrew, coal merchant            Cobridge
(*p. 37*) Clews, Ralph & James, earthenware mfgr.      Cobridge
    *Alphabetical List of Tradesmen.* [Same information]
      (*pp. 51*)    *Coal Proprietors.*
    Stevenson, Andrew (merchant)
                                     Cobridge
    (*p. 52*) *Earthenware Manufacturers.*
    Clews, R. & J.            Cobridge
    Stevenson, Ralph        Cobridge
    *List of Earthenware Manufacturers*
           *in the Potteries.*
    (*p. 128*) Clews, R. & J.    Cobridge
    Stevenson, Ralph        Cobridge
    Stevenson, Andrew     Cobridge

From *The Newcastle & Pottery General & Commercial Directory for 1822-1823*, Hanley:

*Burslem*
(*p. 51*) Stevenson, Andrew, earthenware mfgr.      Cobridge
(*p. 51*) Stevenson, Ralph, earthenware mfgr.        Cobridge
(*p. 36*) Clews, R. & J. china & earthenware mfgr.     Cobridge

It was suggested at the William Salt Library that poll books and jury lists in possession of the County Council might furnish further information. Research disclosed the fact that there were no voters' lists as early as the period under consideration. Among *Jury Lists* was found:

*Sept. 9, 1817*,
An Alphabetical List of Persons liable to serve on Juries for the Township of Burslem, by Thomas Cooper, Constable.
    *Names*     *Place of Abode*     *Description*
             (whether yeoman, gentleman, farmer)
    Stevenson, Andrew Cobridge Manufacturer G. J.

G. J., meaning *Grand Juror*, signified one "proper to serve upon the Jury at the Sessions." *Ralph Stevenson G. J.* occurs on the Jury Lists of 1821, 1823, and 1825.

The Chief Clerk of the County Council ventured the opinion that the non-appearance of Andrew Stevenson on grand jury lists later than 1817 might indicate that he had moved away or that he was over age (the law now exempts all persons over sixty years old; perhaps it was in force then).

We have, therefore, many proofs that Andrew Stevenson did exist as a Staffordshire potter at Cobridge (as per Directories of 1818, 1822 [2], 1828), that he operated until 1818 or 1819 not merely as an earthenware manufacturer but as a coal merchant, and was of sufficient moment to the community to be on the grand-jury list. We have removed the arguments advanced in the editorial for attributing Andrew's three beautiful floral borders to Ralph, whose designs were of a totally different character. Lastly we have shown that Andrew Stevenson's sale of his works to Clews by no means put an end to his activities as a potter, which, indeed, are recognized in Pigot's directory as late as 1828-1829. Are we not then permitted to credit Andrew, and no one else, with pictorial wares made from 1820 to 1825 upon which his mark appears?

*Fig. 3* — NIAGARA (SHEEP-SHEARING SCENE); ENTRANCE OF ERIE CANAL, ALBANY
10-inch plate. Marked *A. Stevenson*

# James and Ralph Clews, nineteenth-century potters

## Part I: *The English experience*

BY FRANK STEFANO JR.

ONLY CONFLICTING OR incomplete accounts have appeared about James and Ralph Clews, makers of Staffordshire ware from 1815 to 1834. Very little has been published at all about the pottery James Clews managed near Louisville, Kentucky, from 1837 to 1842. The present articles, the first about the Clews brothers in England and the second about James Clews in America, are an attempt to clarify and expand the record.

James Clews was born on September 2, 1790, one of six children of John and Ann Clews of Newcastle under Lyme. His father was at first a hatter and later a malt manufacturer. His older brother Ralph (born 1788) first entered the father's malt business, but by November 1815[1] had joined James in the pottery business, as a handbill of that date indicates (Fig. 1).

Many new potteries sprang up in Staffordshire at this time but few firms committed themselves so completely to the export, and especially the American, market as did the Clews brothers.[2] For this reason, even today marked pieces of Clews ware are relatively rare in England.

The brothers appear never to have operated separately nor to have taken in other partners during the nineteen-year life of the firm. It appears too that they always rented their potting works and that they were located at at least two potteries in Cobridge. On September 29, 1817, William Adams rented to the brothers "a potworks and other buildings at Cobridge for 15 years starting 11 November 1817 for 130 pounds annually due the first of November and May, free and clear of and from all taxes and deductions."[3]

Sometime after this the brothers appear to have rented a larger potting works from Andrew Stevenson[4] called the Cobridge Works, where they remained until their bankruptcy in 1834.[5]

It is possible that the Clews brothers lacked capital to buy their own potting works, for when their father died in 1819 they were already in debt to his estate £938/7/11, not including interest.[6]

Although many other potters produced historical views as well as English and decorative designs, only the Clewses offered the three so-called literary series consisting of engravings after Thomas Rowlandson's Dr. Syntax drawings (Fig. 2), illustrations from Don Quixote after paintings by Robert Smirke (Fig. 3), and a series of engravings after paintings of domestic scenes by Sir David Wilkie, R.A. (Fig. 4). The Clews brothers also produced the beautiful Indian Sport series which hitherto has been said to be exclusively Spode (Pl. II, Fig. 5). Perhaps Clews wares in this series were made for export and Spode's for the domestic market. Figure 6 shows another example of the Indian Sport series made by Clews. On the back it bears

**CAUTION**

TO

**PERSONS TIPPLING,**

AND TO

***PUBLICANS.***

THE UNDERSIGNED MANUFACTURERS of Earthen-Ware within the parish of BURSLEM, sustaining the most serious loss and inconvenience, by daily interruptions to their business, in consequence of the habits of idleness and tippling which many of their workmen indulge in, during the regular hours of work, and in which they find encouragement by the very CULPABLE CONDUCT OF MANY PUBLICANS within this parish; Do hereby make known, that from the publication of this Notice, *they are resolved to give every protection and support to such persons as will lay complaints before the Magistrates, against any workmen for the offence of tippling;* and the undersigned Manufacturers have also resolved,

***Individually to notice and to report to the Magistrates***

The conduct of all such Publicans as shall from henceforth suffer any workmen to remain tippling in their houses during the regular working hours, or at any other improper time.

**THE PUBLICANS ARE HEREBY INFORMED,**

That on conviction of the offence of suffering tippling, or unlawful Games in their houses, they are liable to *forfeit their recognizances*, and to have their *licenses suspended* for the space of *three years*, besides being subject to a penalty of ten shillings for every offence by tippling; and that *the Magistrates acting for this Hundred have come to the resolution of putting these laws strictly in force for the future.*

☞ Any person found tippling in a Public-house is liable to a penalty of three shillings and four-pence, to the use of the Poor, besides the costs of the information.

*Burslem, November*, 1815.

| | | |
|---|---|---|
| *Wood & Caldwell* | *Jno. & Rich. Riley* | *Jno. Rogers* |
| *Henshall & Williamsons* | *Tho. & Benj. Godwin* | *Rhead & Goodfellow* |
| *Jno. & Jas. Davenport* | *William Stanley* | *Machin & Co.* |
| *Thomas Heath* | *John Brettell* | *Wm. Bourne & Co.* |
| *Samuel Tomkinson* | *William Moseley* | *James Cartlidge* |
| *Ralph Johnson* | *Stevenson and Bucknall* | *J. and R. Blackwell* |
| *Thomas Bathwell* | *Wm. Walsh* | *Benj. Godwin and Sons* |
| *Edward Bourne* | *John Haywood* | *F. and N. Dillon* |
| *John & Christr. Robinson* | *John Wood* | *Ralph Stevenson* |
| *John Hall* | *Lindop & Taylor* | *R. and J. Clews* |

*** Every Publican within this parish will be expected to keep one of these Notices conspicuously posted up in his house, as a proof he is determined to maintain good order therein.

TREGORTHA, PRINTER

Fig. 1. This handbill of November 1815 issued in Burslem warns publicans not to serve pottery workers drinks during working hours. As the usual workday extended from 6 A.M. to 9 P.M. with one and one-half hours off for meals, this was a severe deprivation (*The Victoria History of the County of Stafford*, ed. J. G. Jenkins, London, 1963, Vol. 2, p. 52). *City Museum, Stoke on Trent.*

the same impressed mark of Clews as the soup plate shown in Figure 5, but also the circular impressed inscription *John Greenfield, Importer of China & Earthenware, No 77, Pearl Street, New York*. The latter firm was in business at that address from 1817 to 1843[7] and was probably large enough to import exclusive patterns and designs.

One reason for the lack of a thriving domestic white earthenware industry in the United States until about the middle of the century was the low price of Staffordshire wares. The wholesale price asked by the American importer of the Clews teapot in Plate III, for example, was probably about 50¢, to judge by the wholesale prices for teapots of $6.00 a dozen which was quoted in 1833 by the American importers Rudd and Martin of Louisville, Kentucky.[8]

Although much Clews pottery survives today, no complete record remains of the series, patterns, and forms that the brothers produced.[9] Thus, for example, no marked piece from the dark-blue Cities series has been found, although the series has been attributed to Clews on the basis of a bowl with a print from the Cities series at the center and a border known to have been used by Clews on the Don Quixote series. Since Staffordshire potters rarely pirated each others borders, it seems reasonable to believe that the bowl was made by the Clews brothers.[10]

The three Clews teapots in Plate IV show the wide range of styles and shapes of hollow ware produced by Clews. Further classification of their wares could be made on the basis of the molds used to produce the hollow ware.

In 1827 James and Ralph Clews were forced to declare bankruptcy when Job Meigh of Shelton, "Manufacturer of China," and other creditors called the brothers' debt of £13,419/4/0. By an indenture of bankruptcy dated January 29, 1827, the Clewses were forced to relinquish their entire stock of "Glass, China and Earthenware," from their pottery at Cobridge, their London showroom and warehouse at 111 Holborn Hill, and their two warehouses in Liverpool at 52 Castle Street and on Pool Lane. The agreement was sealed not only with the signatures of all parties but by "the delivery of one Tea Cup in the name of and in lieu of" the delivery of the entire inventory.[11]

However, the Clews brothers overcame this financial crisis, continued to manufacture transfer-printed earthenware, and ventured into other businesses as well. Besides continuing to operate a brewery they had inherited from their father, they acquired a flint mill and a colliery to supply raw materials they needed at their pottery. In the early 1830's they built the Waterloo and American Hotel on Waterloo Road, Cobridge, the main route between Burslem and Hanley. The building is now a pub called the American.

The notice of the Clewses' second and final bankruptcy was carried in the *Staffordshire Advertiser* on November 22, 1834. It may have been precipitated by the first major strike at the potteries which had begun on Martinmas (November 11). Workers at the potteries were hired only on that date for wages that remained fixed for the next twelve months. However, in 1834 they refused to sign the agreement and struck the potteries for four months.[12] The brothers' assets[13] were dispersed at a series of sales over the next six months. The two-week-long sale of the potting fixtures in February 1835 comprised:

All the potters fixtures, stock of materials and utensils; Consisting of block and working moulds, of the most approved shapes and

Fig. 2. *Dr. Syntax Reading his Tour*, from the Dr. Syntax series. Dark-blue transfer-printed plate by James and Ralph Clews. This is one of the thirty-one designs in the Dr. Syntax series after drawings by Thomas Rowlandson (1756-1827) originally made to illustrate William Combe's three-volume satire on the published tours of William Gilpin (1724-1804). (Another plate from this series appeared in ANTIQUES for January 1974, p. 170.) Diameter 8½ inches. *Collection of Robert Scanaff*.

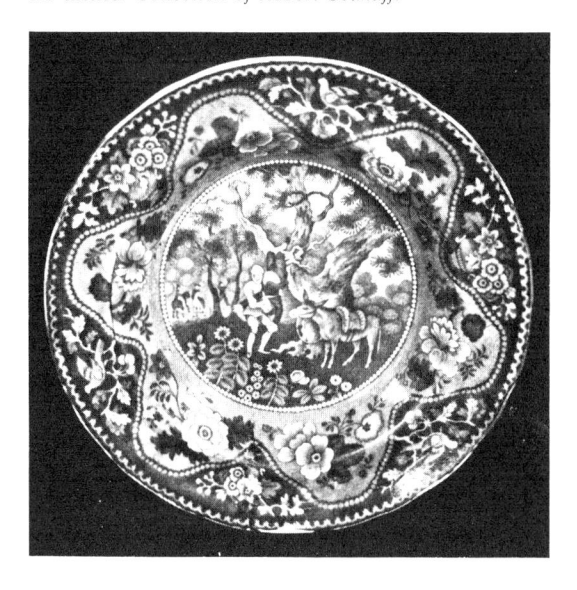

Fig. 3. *Sancho Panza at the Boar Hunt*, from the Don Quixote series. Dark-blue transfer-printed soup plate by James and Ralph Clews. This is one of twenty-one designs in the series after paintings by Robert Smirke (1752-1845) which were engraved and then used to illustrate a translation made by his daughter, Mary, of Cervantes' *Don Quixote*. Diameter 9¾ inches. *Photograph by courtesy of Garry Stradling*.

Fig. 4. *The Escape of the Mouse*, from the Wilkie series. Dark-blue transfer-printed plate by James and Ralph Clews. This is one of seven designs done after paintings of English cottage life by Sir David Wilkie, R.A. (1785-1841). Diameter 10¼ inches.

Pl. I. *Landing of Gen. LaFayette at Castle Garden, New York, 16th August 1824.* Transfer-printed platter by James and Ralph Clews. The engraving was done by Samuel Maverick of New York. Length 19 inches. *National Museum of History and Technology.*

Pl. II. *Chase After a Wolf,* from the Indian Sport series. Transfer-printed soup plates, the one at the left by Spode; the one at the right by James and Ralph Clews. Diameter of each, 9¾ inches. *Photograph by Helga Photo Studio.*

Pl. III. *Christmas Eve*, from the Wilkie series. Transfer-printed teapot by James and Ralph Clews. This is one of seven designs in that series (see caption to Fig. 4). Height 7½ inches. *Helga photograph.*

Pl. IV. Transfer-printed teapots by James and Ralph Clews. The one at the left, showing children playing with a dog, has on the bottom the blue printed mark CLEWS in a Chinese-style seal; the one at the center has on the bottom the pattern name, *Summer Rose* in a blue cartouche and the impressed words CLEWS WARRANTED STAFFORDSHIRE in a circular mark surrounding a crown; the one at the right is the so-called Neptune pattern. The first two teapot patterns have not previously been classified as being made by Clews; the Neptune pattern appears in Laidacker, *Anglo-American China*, Part 2, p. 36. Height of tallest pot, 7½ inches. *Helga photograph.*

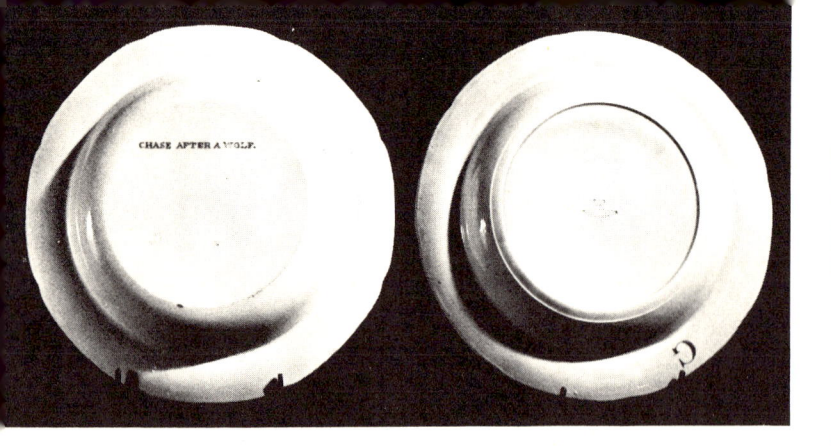

Fig. 5. Reverse of the soup plates shown in Pl. II. The plate at the left bears both the printed and impressed name SPODE as well as the printed name of the design, *Chase After a Wolf.* The plate at the right has impressed at the center beneath a crown CLEWS/WARRANTED/STAFFORDSHIRE. The *G* at the edge is printed in blue.

patterns, adopted for the home trade and American Markets. With most extensive and valuable sets of copper plate engravings, in table, desert, toilet, jug and tea services, many of which are quite new, and the production of some of the most approved artists in the trade; also an extensive stock of Blue and Black Ball Clay, China Clay and other materials. Throwing wheels, lathes, benches, headpoles, pegposts, stillages and stovepots. About 30 printing presses, printing stoves, bakeplates. Upwards of 2000 work boards, lead and colour mills, buckets and wheelbarrows. About 6000 biscuit and gloss saggers. 300 saggerhoards and drums. Large and small mortars and pestles, crane weighting machine, dropping tubs, washing out tubs, beating flags, stove flags, plater do, and frames and a great number of other utensils requisit for that line of business. Also a general and large assortment of colour, cobalt and zaffre calx; cording, printers flannel, soda borax, etc; 4 tons of cullet, nearly 1 ton of old copper; counting house desks and cupboards, copying machine, iron chests, valuable iron door and door case and frame, several sets of scales, etc.[14]

The inventory of earthenware was sold on March 27, 1835. The advertisement for that sale reads in part:

Manufactured Earthenware—on the premises at the Large and Small Manufactories, at Cobridge, on Friday 27 March 1835, in one or more lots. The entire manufactured stock of Earthenware consisting of a general assortment of Blue and Coloured Printed Table Ware, Tea Service, Ewers and basins, Jugs, Toilet, and Desert Sets. Edged, Painted, Cream Color and a great variety of other articles of Earthenware.[15]

Thus ended the partnership of the Clews brothers and the production of Staffordshire ware at their works in Cobridge. Ralph was content to remain in Newcastle under Lyme, but James, who had been the driving force in the firm, emigrated with his family to America in 1836 to superintend a potting venture near Louisville, Kentucky. Part two of this article, to appear in ANTIQUES in March, will relate the history of that venture.

Fig. 6. *Driving a Bear out of the Sugar Cane,* from the Indian Sport series, based on drawings by Samuel Howitt (1765?-1822). The reverse bears the same impressed Clews mark as the soup plate shown in Fig. 5 (right). It also has the circular impressed inscription *John Greenfield, Importer of China & Earthenware, No 77, Pearl Street, New York.* Length 17 inches.

[1] The partnership did not begin in 1818 as maintained in W. E. Little, *Staffordshire Blue* (New York, 1969, p. 56); or 1819 as maintained in E. B. Larsen, *American Historical Views on Staffordshire China* (New York, 1950, p. 53).

[2] The firm also exported to Russia and printed on their billhead "Potters to Her Imperial Majesty, the Empress of all the Russians" (Geoffrey A. Godden, *Encyclopaedia of British Pottery and Porcelain Marks,* New York, 1964, p. 152).

[3] The lease is preserved in the archives of the Stoke City Library, Stoke on Trent, Staffordshire.

[4] There is no evidence to support the suggestion that the Clews brothers bought Stevenson's pottery works as implied in Llewellyn Jewitt's *Ceramic Art in Great Britain* (London, 1878, Vol. 2, p. 290) and stated in Larsen, *American Historical Views* (p. 44). Neither of the two bankruptcy proceedings against the Clews brothers mentions their owning the facilities for manufacturing earthenware.

[5] In 1836 these works were taken over by the firm of Robinson, Wood and Brownfield.

[6] When John Clews died on October 31, 1819, his will placed his estate in trust for his six children. One of the provisions of the will, which was dated October 23, 1819, was that advances made to James and Ralph Clews "at diverse times . . . to enable them the better to carry on their trade and partnership in the Earthenware Manufactury . . . now indebted to 938 pounds 7 shillings and 11 pense be repaid, with interest into the estate." (The will is filed among the Bishops' Transcripts, Litchfield, Staffordshire.)

[7] New York City directories.

[8] The Rudd and Martin daybook entry of March 30, 1833, quotes the following wholesale prices for Staffordshire in Louisville, Kentucky.

| | | | |
|---|---|---|---|
| Edged Twifflers | .50 | per dozen | |
| " Plates | .70 | " | " |
| " Muffins | .40 | " | " |
| " Cup Plates | .30 | " | " |
| Printed Hollow-ware | | | |
| Pitchers | 4.00 | per dozen | |
| " | 7.50 | " | " |
| Tea Pots | 6.00 | " | " |
| Creamers | 2.75 | " | " |
| Sugars | 4.00 | " | " |

"Twifflers" and "muffins" correspond to today's salad and bread-and-butter plates. The daybook is preserved in The Filson Club, Louisville, Kentucky.

[9] The first research into Staffordshire patterns was Edwin Atlee Barber's *Anglo-American Pottery* (Indianapolis, 1899). A much more complete and detaiied study was E. B. Larsen's *American Historical Views on Staffordshire China.* There is also Sam Laidecker's *Anglo-American China* (Bristol, Pennsylvania; Part 1 [revised 1954]. Part 2 [1951]).

[10] ANTIQUES, March 1954, p. 238.

[11] The indenture of bankruptcy is preserved in the William Salt Library, Stafford, England.

[12] Harold Owen, *The Staffordshire Potter* (Bath, 1970, p. 29).

[13] These assets were their brewery at Shelton, carried on in the name of Clews and Malkin; their interest in the estate of their late father, John Clews of Newcastle under Lyme; their flint mill at Tunstall; their colliery called the Jackfield Colliery in Burslem; settlement of a suit against Joseph Heath for rent on the flint mill; the Waterloo and American Hotel and its contents; all potters' fixtures, materials, and utensils; James Clews' newly erected dwelling, called Oxleasows, near Cobridge, plus 110 acres of land, nearly all of it in turf; cattle, horses, sheep, pigs, and other livestock, wheat, oats, straw, and other feed at Spot Farm near Hilderstone; two dwellings in "The Twenty Row," Burslem; two freehold houses in Merrill Street, Newcastle; and (subject to a mortgage of £1000) the dwelling and malthouse, Marsh Street, Newcastle, belonging to Ralph Clews. (The above is a digest of the information contained in the *North Staffordshire Mercury, Pottery Gazette & Newcastle Express,* December 20, 1834.)

[14] *North Staffordshire Mercury,* January 24, 1835.

[15] *Ibid.,* March 14, 1835.

# James Clews, nineteenth-century potter

## Part II: *The American experience*

BY FRANK STEFANO JR.

AT THE BEGINNING of the 1830's the United States made no equivalent to the white-clay Staffordshire ware that was imported so successfully and in such large quantities from England. The domestic earthenware industry was limited to redware, brownware, and the stoneware used for jugs and crocks.

In 1837 the Indiana Pottery Company was started near Louisville, Kentucky, to produce the white earthenware known as queen's ware. The three principals in the venture were Jacob Lewis, a Louisville potter, Samuel Casseday, a Louisville importer of earthenware, and James Clews (Fig. 1), the Staffordshire potter whose career in England was reviewed in Part I of this article, which appeared in ANTIQUES for February.

Jacob Lewis had been interested in producing whiteware from local clays since the early 1820's, and in 1828 he sent samples of those clays to England with John P. Bull, a partner of Casseday's in the Louisville earthenware importing firm of Bull and Casseday. As Bull wrote: "I had a small pitcher made of it: it was mixed up and made in my presence, and marked with my name on the bottom. . . . It can be easy seen that the quality is finer than the English ware. I gave it to Mr. Lewis when it arrived in 1829."[1] In 1828 and 1829 Lewis furnished local whiteware clays to William Frost and Jabez Vodrey who in 1827 had started a pottery in Pittsburgh. Lewis later persuaded Frost and Vodrey to come to Louisville and work for the Lewis Pottery Company, incorporated there in 1829 to make queen's ware.[2] About the enterprise Vodrey later wrote: "We did not succeed in making all good ware in the first attempt of new materials. The company became discouraged, and all of them abandoned it except Mr. Lewis. He continued, and saved it from being lost to the State and country."[3]

When Samuel Casseday first came to Louisville in 1822 he worked as a clerk in a crockery store.[4] In June 1824 he and John P. Bull started a business as dealers in queen's ware, chinaware, and glass. The firm was one of the first west of the Alleghenies to import Staffordshire directly. The vegetable dish shown in Figure 2, with a view of Louisville, was one of the many patterns which Bull and Casseday probably imported from Staffordshire. It is from the unmarked Cities series attributed to James and Ralph Clews.[5]

Casseday also recognized the importance of promoting a domestic earthenware industry and was the first of more than fifty signers of a "Memorial of Certain Citizens of Louisville, Kentucky" dated May 14, 1834, asking Congress to grant Jacob Lewis a tract of land "for the establishment of a manufactory for fine earthenware."[6] Two years later Casseday bought land near the village of Troy, Indiana, some distance downriver from Louisville,[7] on which the Indiana Pottery Company came to be estab-

Fig. 1. Portrait of James Clews (1790-1861), artist unknown. Oil on canvas. *Collection of John E. Parsons.*

lished. The location was chosen because of the availability of the necessary clays and coal. The company was incorporated by a special act of the Indiana legislature on January 7, 1837, and started with a capital of $100,000 and eleven partners, most of them Louisville businessmen.[8] One of the partners was James Clews, who had come to Louisville in 1836 on Casseday's invitation. Late in that year Clews imported thirty-six potters from Europe to staff the Troy pottery,[9] a task doubtless facilitated by the fact that thousands of workers had struck the British potteries that autumn.[10] The new venture also drew other British potters who had previously emigrated to America, including James Bennett, who had come to the United States in 1834 at the age of twenty-two and worked in Jersey City. Bennett was one of the real founders of the American earthenware industry, not at the Troy works, which he subsequently left, but at East Liverpool, Ohio.

The Indiana Pottery Company's first kiln of ware was pulled in June 1837.[11] The snuff bottle in Figures 3 and 3a was made and transfer printed by the company while Clews was associated with it. The glaze flowed imperfectly so that it is lighter on the front than on the back, and although the transfer is in blue, it is not the rich dark blue of the English wares. Nonetheless this snuff bottle is one of the first examples of transfer-printed earthenware produced in America.[12] No examples are known of white earthenware marked with the firm's complete name, perhaps because it was felt that Clews' name (Fig. 3a) would sell better.

At the end of the first year of operation the directors of the company petitioned Congress for a donation of public land containing the raw materials the pottery needed. The petition, dated January 4, 1838, stated:

That, for a number of years, many of them have been engaged in examining and experimenting upon the clays and other materials west of the Alleghany Mountains necessary for Manufacturing Queensware and China; that they so far satisfied themselves of the abundance and quality of these materials, in the western country that they obtained a year ago an act of incorporation from the State of Indiana, under the style and name of 'The Indiana Pottery Company'. That they located the establishment at Troy, in said state, and erected large and suitable buildings and machinery, for the said manufactory, and sent to Europe and imported a number of potters, say in all, thirty-six, at very great expense and trouble. That their manufactory is now in operation, and the company have fully and completely tested and proved the practicability of rendering our country independent of foreign nations, for the articles of queensware and china; but then find that it will be impossible ever to make the business yield a profit until workmen can be made of American citizens. They are, therefore, convinced that they must pursue this business at a heavy loss for several years to come, and having already expended over fifty thousand dollars, and their means being so far exhausted that they can not divert them from the works, they respectfully represent that there is in the States of Indiana, Illinois and Missouri, clay, marl, flint, spar and other material necessary for the manufacturing of queensware and china; that they are to be found, generally, on poor and broken public lands, that they have been many years in market and remain unsold, that it is necessary for the future prosecution of their manufacurery that the company should possess some of these lands, and they are of the opinion that their success is of great national importance.

James Clews remained part of the management of the ailing company until 1842, when he sold his three shares back to the company.[13] He must have remained in America until at least 1847, for in that year ''James Clews of the City of New York''[14] sold the five acres of property in Troy that he had bought in 1838, after being in Troy for about two years.[15] British records show that Clews had taken up residence near Hilderstone, which is near Stoke on Trent, in 1849, and that he died there on July 7, 1861.[16]

The Indiana Pottery Company continued under that name and was managed by Jabez Vodrey until 1846. From then until 1859, when he sold it, the property continued to be owned by Samuel Casseday but was leased and operated by others.

Fig. 2. View of Louisville, Kentucky, from the Cities series attributed to James and Ralph Clews. Dark-blue transfer-printed vegetable dish. The view shows the city and the Ohio River in the early 1830's with Sixth Street the broad thoroughfare leading down to the water. *National Museum of History and Technology.*

[1] From "A brief view of efforts made to get a Fine Ware Pottery established in Louisville," appended to the "Memorial of Certain Citizens of Louisville, Kentucky," of May 14, 1834, addressed to the 23rd Congress, First Session. Pamphlet in The Filson Club.

[2] That the Lewis Pottery Company was making queen's-ware pottery was noted in the following advertisement, which appeared in the Louisville *Public Advertiser* for March 2, 1830: "STONEWARE: Issac Dover informs the Public, that he has established a Pottery, east end of Main Street (North Side), a short distance from the Queensware Pottery of Mr. Jacob Lewis, where he keeps on hand an assortment of Stoneware. . . ."

[3] From "A brief view . . ." appended to the "Memorial of certain citizens. . . ."

[4] A summary of the life of Samuel Casseday appears in *History of the Ohio Falls Cities & Their Counties*, Cleveland, 1882, pp. 565-566.

[5] The attribution was made in ANTIQUES for March 1954, p. 238. Also in the Cities series are other views of the growing Midwest showing Chillicothe, Columbus, and Sandusky, Ohio; and Detroit, Michigan.

[6] The memorial says, in part: "Your memorialists, citizens of the city of Louisville and its vicinity, respectfully represent to your honorable body, that they are deeply impressed with the opinion that it is the true policy of every enlightened nation to encourage and promote domestic manufactures, particularly the manufacture of such articles of necessity, comfort, and convenience, as can be introduced without increasing the burden of the people; and that it should be the policy of our Government to aid and support such manufactures, as the country will thereby be rendered less dependant upon the skill and industry of foreign nations.

"Amongst other manufactures of daily domestic use for which the people of the United States have been, and still are dependant upon other nations, are the various articles of queensware, or white earthenware, which your memorialists believe can be advantageously manufactured in the United States, if suitably encouraged, of a quality fully equal in all respects to similar articles imported from Great Britain."

[7] Indenture for fifty acres of land dated June 18, 1836, from Samuel and Nancy Connor to Casseday; indenture for six acres of land dated August 4, 1836, from Alexander M. Fountaine *et al.* to Casseday. Courthouse records, Cannelton, Indiana. I am indebted to Frank Baertich for making these and other Indiana records available to me.

[8] The partners were: James Clews, Samuel Casseday, Jacob Lewis, Willis Ranney, Reuben Bates, William Bell, James Anderson Jr., Edmund T. Bainbridge, Perly Chamberlin, John B. Bland, and William Garvin (Edwin Atlee Barber, *The Pottery and Porcelain of the United States*, New York, 1893, p. 159). Ranney was Casseday's current partner in the earthenware importing business. Bates was a merchant from Troy who also contributed some land to the venture. Except for Lewis and Clews the other partners were Louisville merchants.

[9] Petition to the 25th Congress, Second Session, by the Indiana Pottery Company dated January 4, 1838, William Henry Smith Memorial Library, Indianapolis.

[10] In anticipation of the annual hiring date of Martinmas (November 11) some 3,500 employees at fourteen manufactories in Staffordshire came out on strike in September 1836. They were followed on Martinmas itself by a total of some 20,000 employees of sixty-four manufactories (Harold Owen, *The Staffordshire Potter*, Bath, 1970, pp. 36-37).

[11] John Ramsay, *American Potters and Pottery*, Clinton, Massachusetts, 1939, p. 106.

[12] Transfer printing was also being developed by David Henderson at his American Pottery Manufacturing Company in Jersey City, New Jersey, in the early 1840's.

[13] In return for the shares he was allowed $500 for bringing out his family from England and $2740 for bringing out hands for the pottery from England. Each party released the other from all liability arising out of James Clews' management of the concern. (James Clews vs. Samuel Casseday, May 1842 term of the Perry County, Indiana, court. Courthouse records, Cannelton.)

[14] Indenture dated August 25, 1847, Clews to Taylor Basye, Perry County courthouse records.

[15] Indenture dated November 13, 1838, Catherine and Denison Mason to Clews, Perry County courthouse records.

[16] Staffordshire directories 1848 to 1861; death notice in the *North Staffordshire Mercury*, July 13, 1861: "on the 7th instant, James Clews, Esq., of the Ox Leasows, near Hilderstone, in his 71st year."

Fig. 3. Whiteware snuff bottle made by the Indiana Pottery Company, c. 1837-1842. The Baltimore directory for 1835-1836 shows "Starr, Tobacconist 27 S Calvert Street." The next available directory, of 1845, gives Starr's address as "31 S Calvert Street." Height 6¼ inches. *Collection of Mrs. Spencer Woodbridge.*

Fig. 3a. Bottom of the snuff bottle in Fig. 3 showing the mark CLEW'S MANUFACTURER'S. Diameter 3⅜ inches.

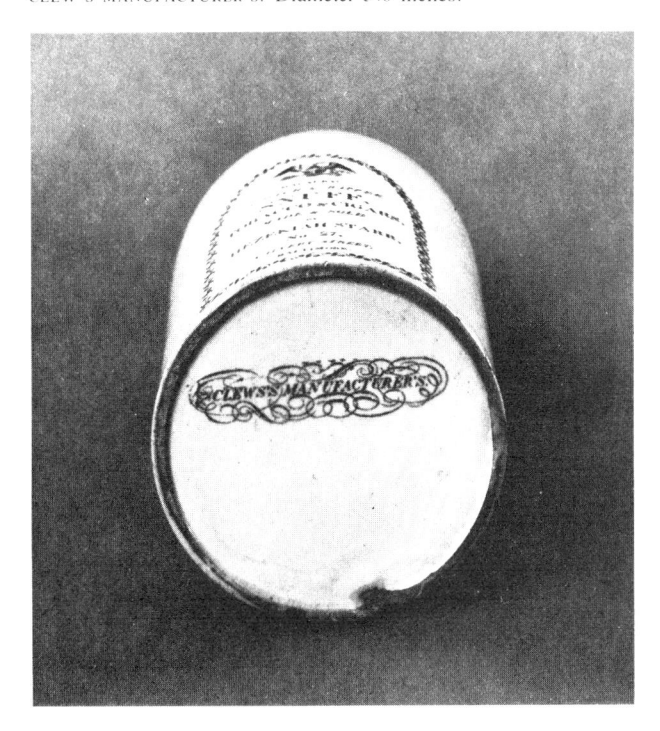

# Enoch Wood earthenware found in St. Paul's Church, Burslem

BY PAMELA D. KINGSBURY

WHEN ST. PAUL'S Church in Burslem, Staffordshire (Fig. 1), was demolished in 1974 a large cache of ceramics placed there by Enoch Wood (1759-1840) was discovered in the foundations of the walls. The church, erected in 1828, had become structurally unsound and the decision was made to demolish rather than remodel it. The demolition agreement gave the contractor complete salvage rights. However, after consultation with the staff of the City Museum and Art Gallery, Stoke-on-Trent, the contractor donated nearly three hundred pieces of the earthenware found in the church to the museum.[1] The bulk of the gift comprises dark- and light-blue underglaze transfer-printed earthenware and red and black overglaze transfer-printed earthenware. There are also a number of pieces of earthenware hand painted with large red roses, some copper and gold lusterware jugs and teapots, and ninety-one hand-painted lids to now-vanished hollow ware. A large polychrome enameled earthenware statue of Shakespeare modeled after the statue by Peter Scheemakers in Westminster Abbey and a very curious pearlware statue of what appears to be an American Indian in European dress complete the gift.

Among the objects found in the church, but not included in the gift, are said to be[2] a white on blue jasper-ware plaque of the Descent from the Cross after a Rubens painting; a black basalt bust of Enoch Wood Jr.; a black basalt bust of George Washington; a large earthenware statue of the duke of Wellington painted black; and a jasper-ware urn which contained a number of small jasper-ware medallions of John Wesley.

Enoch Wood, who has been called "this venerable Father of the Potteries and truly eminent Antiquarian,"[3] knew all aspects of the pottery business. He was briefly apprenticed to Josiah Wedgwood and was a modeler and sculptor before establishing his own firm, which by 1820 had become one of the largest and most important of the Staffordshire potteries. Wood's interest in the historical aspects of ceramics led him to form a comprehensive collection of English pottery which he exhibited in his own museum. In 1835 he exchanged part of his collection with the Royal Museum of Dresden.[4]

Another facet of Enoch Wood's antiquarian interest was his practice of depositing examples of his wares in buildings under construction throughout Burslem.[5] Because of the way in which the St. Paul's Church cache was discovered, all the earthenware given to the museum is fragmented. Of the dark-blue underglaze transfer-printed wares, the largest group is from the series entitled London Views which is based on James Elmes, *Metropolitan Improvements: Or London in the Nineteenth Century* (London, 1827) with engravings after drawings by Thomas H. Shepherd. The majority of views in *Metropolitan Improvements* are of Regent Street and Regent's Park, as transformed by John Nash. Of the nineteen pieces in this group—platters, plates, tureen stands, perforated baskets, and a bowl—eighteen depict Regent Street and Regent's Park and one the Bank of England.

The transfer printing on the London Views series is of a high quality, although the labeling is sometimes careless.[6] Stipple and line engraving were used in conjunction to

Fig. 1. *St. Paul's Church, Burslem,* engraved by John Taylor Wedgwood (c. 1783-1856). The print was published in John Ward, *The Borough of Stoke-upon-Trent* (London, 1843), facing p. 252. *Victoria and Albert Museum.*

Fig. 2. *Part of Regent Street*, from the London Views series. Dark-blue underglaze transfer-printed tureen stand made by Enoch Wood and Sons (1818-1846), 1827-1828. Impressed on the back, WOOD. *Approximate length, 13 inches. Except as noted, the objects illustrated are in the collection of the City Museum and Art Gallery, Stoke-on-Trent; photograph by the author.*

produce a dotted, granular transfer which resulted in a sharper, more distinct impression on the biscuit. View and border have been carefully applied so that the sections of the border do not overlap, as they frequently do on underglaze transfer-printed earthenware.

The tureen stand shown in Figure 2 is typical of the London Views series. It is thickly potted, and a small amount of cobalt blue—the blue used for the transfer printing—was added to the glaze to counteract the tendency of the lead glaze to yellow. The back of the stand bears an impressed WOOD mark and an underglaze-blue transfer-printed label enclosing in a cartouche the series title and the name of the view. Other pieces have only the impressed WOOD mark. Many pieces bear impressed and transfer-printed numbers, letters, and triangles, presumably for the benefit of the factory.

The St. Paul's cache also included nineteen dark-blue underglaze pieces decorated with American scenes and intended for export to America. Among them are the views *Union Line*; *Gilpin's Mills on the Brandywine Creek*;

Fig. 3. Fragments of dark-blue underglaze transfer-printed plates made by Enoch Wood and Sons. Left to right: *Vue Prise aux Environs de Francfort*. Approximate diameter, 6½ inches. *Vue de la Port Romaine a Andernach* (mislabeled on the back, *Vue Prise aux Environs de Francfort*). Approximate diameter of fragment, 4½ inches. *Vue de la Porte Romaine a Andernach*. Approximate diameter, 6½ inches. *Author's photograph.*

*Washington Standing at Tomb, Scroll in Hand*; *Lafayette at the Tomb of Franklin*; and *Commodore Macdonnough's Victory*.[7]

By far the most interesting of these American views is a plate commemorating the opening of the Erie Canal which has an inscription praising Governor Clinton in the center. The four reserves on the rim, separated by four small floral cartouches, show alternating scenes of canal locks and boats. Unfortunately, the plate, which is privately owned, has no manufacturer's mark.[8]

Compared to the London Views series, the American views are more heavily potted, the cobalt blue is darker and muddier, the transfer printing is more carelessly executed, and sections of the borders overlap. On the back of many pieces particles of cobalt blue are suspended in the lead glaze, indicating that the transfer-printed biscuit piece was dipped into the glaze pot before the printing had dried.

Although less care was taken in the production of the ware made for the American market, the system of marking on the American views is more consistent and comprehensive than that used on the London Views series. The majority of the American pieces have on the back either an impressed WOOD mark or an underglaze transfer-printed cartouche enclosing the name of the view. A few pieces have both marks. In some instances where no label was used on the back, the title of the scene was incorporated

Fig. 4. Dark-blue underglaze transfer-printed plate with a view of a chinoiserie garden pavilion, made by Enoch Wood and Sons, c. 1828. Impressed on the back, WOOD. Approximate diameter, 8 inches. *Author's photograph.*

into the border or placed in the scene itself. The American, like the London views, bear a variety of factory marks on the back.

The St. Paul's cache includes six plates of the same size with two views of the German cities Andernach and Frankfurt (see Fig. 3). The titles are transfer printed in French on the back of each plate, perhaps indicating that the plates were made when Andernach and Frankfurt were part of Napoleon's empire (until 1815). One of the plates is mislabeled (Fig. 3, middle). On none of these plates is there a manufacturer's mark or a series title, but there are numerous factory marks. The six plates are very similar to the American export ware in that they are heavily potted, the cobalt blue is dark and muddy, the transfer printing is carelessly executed, and particles of cobalt blue are suspended in the lead glaze on the backs. These similarities and the French titles suggest that this group of plates was intended primarily for export to the Continent.[9]

Four remaining dark-blue underglaze transfer-printed patterns in the St. Paul's cache do not fit into either the export or the home market category. The chinoiserie plate shown in Figure 4 is one of the finest pieces in the cache. In contrast to the export wares, this plate is thinly potted, the transfer printing is clear, the impression is carefully applied, and the color is a rich, deep blue which heightens the luxuriance of the scene. The plate is marked with an impressed WOOD mark on the back, but unfortunately it does not bear a series name.

Both sides of the teapot shown in Figure 5 depict the same sleighing scene. The teapot bears no manufacturer's mark, but another teapot in the cache with the same scene has an impressed WOOD mark on its bottom. Four other pieces in the cache are decorated with the scene: an unmarked tea bowl and three sugar boxes, two with an impressed WOOD mark. All six pieces have factory markings and none has a series title or the name of the view. All are similar in quality to the American export ware.

The two other unrelated patterns found in the cache share an identical ornate border of roses and passion flowers. The pattern commonly called *The Young Philosopher* (Fig. 6) is found on two plates bearing the impressed WOOD mark but lacking a label with the title. The other pattern, called *Cupid Imprisoned*, is represented by a plate and a saucer. Cupid stands behind prison bars with his left hand outstretched through the bars. Neither piece bears a title, but the saucer does have an impressed WOOD mark. The examples in the St. Paul's cache neither repudiate nor substantiate the claim that these two patterns are companion pieces belonging to the same series.[10] The wares of both patterns are closely allied to export ware because they are heavily potted, have particles of cobalt blue suspended in the lead glaze, and are printed with a dense, muddy blue. The patterns were probably produced for export as well as for the home market.

The St. Paul's cache yielded forty-two pieces of light-blue underglaze transfer-printed ware. Two soup plates show a park with a swan on a lake and a chinoiserie temple on the far bank; several pieces are decorated with an asymmetrically placed butterfly, bird, and flower design; and thirty-one pieces in the English Cities series are marked with the name of the view and E W & S, the initials of Enoch Wood and Sons.

The source of the English Cities series is *Picturesque Views of The English Cities*, edited by John Britton (London, 1828), with engravings after drawings by George Fennel Robson.[11] The book is composed of thirty-one engravings of urban abbeys and cathedrals, each of which is depicted from a point outside the city so that the church becomes the focal point in a bucolic panorama. Eleven of the views are represented in the St. Paul's cache: Canterbury, Durham (Fig. 9), Ely, Hereford, Lincoln,

Fig. 5. Dark-blue underglaze transfer-printed teapot with a sleighing scene, attributed to Enoch Wood and Sons, c. 1828. Approximate height, 5⅝ inches. *Author's photograph.*

Lichfield, London, Peterborough, Rochester, Worcester, and York. Wood's label on the English Cities series (Fig. 7) is composed of elements from the title page of *Picturesque Views of The English Cities* (Fig. 8).

The series represents the finest underglaze transfer printing in the St. Paul's cache, in keeping with Wood's desire to offer the best-quality ware to the home market. Unlike the dark-blue underglaze ware, where the entire surface is covered, large areas of the English Cities series are left undecorated. This is probably because the earthenware body is of a finer quality and thus could be used as a foil for scenes that are carefully rendered in several shades of light blue. In the English Cities series each view is surrounded by a light-blue brocade border alternating with dark-blue floral medallions, and each piece has a molded edge.

One of the primary objectives of *Picturesque Views of The English Cities* was to capture atmospheric effects and the changing light at different times of day. Often such subtleties could not be re-created on the earthenware surface because of the nature of transfer printing. The dilemma is well illustrated by Figures 9 and 10. The engraved view has been accurately copied, yet the transfer-printed scene fails to convince the viewer that the time of day depicted is evening.

Enoch Wood placed twenty-three pieces of overglaze transfer-printed ware in St. Paul's Church. The overglaze technique was invented in England during the mid-eighteenth century and was used to decorate enamels, various kinds of earthenware, and porcelain.[12]

Thirteen of the overglaze-printed pieces found in St. Paul's are decorated in red. All thirteen are thinly potted and there is a slight blue tint to the lead glaze. The crisply printed scenes are composed of outlines filled in with innumerable small dots. None of these pieces bears a manufacturer's mark, a series name or title, or factory marks.

The design on the thirteen red overglaze bowls, plates, cups, and saucers shows a young girl standing in a landscape holding a parrot on her right hand (Fig. 11). On some of the hollow ware the girl-and-parrot scene is used in conjunction with a landscape in which a seated cupid

Fig. 6. *The Young Philosopher*. Dark-blue underglaze transfer-printed plate made by Enoch Wood and Sons, c. 1828. Impressed on the back, Wood. Diameter 10¼ inches. *Author's photograph.*

leans on a goat. No source has been found for these scenes, but the girl's high-waisted dress is in the Empire style that was fashionable for several decades after about 1815. The neoclassical temple and the static nature of the landscape are also characteristic of that time. Also in the cache were several pieces of overglaze-printed ware decorated in black with a scene entitled *Winchester College.*

The question arises as to why the Wood firm was still making overglaze-printed ware when the underglaze method was easier, less expensive, and popular. The firm presumably felt the overglaze method better suited to the requirements of the neoclassical taste, which was one of several vogues prevailing early in the nineteenth century. By overglaze printing a single color on a white ground, a ware suggesting more expensive porcelain could be made available to a wide market.

Because of the unfortunate circumstances surrounding the demolition of St. Paul's Church, there is no accurate record of exactly what was placed in the cache of ceramics. But considering the earthenware given to the museum, it is possible to conclude that Enoch Wood placed a broad sampling of his current production in the wall foundations of the church, and that that production included a variety of decorative styles popular in the late eighteenth and early nineteenth centuries: chinoiserie, neoclassical, and picturesque.

Fig. 7. Light-blue underglaze transfer-printed stamp on the back of a plate decorated with a view of Worcester from the English Cities series, made by Enoch Wood and Sons, 1828.

Not all the pieces in the cache are marked, but the uniform standards of potting, design, and workmanship strongly suggest that the entire cache was produced by one manufacturer, Enoch Wood. The cache proves that the potter was making overglaze and underglaze transfer-printed wares at the same time, and that he was printing the latter in both light and dark blue. Finally, knowing the source for the London Views and English Cities series, and the date when the cornerstone of the church was laid, one can date the introduction of those two patterns to within a few months.[13]

I am indebted to Arnold Mountford, the director of the City Museum and Art Gallery, Stoke-on-Trent, for permitting me to study and publish the Enoch Wood collection and for his invaluable guidance and support. I am also indebted to the staff of the museum for their assistance and, in particular, to Joy Greaves, who answered my many inquiries.

---

[1] There are 297 pieces in the collection, but only two hundred are in a suitable state for study and analysis.

[2] These are verbal descriptions of objects I have not seen.

[3] Simeon Shaw, *History of the Staffordshire Potteries* (Hanley, 1829, reprinted 1968), p. 30.

[4] The collection is now in the Museum für Kunsthandwerk, Dresden. For a brief history and description of the collection see Gunter Reinheckel, "Zur Erwerbung einer englischen Keramiksammlung im Museum für Kunsthandwerk Dresden," *Dresden, Staatliche Kunstsammlungen Jahrbuch*, 1965-66, pp. 129-139.

[5] Earthenware statues of Bacchus and Ariadne, Shakespeare, and others were found in a wall at the back of the Big House in Burslem, the residence of John and Thomas Wedgwood (Frank Falkner, *The Wood Family of Burslem*, London, 1912, p. 92). In 1835 Enoch Wood placed an oval salt-glazed dish inscribed by himself and modeled by his father, Aaron, in the foundation of the Old Market in Burslem (Arnold Mountford, *Stafford-*

Fig. 8. Title page from John Britton, ed., *Picturesque Views of The English Cities* (London, 1828). *Victoria and Albert Museum.*

Fig. 9. *Durham*, from the English Cities series. Light-blue underglaze transfer-printed platter made by Enoch Wood and Sons, 1828. Length 18½ inches. *Author's photograph.*

Fig. 10. *N.W. View of The City of Durham*, from Britton, *Picturesque Views*, Fig. 12. *Author's photograph.*

Fig. 11. Red overglaze transfer-printed saucer showing a girl holding a parrot, attributed to Enoch Wood, 1815-1828. Diameter 7½ inches. *Author's photograph.*

shire Salt-Glazed Stoneware, London, 1971, p. 47). The deposit that most closely parallels the St. Paul's find in content is a cache Enoch Wood placed in the walls of his vault in St. John's Church, Burslem. This comprised a jasper-ware plaque of the Descent from the Cross, a crucifix modeled by Wood at the age of fourteen, and a bust of his son Enoch Jr. with an inscription on the back that epitomizes the elder Wood's attitude about history and his place in it: "The inscription on the back of this Junior Enoch Wood's bust will endure to the end of time which some learned Divines believe this world by Divine Providence is pre-destined to exist; however, if this should at any distant day again appear upon the surface of the earth it may be preserved in some future museum when my whole family and friends are no more known or thought of than if we never had an existence upon this terrestial globe" (Falkner, *The Wood Family*, p. 42).

[6] For example, the tureen stand shown in Fig. 2 is labeled *Part of Regent Street*, which is less precise than the corresponding engraving, *Buildings on the East Side of Regent Street*. Spelling mistakes also occurred: two plates are labeled *The Colisseum, Regent's Park*.

[7] For a more thorough discussion of Enoch Wood's American production see Ellouise Baker Larsen, *American Historical Views on Staffordshire China* (New York, 1950 edition), pp. 7-29.

[8] The only mark on the back of the plate is an underglaze figure 7. The pattern is illustrated in Larsen, *American Historical Views*, p. 236, No. 638.

[9] In all probability these plates belong to the series of French views discussed by Larsen, *American Historical Views*, pp. 29-30, and Sam Laidecker, *The Standard Catalogue of Anglo-American China* (Scranton, Pennsylvania, 1938), pp. 68-69.

[10] Falkner considers the two patterns companion pieces in the same series without citing a source for this idea *(The Wood Family*, p. 85). Edwin A. Barber also refers to them as companion pieces, and he too gives no reason for making this assumption ("Printed Decorations of Old Staffordshire Potteries As Shown By Old Copper-Proofs," *Old China*, March 1903, pp. 118-119).

[11] I am indebted to Iver Atkinson of the Cathedral Library, Durham, for first bringing this source to my attention.

[12] The underglaze technique followed soon and had the distinct advantage of placing the design under the protection of a transparent glaze. By the last quarter of the eighteenth century the underglaze technique was being used successfully on all types of earthenware.

[13] The cornerstone of St. Paul's Church was laid on June 24, 1828 (John Ward, *The Borough of Stoke-upon-Trent*, London, 1843, p. 248). The source for the London Views series, James Elmes' *Metropolitan Improvements*, was published on May 5, 1827, and the source for the English Cities series, John Britton, ed., *Picturesque Views of The English Cities*, was published on January 1, 1828.

A GROUP OF CHILDREN'S MUGS. *Left to right. Jefferson*, black transfer with luster bands; *Ring Taw*, from one of the children's games series; *Search the Scriptures*; and a mug from the alphabet series. *Photographs courtesy of The Society for the Preservation of New England Antiquities.*

# CHILDREN'S MUGS

## By KATHARINE MORRISON McCLINTON

*From time to time Mrs. McClinton contributes a note to* ANTIQUES *on some intriguing bypath of collecting interests. This one, which offers an appealing approach to nineteenth-century ceramics, will be incorporated, in expanded form, in her forthcoming book on antiques, to be published next year by McGraw-Hill.*

NINETEENTH-CENTURY CHILDREN'S MUGS have long attracted collectors, but few are perhaps aware of the wide variety of patterns in which these mugs may be found. The collection of pottery mugs formed by Margaret H. Jewell, now on display at the Harrison Gray Otis House in Boston, includes no less than 1200 examples, with hardly a duplicate.

Among the earliest, made before 1840, are mugs decorated simply with a name and inscription, sometimes adding a wreath of leaves. Today these mugs are rare. They were made in canary as well as cream color, with transfer decoration most commonly in black, though other colors, such as vermilion transfers on canary, occur.

Sometimes there are pictures in addition to the inscriptions. One group of early transfers on canary ground carries such inscriptions as *A Carriage for Ann, A Pony for Edward,* or *A New Doll for Margaret,* together with pictures of the object mentioned. One canary mug with black transfer has an alphabet border and the words *Come dear child and let me see how you can do ABC.*

Transfer portraits in black on cream and canary grounds form a small group of mugs. The rarest is the Washington and Lafayette, made in about 1824-1825. A portrait of Adams also appears, in black transfer on yellow.

There is a large group of mugs with luster decoration. Copper luster occurs in bands of blue, cream, or tan, or a flower design. Luster decoration is also used on about six different varieties of Gaudy Welsh—ironstone pottery dating about 1840 or 1850. A rare group of mugs has silver resist decoration, sometimes with luster bands in addition to a transfer-printed scene in red, brown, or black. Pink luster is also found, with and without transfer scenes. A Sunderland pink luster mug bears the inscription *Forget and Forgive,* in a wreath.

One group of creamware mugs has hand-painted sprays of flowers and borders. Among the earliest, decorated with roses, yellow flowers, black foliage, and brown bands, is one marked *Bristol.* An early creamware mug with *Bird's Nest* design in black transfer is probably Liverpool. Others are attributed to Leeds or Bristol, while some toy mugs with flowers are thought to be late Staffordshire.

Various patterns of mocha ware include checkered designs, rope, and cat's eye patterns. Mocha mugs with simple bands of color also occur in children's sizes.

Blue and white pottery mugs form another

EARLY MUGS with wreaths and mottoes (*c.* 1830). *Top left,* from one of the animal series, inscribed *Foxes are Mischevious.* The others, some of them with wreaths, are inscribed *A Present for Hannah, A Grandmother's Gift, A Present for a Friend, From an Affectionate Father,* and *A Token of Affection.*

September, 1950

THREE PRESENTATION MUGS, that on the left inscribed *Accept this trifle/From a friend,/Whose love for thee/Will never end*, the next two *For My Dear Boy*, the center one having copper luster bands; PLAYING HOOPS, from children's games series.

group, the color varying in tone from light blue to a rich dark shade. One little mug has a stippled border and the old English potter's rhyme:

> No Handycraft can with
>   Our art compare
> We make our pots
>   Of what we are.

A rare mug of special interest is a souvenir of the New York fire. The inscription, printed in black, reads "Conflagration/ City of New York/ 16th Decr. 1835/ 700 houses burnt/ Amount Property destroyed 25,000,000 Dollars/ Did not affect Public Credit."

Among the later mugs which are more readily available today are some with rhymes from children's poems, and scenes from such children's books as *The Boys Treasury of Sports and Pastimes*. The latter provided the subject matter for a series of mugs depicting children's games. There are many of these game mugs, in different series. Among the earliest is that which includes *Ring Taw, Whip Top, Walk My Lady Walk, Shuttlecock, Pyramid,* and *French and English*. Later ones illustrated *Blind Man's Buff, Leap Frog,* and *Marbles*. These were printed in black, brown, red, or blue, with crude splashes of red, yellow, and green.

Franklin's maxims from *Poor Richard's Almanac* appear on another series of mugs, made by several different companies. The common number of maxims on each mug is two, but sometimes there are four. One of the most available is *Keep thy shop and thy shop will keep Thee*.

Among other maxims found on mugs are *Idleness is the Parent of Want and of Misery, Industry is Fortunes Handmaid,* and *Never Speak to Deceive nor Listen to Betray*. Sometimes religious verses were used, enclosed in wreaths of flowers.

The Reward of Merit series forms another group of mugs, with inscriptions which include *A Present for Knitting Well, For Attention to Learning, Present for Going to School,* and *Present for Writing Well*.

One of the prettiest groups is that of the

Months. Each has a verse. The one for January reads:

> How the rolling seasons Vary
> Through the years from January
> When the Infant Smile Awakes
> On New Year's gifts and sugared cakes.

There is another series which shows children and their pets. Included in this are *Puss's Breakfast, Little Playfellow* (dog), *Beggar's Petition* (dog), *Billy Button* (horse), and *Bird Catchers*. Still another animal group featured elephants, tigers, goats, dogs, and all sorts of birds. A lion with a palm tree printed in blue is marked *Davenport,* as is also a mug with a zebra design.

There is quite a variety of alphabet mugs, which even include the deaf and dumb symbols. At least two different series are known. On one of them, for instance,

> E was an eagle chained to his perch,
> F stands for Fanny returning from church.

According to the other,

> E was an Emperor who ruled in fear,
> F was a fiddler who fiddled for beer.

Today a collection of mugs with late transfer scenes may still be acquired at a moderate price. Early transfers and patterns in silver resist, however, are scarce and expensive.

LUSTER MUGS. *Top row, left to right,* Gaudy Welsh with copper luster; silver resist; copper luster with pink and green hand-painted decoration. *Bottom row,* Children's Pets mug, with copper luster and black transfer; silver luster mug in Reward of Merit series; silver luster mug in Mottoes series, inscribed *Idleness Brings Disgrace*.

217

# VI Victorian and Later Pottery and Porcelain

A curious feature of the English ceramic specialist is that he tends to assume that, as far as his interests are concerned, the world ended in 1820 or, at the very latest, 1830. He will rather grudgingly turn his attention to the products of obscure early 19th century factories such as Nantgarw, particularly if they can be mistaken for 18th-century objects, but he has a total inability to come face to face with the products of the major Victorian manufacturers. As a result, for every one article or book about Minton, Copeland, or Doulton, there are at least ten about comparatively insignificant factories such as New Hall or Swansea. In fact, it seems a necessary prerequisite of an English porcelain collector that the target of his admiration should be trivial, irrelevant, and preferably unsuccessful. How else can one explain the many Victorian potteries of international status whose histories are completely unrecorded?

This apparently congenital refusal on the part of both collectors and so-called learned societies to face the products of the Victorian era is not only unjust, but is also actively misleading. For it is possible to argue that all the interesting and significant developments in English ceramic history actually took place *after* 1800. Certainly the English were not able to make porcelain with any degree of artistic or economic stability until they had created bone china. Once they had this marvelous new material, however, they were able to dominate Europe for the next 150 years. In the 1860s Minton was able to reproduce the Sèvres styles of the 18th century with such precision that their only fault was that the replicas were actually better made than the originals. The control of technology that occurred during the early 19th century in reality increased artistic freedom, for it enabled designers, painters, and manufacturers to predict with some certainty just what would emerge from the kiln. The pâte-sur-pâte wares produced at Minton by the French artist L. M. Solon simply could not have been made in the 18th century.

Bone china apart, there were many other Victorian developments of equal significance. Many of these are featured in the articles in this section, for example liquid lustre glazes, ironstone, and semi-porcelain tablewares that overcame the fragility problems inherent in creamware, multicolor printing, the parian modeling material that allowed contemporary sculptors to work alongside potters and, last but not least, the close artistic links between England and the rest of Europe. These last two are particularly important for—for the first time—they enabled ceramics to be judged as an independent art form, capable of taking its place alongside painting, sculpture, and the other fine arts. Throughout the middle and latter decades of the 19th century, the ceramic industry, confident in its new artistic status, was able to flower as it has never done before; the English potters, proud in their new mastery of technology and art, were able to show the world their skills at the various international exhibitions that followed the Hyde Park display of 1851. How trivial the 18th-century porcelains look beside these High-Victorian masterpieces.

Inevitably, there was a reaction against the ornamental technology of the Victorian period. In the 1870s and 1880s many individual potters and decorators moved away from the factory system in an attempt to re-establish traditional studio practice. Many of these early art pottery studios, for example those operated by Minton and Doulton, were actually developed within the factory system, but they were staffed by the products of the new art schools. This revolutionary movement spread, its influence becoming equally strong in Europe and America, where potteries such as that established at Rookwood were able to produce individually designed and decorated wares of a quality and originality probably unmatched anywhere in the world.

In the 20th century, the studio potters finally broke away from industry and abandoned technology and traditional aesthetics to return to some pseudo-oriental handicraft ideal, a divorce that has caused only harm to both parties. However, some potters in this century, such as Charles Vyse, have been prepared to draw on their industrial experiences when establishing their studios. By so doing they have kept alive the main theme of the Victorian period, namely that a modern ceramic industry could only exist when built out of a spirit of cooperation between manufacturers and artists.

# A Collection of Swansea and Nantgarw Porcelain

BY AUBREY NIEL MORGAN

DEVOTEES OF *The Forsyte Saga* will remember when old Jolyon, attempting to dry the tears of Irene, "could think of nothing better than china and moving with her slowly from cabinet to cabinet he kept taking out bits of Dresden and Lowestoft and Chelsea... 'Now what would you say this was?' And he was comforted, feeling that with her taste she was taking a real interest in these things for after all nothing better composes the nerves than a doubtful piece of china." How well an unmarked piece attributed to Swansea or Nantgarw would have served his purpose!

The story of the production of the beautiful china by these two Welsh factories is one of high hopes and sad frustrations. In November 1813 William Billingsley, a ceramic artist of great skill, went from Worcester to the village of Nantgarw in South Wales and with the help of his son-in-law Samuel Walker built a small porcelain factory alongside the Glamorgan Canal. The canal was an important asset. It carried to the works inexpensively the clays, sand, and other materials which ships took to Cardiff docks eight miles away; and the output of the factory could make the reverse journey to the ships bound for London by barge, avoiding the exceedingly bad roads. Billingsley probably chose this isolated spot and used a different name—Beeley—to avoid the attention of debt collectors.

All Billingsley's life was spent in pursuit of a dream: he was obsessed by a vision of the perfect soft paste which would produce a brilliant translucent porcelain of the highest quality. Like many others in this craft he had a strong touch of the alchemist in him, and kept to himself and his son-in-law Walker the secret of the ingredients used in their attempt to reach perfection. Eventually he was paid £200 by Barr, Flight and Barr of Worcester for his formula but ironically the famous firm made almost no use of it.

In his search for a faultless formula Billingsley was continually making experiments. He needed benevolent employers who would back him in these efforts. He worked in a number of factories: Derby, where he started as an apprentice in 1774, Pinxton, Mansfield, Torksey, Worcester, Nantgarw, Swansea, Nantgarw again, and finally Coalport, where he died in 1828 aged seventy years.

At Nantgarw he was for the first time his own master, and with a capital of £250 he was prepared to challenge the acknowledged perfection of the porcelain from the state-subsidized works at Sèvres. This remarkable goal was set forth in a letter requesting financial support, addressed by the Nantgarw potters to the government's council for trade and plantations. Written by William Weston Young in September 1814, the letter stated:

> The porcelain manufactured by us, altho on the same Principles with the French, is not borrowed from them, but is the result of a series of experiments pursued for years ... the further improvement hinted at in the Memorial is a combination of the Qualities of the best French Porcelain, Whiteness and semi-transparency, with the firmness and closeness of Grain peculiar to the Saxon or Dresden Porcelain. [Quoted by W. D. John in *Nantgarw Porcelain*, Newport, Monmouthshire, 1948.]

Billingsley proved this claim by producing plates at Nantgarw so close to early Sèvres examples that the London dealers were prepared to take the entire output in white for their enamelers to decorate. Because of this ready acceptance, Billingsley and Walker concentrated on making plates, reaching a production of about three hundred a week. The mark was NANT-GARW impressed with the initials C. W. (probably for China Works) below. The finished article, when decorated in the Sèvres style, was virtually indistinguishable from the original.

A large gilt-decorated soup tureen, of which W. D. John says, in *Nantgarw Porcelain*, "This was probably one of the most difficult shapes potted at Nantgarw. . . . There is a well known and particularly fine example from a very large dinner service which bears an armorial design with the motto *Migro et Respicio*." All illustrations are from the author's collection.

Two pairs of Nantgarw vegetable dishes from the *Migro et Respicio* dinner service with covers differentiated by the finials. These are extremely rare shapes.

But unfortunately there was a large fly in this exquisite ointment: the shapes were very much given to warping, wilting, and shivering when fired in the kiln.

Lewis Weston Dillwyn, a man of substance who, among his many business interests, was the owner of the Cambrian Pottery Works in Swansea, Glamorgan, had come to inspect the Nantgarw product at the request of a member of the council for trade and plantations. Dillwyn was so impressed by the superb quality of the porcelain that, despite his observation that nine-tenths of the contents of the kiln proved faulty, he allowed himself to be persuaded that the faults could be corrected if money were available to build a proper kiln. He proposed moving Billingsley, Walker, their families, and their modeler, Isaac Wood, to Swansea where he would build two kilns for them. The move took place in October 1814, less than one year after the Nantgarw works had opened.

Dillwyn was a very competent and successful businessman with an artistic bent, who took great interest in his venture into pottery and porcelain. After a few trial runs with the new kilns he saw there was no commercial future in Billingsley's soft paste unless some ingredients were introduced to give it greater stability. Thus only a very small quantity of Billingsley's own paste was produced for test purposes at Swansea.

A series of experiments was then undertaken by Walker, resulting in the fine Swansea soft paste known as "duck egg" because the body, though as white and translucent as before, appears green when looked at by transmitted light. This green color varies as a consequence of experiments with the formula.

Swansea duck-egg porcelain, though quite different from the Nantgarw product, was very well received by the London dealers and they were prepared to take all that Swansea would send them. Not all of it went to London, however. Dillwyn, who was very proud of this product, kept back a considerable amount for local decoration. He had the master flower-painter Billingsley working for him, and brought to Swansea the great porcelain painter Thomas Baxter. Together with the local artist David Evans, these men decorated some of the most satisfying and beautiful examples of Swansea china.

The factory went into full production and turned out many tea sets and dinner and dessert services, a number of which earn the description magnificent. Among these were the Burdett-Coutts dinner and dessert service, and Baxter's Garden Scenery service which Dillwyn kept for himself. There was also a wide range of other forms, including ornamental vases, potpourri containers, spill jars, cabinet cups and saucers, inkwells and writing sets, pen trays, and the charming small cabaret sets which consisted of a teapot, cream jug, sugar container with lid, cup and saucer, and bowl on a tray.

Another and quite different formula produced the glassy Swansea ware which has come to be known as "sodden snow." Because of the difficulty of working this paste and the ensuing high cost of production, only a small amount was made. Its whiteness and remarkable translucence make it highly prized among collectors of Swansea.

Unfortunately, the attempt to approach the quality of the Billingsley paste carried risks with it. No matter how successful the sales, the cost of production remained far too high. Dillwyn made one more effort: Walker came up with a formula that eliminated the loss in firing, but this porcelain, marked with an impressed trident, lacked the quality and translucence of its fragile predecessors and the London dealers would have none of it, leaving only a limited local market.

With the rejection of the trident china by London, Dillwyn lost hope, and increasing family and business responsibilities decided him to lease the Swansea works to T. and J. Bevington in 1817. They produced only a very small amount of fine Swansea porcelain.

Plate from the famous MacIntosh service of Nantgarw porcelain.

Plate from the superb Burdett-Coutts dinner and dessert service of over three hundred pieces ordered by the banker Thomas Coutts from the Swansea factory and decorated in London. This service of duck-egg porcelain was Swansea's finest achievement.

Examples from a London-decorated Nantgarw dessert service.

Three types of small tureens. *Left to right:* Nantgarw sauce tureen and stand from the *Migro et Respicio* service; sugar tureen, or *sucrier*, from a Swansea dessert service; Nantgarw sugar tureen with double handles. The plate belongs with the *sucrier* in front of it.

Swansea tea service with two bread-and-butter plates. Faint duck-egg tint with pale *café-au-lait* bands. The pomegranates are coral color.

Before the trident china was evolved the inevitable clash between the ideals of the artistic perfectionist and the practical requirements of the businessman had taken place and Billingsley left Swansea. When Dillwyn sold out, Samuel Walker, finding himself out of a job, joined Billingsley, who had returned to Nantgarw. In 1817 they made a fresh start with the help of William Weston Young, who from the beginning in 1813 had had great faith in the quality and potential of the porcelain made by Billingsley.

Young was a surveyor and as a result of his work knew some of the leading industrialists and landowners of South Wales. From them he raised £2,100 to finance the new venture. With the help of this sizable sum the Nantgarw China Works entered its most prolific period: once again the wonderful soft paste of the highest quality was readily accepted in the white by London dealers.

Benefiting by their experience in Swansea, Billingsley and his associates produced a wide range of forms besides tea services, dessert services, and a small number of din-

Three sizes of cups—breakfast, tea, and coffee—and the bottom of the muffin dish from a royal service made at Nantgarw. E. Morton Nance in *Pottery and Porcelain of Swansea and Nantgarw* (London, 1942) says it was ordered by George III for the Duke of Gloucester on his marriage; W. D. John says it is also known as the Duke of Cambridge service. The ground color is a beautiful deep apple green, and John ranks this with the MacIntosh as the most colorful and decorative of all Nantgarw services.

In *Swansea Porcelain* (Newport, Monmouthshire, 1958) W. D. John states, "The Swansea cabaret tea set with the square tray has never been equalled for elegance by any other porcelain factory." According to John, in 1816 Mortlocks of London "were very proud to announce in the current newspapers that they were supplying splendid Swansea cabaret tea sets to the Royal Princesses." The cream jug is missing from this set, which is believed to have been decorated by Billingsley.

On the underside of the tray of the cabaret set is written in ink above the impressed mark SWANSEA: *Nantgarw China This little breakfast service was the gift of a very kind old Friend Mrs. Wyndham of Dunraven Castle Feb. 7th 1819.* This is an interesting example of the confusion between Nantgarw and Swansea porcelain that exists among some of the local inhabitants.

ner services. All but very few of the services have been dispersed among many collectors; the most highly prized of these is the MacIntosh dessert service. There is also a large Nantgarw dinner service still in the hands of one owner, which is known by the motto encircling its crest, *Migro et Respicio*. Because the modeler Isaac Wood had stayed on at Swansea, the new Nantgarw designs were most probably the work of Billingsley. However, with the need to concentrate on production and the demands of London for china in the white, Billingsley decorated only a small amount of his inspired porcelain in this period at Nantgarw.

Once again the old story repeated itself. The losses in the firing of the paste devoured the capital, which was all gone by early 1820. It was the end of the manufacture of porcelain by Billingsley's formula.

Production of fine porcelain at Swansea and Nantgarw lasted not quite seven years. It was limited by the immense loss in firing, by the small size of the factories, and by the scarcity of capital.

A considerable amount of porcelain that had not been sent to London, some because of slight defects, remained after Billingsley left Nantgarw and after the Swansea works stopped making the duck-egg paste. At Nantgarw much of this was decorated by the experienced and gifted Thomas Pardoe. William Weston Young also painted a small amount after Billingsley left the works (his efforts on behalf of the Nantgarw factory finally left Young bankrupt). At Swansea several artists of great merit worked on the remaining stock. The best known of these were David Evans, William Pollard, Henry Morris, and George Beddow. With the exception of Beddow, who painted rural scenes, all these men were outstanding floral decorators.

The marks on Swansea porcelain are varied. Among them are the impressed mark SWANSEA in block letters and in script which varies according to the hand of the inscriber; the script is nearly always in red, but occasionally in another color. There is also the red transfer of SWANSEA in capital letters. The impressed trident mark usually carries with it SWANSEA impressed.

The decoration of Swansea and Nantgarw porcelain raises many problems for the collector. Since a high proportion of their output was decorated by independent artists in London, it was inevitable that similar decoration would appear on porcelain from other factories. Additional problems of identification are created by the work of itinerant decorators. When the collector is considering an unmarked piece from Swansea or Nantgarw he should first compare the quality and color of the paste with those of a marked piece. Then he should carefully examine the design and shape, not allowing himself to be too quickly influenced by the decoration.

There has been an unfortunate tendency to attribute a wide range of floral designs to Billingsley whenever the rose is the dominant feature. While he could not have painted all the pieces today's collectors give him credit for, he did introduce an entirely new method of creating the highlights in floral decoration: instead of leaving small portions of the porcelain unpainted to provide the highlights, he made them by wiping off most of the wet color with a dry brush, thereby more clearly defining or modeling the structure of the petals.

Billingsley could not have pursued his goals or inspired others to follow and support him if he had not been a master of all aspects of the making of fine porcelain. He was a great expert in the techniques of practical pottery and a designer of beautiful classic shapes, as well as one of the greatest flower painters in English ceramic history. His impractical formula for a soft paste produced a body of a quality and beauty unsurpassed in British porcelain.

This is an astonishing record, and one which met with little or no reward. Would Billingsley feel that at last he was justly and deservedly appreciated if he knew that a single Nantgarw plate of the MacIntosh service fetched six hundred and eighty pounds in a London auction room in 1968? At least it shows that the creations of his frustrated dreams have become our cherished treasures.

Three examples of Swansea shell inkwells. The center one could have been decorated by Billingsley, to judge from the appearance of the roses; the other two have gilding on the ridges of the shells.

# Diversity in old Spode

BY EDGAR AND ELIZABETH COLLARD

JOSIAH SPODE I (1733-1797) and his son, Josiah Spode II (1754-1827), were outstanding industrial figures of the years that brought the stately world of the eighteenth century to its close and raised the curtain upon the vital and unabashed days of the Regency. It has been said that the products of the Spode factory, from the very fact that they were admittedly "industrial potting" and intended for mass consumption, are without the distinctive charm of the work of earlier English potters. But old Spode should be appreciated for what it is, rather than condemned for what it is not. It is important because of the wide variety of uses for which it was made, the styles in which it was designed, and the chemical compositions that entered into its manufacture.

Greatest of all the demands that the Spodes sought to fill was, of course, that for tableware; the very tendency of the time to eat to excess and to demand all manner of courses and dishes was in itself a stimulus to the potter. But the Spodes did not stop at the table. By the time of Josiah the second, Spode wares might be found in every room of the house: fine Spode vases on the drawing-room mantel, and ornamental plaques on the walls; on the desk a Spode letter rack, inkwell, penholder, and, perhaps, a snuffbox; in the boudoir a Spode footbath, rouge pots, scent jars, and pin holders. The air might be perfumed by Spode potpourri jars and pastille burners. For lighting the rooms, there were Spode candlesticks, snuffer trays, and spill vases. In the wine cellars were Spode bin labels, and outdoors could be found Spode flowerpots and garden seats.

Nor did the Spodes stop at meeting the varied needs of the household. They manufactured wares useful to industry and the professions, such as the spouted tea tasters with which the East India merchants tested their teas from China; and for the apothecary, jars for medicinal herbs and mortars and pestles to grind them.

Not only did this Staffordshire factory produce wares for all purposes: it produced them in all manner of styles. The Spodes set out to challenge the skilled and experienced manufacturers of the Orient and of the Continent. They turned out a vast number of pieces in the Chinese manner; they imitated Japan's Imari patterns; and they

The famous Peacock pattern, an example of Spode's adaptation of Chinese designs, used here against a fawn-color background, c. 1815; transfer-printed outline, with colors filled in by hand. This pattern is found on Spode porcelain, earthenware (as in this specimen), and "stone china." Marked SPODE impressed and SPODE in blue. *Except as noted, illustrations are from the authors' collection, photographs by Jack Markow & Co.*

Bone porcelain dish, c. 1792-1794; Chinese tree-of-life design enameled in bright colors with gold. Length 12 inches. *Spode Museum, Stoke-on-Trent.*

Earthenware baskets showing Japanese influence, c. 1790; brilliantly decorated in red, blue, pink, and green, with touches of gold. Rare mark SPODE impressed and two concentric blue circles.

Large potpourri jar, with perforated cover and inner lid, decorated in anglicized Chinese manner, c. 1810; design printed in light brown outline with colors filled in by hand. Height to top of gilded knob, 10 inches. Marked *Spode Felspar Porcelain.*

Black basalt chocolate pot, c. 1785; unglazed; engine-turned decoration on body and lid. Height 9¾ inches.
Marked SPODE impressed in very small letters. *Posen photograph.*

Bone porcelain teapot, sugar bowl, creamer, cup and saucer, c. 1800. Uncolored floral motifs in cobalt bands, with rich gilding. *Spode Museum*.

Bone porcelain dessert plates, c. 1800. English scenes finely painted in full color; pale fawn-color border with gold scrollwork and dots, and gilding on gadroon rim. *Left*, Richmond Bridge; *right*, Maidstone, Kent. Place names and *Blades, London* inscribed on backs. *Spode Museum*.

Creamware dish with decoration of leaves and berries painted in bright red and green, c. 1795. An example of the bright simplicity that characterizes many early Spode productions. Marked *Spode* impressed.

produced a variety of wares in the French spirit. It is true that these were rarely literal reproductions (except when replacements had been ordered for imported services). They offered, rather, English interpretations of foreign models; and the English purchaser, far from being displeased at the transformation, seems to have found this very Englishness to his taste—even when the Chinese figures on the Spode ware looked rather like Staffordshire workmen on parade. Indeed, these English interpretations are cherished for just this amusing inconsistency. In addition to adaptations of foreign designs, such notably English patterns as the "Girl at the Well" and the "Milkmaid," the views of English country residences, and the English floral patterns even today evoke the stir of a warm summer's breeze in the hedgerows.

Josiah Spode the second exploited the English interest of his day in the scenery of foreign lands with printed views of Italy and Asia Minor and India on his splendid blue and white earthenware, and these services have a rugged Staffordshire honesty in shape and feeling that places them among the chief glories of the factory. When, however, the Spodes sought to make wares in classic-revival shapes, the classic lines were so transformed by the Spodes' essentially English touch that the result was often unconvincing.

Finally, Spode wares show a vigorous variety in their range of chemical composition.

The Spodes had a fine feeling for the possibilities of earthenware, and the elder Spode experimented early with "Egyptian" redware, cane-color stoneware, and black basalt; "The vitrified basaltes, or black Egyptian ware, were much improved by his efforts," according to a contemporary account. Examples of these wares are now rare. More commonly found by today's collector are examples of his cream-color ware and of his early attempts at under-glaze blue transfer printing.

Later his son introduced special types of earthenware, such as "Spode's imperial" (a superior body) and "Spode's new fayence" (a ware commonly covered by over-all patterns). Within the field of porcelain the

227

Potpourri jars and vase with painted decoration in the Imari style, c. 1804; red, cobalt, and green, with rich gilding. Perforated cover and inner lid of one jar shown in foreground. Height of vase, 12½ inches. Marked SPODE in red. *Spode Museum.*

Below, left. Mortar and pestle in unglazed stoneware for the use of apothecaries, c. 1805. Marked *Spode* impressed. Height 3¾ inches.

Below, right. Bone porcelain pastille burner in the form of a cottage with applied embossed flowers; naturalistic colors with gilding; c. 1820. Marked SPODE in red. *Spode Museum.*

Spodes were no less enterprising. Josiah the first is credited with making porcelain, and his experiments laid the groundwork for his son's achievements. Chief among the commercial triumphs of the Spode factory was the use of a dependable formula for bone porcelain—the same practical formula for a porcelain evenly translucent, but strong, that is in general use today. Bone had been known as an ingredient for English porcelain since the middle of the eighteenth century. It was at the Spode factory, however, that the competitive possibilities of an adjusted formula for "bone china" were first fully realized. One factory after another had to follow the lead of the Spodes. By greatly reducing losses in the kilns this formula made porcelain available to far larger markets, and its widening use marked one of the turning points in English ceramic history; therefore, specimens of early Spode bone porcelain have a particular historic significance.

Early in the 1800's Spode the second arrived at a formula for a special type of luxurious porcelain which created a rich, translucent body with a luscious appearance. This "felspar porcelain" was used for many of the more costly and ambitious productions of the factory. The last of these pieces was made by the factory a few years after Josiah the second's death. Specimens of "Spode felspar porcelain" (most of which are clearly marked as such) are likely to be among the major attractions of any collection of old Spode.

In 1805 Spode the second produced his famous "stone china," which, with its dense body, fine texture, and extreme hardness, was the link between earthenware and porcelain. Its grayish blue color was particularly suitable as a background for Chinese decoration. A few years later Spode whitened the body considerably and called it his "new stone china."

Old Spode represents old England, ready to learn and adapt, but insisting at the same time on being itself. The restless, many-sided enterprise of the men who produced it—the result of the Spodes' acute sensitivity to the public demand of their times—has left an exceptionally varied heritage for the collector of today.

Earthenware platter with "Girl at the Well" design and floral border transfer-printed in blue, c. 1820; a distinctly English pattern. Marked SPODE impressed.

# English yellow-glazed earthenware from the Eleanor and Jack L. Leon Collection

## Part I. *Rarities*

BY J. JEFFERSON MILLER II, *Curator of ceramics history, Smithsonian Institution*

A CURSORY EXAMINATION of the literature on eighteenth- and early nineteenth-century English ceramics reveals that most of the various types of porcelains, stonewares, and earthenwares of this period have been the subject of numerous studies of varying degrees of scholarship. Few stones have been left unturned, but one has only recently been turned up. The presentation by Mr. and Mrs. Jack L. Leon to the National Museum of History and Technology of the Smithsonian Institution of a splendid collection of over six hundred pieces of yellow-glazed English earthenware dating from about 1785 to about 1835 required the curators involved to familiarize themselves with the literature on the subject. In a very short time it became apparent that with the exception of a few brief references in some of the standard studies, these distinctive wares have been ignored by ceramics historians. This not surprising omission probably results from the fact that no major collection of English yellow-glazed earthenware has heretofore been brought together. At the present time there are a few scattered private and museum collections of such wares in this country and in England, but none of these provides a sampling sufficiently representative to support a detailed study. The Leon Collection makes it possible to begin one more subchapter in the complex story of English ceramics of the eighteenth and nineteenth centuries.

The specific influences leading to the production of these yellow-glazed wares are unknown, English potters, with a few exceptions, having been understandably uncommunicative as to their craft; but prototypes or inspiration can be found in a variety of eighteenth-century ceramics. Imported Oriental porcelains of many decorative types interested eighteenth-century Europeans, and one of these was the Chinese *famille jaune*. Between about 1725 and 1775 a number of major European porcelain factories, including Meissen, Nymphenburg, Sèvres, and Worcester, developed yellow ground colors which proved to be extremely satisfactory. During the same period, quite a number of Continental faïence manufacturers turned out limited quantities of tin-glazed earthenwares with over-all yellow grounds. Another possible point of departure can be found in slip-decorated English earthenwares, which

Strawberry basket and stand, early nineteenth century; length of stand, 9½ inches. Both basket and stand are impressed I/SHORTHOSE. John Shorthose worked at Hanley, Staffordshire, from the 1780's until c. 1823. A number of yellow-glazed pieces with various Shorthose marks are in the Leon Collection. The pierced decoration of diamonds, hearts, and flowers is especially fine, and its similarity to pierced borders on clear-glazed creamware from the Leeds Pottery should be noted.

229

July, 1971

A. Box in the shape of a woman's head, late eighteenth century; height 3¾ inches. Perhaps used as a patch or snuff box, this container has a screw-on base. An identical box in clear-glazed pearlware illustrated in Donald Towner's *The Leeds Pottery* (London, 1963; Fig. 31a) is dated c. 1790 and attributed to Leeds, so it seems reasonable to give this one a similar attribution. There are three marked Leeds Pottery pieces in the Leon Collection, and other marked yellow-glazed Leeds examples are known. The probable prototype for these boxes can be found in an English box which is almost identical except that it is in porcelain, probably Lowestoft or Bow, in the collections of the Victoria and Albert Museum. *All illustrations are from the Eleanor and Jack L. Leon Collection, National Museum of History and Technology, Smithsonian Institution.*

B. Leaf dish, late eighteenth century; length 5¾ inches. Probably made at the Leeds Pottery. The enamel painting on this thinly potted piece is especially fine. A similar leaf dish, in clear-glazed creamware, is in the Schreiber Collection at the Victoria and Albert Museum.

C. Sauceboat, early nineteenth century; height 6½ inches, length 6¾. Sauceboats are exceedingly rare in the yellow glaze. The form of this one, with its high, curving swan handle, and the delineation of the green enamel reserves suggest the possibility that it is Continental. However, body and glaze are typically English.

D. Mug, early nineteenth century, height 6 inches. This handsome presentation piece has the monogram *LM* in an oval. Its enamel decoration of strawberries and leaves differs from the usual foliate themes found on yellow-glazed wares. The borders are painted in silver luster.

E. Pitcher, early nineteenth century, height 12 inches. Relief diamond-quilted creamware and silver-luster pitchers of this type are frequently termed Harlequin pitchers. A number of them are impressed HARLEY or T. HARLEY. Thomas Harley was the proprietor of a pottery at Lane End, Staffordshire, 1802-1808. Though it is unmarked, it seems reasonable to attribute this yellow-glazed pitcher to Thomas Harley.

F. Teapot, c. 1785, height 4 inches. Well modeled, with enamel-painted details in delicate colors, this piece is impressed WEDGWOOD. Many students and collectors of Wedgwood have held the opinion that Josiah Wedgwood did not make yellow-glazed wares. This teapot, and six other marked Wedgwood pieces in the Leon Collection, provide substantial evidence that Wedgwood did manufacture some yellow-glazed wares in the late eighteenth and early nineteenth centuries.

Part II of this article, *American subjects,* will appear in ANTIQUES for August 1971.

Footed bowl, c. 1810; height 2⅜ inches. Decorated with transfer prints in black of a goldfinch and (obverse) a yellow bunting. The prints are copied from Thomas Bewick's woodcuts in *History of British Birds,* Vol. I (1797). This bowl, which may have been made at the Cambrian Pottery, Swansea, Wales, was presented to the Leon Collection by Mr. and Mrs. W. J. Grant-Davidson.

frequently were covered with a cream-color slip that came very close to being yellow. Finally, Josiah Wedgwood, and no doubt many others, worked from the mid-eighteenth century onward to achieve a good yellow lead glaze.

Any (or none) of these ceramics could have provided the impetus for the development of the yellow lead glaze eventually used on the yellow-glazed wares. In any event, emulation or commercially inspired experimentation led in the final years of the eighteenth century to limited production of yellow-glazed earthenware by a number of English potteries. In most cases bodies of the standard cream-color earthenware or the newer pearlware were employed, with the lead-glaze recipes altered by the inclusion of antimony to give the yellow color. The fact that so few yellow-glazed pieces have survived, combined with an almost total absence of contemporary references, suggests that comparatively small amounts were made.

English yellow-glazed wares are found in almost all of the forms in which creamwares and pearlwares were made. Tea and coffee services, vases, toys, pitchers, mugs, and plates were not uncommon. The absence of large serving pieces—platters and tureens—from any presently known collections indicates that entire dinner services of yellow-glazed wares probably were not made. As in the case of the majority of creamwares and pearlwares with a clear glaze, most of the yellow-glazed pieces are unmarked, but the few marked examples suggest that a rather representative cross section of English manufacturers made them. Wedgwood, the Leeds Pottery, Enoch Wood & Sons, Sewell, John Shorthose, Fell, Brameld (Rockingham), and the Sunderland Pottery are represented in the Leon Collection by one or more marked pieces, and certain unmarked pieces can be attributed to other factories such as the Herculaneum Pottery in Liverpool and the Cambrian Pottery in Swansea on the basis of comparative studies. The examples shown in the illustrations here represent a selection of some of the more unusual forms and decorations found in yellow-glazed English earthenwares.

Casters and salt, early nineteenth century; heights 4⅝ inches, 1½, 4¼. The caster on the right has sponged enamel decoration in green, the salt has red and green sponged decoration, and the caster on the left has black, red, and green dots and is painted in the same general style as some of the so-called banded wares of the early nineteenth century.

232

Furniture supports, early nineteenth century; height 4¼ inches. Painted in black, red, and green enamel with details in silver luster, these supports possibly represent Wellington. So-called furniture supports were evidently made in sets of four, and their exact function is open to some conjecture. A single support from the same mold, but decorated only in gold luster, is shown in W. D. John and Warren Baker's *Old English Lustre Pottery* (Newport, England, 1951), Illus. 92A. Colonel David Lloyd-Lowells of London has a collection of over two hundred ceramic supports, but none has the over-all yellow ground.

Cow creamer, late eighteenth or early nineteenth century; height 4 inches, length 5 inches. Decorated with brown enamel sponged over the yellow ground; the lid is a replacement. This piece is from the well-known C. B. Kidd collection of English figures and earthenware sold at auction in 1966 and 1967. Of over five hundred cow creamers in one part of the collection, this was the only one with an over-all yellow ground.

Jug, c. 1820, height 5 inches. Decorated with a black transfer-printed portrait of Sir Francis Burdett (1770-1844), Parliamentary reformer and a leader of liberal causes. Burdett's popularity is attested by many surviving printed portraits on English ceramics, but the print on this jug is especially rare. It is inscribed *Engraved by T. Robson, Sunderland Potery*. Robson was a well-known Yorkshire engraver of maps and book plates. The Sunderland Pottery was operated by various partnerships c. 1807-1865. The three black enamel bands circling the pitcher's neck are characteristic of many jugs made in the Sunderland area in the early nineteenth century.

Coffeepot and cover, late eighteenth or early nineteenth century, height 10¾ inches. The simple black-enamel painting of morning glories demonstrates the effectiveness of the yellow glaze as a background for the most restrained type of decoration. Mugs and pitchers are perhaps the most usual forms encountered in yellow-glazed wares and teapots are not uncommon, but coffeepots are particularly rare. The shape of this piece is sometimes associated with Staffordshire. A marked New Hall porcelain coffeepot of rather similar shape in the collections of the Victoria and Albert Museum is illustrated in Geoffrey A. Godden's *An Illustrated Encyclopedia of British Pottery and Porcelain* (New York, 1966), Fig. 444.

Plate, c. 1820-1830, diameter 8⅝ inches. Marked E. WOOD & SONS, BURSLEM, impressed. The tower and landscape are printed in red, but the same scene is also found printed in black on other marked yellow-glazed Enoch Wood plates. The distinctive anthemion relief border on this piece permits tentative attribution of other unmarked printed wares with the same border to Enoch Wood & Sons.

# English yellow-glazed earthenware from the Eleanor and Jack L. Leon Collection

## Part II. *American subjects*

BY J. JEFFERSON MILLER II, *Curator of ceramics history, Smithsonian Institution*

Part I of this article, *Rarities*, appeared in ANTIQUES for July 1971.

SO-CALLED AMERICAN VIEWS have long interested collectors and ceramics historians in the United States and in England. The great majority of English ceramics decorated with these American subjects are transfer printed and date from the late eighteenth century to the present. With some possible exceptions, they were manufactured primarily for the American market. In fact, the English potteries' profitable business in American subjects has continued, virtually uninterrupted, for nearly two hundred years. The two most common types can be described roughly as earthenwares (creamwares or pearlwares) printed under the glaze in blue or other colors, and earthenwares printed over the glaze in black, red, brown, or purple. Ellouise Baker Larsen's *American Historical Views on Staffordshire China* (rev. ed., Garden City, 1950) is the standard reference work dealing with the first type; Robert H. McCauley's *Liverpool Transfer Designs on Anglo-American Pottery* (Portland, 1942) is concerned with the second. Both are surprisingly comprehensive, and only a modest number of unrecorded American subjects have come to light since the publication of Mr. McCauley's volume and the second edition of Mrs. Larsen's book.

English yellow-glazed earthenwares decorated with American subjects may be considered a special category of the overglaze-printed creamwares and pearlwares. Examples dating from the late eighteenth century to about 1825 are notable for their rarity. In nearly every case, similar printed decoration can be found in far greater numbers on clear-glazed creamwares and pearlwares. The very few American subjects on yellow-glazed wares are not aberrations; rather, they reflect the comparatively meager production of all yellow-glazed wares by the English potteries. With this in mind it seems worth while to enumerate the more important members of this small group in the hope that, in time, the list can be expanded. The pieces discussed and shown here are from the Eleanor and Jack L. Leon Collection in the National Museum of History and Technology, Smithsonian Institution.

An oval medallion printed in black with a portrait of George Washington (Fig. 1), perhaps the only extant example in yellow, can be attributed to the Herculaneum Pottery (c. 1796-1840) in Liverpool. The portrait is after Gilbert Stuart, and the engraver of the copper printing plate no doubt copied a contemporary print. On the basis of its style and character the medallion would be assigned a date in the last years of the eighteenth century or the first decade of the nineteenth; it may have been made as a memorial shortly after Washington's death in 1799. Alan Smith in *Liverpool Herculaneum Pottery 1796-1840* (New York, 1970, pp. 39, 40) notes that identical prints exist on three clear-glazed creamware

Fig. 1. Medallion, c. 1800; length 5 inches. Probably made at the Herculaneum Pottery, Liverpool. The black transfer print of George Washington is after a portrait by Gilbert Stuart. *All pieces illustrated are from the Eleanor and Jack L. Leon Collection, National Museum of History and Technology, Smithsonian Institution.*

Fig. 2. Mug, c. 1825-1840; height 2½ inches. Transfer print in underglaze blue of an American eagle and trophies on a shell with the legend *To Washington/The Patriots of/America*.

Fig. 3. Beaker, c. 1790-1810; height 3½ inches. Transfer print in black of Benjamin Franklin after a drawing by Charles Nicolas Cochin the Younger (1715-1790).

examples (one is in the Smithsonian's McCauley collection). The basis for the Herculaneum attribution is a group of distinctive clear-glazed pearlware pitchers with the same transfer print of Washington under the spout. One of these is in the Essex Institute and another is owned by the Chicago Art Institute (Smith, *op. cit.*, Pl. 90). Both are impressed HERCULANEUM.

A small yellow-glazed mug in the Leon Collection (Fig. 2) is of interest for two reasons. First, it is printed in underglaze blue. As practically all of the transfer-decorated yellow-glazed wares are printed over the glaze, this technical difference is significant. Second, a nice question is presented by the decoration itself: an eagle, American shield, and trophies on a wave-borne sea shell with the wording *To Washington/The Patriots of/America*. This particular print of eagle and shell is unrecorded, though a very similar one, differing only in detail, is illustrated in Larsen (No. 501). The cup and saucer with this print in the Larsen collection at the Smithsonian Institution has a printed mark R. HALL & SON and the pattern name *Eagle*. Ralph Hall operated a pottery at Swan Bank, Tunstall, from about 1822 to 1849. The Larsen cup and saucer probably date from the 1830's, but may be later. A similar print (but not necessarily the source) was found by Mrs. Larsen on a diploma dated 1848. The close similarity of the prints might indicate that the yellow-glazed mug was also made by Hall & Son, but it would be rash to make such an attribution solely on this evidence.

A beaker (Fig. 3), a shape seldom encountered in English yellow-glazed earthenware, is printed in black with two American subjects: a fur-hatted and bespectacled Benjamin Franklin labeled *Benj.ⁿ Franklin Born at Boston in New England, 17 Jan. 1706. L.L.D. F.R.S.* and, on the reverse, a standard print of the Great Seal of the United States. A creamware pitcher decorated with the same Franklin print is illustrated in McCauley (Pl. I, No. 15) and described in Larsen (No. 503). The source of this particular portrait was probably an engraving published in 1784 by Whitworth and Yates of Birmingham. This engraving, in turn, probably derived from a 1777 engraving by Augustin de Saint-Auban which was made from a drawing (now lost) by Charles Nicolas Cochin the Younger. The print of the Great Seal can be found in numerous versions on the printed clear-glazed creamwares and pearlwares of the period, but it is very rare in the yellow-glazed wares.

Perhaps the most handsome piece decorated with an American subject in the Leon Collection is a large pitcher with a symbolic representation of *America* printed on each side (Fig. 4). One could quibble and say that this theme should be excluded from the group because it does not relate to the history of the Colonies or the early Republic, but it may well be that this print of America represents an iconographical starting point for the other American subjects. Allegorical representations of the four continents probably originated during the Renaissance and seem to have been especially favored by North German and Netherlandish artists. In the seventeenth century this theme was used in ceramic decoration, and by the eighteenth century the continents were produced as figure groups by many European porcelain factories. The continuation of the theme in ceramic decoration into the early nineteenth century is of interest in itself. The rarity of the subject and the fine printing make this pitcher indeed an exceptional piece of English yellow-glazed earthenware.

A mug (Fig. 5) is printed in black with an unusual view that is possibly of the White House. Though badly printed on one of the forms most often found in yellow-glazed wares, this mug is significant because the transfer print seems to be an unrecorded one. Comparison with prints of the White House prior to the burning in 1814

Fig. 4. Pitcher, early nineteenth century; height 8¼ inches.
Transfer print in black of *America*.
Silver luster borders.

Fig. 5. Mug, c. 1808-1828; height 3½ inches. Transfer print in black, possibly of the White House; probably copied from a print made some time after the Jefferson portico (the low arcade on the left side) was added in 1807. Copper luster border.

Fig. 6. Pitcher, early nineteenth century; height 7 inches.
Transfer print in brown of *Arms of the United States*. Borders and details enameled in brown.

Fig. 7. Mug, c. 1800; height 6 inches. Transfer print in black of Washington, Franklin, and allegorical figures, and a map of the east coast of North America.

Fig. 8. Pitcher, early nineteenth century; height 7½ inches. Transfer print in black of the Great Seal of the United States, names of ten states and *Boston*, allegorical figures of Peace and Plenty, and the legend *Peace/Plenty/and Independence*. Borders in silver luster.

and after reconstruction strongly suggests that the building depicted here is indeed James Hoban's President's House. The presence of a low extension at the left of the building (the Jefferson portico?) provides some additional confirmation for this attribution. The rolling hills in the background may be a fanciful addition by the engraver of the copperplate; such artistic modifications of the landscape were a common practice. However, English country houses were popular subjects for transfer prints on ceramics, and the possiblity that this view is of such a house cannot be entirely dismissed.

American patriotic fervor preceding and during the War of 1812 supplied the English manufacturers with new subject matter for decorative devices on ceramics intended for sale in the United States. The fact that England and this country were mortal enemies failed to diminish the enterprise of the English potters, who supplied both sides with pots printed and enameled with all sorts of patriotic emblems. A yellow pitcher (Fig. 6), printed in brown with a version of the *Arms of the United States*, typifies this sort of decoration. Complemented by brown-enameled borders and details on handle and spout, the meticulously detailed brown overglaze transfer print contrasts well with the yellow ground. The same print appears on both sides of the pitcher, and a wreath surrounding the legend *Free Trade and Sailors/Their Rights* is beneath the spout. There is a similar yellow-glazed pitcher in the Larsen collection (No. 722), as well as a clear-glazed pearlware pitcher with pink-luster trim and a variation of the arms print, overpainted in enamel colors. The Washington mug printed in underglaze blue (Fig. 2) and this pitcher are the two pieces with American subjects in the Leon Collection printed in colors other than black.

One of the more interesting and better-known American subjects depicts a map of the eastern part of North America surrounded by a cluster of patriotic symbols, an iconographical hodgepodge somewhat relieved by numbered references to a legend at the bottom identifying *Fame, Washington securing Liberty to America*, and *Wisdom & Justice dictating to Dr. Franklin*. This print is not uncommon, and can be found in several versions on clear-glazed creamware bowls, pitchers, and mugs transfer printed over the glaze (McCauley, No. 58). Some of these prints, including one on a yellow-glazed pitcher in the collections of the Chicago Art Institute, are signed *F. Morris, Shelton*. The yellow-glazed mug in Figure 7 is decorated with this subject, though it must be admitted that this particular example has its shortcomings: the copper engraving was a bit too large for the mug, so when the decorator applied the inked transfer paper, the encircling wreath ran out of space at both top and bottom. But never mind, these printed ceramics essentially served as patriotic emblems or commemorative souvenirs, and the buyers probably were far less interested in aesthetics than in the noble sentiments so unabashedly indulged in by that first post-Revolutionary generation.

A pitcher (Fig. 8) has another decoration with elaborate iconography. It is printed on both sides in black with a somewhat belligerent version of the Great Seal of the United States surmounting a coiling ribbon that bears the names of ten states and *Boston*. The ribbon circlet is flanked by allegorical figures of Peace and Plenty, and in the center is the legend *Peace Plenty and Independence*. The legend *Peace and Prosperity to America* is printed in a wreath under the spout. The rims, spout, and handle details, and the borders of the main transfer prints are all

Fig. 9. Cup plate, c. 1820-1830; diameter 3½ inches. Great Seal of the United States in silver luster. Circular impressed mark of eagle and ENOCH WOOD & SONS BURSLEM on underside.

Fig. 10. Plate, c. 1810-1825; diameter 3½ inches. Great Seal of the United States in enamel colors.

done in a strong silver luster. Though encountered frequently on clear-glazed creamwares and pearlwares (Larsen, No. 777; McCauley, Nos. 187, 188, 189, 190), this *Peace Plenty and Independence* subject is seldom found on yellow-glazed wares. In addition to the jug in the Leon Collection, which is illustrated in W. D. John and Warren Baker's *Old English Lustre Pottery* (Newport, England, 1951, Illus. 44E), at least two others are known, one in the Rose collection at Brandeis University and the other in the collection at Valley Forge Historical Park, and it is possible that still others exist in private or public collections.

Though the majority of the American subjects in the Leon Collection are transfer printed, two are painted in enamel colors and silver luster over the glaze. Both of these are representations of the Great Seal of the United States. The arts of the early Republic—both domestic and imported—reveal the popularity of this decorative device, a popularity attested in ceramics by its ubiquity on China Trade porcelain and on English transfer-printed earthenwares. English clear-glazed pearlwares, especially those edged in blue and green, were sometimes hand painted with versions of the Great Seal. The two plates in the Leon Collection fall within this general category. A cup plate (Fig. 9) with a feather edge and scale-molded border has, in its center, a crude and sketchy Great Seal painted in silver luster. The significance of this piece lies in its circular mark of an eagle and ENOCH WOOD & SONS BURSLEM impressed on the back. Enoch Wood & Sons manufactured large amounts of underglaze blue transfer-printed wares for sale in the American market, many of which are impressed with a similar mark which seems to have been used on pieces intended for the United States from about 1818 to 1846. Though the relief border on this cup plate is not without merit, the amateurish painting (which is not necessarily suspect) indicates a considerable range in the quality of decoration on this particular factory's output intended for the overseas trade.

The second plate (Fig. 10), dating about 1810 to 1825, is more pleasing. The deep border has a scaled relief pattern upon which is superimposed an enameled seven-pointed star design in black, green, and red. In the center is a somewhat awkward Great Seal with the shield painted in blue and red, and the eagle and its accouterments in black and gray enamel. In concept and feeling this design is similar to the more commonly found ones on clear-glazed pearlware plates of the period, but it is not nearly so competently done as the typical Great Seal found on contemporary China Trade porcelains.

In addition to the pieces described here, a few other American subjects are presently known on yellow-glazed wares. Perhaps the most frequently encountered are small mugs and pitchers printed in black or red-brown with vignettes of Washington, Lafayette, and (on some) Cornwallis' surrender at Yorktown. These most probably date from about 1824, the year of Lafayette's triumphant return visit to the United States. Yellow-glazed mugs are occasionally found printed with the names of Adams, Madison, or Monroe. Counterparts of these small mugs in clear-glazed creamware or pearlware also exist.

Considering yellow-glazed wares decorated with American themes as a group, what conclusions should be reached? First, they are rare—but their significance does not stem from this alone. Rather, within the broader picture of English ceramics history, these yellow-glazed wares provide an additional dimension to the large and complex picture of the relationship between the post-Revolutionary English ceramics industry and its ever-growing American market. A definitive history of English ceramic exports to the United States during the period of the early Republic has yet to be written. The pieces illustrated here demonstrate that some small part of that trade was comprised of the yellow-glazed earthenwares that, even in England, seem to have been a particularly exotic subspecies of the popular mass-produced creamwares and pearlwares which were the ceramic staples of the time.

# Banded creamware

BY SUSAN VAN RENSSELAER

A CERTAIN TYPE of cream-color earthenware which has become increasingly popular as a collectible since the 1930's has been the subject of no little discussion among the antiques-minded here and in England. Although students have been hindered by lack of contemporary documentation, some findings have resulted that should eliminate misnomers and remove the aura of mystery concerning so-called mocha ware—which was discussed and renamed banded creamware by Robert J. Sim in ANTIQUES for August 1945 (p. 82).

An early reference to this ware occurs in Simeon Shaw's *Chemistry of Pottery* (1837), which mentions "mocha dip." Then in 1846 William Evans (*Art and History of the Potting Business*) wrote that when a drop of saturated infusion of tobacco in stale urine and turpentine is let fall on colored dip it spreads into forms resembling trees, shrubs, and so forth. He also divides decoration of "dipt" pottery into three categories: marbled slip ware, mocha, and banded.

After this ware was turned, smoothed, and air-dried to leather hardness, bands of color were applied and then, on the still wet surface, the mocha "tea" was added. The tea, made as has been indicated, brought about a capillary reaction resulting in delicate brown traceries like the dendritic markings of the Mocha stone, a variety of quartz from Mocha on the Red Sea in Arabia which was used in fashionable jewelry in eighteenth- and nineteenth-century England. In the later wares, hops, tansy, ground brown oxide of iron, citric acid, and dry printer's black color were used to make the mocha tea.

William Turner, in *William Adams, an Old English Potter* (1904), wrote that "attractive Mocha was first produced by Adams at Tunstall" about 1789. The earliest extant dated example of banded creamware known is a child's mug inscribed *M Clark/ 1799* on the bottom; this is owned by the Christchurch Mansion Museum in Ipswich, England, and illustrated in Godden (*British Pottery and Porcelain 1780-1850*, 1963). It has mocha trees, and five narrow colored bands at top and base. In general, the first banded creamware had bands in various widths of blue, ocher, and dark brown, with mocha decoration. Later on, tones of chestnut brown, slate green, dark green, olive green, orange, tans, grays, and blue-greens were introduced. Presumably potters began about the same time—that is, in the first quarter of the nineteenth century—to develop such additional decorations as those known as the worm, the twig, and the cat's-eye, and marbleized and combed effects. Most of these designs are found on lightweight creamware, made in several of the Staffordshire potteries, though cane ware, with its dense, compact body, and a cheaper white earthenware were used as well.

By 1836 more than one potter was producing this ware. Mocha ware is listed under the heading "Dipped Ware"

Plain banded bowl and matching pitcher striped in shades of brown and tan; impressed pattern on pitcher rim, in black covered with blue slip; lathe-turned rim of washbowl banded with blue and black slip. Height of pitcher, 9 inches. *Old Sturbridge Village.*

Specked and checkered teapot with bamboolike molded border, acorn finial; gray, black, and cream. Height 4¼ inches. *Brooklyn Museum.*

Pitcher, true mocha with cat's-eyes; blues, browns, and black on grayish-tan field, with impressed diaper band washed with translucent green. Height 8½ inches. *Collection of Mr. and Mrs. Robert H. Carew.*

along with "painted," "blue-painted," and "common cable" in the working price list in the *Declaration of the Chamber of Commerce for the Potters* issued in June of that year. Makers listed by various authorities include, besides Adams, Copeland & Garrett of Stoke-on-Trent; Cork & Edge, Pinder & Bourne, and I. & R. Riley of Burslem; Broadhurst of Fenton; Tams of Longton; MacIntyre of Cobridge; Green of Church Gresley; Maling of Newcastle-on-Tyne; and William Chambers Jr. at Llanelly in Wales. Another source was the old Cambrian (Swansea) pottery: E. M. Nance (*The Pottery and Porcelain of Swansea and Nantgarw*, 1943) illustrates shards of banded creamware dug from its site, and says it is obvious from the large percentage of "dipt"-ware fragments found in the refuse piles that great quantities were manufactured there.

Nance (*op. cit.*) also clarifies another puzzling aspect: "We are told that the 'dipped' body was mixed in the usual way, that it was then thrown and handed to the 'dip turner,' who smoothed it on the lathe, and even gave it 'a pattern, if thought desirable, by engine-turning.' After that, rings of coloured slip were trailed on to it from a vessel with a spout as it turned slowly on the lathe. Variations of pattern were produced by using different slip mixtures, and arborescent designs were also obtainable by dropping one slip upon another while still wet. The article was completed and finished for the market by firing . . ." He added that such pieces were seldom if ever marked and are not usually seen in widely representative collections of Swansea ware, even though they are very attractive.

Leeds is another possible source. Donald Towner seems to have had banded creamware in mind when he wrote, in his *Leeds Pottery* (1963 ed.), "A form of creamware . . . introduced by the Leeds Pottery early in the nineteenth century . . . was decorated with coloured clays or slips which are referred to in the Leeds Drawing Books as 'dips' and judging by the very great variety of patterns of this kind of ware illustrated in the *New Teapot Drawing Book* (page 53), it must have been produced in vast quantities . . . Dip decoration was also combined with other treatments such as an *agate* ware formed by a dip of mixed slips; *pepper*, which is a putty colour peppered with minute particles of black . . . Most of these types were bordered with chequer patterns . . ."

Archeological evidence that banded creamware was used in America has been found at nineteenth-century

241

Two-piece true mocha jardiniere in one shade of rich deep brown against cream. A rare form made more notable by the incised mark MONTEREAU; height over all, 7½ inches.

Checkered mug in black and white, with typical wide light blue and narrow black bands at top and base; a variant of lathe-turned ware. Height 4 inches. *Carew collection.*

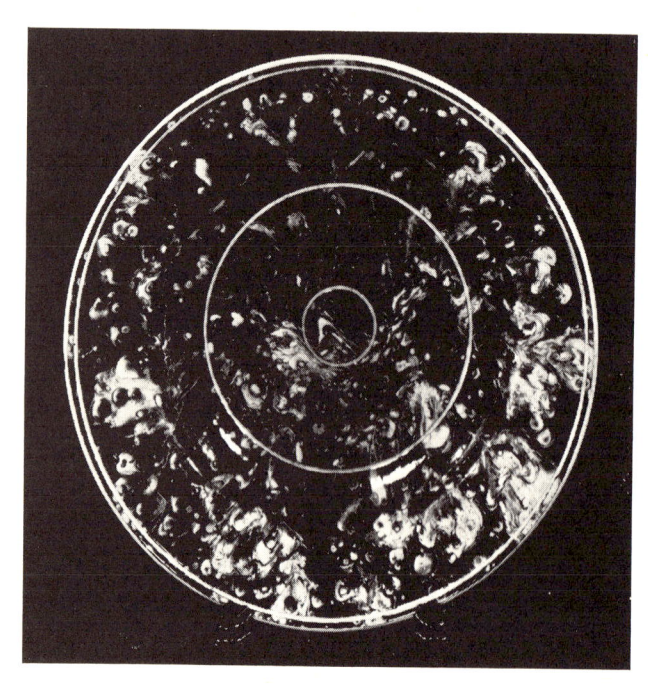

Plates are a rarity in banded creamware. Scrambled slip in dark reddish brown with yellow mottling, and cream-color bands. Diameter 9 inches. *Carew collection.*

levels in southern New Jersey; Newburyport, Massachusetts; and Williamsburg, Virginia. In his pioneering article "Mocha Ware" (*Old China*, January 1903) the American authority Dr. Edwin A. Barber described the type as a "variety of white crockery, which is rudely decorated with sea-weed or tree-like designs in black, brown, green, and other colors, usually on a tinted zone which is outlined with lines or narrow bands of darker color, while occasionally at top or bottom of a piece will be found another zone of a different tint. This is what is known as Mocha Ware in the English potteries . . . Vast quantities of this ware must at one time have been made and sent to this country, judging by the abundance of examples that are constantly turning up [those were the good old days!]. Of late, collectors have been giving considerable attention to this homely and humble ware. The style of decoration is among the simplest, yet the effect is often pleasing and always characteristic."

Banded creamware is rarely collected in England. The collection started there by N. Teulon-Porter about 1910, which he limited to examples with true mocha decoration, is now owned by the City Museum and Art Gallery at Hanley, Stoke-on-Trent. It comprises about one hundred and fifty pieces ranging from miniature tea and washstand sets to commodious two-gallon jugs and delicate potpourri bowls.

Banded creamware of any type is seldom marked. G. Bernard Hughes (*Victorian Pottery and Porcelain*, 1959)

Marbleized (scrambled) teapot in subtle tones of brown and tan combined with gray and black. Height 5¾ inches. *Carew collection.*

Jug combining marbleized medallions in gray, tans, and browns with blue sponged decoration; top and base bands, canary yellow outlined in dark brown. Height 6¼ inches. *Henry Ford Museum.*

says that Adams' impressed mark has been found on a group of mocha mugs, and the only other marked piece I have found reference to in the literature is a covered jug of about 1835 decorated with loopings and marked COPELAND & GARRETT, illustrated in Geoffrey Bemrose's *Nineteenth Century English Pottery and Porcelain* (No. 27). However, banded creamware mugs and jugs made after 1824 for use in public houses or as measures for produce can often be dated by the excise mark which certifies their capacity; this was sometimes stenciled, sometimes molded and applied. Where the initials *G.R., W.R.,* and *V.R.* occur, they indicate the reign in which a particular piece was made.

Use of mocha decoration spread into France when English potters migrated there during the last quarter of the eighteenth century; it appears on wares manufactured at Creil as early as 1809. English pottery influence may have been exerted by Clark, Shaw & Company, who reputedly absorbed the Creil works at Montereau and produced a creamware in the English manner there. A hitherto unpublished example bearing the mark of this factory is illustrated here.

Other French factories producing banded creamware—with decoration simulating agate, marble, granite, and porphyry—were those at Douai and Utschnieder. Douai was founded in 1780 or 1781 by Charles and James (or Jacob) Leigh of Staffordshire; they obtained permission to make "*fayence en grès pâte tendre blanche connue sous le nom de grès d'Angleterre.*" The Utschnieder factory was established at Sarreguemines about 1770 by Paul Utschnieder and its products, like Wedgwood's, were extremely varied.

In the main, banded creamware was produced as an inexpensive, utilitarian ware for use at home and for export. A common earthenware, it did not meet later, more sophisticated standards of taste which approved ornamentation irrelevant to the form or function of the ware, and it was little appreciated until the twentieth century. However, from late in the eighteenth century until the middle of the nineteenth it reflected a vigorous and spontaneous English potting tradition that was gradually lost with the adoption of mass-production methods. Surviving examples are usually worn, chipped, cracked, and discolored, but the ware has a special appeal because of its free use of color and the element of originality in its application.

I wish to express my gratitude to A. R. Mountford and Reginald G. Haggar, as well as to many other authorities in this field, for help most generously given. The categorical distinctions in the captions here—with the exception of "lathe-turned"—are those used by Mr. Sim in the article cited above.

Pepper pot in variegated wave and loop; light green, white, black, and bright orange on blue ground, with blue rim and top. Height 4¾ inches. *Carew collection.*

Covered tureen is another rare form, especially with this decoration on—as here—creamware. Variegated wave and loop ("worm") in tans, blues, and light cream on light brown band bordered with black and light blue. Height 7 inches. *Carew collection.*

Bowl with cat's-eye decoration in white, blue, and black on burnt orange band bordered by chocolate brown; impressed diaper pattern on rim has typical green translucent wash. Height 3½ inches. *Currier Gallery of Art.*

A mug in the "miscellaneous slip decorated" category; monochromatic color scheme has undulating lines of cream-color slip on brown background with stripes ranging from light to deep chocolate brown. Height 5¾ inches. *Carew collection.*

Extraordinary lathe-turned mug in quart size. Patterns are cut on lathe, then slip is applied as the piece revolves; the result is so even it resembles printing. Chocolate-brown pattern and bands on cream-color ground, with translucent green slip at top and base. Height 5 inches.

244

*Fig. 1* — CREAMER, TEA POT, AND SUGAR BOWL
Of a set of twenty pieces. This is most attractive, with sprigged panels, two tones of deep rose, and coral pink lustre.

# Pink Lustre

*By* DANIEL CATTON RICH

(The author wishes to express his appreciation to Emma B. Hodge, Curator of Ceramics, the Art Institute, Chicago, to whom he is indebted for valuable information on the Staffordshire potters.)

(*Illustrations from the collections of Mrs. F. S. Fish; Mrs. Hugh Miller; Mrs. C. D. Tiedemann; Mrs. W. P. Harmon; Mrs. T. E. Standfield; Mrs. E. H. Carleton, and the author.*)

IN 1816, Caleb Adams, urged by his wife, Martha, sent to England for a new tea set. The old Chinese Armorial dishes were chipped and worn, while the new ware of "floreated designs in pink," was the talk of the fashionable dames as they sipped their tea. What was true of the Adamses, was true of other New England families. And so pink lustre came into its own, in the late eighteenth and early nineteenth centuries, replacing the once-popular Lowestoft and gracing many an Empire tea table.

The term "pink lustre" rather generally includes all types of china that are decorated with any amount, large or small, of precipitated rose gold. It comprises the splotchy pink Sunderland, and the creamy white with golden pink decoration of New Hall. Under this general head, also, comes the Staffordshire printed ware employing lustre lines, the Castleford ware, and some Swansea ornamented with raised figures, coloured pink.

This particular kind of lustre, so universally used and admired, was manufactured only in England. Some authors credit the great Josiah Wedgwood with its invention, and certain it is that he employed it to line shell-shaped dishes at an early date. Pink lustre was made sparingly from 1780, until 1800; from 1800 to 1810 in gradually increasing amounts, and from 1810 until the decadence and shutting down of many of the plants in 1830, it was manufactured in great quantities, chiefly for the Dutch and American trade.

It is a thin, irridescent, metallic coating of deep rose or pink, produced from gold thinly applied. The depth of colour depends on the thickness of the gold, while the play of light comes from the reduction of the metallic salts in a reverberatory furnace.*

Pink lustre was mainly used to ornament tea sets. These usually consisted of twelve plates, often of varying design and paste; twelve cups, with or without handles, and accompanied by deep saucers; sugar bowl, creamer, waste bowl and tea pot. The cups without handles are generally older than the other type. There is no great difference in the other pieces as to period although the helmet shape (*Figs. 1 and 5*) is the oldest, and shows the influence of Lowestoft contours. Mugs, intended for chocolate, were included in some of the later sets, and are often quite charming.

Besides these it was employed to a great extent in decorating occasional pitchers. Wine cups, salts, and punch bowls are more rarely found, though I have in mind a fine punch bowl, 14 inches in diameter and 8 inches deep, with a design of sprigged lustre around the sides, the interior in the variegated Sunderland style.† Lustre in stripes or patterns is likewise met with in Staffordshire cottage ornaments. "The Four Seasons," by Dixon, Austin & Company is an excellent example of this kind.

Of the many factories making pink lustre, among the most important are those of Sunderland, where, from the early part of the nineteenth century until past its middle years, there was active production of various wares. Chaffers, in his *Marks and Monograms*, edition of 1876, recites the names of Dixon, Austin & Company; Scott Brothers & Company, which in 1837 became Anthony Scott & Sons; Phillips & Company, active in 1813; Thomas Dawson & Company, and other minor concerns. All of these factories produced lustre ware. Perhaps, as is claimed by some, Dixon, Austin & Company are to be credited with the major part of the rose marbled ware. It is a deep pink, splotched lustre, this effect being obtained either by blowing on the ware when wet, or by the brush of the workman. This was very popular at one time, and is more commonly

---

*This is a kiln so constructed that ceramics fired in it do not come in direct contact with the fuel. The flame goes over a fire bridge of brick, and is reflected or reverberated on the material beneath.

†Vases or urns of classic outline and fine coloring occur in marbled pink lustre.

*Fig. 2* — THE CUP AND SAUCER
At the right is the handsomest cup and saucer of the lustre worker's art I have ever seen. The colours are brilliant and perfectly blended into a free and beautiful design.

found than any other pink lustre today. It is less carefully decorated, and is of rather coarse, yellow paste; two facts which detract from its value.

The Sunderland potteries also turned out pieces bearing sailor verses—mugs and pitchers with quaint sea rhymes, conceived in a salty sentimentality calculated to assuage the grief of the Nancy Lees who waved their wandering Jacks good-by. Attractive as these are, one of the rarest achievements of Sunderland is the pitcher bearing the engraving of the Wear Bridge at North Hylton. This is the work of Phillips and Company. In the Mayer Museum at Hanley in Staffordshire is a large jug of this lustre ware. It is creamy white, ornamented with panels surrounded by wavy lines of purple. On one side occurs a coloured view of the Iron Bridge over the River Wear, and underneath it the inscriptions: "A South-east view of the Iron Bridge over the Wear near Sunderland. Foundation stone laid by R. Burden, Esq., Sept. 24th, 1793. Opened Aug. 9th, 1796." "Nil Desperandum Auspice Deo." "Cast Iron 214 tons; Wrought, do., 40; Height 100 feet; Span 256," and the name of its maker and the pottery "J. Phillips, Hylton Pottery." The frontispiece shows one of these pitchers similar but not identical. The background is of spotted lustre and the ovals are engraved views.

The Castleford Pottery, established in 1770, produced some pink lustre ware, of which the most notable examples are the pitchers. These have a ridged or fluted surface, and nearly always carry decoration of a patriotic nature. The eagle and thirteen stars, in high relief, proud in pink lustre, or a wobbly figure of Liberty with a flag, are among the designs most often encountered. These English conceptions of American freedom were often further adorned with pink monograms under the spout. Castleford pieces are rather rare in this country, but are always nicely coloured, and quaint in design. This lustre ware is easily recognized by its pitted surface and raised, coloured designs.

There is another variety of pottery which, while not strictly pink lustre, combined the printed views of Stafford-

*Fig. 3* — PINK LUSTRE
Cheerful designs and pleasing forms.

engraving in pink, displaying three orphans wailing in a cemetery. It is tearfully inscribed "The Mother's Grave."† Other lachrymose subjects are common. They usually offer a weeping willow or a tombstone bearing the touching legend "To Lucy in Heaven." Patriotic designs were often tinged with grief too. A rare pitcher eight inches high, with a medallion, set on a white ground, shows a monument to Washington. On it is a wretched portrait of the Father of His Country, bearing a most unfatherly expression. At one side is a plump Fame, weeping lugubriously. At the top appears the comforting assurance, "Washington in Glory," with its companion band below which reads, "America in Tears." On the front is placed the coat of arms of the Washingtons; the edges and handle have lustre lines.

Many masonic and guild pitchers were sold in the early

---
†Early nineteenth-century decoration in England and America is full of this kind of mawkish romanticism—a natural reaction from classical grandiloquence.

*Fig. 4*

*Fig. 5*

shire, in brown, black, or pink, brightened with lines or borders of the lustre. This includes ware made at New Hall, at Sunderland, and at The Sheepfold Pottery, by T. J. Rickby. Some of these are, rarely, inscribed, "Bently, Wear and Browne, Engravers and Printers, Shelton Staffordshire." A favorite pattern shows a mother languidly reclining on a chaise longue, playing with her ringletted daughter at battledore and shuttlecock.* The design is in black, printed on a white ground, and is enclosed in concentric circles of pink lustre. Figure 8 shows a bowl of this general sort, with an en-

---
*Contemporary with mirror panels bearing very similar representations of maternal solicitude.

*Fig. 6* — Pink Lustre
Of the three pieces shown, the tea-pot is best.

247

nineteenth century. Some quite handsome examples show the symbols of the fraternal orders. Hunting pitchers are not uncommon either and I have seen one recently that is extremely attractive. It is seven inches high and displays two raised figures—engaging, dotted lustre hounds on the scent. The reverse discloses a chimpanzee, hidden high in branches, with a malicious pink lustre cocoanut in his arms, ready to hurl on any unfortunate pleasure seekers below.

While many of the foregoing designs are merely interesting or amusing, the New Hall tea sets are the triumph of the lustre potter's art. In these the pattern in lustre was combined with colours to produce original and charming flowers and fruit. These decorations are in flat brush work, done in enamel and lustre and are painted on a ground colour of ivory. The finest of these sets are light in weight, of a delicate paste. Some are signed "New Hall," in running characters. Figure 5 illustrates a tea pot in New Hall, made somewhere before 1825 when the factory closed. The design is a good "flowing" one, and the helmet shape unusually graceful. It is the last remnant of a tea set brought across the Alleghanies in 1832.

Figure 2 shows tea cups and saucers in a design of brilliantly coloured flowers, in deep rose lustre, set in leaves of green, enlivened with almost harsh touches of blue. Figure 1 illustrates the creamer, sugar bowl, and tea pot of a wonderfully preserved set of twenty pieces. The design is a charming motif borrowed from the French, and surprises one by the delicacy of its handling. It shows dull violet and green in combination with the lustre, and is a rare and valuable acquisition.

Patterns are often found utilizing fruit. The strawberry design is typical of the best of these. Figure 4 shows a tiny mug in this pattern. The little vines and tendrils are carefully painted, and the berries are achieved by the print of the thumb when the paint is wet.

But perhaps the most original, and naive, was the house design. In Figure 7 three variations are shown. The first is a pitcher encircled with a band of yellow, with a pink lustre dwelling gaily painted on it. This is more pretentious than many found and I am inclined to place it a little later than the other two. The *petite maisonette*, with the sloping roof,

*Fig. 8* — EMPIRE GRIEF
Three orphans before their mother's grave. A distant church and funeral urns, complete the saddening picture. This ware was made for sale to rather simple folk. It illustrates the type of romanticism that developed concurrently with the closing years of Empire style.

on the mug, and the cup and saucer, with its painted cottages set in panels, are entirely of lustre of unusual brilliance.

This design is so attractive, and so often really artistic that it makes an irresistible appeal to collectors. Indeed, I know of one collector who is specializing in it, and very gay her corner cupboard must appear, full of these shining but tiny dwellings of a hundred years ago.

Very exquisite, too, are the cups and saucers shown in Figure 3. Crude red lustre flowers, with sea green leaves bloom on some of them, while others have bunches of gaudy sunflowers in orange and lilac pink.

The greatest difficulty faces the collector in classifying these designs. There are so many and the dilemma is made so much worse by the fact that most of the pieces are unmarked. A few of them bear the New Hall mark or "Wood," impressed, the latter designation dating from 1800 to 1819. The most common mark is simply a string of gold or lustre numerals, which steadfastly refuse to disclose the mystery of their meaning. A few pieces are marked for trade in the States with an impressed eagle, and for this reason it has been ignorantly argued that pink lustre was manufactured in this country.

*Fig. 7* — PINK LUSTRE IN THE HOUSE DESIGN
To the left is a very English-looking cottage with sloping roo. and formal hedge. In the middle of the group are a cup and saucer with views of a farm set in panels. The pitcher at the right is a yellow band which flaunts a pink lustre mansion with a background of cubistic trees.

# WHO MADE OLD ENGLISH LUSTER AND WHEN?

## By W. D. JOHN

*Mr. John is a noted student and writer in the field of ceramics and glass paperweights. He is the author of the authoritative volume on Nantgarw porcelain, and has recently completed a book on English luster.*

COLLECTORS OF OLD ENGLISH LUSTER have for long been handicapped by the lack of authoritative knowledge on the whole subject, and they have often been wrongly informed and misled by the many writers who have attempted to deal with its development. The two small volumes, *Collecting Old Lustre Ware,* by W. Bosanko (1916) and *Pink Lustre Pottery,* by Dr. Atwood Thorne (1926), are both unreliable and have been of value only for their enthusiasm and some illustrations.

It has frequently been stated that, as the result of information imparted to him by his friend Dr. Fothergill, Josiah Wedgwood was experimenting with the lustering process as early as 1776 and that he was making commercial luster ware by 1790. From Wedgwood's correspondence, however, it is evident that such information related only to the preparation of metallic bronze mountings for certain vases, and the Wedgwood catalogue of seventy-eight pages, of the year 1787, does not list a single luster item. Actually, Josiah never made any luster himself, and it was not until some ten years after his death that such wares were first prepared at Etruria.

Another myth which has persisted is that copper luster was made at Brislington near Bristol by Richard Frank between 1782 and 1785. This was disproved by W. J. Pountney, who in 1914 completely excavated the pottery site and found only fragments of blue and white delft ware.

The introduction of metallic lustering on English earthenware was a new and independent discovery, and it was made by John Hancock of Hanley, Stoke-on-Trent. He has pronounced his own claim to this quite fearlessly in an issue of the *Staffordshire Mercury* for 1846: "I was the original inventor of luster, which is recorded in several works on Potting, and I first put it in practice at Mr. Spode's Manufactury for Messrs. Daniels and Brown . . . I shall be very happy to furnish proof on the subject."

There was no contradictory statement in any succeeding issues of the Staffordshire newspaper, and in view of the downright nature and forcible language of the Staffordshire workmen of those days such statements would certainly have appeared if Hancock's claim had not been truthful and accurate.

John Hancock was born in Derby in 1758 and was apprenticed to the Derby porcelain works to learn the art of painting and gilding. Later he went to Swansea and then settled in Staffordshire about 1786, where he was employed by W. and J. Turner of Lane End. It is not too difficult to determine when Hancock's process began to be employed on a commercial scale. This was certainly not before 1800, for careful examination of the directory of the Staffordshire pottery district for 1802 shows that luster is not mentioned at all, either in connection with the 139 manufacturers of

SHELL WALL POCKET, Spode, pink luster, impressed mark *(c. 1805).* Collection of Dr. Warren Baker.

PASTILLE BURNER, Wedgwood, gold luster, marked *Josiah Wedgwood Feby 2 1805.* Collection of Mrs. M. L. Rueter.

OVAL DISH, Lakin, pink luster, impressed mark *(c. 1808).* Collection of Dr. Warren Baker.

SHELL DISHES, Wedgwood, moonlight luster, impressed mark *(c. 1810)*. *Courtesy C. W. Lyon, Inc.*

earthenware or with the associated craftsmen who prepared the colors, glazes, and enamels. Later directories, after 1808, describe many of the manufacturers as lusterers.

The introduction of lustering was also closely associated with the availability of the metal platinum. This had been isolated from its ores in 1780, but industrial supplies in the pure state could not be purchased in England until after 1795, when the Staffordshire potters quickly realized the possibility of using it to produce metallized earthenware which would replace the more expensive plated metal utensils.

The first reliably dated examples of luster ware are the tripod pastille burners in over-all gold luster made by Josiah Wedgwood, II, which bear the impressed mark *Josiah Wedgwood/Feby 2/1805*, and which appear to be quite early examples.

It is well to emphasize that the English luster wares are coated with a thin film of either metallic gold (to impart the gold, copper, pink, and purple colorings), or platinum (for silver effects), whereas the Islamic and Hispano-Moresque luster is a combination of staining and iridescence produced by the two quite different metals, copper and silver.

The dating of the first English luster wares has always been too early. It is much more in accord with available evidence to date Staffordshire silver and gold luster about 1800 to 1805, and Staffordshire pink and resist luster about 1805 to

KRATER VASE, Wedgwood, moonlight luster, impressed mark *(c. 1812)*. *Burnap collection, William Rockhill Nelson Gallery.*

1815. It is the luster ware of the period 1805 to 1815, with its careful finish and intensity of metallic coloring, which is principally of interest to present-day collectors. Most of the important Staffordshire potters of this period participated in its production, and marked examples are known by Spode, Wedgwood, Wood and Caldwell, Bailey and Batkin, David

LARGE OVAL DISH, Leeds, silver resist luster, impressed mark *(c. 1812)*. *Burnap collection, William Rockhill Nelson Gallery.*

SPORTING JUGS, Wood & Caldwell, pink luster, impressed marks *(c. 1815)*. *Collection of Mrs. M. L. Rueter.*

250

FIGURE OF BRITANNIA, Wood & Caldwell, silver luster, impressed mark *(c. 1818)*. *Art Institute of Chicago.*

Wilson (not Robert Wilson), Lakin (but not Lakin and Poole), Shorthose, Warburton, Davenport, Barlow, Harley, Ridgway, Stevenson, Aynsley, and Adams.

The Leeds pottery in South Yorkshire was the first one away from Staffordshire to use the lustering process. It was introduced there about 1808 by Thomas Lakin, experienced Staffordshire enameler and color mixer. After dissolving his partnership with Poole in 1796 and working on his own account for a few years, Lakin had quickly appreciated the possibilities of Hancock's invention and evidently profited by taking the receipts to the Leeds pottery, of which he later became the manager. The Leeds luster, made from 1808 until about 1815, is of first-class quality, including some of the finest silver-resist types.

It can be stated quite definitely that no luster ware was made at any of the other four contemporary Yorkshire potteries—Castleford, Swinton, the Don, and Ferryside. Similarly, none of the many early Liverpool potteries made luster, with the possible exception of the Herculaneum, which was worked in the Staffordshire tradition by the many workmen who had migrated there from Burslem. Furthermore, luster ware was never made in Bristol.

Apart from Staffordshire and Leeds, luster was produced only in two other districts of England—in the northeastern counties and at Swansea in South Wales, both of which were some two hundred miles away from Staffordshire, but in opposite directions.

Early experimentation in the lustering process was made by Thomas Pardoe at the Cambrian pottery, Swansea, and a few silver-resist examples were produced by him before 1810. By far the larger proportion of recognizable Swansea luster ware, however, was manufactured during the period from 1825 to 1830 and comprises much pink luster in the form of basket-edged plates, jugs, and milk containers in the shape of cows. A second pottery in Swansea, the Glamorgan, also made pink

WIG STAND, Bailey & Batkins, silver luster, marked *(c. 1818)*. *Collection of Mrs. M. L. Rueter.*

SET OF SEASONS, Sunderland, pink luster, impressed *Dixon, Austin & Co. (c. 1820)*. *Collection of Dr. Warren Baker.*

luster wares about the same period, and in later days *(c. 1845-1860)* some average gold lustered earthenware was made at the South Wales Pottery, Llanelly, some twelve miles beyond Swansea.

In Sunderland, between 1815 and 1840 (mostly of the later dating) there were at least five manufactories making large quantities of mottled pink luster wares, usually engraved with shipping scenes and sentimental verses. The most important makers were Phillips & Co., and later Dixon, Austin & Co., who worked both the North Hylton and Sunderland potteries, Scott & Sons of the Southwick pottery, S. Moore & Co. of the Wear pottery, John Dawson & Co. of the Low Ford pottery, and Wm. Ball of the Deptford Pottery.

Twelve miles to the north of Sunderland, pink lustered wares in a similar style were also made by the Newcastle-upon-Tyne potters, whose names are not so well known: Sewell, Fell & Co., Maling & Co., and Paterson. Twenty-five miles to the south of Sunderland, the Middlesborough and Stockton potteries produced like types of pink luster wares. Marked ex-

251

amples are often available from all the northeastern potteries, and although they never equaled in quality those of the earlier Staffordshire potteries, they are perhaps more expressive of the social life of the period.

Many of the desirable sporting jugs with richly colored grounds and intricate silver-resist designs have often been attributed to the Swansea pottery, but confirmation is lacking and most of them are more likely to have been made in the Staffordshire potteries between 1808 and 1815.

The manufacture of luster wares was thus never as widespread in England as has been so frequently assumed and declared. The main center was always Staffordshire, though the Leeds pottery followed almost immediately during the years from 1805 to 1815. There were only two other important areas of production, and mainly for pink lustering—South Wales and the Northeastern counties of England—into both of which it was introduced only after it had been fully established in Staffordshire.

The pieces illustrated are all marked examples, and indicate the various types of luster wares made by the early and important English manufacturers.

FLOWER POT HOLDER, Stevenson, pink luster, marked *(c. 1820)*. *Art Institute of Chicago.*

Luster has been made continuously since its introduction, and while the original forms, principally in gold and copper coloring, are still being reproduced, it is not unduly difficult to identify the more modern examples.

Lustering of the resist type has also been adopted for present-day pottery designing. Recently a Wedgwood dinner service of 161 pieces was chosen by H. M. Queen Elizabeth for presentation to President and Madame Auriol of France on the occasion of their state visit to England; it was designed by Miss Star Wedgwood, in grey with a ground-laid border and stenciled flowers outlined in platinum luster.

CUP AND SAUCER, Shorthose & Co, pink luster, impressed mark *(c. 1818)*. *Art Institute of Chicago.*

JUG, Newcastle, pink luster, impressed *Sewell* *(c. 1820)*. *Art Institute of Chicago.*

PLATE, Swansea, pink luster, impressed mark *(c. 1825)*. *Collection of Dr. Warren Baker.*

# Stoneware gin flasks: legacy of the damned

BY IVOR NOËL HUME, *Director, department of archaeology, Colonial Williamsburg*

A GROWING INTEREST in ceramics as artifacts of history, coupled with the increasing desirability of nineteenth-century pottery (as the scarcity of earlier wares prices them beyond the means of many collectors), has sparked an enthusiasm for a large group of hitherto neglected British stonewares. They are the brown, salt-glazed spirit flasks that had evolved from the simple pocket bottles of the eighteenth century into elaborately slipcast creations catering to the gin-palace taste of the second quarter of the nineteenth century. Such flasks were designed to amuse then, just as they still do today; but behind the comic and patriotic ceramic artistry lurked a sinister purpose, and thus speculation as to where these bottles have been and what damage they may have done gives them a macabre interest uniquely their own.

"Drunk for a Penny/ Dead drunk for two pence/ Clean Straw for Nothing." That grim advertisement inscribed on an arch in William Hogarth's engraving *Gin Lane* is believed to have been copied from a sign outside a London tavern in the 1730's. In commenting on it, Hogarth's biographer John Ireland drew his readers' attention to another: "Even now," he wrote in 1791, "there is inscribed on a barber's shop, in the vicinity of Drury Lane, 'Shave for a Penny, and a Glass of Gin into the Bargain!'"[1] Both are eloquent testimony to the magnetism of geneva (from the Old French *genevre*, juniper), and to gin's ready

Fig. 1. Three small brown stoneware bottles found in London and thought to be of London manufacture. *Left:* Flask flattened on the back for easy pocketing and incised on the front *N M/1742*, making it the earliest recorded spirit flask of its type. Height 5½ inches. *Center:* Flask flattened on both sides and pricked on the surface to provide a sure grip for uncertain hands; probably second quarter of nineteenth century. Height 6¼ inches. *Right:* Cylindrical bottle with the purveyor's name *Howe* impressed in printer's type; probably last quarter of eighteenth century. Height 3¾ inches. *Guildhall Museum.*

availability to the city's poor. Like another hazard to British physical and moral health, the scourge of the "infernal broth"[2] could be blamed on the French, for it was in an effort to discourage the importation of French brandy that an act of Parliament was passed in 1690 promoting the distilling of spirits from home-grown grain. A related parliamentary act was made law early in the reign of Queen Anne, at which time controls previously vested in the Distillers' Company were cancelled, permitting anyone with a still and a supply of mash to produce whatever kinds of rotgut he could conceive.

So detrimental to health and labor were the results of these laws that in 1736 the celebrated but ineffectual Gin Act was passed in an effort to tax it out of reach of the masses. In spite of this, and a series of similar measures enacted from time to time through the rest of the eighteenth century, gin drinking continued to increase. In 1742 twenty million gallons of gin were distilled in London alone. Eleven years later, Chambers' *Cyclopaedia* reported that the city's gin no longer contained juniper berries, "our rascally chemists" having taught the distillers that oil of turpentine served just as well. Never, the encyclopedist added, had a greater quantity been made.

Yet another anti-gin act was passed in 1830 permitting the general sale of beer and cider by anyone willing to invest in a two-guinea license. The move uncorked a veritable Pandora's bottle of drinking shops freed from controls long imposed by statute on inns and taverns. Because such places were soon found to be selling bootleg gin, their proprietors were encouraged also to acquire licenses to sell spirits. Thus, by 1840, beer drinking had gone up by twenty-eight per cent and licensed gin sales by thirty-two per cent.

Although much gin was consumed on licensed premises, it was the gin-to-go trade that added a colorful and historically important chapter to the history of British ceramics. As early as 1724 one finds a thief being tried at the Old Bailey for, among other crimes, snatching a woman's "pocket" containing "37 shillings, and some halfpence, a silver snuff-box gilt, a pocket bottle of geneva, and a tortoise-shell tobacco-box."[3] In all likelihood that pocket bottle was of glass cased in leather, for it clearly had belonged to a lady of substance. Much stouter containers would be needed to endure the rough and tumble of eighteenth-century slum life, a need well served by flattened bottles of brown salt-glazed stoneware such as that at the left in Figure 1. It is inscribed *N M / 1742* and is the earliest dated example known to me. The bottle at the right in the same illustration bears the name *Howe* in letters impressed with printer's type, a technique commonly used on brown stoneware tavern mugs between about 1760 and 1790. This bottle is not flattened for pocketing, however, and it may be argued that it was not intended for gin but for a more beneficial potion manufactured by the chemist and druggist Nathaniel Howe of West Smithfield, who was listed in *The New Patent London Directory* for 1793.

A hitherto unrecorded flask marked PUBLISHED BY S GREEN LAMBETH JULY 20th 1837 recalls the accession of Queen Victoria in that year (Fig. 4). On one side is an extraordinarily swan-neck portrait of the queen and on the other a more elegant rendering in high relief of the British royal arms. Unfortunately, elegance is a poor substitute for accuracy, and these arms are incorrect in that they retain the central escutcheon charged with the crown of Hanover.

Fig. 2. Brown stoneware flask flattened on two sides, both decorated with an applied female profile; c. 1790, Lambeth or Fulham. Lip reconstructed. This sprig-decorated type is thought to be the precursor for the press-molded and slip-cast flasks of the nineteenth century. Height 4⅞ inches. *Private collection.*

Although part of the British arms from 1714 until 1837, the Elector of Hanover's ermine cap (a crown after 1815) was omitted after the death of William IV since Victoria was ineligible under Hanoverian law to succeed to the kingdom of Hanover.

The maker of the Victoria portrait flasks (Figs. 3, 4), Stephen Green, established his factory at Lambeth about 1820 and it continued under his management as the Imperial Pottery until 1858. When he began, Green was one of six or seven stoneware potters working in Lambeth, all of them (according to Llewellyn Jewitt[4]) specializing in bottles for blacking, ginger beer, porter, cider, spruce beer, and ink. Curiously, there was no reference to gin.

Another bottle commemorating the accession of Victoria was manufactured at Joseph Bourne's Denby Pottery in Derbyshire, a center second only to Lambeth in the mass production of stoneware flasks. The Denby example in the London Museum is impressed on the back *Queen Alexandrina Victoria* and was made before it was known that the young queen would use but one name. The modeler has done her little justice, and she is seen as a rather frowsty and fat-faced matron holding a scroll reading *May Peace and Prosperity Prevail*. Her pose is similar to that of the better-looking young lady holding a bird shown in Figure 5, and the master matrices for both figures are almost

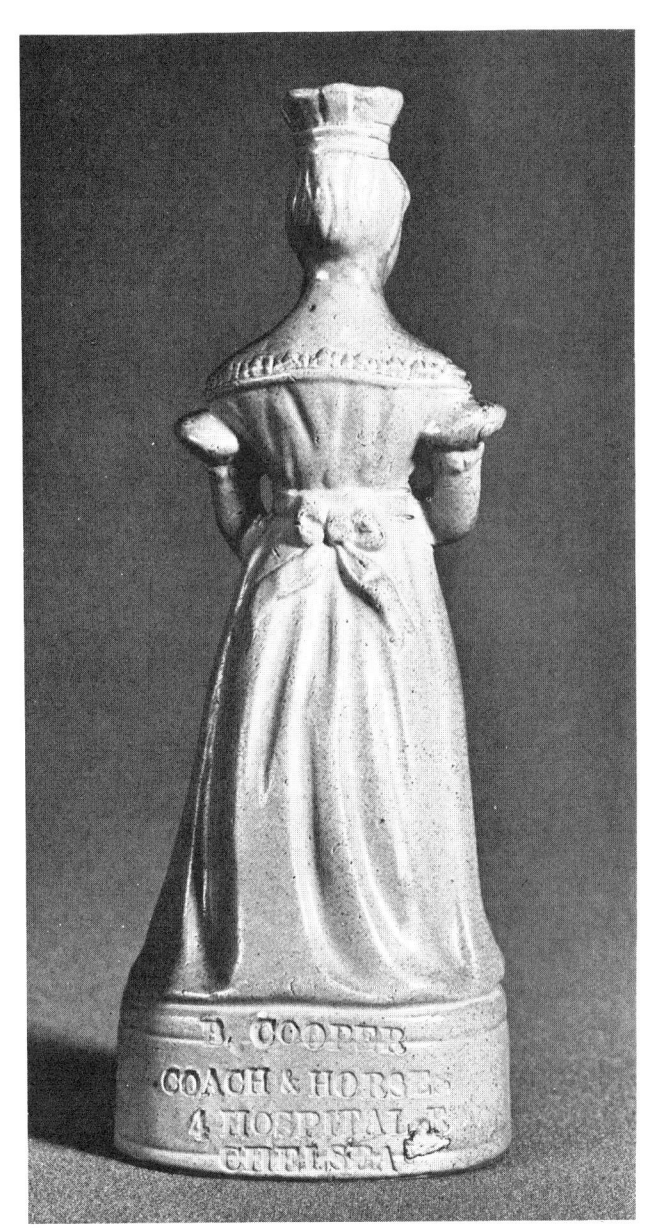

Fig. 3. Front, back, and bottom of a rare standing portrait flask of Queen Victoria marked as being of half-pint capacity. The queen's name is cast in Tuscan lettering in high relief, while on the back the name B. Cooper and his Chelsea address are impressed in printer's type. As Benjamin Cooper was landlord of the Coach and Horses for only a short time between 1837 and 1838, this may be the most tightly documented of all portrait flasks. Additional information is provided by an impressed, script-lettered inscription on the bottom revealing that the bottle's design was registered by the stoneware potter Stephen Green of Lambeth on July 20, 1837, a month after Victoria's accession. Height 9 inches. *Private collection.*

Fig. 4. Front and back of a seven-ounce flask commemorating the accession of Queen Victoria in 1837. This hitherto unrecorded example is marked on the bottom as having been registered by the potter Stephen Green on the same day as the matrix for the flask shown in Fig. 3. On one side is an anatomically odd portrait of the queen and on the other a heraldically inaccurate rendering of her royal arms. Height 5$^{11}$/$_{16}$ inches. *Private collection.*

Fig. 5. A rather ponderous flask sometimes erroneously considered to be a portrait of Jenny Lind; possibly intended to represent the Princess Victoria, c. 1836. Impressed on the back is the mark of the Bourne Potteries of Denby and Codnor Park in Derbyshire. Height 8⅛ inches. *Private collection.*

certainly the work of the same man. Although the bird-gripping damsel was recently sold as a portrait of Jenny Lind, who did not make her British debut until 1847, ceramic-historian Geoffrey Godden possesses a flask from the same Denby mold dated August 19th, 1836, thus eliminating Jenny Lind. It remains possible, however, that the figure is that of the Princess Victoria on the grounds that the hair style parallels that shown in an 1835 self-portrait in the Royal Collection at Windsor.

Impressed marks on the backs of both the Victoria and "Jenny Lind" flasks read DENBY & CODNOR PARK•BOURNES POTTERIES•DERBYSHIRE•, an important dating aid, as the Codnor Park Factory was acquired by Bourne in 1833 and kept in operation until 1861. It had been developed by another stoneware-bottle manufacturer, William Burton, who had acquired it in 1821, manning the factory with workmen brought from the famous stoneware center at Brampton. The Bourne empire began at nearby Belper in about 1800 and expanded to take in the Denby Pottery in 1812; consequently some of the earliest pictorial stoneware gin flasks are marked BELPER & DENBY/*BOURNES POTTERIES/DERBYSHIRE* (Fig. 6). These, therefore, must have been made no later than 1834, when Joseph Bourne closed the Belper works.

Figure 7 illustrates another royal flask which for a time masqueraded under a false identity. It was sold as representing the luckless Caroline, whom George IV rejected as queen in 1820, thus dating the flask to that year. Instead, the figure standing beside the crown and scepter of England is that of the young Victoria in a pose borrowed from her portrait painted by George Hayter in 1833. Only one recorded flask can lay any claim to portraying Caroline,

Fig. 6. Front and back of a William IV portrait flask belonging to the well-known political Reform Bill group. The inscription on the front is impressed with printer's type, a double-strike error at the beginning revealing that the three-line inscription was set up in a single block and applied with a rolling motion from left to right. The slip-cast flask is a superior product of Joseph Bourne's Belper and Denby Potteries and must date between 1830 and 1834. Height 7½ inches. *Private collection.*

and then only because she holds a scroll reading *My Hope is in my People.* Those words are thought to be a plea to the British public's sense of fair play during the Bergami scandal, whose details unfolded through the spring and summer of 1820.

Caroline's principal defense counsel at her trial in the House of Lords was Lord Brougham who himself earned gin-flask immortality for his part in promoting the parliamentary reform bills of 1831 and 1832. Other Reform Bill heroes of the proletariat portrayed in this way were Whig party leader Earl Grey and Lord John Russell. Their bottles were inscribed respectively *The People's Rights, Grey's Reform Cordial,* and *The True Spirit of Reform.* Equally popular was the people's new monarch, the "sailor king" William IV, and he, too, got a cork in his head, and across his ample girth the inscription *William, IV, th's Reform Cordial* (Fig. 6).

William's predecessor George IV is not recorded as a gin-flask subject (other than as a mask decorating a stoneware pistol), supporting the belief that the market favored heroes or individuals for whom the masses felt some sympathy. This thesis may at first glance appear to be damaged by the fact that Sir Robert Peel, prominent among the Reform Bill's Tory opponents, is one of the more common gin-flask politicians. The public memory was short, however, and in the 1840's Peel became a popular figure after leading the Conservative party to victory in 1842 and presiding over the abolition of the Corn Laws four years later. In his full-length portrait flask he is therefore shown holding a scroll inscribed *Bread for the Millions.*

Not all flasks immortalized political or royal favorites; on the contrary, one of the most common recalls the astonishing popularity in Britain of an American entertainer

(Fig. 8). Thomas Dartmouth Rice galloped to stardom as an entr'acte performer in Louisville, Kentucky, in 1828, by aping an aged Negro named Jim Crow. Rice's hit song of that name preceded him to London, where he first appeared at the Surrey Theatre in 1836, and it was either his playbill or the sheet-music cover for "Jim Crow" (Fig. 9) that inspired the flask's design. Either way the bottle merits a place among the memorabilia of the American theater, as well as a niche in the scant artifactual history of the black man in the pre-Civil War United States, recalling as it does the origin of the term "Jim Crow." Two variations of this flask are known, though in each the relief-molded figure is the same. The principal differences are a zone of beading around the central neck cordon and an arc of similar beading at the shoulder. One of these beaded flasks is stamped as having been made for the Black Horse public house in Kingsland Road, Shoreditch.

The London borough of Shoreditch lies northeast of the old walled city and likes to be remembered as the home of Shakespeare when first he sought his fortune there; but by the nineteenth century Shoreditch was known only as the worst of slums. The London historian Arthur Mee was not exaggerating when he wrote that "in the year of Queen Victoria's Jubilee this was a sink of iniquity with hardly a parallel in England."[5] Figure 10 illustrates another flask recalling those days when a saddened Shoreditch vicar could justifiably complain that "managing this parish is like walking on a wall adorned with broken bottles."[6] Decorated only at the shoulder, the flask is impressed *Vemur Stout House Shoreditch* and probably dates from the 1840's. It was dug up in Lambeth, where most of these bottles were made, and it therefore remains anyone's guess as to whether this one had groped its way home from Shoreditch or whether, because of its obvious underfiring, it was simply a factory reject.

Among the more common of the nonpolitical flasks is another having a secondary association with the Surrey Theatre. The latter's onetime resident playwright Douglas Jerrold in 1845 contributed a series of essays to the magazine *Punch* entitled "Mrs. Caudle's Curtain Lectures," and catering to their popularity the flask depicts the scolding Mrs. Caudle sitting up in bed haranguing her luckless husband. The other side of the flask depicts the demure "Miss Prettyman," another of Jerrold's characters. Seeking, as one must, dating criteria for cataloguing unmarked specimens, I had put some store by the fact that the Caudle flask (c. 1845) has a flaring mouth similar to that of the Vemur Stout House example, whereas the Jim Crow (1836) and the after-Hayter Victoria (1837) possess identical triple-cordoned necks and no flaring at the mouths. Unfortunately this neatly datable distinction collapsed with the appearance of the Victoria flask of 1837 shown in Figure 4, for its mouth clearly belongs to the allegedly later Caudle class. It is relatively safe, however, to assume that those portrait flasks whose figures are shaped only to the waist (the Reform Cordial group) belong to the period 1830 to 1835 and were followed by full-length portrayals by about 1837—always supposing that we assume the full-length figure in Figure 7 to be Victoria, not Caroline, and overlook a half-length Victoria made by Oldfield and Company of Derbyshire (c. 1838-1888).

Flasks whose decoration (for example, Victoria or an old woman taking snuff) is placed within a central medallion surrounded by foliate ornament and whose sides slope

Fig. 7. Flask, 1837, flat on two sides, both decorated with the same low-relief portrait of Queen Victoria. The queen holds a rose and stands beside a table on which is a cushion supporting the coronation regalia. The pose predates the accession, having been taken from an 1833 portrait by George Hayter. Unmarked, but almost certainly Lambeth. Height 7¼ inches. *Private collection.*

Fig. 8. Flask with two flat sides, both decorated with the same portrait figure in relief of the American entertainer Thomas Dartmouth Rice in the role of Jim Crow. Rice was the first blackface comedian and the flask commemorates his appearance at London's Surrey Theatre in 1836. The figure is often incorrectly identified as a drunken or dancing sailor, but it is actually derived from the portrait of Rice in his "Jim Crow" costume used on his hit song's sheet music (Fig. 9). It is probable that these flasks had a long life, for the character of "Jim Crow" was absorbed into the Punch and Judy routines recorded by Henry Mayhew in the 1850's. Unmarked, but almost certainly the product of a Lambeth factory. Height 6¾ inches. *Private collection.*

inward toward mouth and base belong to a distinct and later class and were generally the product of William Northen's Vauxhall Pottery, which operated in Lambeth from 1847 until 1892. Also of relatively late date is a group of flasks in the shape of constables' tipstaffs. The example shown in Figure 11 was described in the 1908 catalogue of London's Guildhall Museum as having been made in 1848 to commemorate the swearing in of special constables. There is, however, another, rather similar flask in the British Museum which is there attributed to about 1837. The survival of these and other specimens from slightly differing molds suggests that they were not made to commemorate a single event, and it may be no accident that like the wooden staffs from which they were copied, these flasks would make excellent weapons for Saturday night brawls.

Flasks in the shape of pistols are probably the best known and were produced by two major Lambeth factories, those of Stephen Green (1820-1858) and Doulton and Watts (1815-1858). The former was also the source of the elaborately molded sportsman's powder flask shown in Figure 12. It is uncertain just how late pistol flasks remained popular, but in 1871 William Blanchard Jerrold (the son of Mrs. Caudle's creator) wrote that it was in the nature of Whitechapel louts to shout at any passerby who might be carrying a "bottle or pocket pistol" in the hope of a free drink. We may deduce from that statement either that pistol-shape flasks were still popular or that by 1871 the name had broadened to include any pocketable bottle. Alternatively, of course, the clumsy and none-too-easily pocketed stoneware pistols may have been the potters' humorously literal rendering of an already existing colloquialism.

With the exception of the political flasks of the 1830's bearing such inscriptions as *Brougham's Cordial, The True Spirit of Reform,* and *Irish Reform Cordial* (this on a portrait flask of Daniel O'Connell), there is no certainty that all ornamental stoneware bottles were intended to contain gin. There are, for example, a number of large fish-shape flasks (see Fig. 12) which Geoffrey Godden suggests were made as hot-water bottles.[7] Although the illustrated fish is unmarked, others like it made by Stephen Green must date prior to 1858. His, incidentally, were fish with cordial expressions—in contrast to those made by William Northen whose open mouths display an alarming array of teeth. The largest recorded fish measures fifteen and a half inches in length and admittedly would hold a good deal of gin, but its capacity would almost certainly be less than that of some gin bottles retailed today. Remembering that nineteenth-century gin was imbibed in prodigious quantities and probably was less potent (if more poisonous) than the distillations we are accustomed to, it is reasonable to deduce that most, if not all, of these flasks started life as gin bottles. There was, of course, absolutely nothing to prevent their later use to heat a bed or to attend church as hand warmers concealed in a lady's muff. The fact, however, that the flasks' period of popularity so closely parallels the rise and decline of the nineteenth century's gin palaces strongly suggests that the bottles were manufactured to decorate their shelves and to beguile and befuddle their uneducated customers.

Throughout history the patrons of such places have had a curious taste for freaks, and the large flask illustrated in Figure 13 may have been made to exploit it. Shaped like an elderly humpbacked woman, it may be a portrait

259

Fig. 9. Lithographed sheet-music cover for Thomas Dartmouth Rice's song "Jim Crow." *Victoria and Albert Museum, Enthoven theater collection.*

flask of an as yet unidentified London "character"; alternatively (and more probably) it may represent Mr. Punch's wife, Judy, for Punch and Judy shows were a staple street entertainment throughout the nineteenth century. Then again, it is possible that the potter was pandering to an age-old superstition that the sight of a hunchback was lucky and that to touch the hump was even more so. The flask is certainly less than an aesthetic delight, but like all the rest, it is historically interesting and eminently collectible. Seen simply as objects, they can all be taken at their face value as amusingly "quaint" reminders of once-famous people and events; yet to the social historian they are the artifacts of a grim world that Dickens and Henry Mayhew knew and described so well—though no better than did William Blanchard Jerrold when he wrote of a visit to the slums of Bermondsey in 1870: "Demands for gin assailed us on all sides. Women old and young, girls and boys in the most woeful tatters; rogues of all descriptions; brazen-faced lads dancing in the flaring ball-rooms on the first-floor of the public-houses; even the Fire King who was performing before half a dozen sailors, and the pot-boy who showed the way up the steep stairs—wanted gin—nothing but gin."[8] In reality, therefore, these flasks, with their disarmingly amusing and often pious portraits, were once keys to the portals of oblivion and survive now as a legacy of the damned.[9]

Fig. 10. The brown stoneware liquor flask in its simplest form, decorated only with incuse petal modeling at the shoulder and impressed with printer's type as belonging to the Vemur Stout House in Shoreditch. Found in Lambeth, this flask was almost certainly made there, c. 1840-1850. Height 7¼ inches. *Private collection.*

Fig. 11. Flask in the form of a tipstaff, decorated on one side with the Garter and the arms of England (post-1837) and on another with the initials *V.R.* (Victoria Regina). This example is unmarked, but a number of variations are known, among them specimens made by Stephen Green and by Doulton and Watts of Lambeth prior to 1858. Height 11¼ inches. *Guildhall Museum.*

---

[1] John Ireland, *Hogarth Illustrated* (London, 1791), Vol. 2, p. 332.

[2] *Ibid.*, p. 334, footnote.

[3] James Montague, *The Old Bailey Chronicle* (London, 1788), Vol. 1, p. 328.

[4] Llewellyn Jewitt, *The Ceramic Art of Great Britain* (London, 1878), Vol. 1, p. 136.

[5] Arthur Mee, *London* (London, 4th edition, 1948), p. 736.

[6] *Ibid.*

[7] Geoffrey A. Godden, *An Illustrated Encyclopedia of British Pottery and Porcelain* (New York, 1966), p. 253, Fig. 446.

[8] Gustave Doré and Blanchard Jerrold, *London, a pilgrimage* (reprint, New York, 1970), p. 145. First published in London, 1872.

[9] For biographical information I am deeply indebted to Ralph Merrifield, deputy keeper at London's Guildhall Museum, and to John May and Anthony Oliver, both of London. I am also greatly obliged to Phillipa Glanville, assistant curator at the London Museum for making its reserve collections available to me for study, and I am equally grateful to John Austin, curator of ceramics of Colonial Williamsburg.

Fig. 12. Three examples illustrating the range of inspirational sources culled by brown stoneware spirit-flask modelers. The large fish (length 15½ inches) is unmarked, but the small oval barrel bears the sculptured label S GREEN/POTTER/LAMBETH, dating it no later than 1858. Length 4 3/16 inches. The elaborately modeled powder horn is taken from a metal prototype; indeed, the master pattern may have been cast directly from it. Both sides are decorated with different hunting dogs, and the usual iron-oxide slip has been deliberately confined to the container to leave the "metal" mouth and dispenser a lighter brown. Impressed on the base at the junction of the mold halves: STEPHEN GREEN IMPERIAL POTTERIES LAMBETH. Before 1858. Height 9 5/16 inches. *Colonial Williamsburg and private collection.*

Fig. 13. One of the more elaborate brown stoneware spirit flasks in the shape of an unidentified humpbacked woman; possibly Judy, the wife of Mr. Punch, whose puppet shows were popular throughout the nineteenth century. London or Derbyshire, c. 1840-1855. Height 9 11/16 inches. *Private collection.*

# Mason's patent ironstone china: an underrated ware

BY STANLEY W. FISHER

Fig. 1. Vestibule vase with black transfer and enameled "Chinese" subjects in reserves on a *rouge-de-fer* ground patterned in black and yellow; height 36 inches. *Illustrations are from the author's collection.*

DURING THE FIRST QUARTER of the nineteenth century in England a flourishing middle class began to appreciate the household possessions of the gentry, and to want something like them for its own homes. The wealthy factory owners bought massive, over-elaborate mahogany furniture, and filled vestibules, china pantries, and every available inch of sideboard top and overmantel with ornate china. They soon discovered that the colorful, splendid Chinese porcelain in the great country mansions was out of their reach and sought a substitute, which the Staffordshire potters were only too eager to supply. Porcelain, of course, was still much too expensive for this market, but many found an ideal compromise in a ware that was durable and that bore a close resemblance to the Oriental in design and in quality of color: the earthenware called Mason's Patent Ironstone China.

Charles James Mason (1791-1856) was the son of Miles Mason, who is known to collectors as the maker of one of the first practical Staffordshire porcelains produced on a large scale. Charles, with his brother George, took out a patent in 1813 for "a new process of manufacturing porcelain and earthenware by the introduction of a material not heretofore used in the manufactory of these articles. This material is known in Staffordshire by the names of Tabberner's Mine Rock, Little Mine Rock, and New Rock." No mention was made of ironstone, a slag by-product of iron smelting; and it is a fact that the new ware contained none. "Stone china," with a very similar body, had been made for some years by Spode, Minton, and John and William Turner, but it was left to Mason to invent a name that suggested strength and durability.

In 1815 the Masons moved from the Minerva Works in Lane Delph to the Fenton Stone Works, and there they set out to supply the new market with their wares. Services, of course, and sets of hexagonal and octagonal ewers with "sea-dragon" or snake handles they made in several styles; and in addition enormous vestibule vases, barrel-shape garden seats, potpourri vases, huge loving cups, sets of vases, beakers, and every other kind of useful or ornamental article—whenever possible imitating Chinese shapes and decoration. But that was not all. So sturdy was their material that they were even able to make complete fireplaces and overmantels and bedsteads, some of which have survived to this day. This enormous output continued until labor difficulties forced Mason into bankruptcy in 1848. Works and equipment were taken over by a Francis Morley, who resold them to the present company in 1862. It should be noted that the firm still makes the same kind of ware, using the same shapes and patterns and the same mark.

Fig. 2. *Left*: copy of a K'ang Hsi plate, in sepia transfer and bright enamels; royal blue ground on rim. *Center*: potpourri vase with black-printed and enameled decoration on a sea-green ground. *Right*: ewer in "bandanna ware"; red and black ground colors.

Fig. 3. Loving cup and cover, decorated in gold on a deep mazarin blue glaze; height 13½ inches.

Fig. 4. Pair of vases and ewer. Chinese landscapes, pink transfer and enamels in reserves on a royal blue ground with gold pattern on the vases, yellow enamel on the ewer.

It is all too easy to assume the superiority of "hand-painted" over "printed" decoration on porcelain and pottery, but painting is often slipshod and careless, while the work of the engraver may be first-rate. Mason had a team of very competent engravers and spared no pains or expense in providing them with the best Chinese pieces to copy; and though much of his ordinary printed domestic ware is colored with misplaced washes of enamel, with little regard to the engraved outline, at the other extreme the enamels were carefully, even meticulously, applied.

Much of the printing was in underglaze cobalt blue, but outlines might be done in black, sepia, or pink enamel. A point of note is that Mason evidently had a restricted range of patterns engraved in different sizes and used in varying arrangements. Still further variety was made possible by different combinations of enamel washes, chosen from a vivid palette including a fine *rouge de fer*, a brilliant yellow, a sea-green, a yellow-green, pale orange, royal blue, crimson, and rose-pink. Another Mason specialty was the use of a very deep mazarin blue glaze, principally as a ground for decoration in gold (Fig. 3). Mason's gold was of fine quality, and was used lavishly on handles and cover knobs of every conceivable kind.

It will surprise those whose opinion of Mason's ironstone china has not been high to learn that the decorating shops produced some very fine brushwork without the aid of transferred outline. Landscapes of this quality are known but they are very rare, whereas excellent flower

Fig. 5. Beaker on stand, decorated in underglaze cobalt blue and gold on yellow ground. The stand is made of ironstone china enameled in mat black.

Fig. 6. Dish with black-transfer and enamel Chinese subject; border in *famille* rose style.

Fig. 7. Pickle tray molded in shell form and decorated in black-transfer outline, underglaze blue, and enamels in Worcester-Chinese style.

painting is fairly common. Figure 10 shows two pieces decorated with painted flowers, and also an example of very careful enamel wash over a delicately printed puce outline, with other flower sprays in gold. Another painted style, in the Japanese Kutani manner, used boldly painted stylized flowers and leaves in blue, red, and gold (Fig. 8, left); and sometimes a central motif enamel-washed over printed underglaze blue was provided with an elaborate border painted in a careless, haphazard manner that is superficially most effective (Fig. 8, right). Occasionally one sees a piece that is such an exact copy of the Chinese original that even an expert may at a short distance be deceived (Figs 5, 6).

Not all Mason's ironstone china was marked, and to identify it the collector must rely on his knowledge of shapes, distinctive paste or body, and typical manner and styles of decoration. At first the words FENTON STONE WORKS in a cartouche, printed in underglaze blue, were sometimes used, and another early (and reliable) mark takes the form of the impressed words MASON'S PATENT IRONSTONE CHINA arranged either in a circle or in a line. The other printed marks are found in various forms: a crown alone, MASON'S above the crown, MASON'S and the crown above a cartouche containing the words PATENT IRONSTONE CHINA, and, later, the same but with the word IMPROVED substituted for Patent. Printed marks may be in underglaze blue, black, sepia, or puce, and occasionally on especially fine pieces the mark was washed over with translucent enamel, usually green.

Mason's output was so great that probably large quantities of his ware still exist in many other countries besides Britain, much of it perhaps in daily use. Heavy it may be, certainly often gaudy to the point of ostentation, but it is supremely decorative, and one day it will be valued as a ware whose imperfections are outweighed by its very real merit.

265

Fig. 8. Plates with hand-painted decoration in (*left*) the Japanese Kutani and (*right*) Chinese styles.

Fig. 9. Mug, ewer, and inkpot painted in underglaze cobalt blue and India red enamel, in the Chinese style.

Fig. 10. Examples of floral decoration. *Left:* sprays in pink-transfer outline, enamels, and gold. *Center:* painted bouquet with a yellow-green border. *Right:* flowers with a mat cobalt-blue border; low relief ornament in white.

BY LURA WOODSIDE WATKINS

# Pratt's color prints on Staffordshire ware

Fig. 1. Two plates issued at the time of the Centennial. *Left, Philadelphia Public Buildings, 1876; right, Philadelphia Exhibition, 1876.*

ABOUT TWENTY-FIVE YEARS ago it was the fashion to collect china potlids. They were the covers of ointment or salve boxes, beautifully decorated with color prints which were not only attractive but important, for they were examples of the first color printing on ceramics. The technique followed closely on the heels of the color work of George Baxter and his associates, who had developed the process of printing with oil colors on paper. We now know that this color process on pottery was not confined to the pictures on potlids but appeared as well on tea and dessert services.

The greater part of color-printed Staffordshire was made in the works of Felix and Richard Pratt of Fenton. They were descendants of the earlier Pratt who is familiar in English potting history for his earthenware decorated with modeling in low relief, produced in the late 1700's and early 1800's. They had established their manufacture early in the 1800's on the site of the old Thomas Heath Pottery, and the two sons of Felix were associated with them. It was the son Felix Edwards Pratt who secured, on December 31, 1847, a patent for an improvement in the manufacture of potlids. The patent may have been the result of discoveries made by Jesse Austin, a skilled engraver, who was responsible for most of the designs produced by the Pratts, as well as for a number put out in other factories.

Jesse Austin was born in Staffordshire, February 5, 1806, the youngest of twelve children. His father, William, was a tailor, a native of Devonshire. Jesse was given an education in the Longton grammar school, and also studied drawing in the evenings. He learned copperplate engraving while employed as an apprentice in the Davenport pottery at Burslem.

Between 1835 and 1840, he was engaged in engraving borders for printing on earthenware. This style of decoration was abandoned soon after 1840, when white ware became fashionable, and Austin suffered a setback. He was also handicapped by a chronic lameness and by asthma. The year 1843 he spent at a pottery in Leicestershire. In the mid-forties he went to the Pratts at Fenton. There he remained until his death in 1879, except for a year spent working for the firm of Brown-Westhead, Moore & Company, of Cauldon Place, Stoke-on-Trent, where he went after a quarrel with Thomas Pratt, second son of Felix, and where he produced some of his best plates.

At Fenton Jesse Austin was in charge of all the engravers employed by Pratt. These artisans, among them

Fig. 2. *Interior View of Independence Hall, Philadelphia.* Issued in 1876.

Fig. 3. *Sandringham, the Seat of H.R.H., the Prince of Wales.*

Charles Scrivener, Thomas Goodwin, and one Stevenson, worked in a shop apart from the pottery itself. In this engraving room Austin originated the multitude of designs, some of his own creation and some copied from paintings, which embellished the potlids and the dessert services made in the pottery. Many of his original watercolor drawings have been preserved in a scrapbook, and many of his copper plates still exist. Some potlids and perhaps also dishes were signed by Jesse Austin, but, even when unsigned, a number of his designs have been identified by means of these surviving copper plates.

To produce one of these charming pictures, four or more separate printings in different colors were necessary. In order to obtain exact registration, tiny dots were placed at opposite sides of the plate to serve as guides. The first impression was in buff, the second in blue, the third in pink or red. The fourth, in brown, was the complete engraving in stipple or line. This method of color printing was the reverse of that employed by Baxter, who printed his line engraving first and the colors afterwards. The pictures on the Pratt china are so neatly registered and so delicately tinted that they look almost like real water colors.

The body of Pratt color-printed ware does not seem to be porcelain, though it is said that the Pratts bought a prepared "china" body for their dessert ware, which they printed and fired at their own works. It is actually a refined sort of earthenware, such as we might call a "semi-porcelain." The tea and dessert services were exhibited at the Crystal Palace exposition in 1851, when they were mentioned as being "earthenware, printed in a peculiar style." It was indeed a peculiar style, for it was the first of its kind. All previous color work on ceramics had been either freehand decoration or printed copper-plate engraving colored by hand. The Pratts were awarded a medal for "underglaze color-printing." This dessert ware was sold principally in the United States, and can still be found here, even though rarely. The potlids are less common in America, but had a tremendous sale in England.

Harold G. Clarke and Frank Wrench composed their book *Colour Printed Pictures on Staffordshire Pottery* (1924) with an extensive catalogue of the views on potlids and with detailed descriptions of the engravings and their sources. Most of the pictures were the work of Jesse Austin and, wherever this fact is known, the authors have noted it. Many, perhaps most, of the potlid views appear on tableware. These are occasionally noted by

Clarke and Wrench, but a number described by them as potlid subjects I have discovered also on dishes.

The color-printed tableware of the Pratts may often be recognized by certain small printed borders of conventional design that occur over and over. The plain grounds of blue, red, magenta, green, lilac, or other color surrounding the picture are also distinctive.

The Pratt color-printed ware exhibited at the Crystal Palace included a series of large flat dishes or plaques embellished with reproductions of paintings by well-known artists of the Royal Academy. They are listed as follows: *The Last In,* W. Mulready; *Highland Music,* Sir Edwin Landseer; *The Blind Fiddler,* Sir David Wilkie; *The Truant,* T. Webster; *The Hops Garden,* W. T. Witherington; *Cottage Children,* Thomas Gainsborough. Other forms displayed were a bread platter, a cheese dish, a variety of box covers, and a pair of ornamental vases. A color print from a Scriptural subject by H. Warren was shown in a frame, while two others were set off with frames of earthenware.

Of especial interest to American collectors are the views with American subjects *(Figs. 1, 2).* Scenes showing exhibition buildings seem to have been popular, for the Pratts made prints of the New York Exhibition in 1853, of the Centennial, and of the Columbian Exhibition in 1893. The earliest of these, entitled *Exhibition Buildings, New York, 1853,* shows the main entrance with all flags flying, and people of various nationalities walking in the grounds. The potlid has an oakleaf border.

Austin's view of the Centennial building put out by the Pratts *(Fig. 1, right)* is the largest of three versions, which vary considerably in detail. The title, *Philadelphia Exhibition, 1876,* which appears below the picture on potlids, is printed in maroon on the back of the plate, under an oval containing the words: KERR'S CHINA HALL / 1218 CHESTNUT ST. / PHILADELPHIA. The *Philadelphia Public Buildings* in Figure 1, *left,* is a view of the City Hall with the statue of William Penn on the tower. This bears a brown-printed mark: PRATT & CO / FENTON / STAFFORDSHIRE, with an oval giving the address of another china dealer: R. J. ALLEN, SON & Cº / 309 / 3H MARKET Sᵗ / PHILADELPHIA. *The State House in Philadelphia, 1776* was also brought out for the Centennial. It is an exterior view of Independence Hall, enlivened with figures of passers-by. The title is at the bottom, with the date underneath. The plate showing *Interior View of Independence Hall, Philadelphia (Fig. 2)* appears here with a simple border of color and gold lines. Both potlid and plate are marked below the title: KERR'S CHINA HALL IS OPPOSITE THE ABOVE.

The 1893 exhibition view carries at the top the title *The Administration Building, World's Fair, Chicago, 1893.* It appears on potlids and presumably also on plates.

Other American subjects are *H.R.H., the Prince of Wales, Visiting the Tomb of Washington,* brought out in connection with the prince's tour of the United States in 1860; *Uncle Tom and Eva* and a companion piece, *Uncle Tom and Legree,* both large ovals; a full-length portrait of the philanthropist George Peabody, titled with a facsimile of his signature; and a three-quarter-length portrait of Harriet Beecher Stowe holding a copy of *Uncle Tom's Cabin.* I have not yet run across these subjects on dishes, but nearly all potlid engravings were applied also to tableware.

Some of the most charming English views are of well-known castles or estates, such as the Queen's residence—Osborne House, Isle of Wight; Sandown Castle; Walmer Castle; Strathfieldsay—home of the Duke of Wellington; and Warwick, Windsor, and Ludlow. In this category I have found the dessert plate *(Fig. 3)* showing Austin's design, *Sandringham, the Seat of H.R.H., the Prince of Wales.* Sandringham was purchased by the prince, later Edward VII, in 1862 and ten years later he replaced the original mansion with the brick and stone building seen in the print. This plate, identified by the mark PRATT / 123 / FENTON, has a typical Pratt border and a wide band of color between the print and the rim design. With the same edge are the subjects *Sebastopol* and *Shakespeare's House, Henley St., Stratford on Avon.* The exotic representation of Sebastopol is signed J. AUSTIN INV. on the pot-

Fig. 4. *Shakespeare's House, Henley St., Stratford on Avon.*

Fig. 5. *Haddon Hall. From the collection of Mrs. J. George Gange.*

lids, though not on the plate. The copper plates for this and the Sandringham view are preserved. The Stratford-on-Avon view *(Fig. 4)* exists in an original Austin drawing, which shows that it was first issued with an elaborate leaf and scroll border having a bust of Shakespeare at the top.

Castle views appear on two plates with highly decorative borders that are possibly the work of Jesse Austin for Brown-Westhead, Moore & Company. One of these has a general tone of olive-green and is entitled *Haddon Hall (Fig. 5)*. The other, of brownish-olive, bears an unidentified view in South Wales. The harmony of coloring in these two prints marks the epitome of accomplishment in this imitation of hand painting.

Aside from views of actual places, there are a great many fanciful and romantic subjects in the taste of the period. These are often untitled. The engraving on the cake-plate form by Pratt *(Fig. 6)* may be the *Ruined Temple* listed by Clarke and Wrench. This I have also seen on a dessert plate.

Collectors of potlids sometimes find covers of irregular shape, such as oval box tops with trefoil ends and oblong box tops with square ends. These odd-shaped prints were also applied to cups, spill cups, vases, pitchers, and plates. The oblong country scene on the pitcher in Figure 7 has been given the name *The Torrent* because it appears in Austin's scrapbook with the written title *Le Torrent* and the signature BERGHEM,PX. The design on the reverse, also by Austin, is called *The Stone Jetty*. The pitcher has an orange-red ground and typical Pratt border design. The curious handle ends in a portrait mask.

Besides the examples here noted and illustrated, I have seen a set of cups and saucers, a large platter, a sauce dish, a mug, and a complete tea set, all undoubtedly of Pratt manufacture.

This ware has recently been revived by a firm at Stoke-on-Trent. I have seen one of their small plates entitled *Summer*. Fortunately, the reproductions are carefully marked, thus: REPRODUCED FROM THE ORIGINAL PLATE FOR THE JESSE AUSTIN PROCESS / 1845-1870 / KIRKMAN'S, LTD. / STOKE ON TRENT.

Fig. 6. Cake plate, *Ruined Temple*.

Fig. 7. Pitcher. *Top*, The Torrent, from a painting *Le Torrent*, by Berghem. *Bottom*, reverse, *The Stone Jetty*. From the collection of Mrs. J. George Gange.

*Except as noted, illustrations from the collection of Mrs. O. L. Stone.*

BY GEOFFREY A. GODDEN

# Continental decorators of English ceramics in the Victorian era

IN THE MID-nineteenth century some of the finest Continental ceramics painters left their native countries for England. This migration was occasioned partly by the various international exhibitions of the period, for the English wares displayed there compared most favorably with the Continental, and the English manufacturers, in fierce competition for world markets, sought new talent and fresh ideas abroad. Other contributing factors were the general unrest in Europe during the second half of the 1800's and the calm and relative prosperity of the English trade. Finally, the Franco-Prussian war with its disastrous results for France caused many leading French ceramics artists to forsake their homeland and cross the Channel. There they found that the fine bone-china body and soft glaze produced by English manufacturers gave an added effect to their work, and many turned to modeling figures and groups in the popular parian ware that had recently been introduced.

Marc Louis Solon was perhaps the foremost Continental artist in England, but he was not the first to arrive. This honor goes to Leon Arnoux (1816-1902), who was a potter of renown in France before joining Minton in 1848 and eventually becoming art director there. Arnoux was a true potter, forever experimenting with new glazes and bodies; the famous Minton "majolica" ware with its colored glazes is but one of the many innovations he introduced for the 1851 and subsequent exhibitions. A writer in the *Art Journal* (1874) states that Arnoux "will always be remembered by his countrymen as one of the most skilful pupils of Brogniart [*sic*: Alexandre Brongniart was director of the Sèvres factory from 1800 to 1847], and by Englishmen as among the most talented and accomplished Frenchmen who ever honored our shores and aided us in the development of our Art-Industries."

Although Arnoux was not primarily a ceramics painter, his success in England encouraged others to follow him. Another early arrival was Christian (also known as Carl) Henk, German by birth, who was employed by Minton from 1842 on. His work, mainly Watteau-style figures in landscapes and cupid subjects in the French taste, is of the finest quality and finish but is seldom signed. Henk died in 1905. His son John (1846-1914) was also employed as a modeler at Minton's from 1863, and many of the fine models for their "majolica" wares were his work.

Born in Paris, Emile Lessore (1805-1876) studied painting for a short time in the studio of Ingres, in 1831 exhibited his first picture in the Paris Salon, and in 1851 was invited to join the Sèvres factory, where his free style of painting with its consequent greater output caused resentment among the slow, meticulous painters of the old school. When he first came to England, in 1858, Lessore was employed for a short period by Minton, but soon transferred to the Wedgwood pottery. His experience there and the reason for his return to France in 1867 are given in his own words:

I was engaged by Mr. Wedgwood, free to name my own conditions, to choose my own workmen, my own materials. Mr. Wedgwood reposed confidence in me. I did not abuse it. I have drawn and colored 4,000 pieces in two years. I shut myself up at Etruria as in a tomb, without seeing the sun more than six times a year. I am racked with rheumatism, but my heart is full of joy. I am my own master, and my benefactors are satisfied with me. My poor children! I thought I should have lost them at Etruria; they could not bear the fog and smoke—the black smoke of the furnaces, which never ceased day or night, Sundays excepted.

By 1867 Lessore had returned to France, where he lived at Marlotte, near Fontainebleau, and continued to decorate Wedgwood creamware sent over from England. He is said to have concealed many pieces in the cellar of his cottage during the siege of Paris and these, like all the ware he decorated in France, were later returned to Etruria for firing and sale in England. During his comparatively short career Lessore may be said to have

Leon Arnoux (1816-1902), art director at Minton, at work in his studio.
*Illustrations are from the author's collection.*

August, 1960

Small oval Wedgwood creamware trays decorated by
Emile Lessore (1805-1876); c. 1866.

Wedgwood creamware tazza decorated with the Pesara Madonna
after Titian, an example of Lessore's more ambitious work; c. 1861.

revolutionized the decoration of ceramics in England. His work was included in many international exhibitions of the period and was widely acclaimed.

Charles Ferdinand Hurten (1818-1901) was born in Cologne and at the age of eighteen went to Paris where he specialized in floral painting, working for various decorating establishments and on special commissions for the Sèvres factory. His fine floral paintings shown in the Paris international exhibition of 1858 inspired Copeland to invite him to Stoke; he joined that firm the following year and remained with them until 1897. Copeland, like its predecessor, Spode, had always been noted for the quality of its floral painting, but Hurten introduced new life. His paintings were taken direct from nature, or from *gouache* studies made at conservatories and gardens of the great houses near Stoke. An art student, writing of his visit to Copeland's London showroom in 1876, selects a circular plaque by Hurten as "the finest piece of realistic painting on china I have ever seen."

Hurten's work was included in all the great exposi-

Copeland plaque with a vigorous floral study by
C. F. Hurten (1818-1901); 23½ inches by 18.

Small Minton creamware tray
in Edouard Rischgitz's free style,
showing artist's signature.

272

Minton porcelain vase painted by A. Boullemier (1840-1900), with date cipher for 1871.

Minton porcelain plate decorated by Boullemier; c. 1881.

*Pâte-sur-pâte* Minton vase by M. L. Solon (1835-1912), c. 1895; height 20 inches.

tions and quickly won him international fame. A writer in the *Art Journal*, reporting on the Copeland productions of 1874, observes that Hurten "has no superior in flower painting, especially on pieces sufficiently large to give full scope to his vigorous yet delicate pencil; and his perfect feeling for all the beauties of texture and color in his favorite subjects is sufficiently obvious. He makes us see he is as much a florist as an artist, and as true a student of form as of color."

Louis H. Jahn (d. 1911) came to England from Vienna in 1862. Like most of the Continental artists he was first employed by Minton, with whom he worked as a figure painter for ten years before joining the Brownfield firm as art director. He held this post until 1895, when he returned to Minton to succed Arnoux as art director there. From 1900 until his death in 1911 he was curator of the Hanley Museum.

During Jahn's first ten years with Minton he painted figure subjects, many in the manner of Watteau, on fine vases. Examples of his work were included in the international exhibitions of 1862, 1867, and 1871. The *Art Journal* made the following comment in 1871: "The vase with cupids is a very fine specimen, remarkable for the softness and brilliancy of its color. The decoration is original and Mr. Yahn, the artist, is entitled to great credit."

The productions of William Brownfield & Sons are not very widely known, but this firm produced some of the finest porcelain of the period under Jahn's supervision and during his term as art director the firm produced some of the best examples of tinted porcelain ever made. He also painted on Brownfield's porcelain until he returned to Minton in 1895.

Édouard Rischgitz (w. 1864-1867) came to England at this period, but his employment with Minton was brief and consequently his work, which was mostly in the free style associated with Lessore, is relatively scarce. He usually painted on Minton's earthenware and majolica; examples range from large vases painted with battle scenes, hunting subjects, cattle, and so on, to small panels and trays. He was represented in the Paris exhibition of 1867. He normally signed his work in full.

Marc Louis Solon (1835-1913) came to England in 1870 and was engaged by Minton. Examples of his work in *pâte-sur-pâte* technique are known and appreciated the world over. The Minton stained parian body made a perfect medium for the painstaking process involved, in which semitranslucent white slip was slowly built up in thin washes over the dark ground color until the required gradation of color was obtained. It is recorded that one fine example took seven months to complete.

Solon, who was born at Montauban, got his early training in Paris, and his experiments in *pâte-sur-pâte* were carried out at the Sèvres factory and independently for the Paris art dealer Rousseau. His early work in France is normally signed *Miles*. He went to England because of the Franco-Prussian War, and he recalls that the day after his arrival he was already at work with Minton, experimenting with the new body and glaze in use there. Solon retired from active employment in 1904, but continued to produce plaques until his death in 1913. Much has been written about the man and about his work, which has always commanded a high price (see ANTIQUES, January 1950, pp. 52-54).

Solon, like Jahn, had a great love of early English pottery. He was one of the earliest collectors, and spent much of his time searching every cottage in the district for examples of early slipware, pew groups, and the like, which were not generally appreciated at that period. His *Art of the Old English Potter*, published in 1885, remains an indispensable work in its field.

Antonin Boullemier (1840-1900) was born at Sèvres. He studied in Paris under Hippolyte Evariste Etienne Fragonard (1806-1876; grandson of the famous painter)

273

Detail from a study in *gouache* by William Mussill (d. 1906).

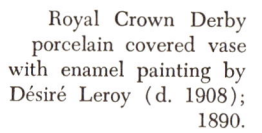

Royal Crown Derby porcelain covered vase with enamel painting by Désiré Leroy (d. 1908); 1890.

and received valuable training in ceramics painting at Dreyfus' decorating establishment in Paris. In 1871 he was employed by Minton. He excelled in figure painting, particularly cupid and child subjects in the French taste, and his delicate touch and high finish, enhanced by the soft Minton glaze, at once brought him to the notice of connoisseurs on both sides of the Atlantic. His work has been spoken of as the high-water mark of modern miniature painting. Shown in the various international exhibitions, it won the highest praise, and examples were purchased by Queen Victoria and other royalty. Boullemier also painted for Brown-Westhead, Moore & Co., makers of the colossal "Shakespeare" vase decorated by Boullemier and shown at the 1893 Chicago exhibition. Contemporaries of Boullemier at Stoke, where he died, wrote: "It would be safe to say that in the whole of North Staffordshire no person was more generally known, or a greater favorite—his work will always obtain for him an honorable position in English ceramics, but he will be long remembered in Staffordshire for his personality alone." Boullemier's son, Lucien Emile, painted for Minton and for the Lenox Pottery in New Jersey, and a third generation continues the tradition in England.

Lucien Besche (d. 1901) also came to England in 1871, where he was employed by Minton for a short period painting figure subjects in the French style. In 1872 he was working for Copeland. The *Art Journal* of that year includes his name in a list of Copeland artists employed on a monumental order, and the following year mentions Copeland vases decorated with Watteau subjects by Besche. His ceramics career was short. In 1885 he moved to London and devoted himself to oil painting, magazine illustration, and costume design for comic opera.

William Mussill (d. 1906) came to England in 1872, after studying in Paris with Hurten and other artists of repute. His early work can be found on examples of Paris porcelain. Employed by Minton, he was the leading exponent of the Barbotine school of ceramics painting, a technique in which thick colors or colored clay slips were laid on in heavy impasto, giving wonderful depth and feeling to the work. Mussill spent long hours making, direct from nature, remarkable *gouache* studies on tinted paper which he later used when decorating the Minton pieces—usually on a dark body especially suited to his technique. His broad style was well suited to large pieces, and his plaques and vases were perhaps his most successful productions.

A writer in the *Art Journal* of 1896 commented: "Some of Mussill's work leaves us in doubt whether he has ever been equaled in flower painting on potteryware. He is an earnest student of nature, and has had the advantage of an early and varied training in art manifest most, perhaps, in the serial and lineal perspective of his compositions."

In 1874 Désiré Leroy (d. 1908) came to England from France, where he and his father were reputedly employed at the Sèvres factory. He first settled with his countrymen at Minton's, where he painted exotic birds and floral motifs in the Sèvres manner. His specialty, however, was fine enamel painting in white on a colored ground. In 1890 Leroy left Minton and joined the Royal Crown Derby Company as art director; there he continued to paint in the same style.

With the exception of Christian Henk all these artists normally signed the pieces they decorated. They were all of international reputation and their work, which appeared only on wares of the finest quality and finish, was highly valued in its own day.

An article by Mr. Godden on English ceramics artists of the Victorian period appears in the *Concise Encyclopedia of Antiques,* Volume Four, 1959.

BY GEOFFREY A. GODDEN, F. R. S. A.

# English parian wares

IN HIS HANDBOOK to the Great Exhibition of 1851, R. Hunt credited Thomas Battam, art director of the Copeland factory, with originating parian ware—a white unglazed ceramic product which successfully imitated marble. At that time parian, or statuary porcelain as it was originally called, was at the height of its popularity. Although its high decorative merits and wide adaptability were now fully recognized, the commercial success of the new body was in the balance for a period of two years, from 1842 to 1844. It was the combined efforts of the editor of the Art Union magazine and the management of the Art Union of London (a form of art lottery) that brought the new ware to the attention of the public. The first Art Union order was for but fifty copies of *Narcissus*, John Gibson's famous Royal Academy diploma piece. But from this small beginning the Art Union commissions grew to gigantic proportions, making the new body known to an extent undreamed of by the makers.

Although the credit for discovering parian was given to Copeland & Garrett, other firms, notably Minton's, were experimenting with a similar body at the same time; and within a few years nearly every manufacturer was engaged in the production of parian, of admittedly varying qualities. Production of the new "statuary porcelain" was not confined to the British Isles: Christopher Weber Fenton of Bennington introduced it in America in the early 1840's (ANTIQUES, June 1956, p. 528).

The name parian reflects Battam's initial idea: to imitate marble, and in particular statuary—which could now be reproduced in such small size and at such low prices that copies of the finest antique statues were within the reach of all. Copeland's early term, statuary porcelain, underlines this point; so does the name carrara, used by Wedgwood. The relative ease with which parian could be molded permitted its use in the production of other decorative and utilitarian objects. As early as 1845 some of the vases made by Copeland in parian were copied from examples in the British Museum; these measure as much as thirty inches in height. In 1846 centerpieces supported by decorative figures

Copeland's famous *Ino and Bacchus* group shown at the 1851 Exhibition. Length 20 inches.
*Except as noted, illustrations are from the author's collection.*

*Miranda*, a popular Minton parian figure modeled by John Bell in 1850.

A finely modeled parian centerpiece, with gilt enrichments. Height 26 inches.

Mid-Victorian parian group showing the charm of these inexpensive models. Unmarked; height 16 inches.

were introduced by Copeland, and such centerpieces, compotes, and so on were at the height of their popularity at the time of the 1851 Exhibition; they were produced by all the leading firms. Some examples bore tasteful gilt enrichments and were fitted with colored glass liners. These parian centerpieces are very decorative when displayed with their intended fruit or floral contents. Other innovations in parian include delicately worked floral jewelry, examples of which were purchased by Queen Victoria.

Parian busts and portrait figures, introduced by various manufacturers, are admittedly not as decorative as some of the other wares, but they are interesting in that they include most of the major Victorian personages and were often modeled on special commissions from leading sculptors of the day. These and other parian figures can be purchased now at a comparatively low price, and are recommended to persons seeking an inexpensive field in which to form a collection. The large range of figures and other objects produced in this body during the Victorian era enables the collector to exercise his personal choice and taste.

In appreciating parian figures and groups it helps to know something about the method of production. Battam, writing in 1849, gave a complete account of the process, which differed from that used for other bisque types (see ANTIQUES, February 1955, p. 143: *The Making of a Porcelain Figure*) mainly in the drying time for casts, the repeated firings, and the chemical elements of the body.

Each figure required many molds: head, arms and hands, legs, body, parts of the drapery, and other details were usually molded separately; a single group might require more than fifty molds. The process of joining the various parts and clearing off the seam marks required great care and judgment because of the fragility of the material at this stage. The parts were joined by being dipped into the slip, or having it applied with a pencil. Only enough was used to soften the surface of the clay so that the parts would adhere to each other; too much caused the edges to yield when pressure was applied, with consequent distortion of outline.

After a drying period of several days the figure or group was fired at about 1100° C. for about sixty or seventy hours. The seams were then rubbed down and the piece refired at a still higher temperature. It was sometimes necessary to fire casts three times, at increasingly higher temperatures and with a repetition of the rubbing-down process each time, to achieve the beauty of surface which the finest specimens present.

The chemical elements of the clay used were essentially alumina, silica, and felspar. The intense heat of repeated firings caused these to agglutinate to form the typical parian body—a body whose perfection is even more apparent at the edges of a break than it is in the finished figure.

Three floral brooches in parian,
probably modeled by Edward Raby of Bristol.

Copeland parian table ornament, with useful panniers.
*Copeland Works Museum.*

Minton parian vase decorated with passion flowers
and foliage in high relief, c. 1854. *Victoria and
Albert Museum, crown copyright.*

# Minton porcelain in the style of Sèvres

BY GEOFFREY A. GODDEN

DURING THE NINETEENTH CENTURY and into the twentieth the Minton factory excelled in copying Vincennes and Sèvres porcelains of the eighteenth century, and a comparison between the products of the two factories is not as farfetched as might be imagined. The special Minton soft glaze and bone-china body matched in effect the glaze and body of the finest Sèvres wares, and both factories employed outstanding men to decorate their porcelain. Each employed a system of year dating, and each allowed its foremost artists to sign their work. Also both factories enjoyed the patronage of royalty, which gave added prestige and publicity to their products.

Many stories have been told underlining the reputation enjoyed by Minton in the nineteenth century. One concerns a well-known and respected Paris dealer of the day who, on receiving an order to fill a large showcase with the finest Sèvres porcelain procurable for one of the world's wealthiest families, left Paris for the Minton factory at Stoke-on-Trent; and there the showcase was filled, to the satisfaction of everybody concerned. The illustrations on these pages indicate that the story might well be true.

Thomas Minton (1765-1836) founded the Minton factory at Stoke-on-Trent in 1793; his son Herbert (1793-1858) succeeded Thomas in 1836. The excellence and range of the Minton wares during the nineteenth century owe much to the fact that in 1848 Herbert Minton engaged as art director the celebrated French potter Léon Arnoux (1816-1902; see ANTIQUES, August 1960, p. 146); and this policy of engaging internationally known artists was continued by Herbert's nephew, Colin Minton Campbell, who became managing director on his uncle's death in 1858.

During Arnoux's tenure Minton began to produce extremely fine copies of the more expensive Sèvres wares. Rich ground colors were employed, of which the most

Fig. 1. Minton potpourri vase with cover, in ship form; c. 1911. Ground of mazarine blue and green with decoration of gilt and birds and flowers in medallion; lion-mask handles. The banner on the cover carries the fleur-de-lis of France. Height 18 inches. *Minton Works Museum.*

Fig. 1a. Sèvres potpourri vase with cover, in ship form *(vaisseau à mât)*; 1764. Deep blue ground, with fishing scene in medallion by Morin (w. 1754-1787); lion-mask handles, and fleurs-de-lis on the banner draping the cover. *Walters Art Gallery.*

June, 1968

Fig. 2. Minton porcelains; c. 1870-1880. The turquoise-bordered plate is copied from a Sèvres set made for Catherine of Russia in 1765 (see Verlet, Grandjean, and Brunet, *Sèvres*, Paris, 1953, opp. p. 68). Other pieces have decoration of exotic birds, flowers, and varied trophies in reserve panels outlined in gilt on a turquoise ground. Height of spill vase, 2¾ inches.

Fig. 2a. Vincennes ewer and basin, before 1753. *Gros bleu* ground with decoration of exotic birds in reserve panels *(panneaux en réserve)* outlined in gilt. *Wadsworth Atheneum.*

Fig. 3. Minton two-handled vase with cover, one of a pair; c. 1862. Mythological scene in medallion on turquoise blue ground; garland-draped handles and base. Painted by Thomas Allen (c. 1831-1915; w. Minton's c. 1845-1875). Height 16 inches.

Fig. 3a. Sèvres two-handled vase with cover, from a *garniture de cheminée*. Mythological scene (Pygmalion and Galatea, after Falconet) in medallion, attributed to Dodin (w. 1754-1802). *Waddesdon Manor.*

279

Fig. 4. Minton jardiniere, early twentieth century. Floral decoration and shipping scene in medallion, probably painted by Lucien Boullemier (1876-1949). Height 8 inches.

Fig. 4a. Sèvres *vase hollandais*, 1761. Decoration of flowers and cupids enclosed in elaborately scrolled, gilt-outlined medallions. *Victoria and Albert Museum.*

Fig. 4b. Minton cups and saucers, c. 1853. Decoration very like that on the *vase hollandais* in Fig. 4a. The painting here is attributed to Thomas Kirkby (1824-1890; w. Minton's c. 1845-1887).

Fig. 4c. Sèvres *écuelle* and platter, 1772. Shipping scenes resemble those on Fig. 4. Height of bowl, 4¼ inches. *Wadsworth Atheneum.*

celebrated is a glossy turquoise blue (like the Sèvres *bleu céleste*)—a color which, when fired correctly, has not been matched by any other manufactory. This particular blue was used extensively during the second half of the nineteenth century and proved most useful for the porcelains showing Sèvres influence.

The charmingly mellow quality of Minton's floral and other painting is due largely to a special soft glaze employed on pieces decorated by the factory's leading artists. This glaze, introduced about 1850, allowed the enamel colors to sink into and merge with it to some extent, as did the enamels of the early Sèvres porcelains—instead of standing above the surface and producing the hard appearance seen on many Continental wares. Pieces treated with this special glaze bear, in addition to the normal factory mark, a small ermine mark.

The figure painter Thomas Allen (c. 1831-1915) was employed at Minton's while in his early teens, and decorated some of the finest Minton pieces shown at the 1851 London exhibition. Apart from majolica wares, Allen mainly painted Sèvres-style figure panels on vases (Fig. 3). His fine figure painting won high and constant praise in various international exhibitions; however, he seldom signed his work. In 1875 this artist left Minton's to join the Wedgwood firm.

The noteworthy Sèvres-style figure painting of Antonin Boullemier (c. 1840-1900, w. Minton's from 1872) is, on the other hand, always signed. Boullemier's son Lucien Emile (1876-1949) painted similar wares at Minton's from about 1895 until about 1911, and his work is normally signed L. BOULLEMIER (Figs. 4, 5). He left England for a few years during which he was employed at the Lenox pottery in Trenton, New Jersey. For a brief period after 1911 Henri Boullemier succeeded his brother at Minton's, and he also painted in the manner of Sèvres.

Thomas Kirkby (1824-1890) painted many Watteau-type figure and cupid subjects in the Sèvres style. He won particular praise for a service shown at the 1851 exhibition which was purchased by Queen Victoria and later given by her to the Emperor of Austria. Kirkby's cupid subjects are not normally signed, but original sketches in my possession indicate that he painted the delightful cups and saucers shown in Figure 4b. The date of the latest entry in the factory records for Kirkby's work is August 3, 1887.

The artists represented here are only a few of the many talented ceramic artists whose work, in collaboration with that of able workmen in every branch of the manufacturing process, prompted a Victorian reviewer to say of Minton's: "They have never been excelled by any firm at any time in resourcefulness leading to complete success in new departures of ceramics. There is scarcely a branch of pottery manufacture which they have not made their own." The factory's Sèvres-type wares are, of course, only part of the output of the factory during these years; however, they make it clear that such praise was well deserved.

A general account of the Minton factory, with a list of the principal artists employed there and keys to its marks and pattern numbers, is given in Mr. Godden's *Victorian Porcelain* (New York, 1961).

Fig. 5. Minton vase, c. 1900. Decorated with elephant heads and a genre scene in medallion on a blue and gilt ground, painted by L. Boullemier. Height 11½ inches. *Minton Works Museum.*

Fig. 5a. Pair of Sèvres *vases à éléphants*, 1760. *Rose Pompadour* ground. Modeled by J. C. Duplessis *père* (d. 1774), with chinoiserie decoration by Dodin. *Walters Art Gallery.*

# CHELSEA TODAY
## The Porcelain Figures of Charles Vyse
### By FRANK STONER

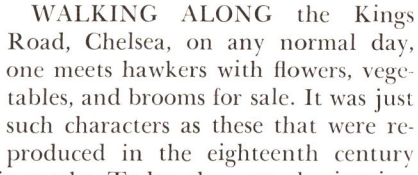

WALKING ALONG the Kings Road, Chelsea, on any normal day, one meets hawkers with flowers, vegetables, and brooms for sale. It was just such characters as these that were reproduced in the eighteenth century by the Chelsea porcelain works. Today they are the inspiration for many of the ceramic figures modeled by Charles Vyse, such as those shown below.

To visit his kiln one continues along the Kings Road to Oakley Street, turns down Oakley Street, and takes the first turning to the right Upper Cheyne Row, the continuation of which is Lawrence Street, where the old Chelsea factory was situated. A little farther on is the Old Chelsea Church, which one occasionally finds reproduced on early Chelsea pieces. It was in this church that many of the artists of the Chelsea factory were married and their children christened. But, alas, it has gone the way of so many other old London churches during the past four years. Turning left into Cheyne Row, past No. 24, which was Thomas Carlyle's house, one reaches a courtyard where Vyse's studio is located.

One end of the studio is used for working, the other for the finished products. The shelves which line the walls are filled with figures and groups. It will be immediately observed that all the Vyse character figures are of the sturdy type, just such types as one sees in the Kings Road. Farther along the shelf are a few of the whimsical figures and groups, such as those shown—a light and delicate contrast to the character studies. There is nothing finicky about any of the products, any more than there is about Charles Vyse himself, a very talented and capable man. He not only models, but makes his own molds, which is a highly skilled and specialized art. Besides this he does his own decorating and firing, and successfully markets his products. His only assistant is Mrs. Vyse, who indeed does a great deal. It is she who models all the flowers for the baskets of the flower vendors, as well as assisting her husband in the decoration of the figures. The Vyse products are marked with his name or *CV/Chelsea,* with the year date.

There are few men who could accomplish all that Vyse does single-handed, and above all give to the world such charming figures and groups. Many collections of his work have been formed both here and in England, and there is no doubt in my mind that future generations will appreciate his art perhaps even more than it is today appreciated. There is much movement and vitality in his products, apart from their remarkably accurate portrayal of London types.

Leaving the Vyse workshop one realizes that twentieth-century Chelsea is producing charming and skillful products which can beautify our homes and enrich our collections, much in the same manner as the figures and groups made in the eighteenth century have for generations enchanted us.

*Illustrations are from the collection of Mrs. W. H. R. Hilliard.*

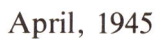

# Index

Adams: John, 125, 126; William, 43, 125, 126, 166, 172, 202, 240, 241, 243
Adams & Bromley, 126
Agate ware, 122, 130, 243
Akeroyd, Henry, 35
Alcock: John & George, 201; S., 198, 199
Allegorical scenes, 236, 237, 238-39
Allen, Herbert, Collection, 66
Allen: Robert, 75; Thomas, 279, 281
American historical Staffordshire. *See* Views, American
American market, 12, 13, 14, 16-17, 46, 50-53, 59, 112, 124, 166, 190, 193, 202, 206, 211, 235, 241-42, 245
Angouleme Sprig pattern, 73
Annular ware, 47
Armorial designs, 186, 187
Arnoux, Leon, 271, 273, 278
Astbury: John, 18, 19, 20, 22, 23, 24, 141, 143, 144, 145, 146, 149, 160; Thomas, 24, 143
Austin, Jesse, 267, 268, 269, 270
Aynsley, 251

Baddeley & Fletcher, 67, 172
Bailey & Batkin, 250, 251
Baker, Warren, 233, 239
Ball, William, 251
Balls, James, 75
Bandanna ware, 264
Banded creamware. *See* Mocha ware
Bang-Up pattern, 176
Barber, Edwin Atlee, 187, 198, 199, 200, 209, 215, 242
Barbotine painting, 274
Barite, 125
Barker, John, 43
Barley rim design, 25, 26
Barlow ware, 251
Barnes, Zachariah, 104, 107
Barnstaple, 12, 13, 14
Barr, Flight and Barr, 219
Bartlam, John, 124
Barwick, John, 35
Basalt, 50, 111, 112, 118, 119, 120, 125, 130, 175, 210, 227
Basket pattern, 26
Battam, Thomas, 275, 276
Battersea enamels, 56-59, 60, 61, 172
Baxter, Thomas, 83, 220, 267
Bead and Reel pattern, 26
Beckett, Isaac, 58
Beddow, George 224
Bell, Samuel, 22, 24
Belper factory, 256, 257
Bemrose, Geoffrey, 243
Bennett Pottery Company, 164
Bennington pottery, 150, 164, 275
Benson, Thomas, 20
Bentley, Thomas, 18, 20, 25, 35, 40, 42, 43, 98, 111, 113, 117, 118, 123
Berryman, John, 12
Besche, Lucien, 274
Bevington, T. and J., 220
Bickerton, L. M., 50, 51

Bickley, Mary, 58
Bideford, 12, 14, 18
Billingsley, William, 83, 84, 219, 220, 222, 223, 224
Bilston enamels, 56-59
Bishop, Collington, 67
Black basalte. *See* Basalt
Blue-and-white porcelain, 91, 93-94, 103, 104
Blue Heron pattern, 176
Bly, John, 77
Boon, Edward, 43
Booth: Enoch, 25, 122; Hugh, 43
Bone, Henry, 91, 94-95, 100
Bone-ash porcelain, 67, 68, 73, 81, 82, 107, 108
Bone china, 42, 82, 102, 228
Bosanko, W., 249
Boullemier: Antonin, 273-74, 281; Henri, 281; Lucien Emile, 274, 280, 281
Bourne: John, 43; Joseph, 254, 256, 257
Bourne & Malkin, 43
Bow, 44, 63, 64, 65, 66, 72, 73, 75, 77, 80, 81, 82, 86, 89, 91, 104, 107, 108, 230
Bow-Pot pattern, 177
Bradley, Samuel, 60
Brannam, C. H., 12, 13, 14
Briand, Thomas, 97
Brindley, 111
Bristol, 39, 43, 82, 91-102, 108, 124, 150, 277
British Ceramic Research Association, 19, 26
Brittan, John, 91, 94, 95
Britton, John, 213, 214, 215
Brongniart, Alexandre, 271
Broome, Isaac, 164
Browne, Robert, 72, 73, 74
Brownfield, William, & Son, 273
Brown-Westhead, Moore & Company, 267, 275
Bucknall & Stevenson, 198, 199, 200, 201
Buff. *See* Cane ware
Bull, John P., 207
Burslem, 19, 23, 29, 42, 43, 122, 191, 193, 200, 201, 210-215
Burton, William, 256

Cambrian Pottery Works, 220, 232, 241, 251
Camehl, Ada Walker, 187, 193, 194
Cameos, 112, 118, 119, 128
Campbell, Colin Minton, 278
Canals for transport, 111, 219
Cane ware, 119, 120, 125, 130, 227
Carr & Patton, 133, 135
Carrara. *See* Parian ware
Casseday, Samuel, 207, 208
Castleford, 34, 35, 36, 50-53, 122, 124, 126, 127, 171, 245, 246, 251
Catskill Moss series, 197
Caughley, 48, 65, 66, 67, 75, 82, 83, 94, 104, 107, 108, 167, 171, 172, 173, 176
Celtic China series, 190
Chaffers: Richard, 67, 68, 69, 107; William, 71, 73, 74, 77, 198, 200, 245
Chambers, William, Jr., 241
Champion, Richard, 43, 91, 92, 94, 96, 97, 99, 102

Che-lin (kylin), 93
Chelsea: 66, 68, 72, 73, 79, 82, 83, 86, 87, 88, 89, 91, 106-07, 108, 160, 282; Gold-anchor period, 82, 86, 89, 106-07, 108; Raised-anchor period, 86, 88, 89, 106, 108; Red-anchor period, 82, 86, 89, 106, 107, 108; Triangle period, 79, 86, 87, 88, 106, 108
Cherokee china clay, 80, 110
Chetham & Woolley, 126, 166
Ch'ien Lung period, 189
China Body formula, 107
China glaze, 43, 44, 49, 122
Chinaman-and-parrot teapot, 87; Chinaman-and-snake teapot, 87
Chinese Crackle, 177
Chinese export porcelain, 76, 78, 91, 107, 239
Chinese House design, 44
Ching-tê Chên, 91
Chisholm, Alexander, 123
Christian, Philip, 67, 69
Cities series, 203, 207
Clarke, Harold G., 268
Clementson, Joseph, 166
Clews: 46, 179, 180, 183, 186, 187, 198, 199, 200, 202-06, 207; James, 168, 200, 202-06, 207-09; Ralph, 202-06
Clouded-glaze ware, 25, 26
Cloume ovens, 14
Clulow, Robert, 126
Coalport, 83-86, 171
Cobridge, 43, 172, 199, 200, 201, 202
Cocker, George, 84
Cockpit Hill. *See* Derby Pot Works
Codner Park, 256
College views. *See* Views
Color printing, 168, 169, 267-70
Columbia College, views of, 179-80, 182
Cookworthy, William, 82, 91, 92, 93, 98
Copeland: 272, 273, 274, 276, 277; Ronald, 175; William Taylor, 175, 176
Copeland & Garrett, 241, 243, 275
Cottage pottery, 75, 96, 161, 163, 169, 245
Cream-colored earthenware. *See* Creamware
Creamware, 16, 25, 26, 27, 29, 30, 34, 36, 37-41, 42, 44, 47, 50, 110, 122-24, 145, 130, 131, 133, 175, 207, 208, 216, 232, 235, 271; Banded, 240-44
Creil earthenware, 124, 243
Crisp, Frederick A., 72
Crocker pottery, 12, 13, 14
"Crouch" ware, 19
Cupid Imprisoned pattern, 212
Curtis, Thomas, 75, 78

Davenport, 46, 83, 124, 171, 251, 267
Dawson Company, 245, 251
Decoration: *See* Barbotine painting; Color printing; Enamel work; Hand-painting; Precipitated Rose Gold; Transfer printing; Underglaze-blue printing
Delftfield Pottery, 39
Delftware, 14, 16, 24, 30, 42, 65, 122, 150, 249
Denby Pottery, 254, 256
Deptford Pottery, 251
Derby, 66, 68, 72, 79, 80, 81, 82, 83, 84, 86, 89, 91, 93, 107, 108, 176, 177, 249

Derby Pot Works, 39, 40
Diaper pattern, 26
Dillon, N., 198
Dillwyn, Lewis Weston, 220, 222
Dipped ware, 16, 17, 19, 20
Dixon, Austin & Company, 245, 251
Dodd, A. E., 26
Donaldson, John, 62
Don Pottery, 124, 251
Don Quixote series, 202, 203
Door pattern, 119
Dot pattern, 26
Douai factory, 243
Doulton & Co., 150
Doulton and Watts, 161, 259, 261
Dresden china, 122
Duché, Andrew, 80
Duck-egg porcelain, 220, 221, 224
du Halde, J. B., 91
Duncan, E. MacGregor, Collection, 94, 95
Dunderdale, David, 36, 50, 52, 124, 127, 171
Dunderdale and Company, 36
Duplessis, J. C., 281
Dutch-enameled English wares, 30-33
Dwight, John, 140, 160

Earle, Alice Morse, 187
Earthenware, 12-15, 16-23, 24-29, 30-33, 138, 167, 175, 206, 207-09, 210-15, 229-34, 235-39, 263
Egyptian black. *See* Basalt
Egyptian wares, 118-121
Elers, David and John Philip, 143
Elmes, James, 210, 215
Enamel work, painted, 56-59, 60
Encrusted wares, 84
English Cities series, 212, 213, 214, 215
Engobe-covered ware, 17, 19
Entwistle, Peter, 68
Etruria, 31, 98, 113, 128
Evans: David, 220, 224; William, 240

Fable series, 88
Faience, 30, 37, 124, 166
Falkner, Frank, 147
Fawkes, Francis, 148
Featheredge design, 26, 27, 44, 45
Feldspathic glaze, 84
Fell & Co., 251
Felspar porcelain, 228
Fenton, Christopher Weber, 275
Fenton Stone Works, 263, 265
Ferrybridge Pottery. *See* Knottingley Pottery
Ferryside, 251
Figures, earthenware and porcelain, 62, 79-82, 84, 89, 93, 131, 138, 143-47, 148-50, 151-52, 153-58, 160-61
Fillpot, Toby. *See* Toby jugs
Fisher, Alvin, 179
Fishley family, 12
Fitzhugh-type borders, 78
Flaxman, John, 111, 113-17, 118
Flint, calcined, 19, 20, 22, 122
Flintporslin, Swedish, 124

Flow blue. *See* Staffordshire, blue
Flower, Joseph, 150
Frank: Richard, 250; Thomas, 91
Franks, Wollaston, 71
Fremington, 12
Frost, William, 207
Frye, Thomas, 82

Gallimore, W. W., 164
Garrett, Thomas, 175
Giles, James, 82, 107
Girl at the Well pattern, 227, 228
Glamorgan Pottery, 251
Glasgow Pottery, 122
Godden, Geoffrey A., 131, 206, 234, 240, 256, 281
Godwin, Thomas, 179, 180, 182, 191
Gold-anchor period. *See* Chelsea
Goodwin, Thos. & Benj., 43
Gorely, Jean, 44
Gothic Castle pattern, 172
Gould, F. Carruthers, 160
Graham, John, Jr., 29, 43
Granite ware, 42, 130, 167, 169, 243
Grasshopper pattern, 176
Gravel-tempered wares, 13, 14, 15
Greatbatch, William, 131
Greek pattern, 176
Greek Key pattern, 119
Green: Guy, 48; John, 35; Joshua, 35; Saville, 35; Stephen 161, 254, 255, 256, 259, 261, 262
Green Festoon pattern, 96
Gypsy Fortune Teller pattern, 61

Hale, Owen, 160
Hall, Ralph, 236
Halsey, R. T. Haines, 187, 199
Hancock: John, 249; Robert, 61, 172
Hand-painting, 175, 177-78
Hanley potteries, 193, 200
Hard paste porcelain, 73-74, 82, 91-102, 107, 108
Harley, Thomas, 231, 251
Harrison, John, 35
Hartley, William, 35
Hartley, Greens, & Co., 26, 38, 44
Harvard College, views of, 179, 181, 182, 184, 185, 186, 198
Heath, Lewis, 126
Heath pottery, 31, 126, 267
Henderson, D. & J., 150
Henk: Christian, 271, 274; John, 271
Herculaneum Pottery, 31, 46, 124, 232, 235
Heylyn, Edward, 82
Historic views. *See* Views
Hobson, R. I., 26
Hollins, Samuel, 126, 130
Hollow ware, 210
Hot Lane Pottery, 42, 44
House pattern, 248
Howitt, Samuel, 188, 206
Hudig, Ferrand, 33
Hughes, G. Bernard, 242-43
Humble, Green and Company, 35
Humble, Hartley, Greens and Company, 35

Humble, Richard, 35
Hurst, A., 50
Hurten, Charles Ferdinand, 272-73

Illustrious Moderns series, 116
Indian Sports series, 173, 174, 188, 204, 206
Indian Pottery Company, 207, 208, 209
Intaglios, 112, 118, 128, 130
Ironstone china, 42, 166, 175, 263-66
Ivory. *See* Creamware

Jackfield ware, 24
Jackson, J. & J., 166, 169, 179, 180, 181, 182, 183
Jackson's Select Views, 185, 186
Jacobsen, Mrs. Jacques Noel, 76
Jahn, Louis H., 273
Jamestown, Virginia, 13, 15
Janssen, Stephen Theodore, 56
Jasper ware, 110, 112, 113, 118, 119, 125-27, 130, 175, 210
Jersey City Pottery, 150
Jewitt, Llewellyn, 13, 22, 48, 73, 198, 200, 206, 254
John, W. D., 219, 223, 224, 239

Kakiemon style, 89
K'ang Hsi period, 63, 189, 264
Kaolin, 91, 99
Kaufman, M. G., Collection, 86-90
Kirkby, Thomas, 280, 281
Knottingley (Ferrybridge) Pottery, 122, 132

Laidacker, Sam, 193, 194, 195, 206, 215
Lakin, Thomas, 250, 251
Lambeth, 254, 255, 258, 259, 261
Landre, Mary, 119
Lane End Pottery, 31, 43, 172, 231, 249
Larsen, Ellouise Baker, 190, 193, 195, 206, 215, 235, 236
Lead glazing, 24, 25, 26, 122, 232
Lead oxide in porcelain, 79
Lead poisoning, 122
Leeds: 30, 31, 34-36, 37, 38, 39, 40, 41, 46, 47, 50, 122, 124, 171, 230, 232, 241, 250, 251
Leigh & Cie, 124, 243
Lenox Pottery, 274, 281
Leon Collection, 229-34, 235-39
Leroy, Désiré, 274
Lessore, Emile, 271-72, 273
Lewis, Jacob, 207
Litchdon Street Pottery, 12
Litchfield, Frederick, 71
Little, W. F., 206
Littler, William, 27
Littler's blue, 28
Liverpool, 37, 39, 47, 66, 67-70, 82, 94, 104, 108, 122, 173
London enamelers, 82, 83
London Views series, 210, 211, 214, 215
Longport, 122
Longton Hall, 28, 66, 69, 79, 80, 81, 82, 84, 86, 93, 107, 108
Lowdin's factory, 60
Lowestoft, 66, 70, 71-75, 76-78, 82, 107, 108, 230
Low Ford Pottery, 251
Low Lights Pottery, 133
Lund's manufactory, 82, 91, 107, 108

Luscon, Hewlin, 72
Lusterware, 210, 216, 245-48, 249-52
Luxmoore, Charles, 22

McCauley, Robert H., 235, 236, 238
Mackenna, F. Severne, 86, 87, 88
Majolica, 30, 125, 271
Maling & Co., 241, 251
Mankowitz, Wolf, 46
Mansfield & Hackney, 198
Marbled ware, 175, 245-46
Maryland, University of, views of, 179, 180, 183
Mason: Charles James, 166, 263, 264, 265; George: 263; Miles, 263
Mayer: Elijah, 126, 130; Joseph, 117; Thomas, 185, 186, 187
Meander pattern, 119
Medallions. *See* Plaques
Medallion series, 199
Meigh: Charles, 179, 180, 182, 185, 186; Job, 203
Meissen porcelain, 63, 65, 79, 92, 125, 164, 229
Melbourne Pottery, 38
Metcalfe, Percy, 160
Miles, Thomas, 18, 19
Milled edge, 25
Minerva Works, 263
Minton: 271, 273, 274, 275, 276, 277; Herbert, 278; Thomas, 48, 167, 171, 176, 278
Mocha ware, 47, 216, 240-44
Mollershead, James, 75
Moons, 79, 80
Moore, N. Hudson, 187, 189, 200
Morley, Francis, 263
Morris: F., 238; Henry, 224; John R., 127
Morton, John Thomas, 41
Mountford, Arnold, 214
Mugs, children's, 216-17
Mussill, William, 274

Nance, E. Morton, 223, 241
Nankin porcelains, 103
Nantgarw, 83, 219-24
Naval views. *See* Views
Neale & Co., 149
Neptune pattern, 205
New Canton factory, 72, 73
Newcastle, 251, 252
New Hall, 67, 102, 108, 245, 247, 248
New stone. *See* Stone china
Norman-Wilcox, Gregor, 187, 198
North Devon pottery, 12-15
Northen, William, 259
North Hylton Pottery, 246, 251
Nowonty earthenware, 124

Old blue. See Staffordshire, blue
*Old China* magazine, 215
Old Paris ware, 163
O'Neale, Jeffrey Hamet, 62
Opaque china. *See* Stone china
Oriental Field Sports. *See* Indian Sport series
Oriental influence, 61, 62, 63-64, 66, 68, 70, 75, 76-78, 87, 89, 103-04, 143, 167, 172, 174, 175-78, 188-89, 225, 226, 263, 265-66
Overglaze-printed ware, 210, 215, 235
Owen, Harold, 206

Palmer & Neale, 126
Pardoe, Thomas, 224, 251
Parian ware, 271, 273, 275-77
*Pâte dure*, 91
Paterson Pottery, 251
*Pâte-sur-pâte*, 273
Peacock pattern, 176, 225
Pearlware, 16, 25, 27, 29, 42-49, 126, 166, 210, 230, 232, 235
Pearl White. *See* Pearlware
Penciled ware, 60, 61, 62
Pennington, John, 107
Perry, Thomas, 58
Petit, Jacob, 163
Petuntse, 91, 99
Pew groups, Staffordshire, 138-42
Philadelphia Society for the Encouragement of Manufactures, 124
Philips, Richard, 75
Phillips & Company, 46, 245, 246, 251
Piccardt. H. A., 33
Picturesque Views series, 180
Pilgrim bottles, 71, 75
Pillement, Jean
Pinder & Bourne, 241
Pitt, Thomas, 91
Plaques, 74, 97, 98, 101, 102, 116
Plymouth factory, 91, 92, 93, 96, 108
Podmore, Robert, 67, 68
Podmore, Walker & Co., 132
Pollard, William, 224
Pont-aux-Choux, 37
Porcelain: Chinese 24, 62, 63, 75, 76-78, 79, 122, 125; French, 63, 84, 91, 94, 124, 163, 219, 229, 243, 271, 273, 274, 278-79; English, 43, 44, 47, 60-62, 63-66, 67-70, 71-75, 76-78, 79-82, 83-86, 86-90, 91-102, 103-04, 105-08, 130, 177-78, 219-24, 227-28, 230, 278-81, 282
Portraiture, ceramic, 159-164; *see also* Plaques
Poskochin, Sergei Yakovlevich, 40
Potlids, 267-68, 269, 270
Pountney, W. J., 249
Powder blue ware, 63-66
Powles, Richard, 75
Pratt: 127, 157, 267-70;. Felix, 127, 157, 160, 267; Richard, 267; Thomas, 267
Precipitated rose gold, 245
Pyrometer, 112

Quail pattern, 65
Queen's pattern, 25, 26, 122
Queen's ware. *See* Creamware

Raby, Edward, 277
Rackham, Bernard, 198, 200
Railroad views. *See* Views
Raised-anchor period. *See* Chelsea
Randall: John, 83; Thomas Martin, 83
Red-anchor period. *See* Chelsea
Redcliff Backs, 82, 103, 104, 150

Redgrave: 77; James, 75; John, 75
Redware: lead-glazed, 24; unglazed *(rosso antico)*, 110, 119, 120, 121, 125, 130, 227
Reverberatory furnace, 245
Rhead, G. W. & F. A., 198, 200
Rickby, T. J., 247
Ridgway, William, 166, 167, 179, 181, 197, 251
Riley, I. & R., 241
Ring, Joseph, 39
Rischgitz, Edouard, 272, 273
Robinson, John, 43, 44, 48
Robinson, Wood, and Brownfield, 198, 201, 206
Rockingham, 75, 83, 84, 160, 162, 232
Rogers, John & George, 43
Rose: John, 83, 84; Thomas, 75, 84; W: F., 84
*Rosso antico. See* Redware, unglazed
Rothwell Potworks, 39, 40
Rowlandson, Thomas, 202, 203
Royal Crown Derby, 274
Royal pattern, 26, 27, 122

Sadler, John, 48, 107
Sadler and Green, 56, 122, 123, 167
Saint-Yrieix quarries, 91
Salopian porcelain, 48, 65, 66, 83, 104, 173
Salt, Ralph, 158
Salt-glazed stoneware. *See* Stoneware, salt-glazed
Salt-glazing, 139
Samian ware, Gaulish, 43
Samson & Company, 75
Sanderson and Bellaert, 33
Schreiber, Charlotte, 34
Schreiber Collection, 34, 63, 65, 66
Scott & Sons, 245, 251
Scratch: blue, 28, 47; brown, 21
Scrivener, Charles, 268
Senior: George, 41; James, 41
Sèvres: 63, 84, 91, 94, 163, 219, 229, 271, 273, 274, 278-81
Sewell Pottery, 232, 251, 252
Sewells and Donkin, 31
Sgraffito ware, 12-15
Shaw: Aaron, 20; Ralph, 22, 23, 24; Simeon, 18, 19, 22, 23, 25, 28, 49, 170, 198, 201, 214, 240
Sheepfold Pottery, 243
Sheldon, Edward, 147
Shell-edge design, 26, 44, 45, 46, 48
Shelton, 18
Sherratt, Obadiah, 158
Shorthose, John, 232, 251
Sim, Robert J., 240
Skinner, George, & Co., 133
Slave cameos and intaglios, 112
Smear glaze, 50
Smirke, Robert, 202, 203
Smith: Alan, 235; A. Merrington, 72; Mabel Woods, 187; Sampson, 158; William, 124, 133
Soaprock porcelain, 68, 73, 82, 107, 108
Society for the Encouragement of Arts, Sciences, and Manufactures, 122
Sodden snow ware, 220
Soft paste porcelain, 73, 77, 79-82, 91, 103
Solon, Louis Marc, 139-40, 271, 273

South Wales Pottery, 251
Sparham, John, 75
Spelman, W.W.R., 72, 73, 74, 75
Spiral wreathing, 94
Spirit flasks, 253-62
Spode: 124, 171, 172, 173, 174, 175-78, 188, 202, 225-28, 249, 263, 272; Josiah I, 82, 167, 172, 175, 189, 225, 227, 228; Josiah II, 126, 166, 175, 225, 227, 228; Josiah III, 175
Sprimont, Nicholas, 88
Spur marks, 79
Staffordshire, 19, 25, 37, 39, 42, 46, 47, 58, 67, 73, 122, 124, 125, 138-42, 143-47, 151-52, 153-58, 160, 162, 163, 166-70, 171-74, 175-78, 179-83, 184-87, 188-89, 190-92, 193-97, 198-201, 202-06, 210-15, 234, 245, 246-47, 250, 267-70
Staffordshire, blue, 167-70, 171-74, 175-78, 179-83, 184-87, 188-89, 190-92, 193-97, 198-201, 202-06, 210-15
Starkey, S. W., 164
Statuary porcelain. *See* Parian ware
Steamship views. *See* Views
Steatite. *See* Soaprock porcelain
Steingut, German, 124
Stephan, Pierre, 93
Stephens, William, 91, 95
Stevenson: Andrew, 166, 168, 179, 180, 182, 186, 198-201, 202; Chas., & Sons, 43; R[alph], & Williams, 168, 179, 180, 181, 182, 198, 199, 200
Stevenson & Dale, 198, 200
Stilt marks, 79
Stoke-on-Trent, 43, 83, 172, 193, 200, 278
Stone china, 166, 167, 173, 228, 263
Stoneware, salt-glazed, 16-23, 24-29, 42, 122, 143, 167, 253-62
Strikes, pottery workers,' 203, 208
Stubbs, Joseph, 194, 195
Summer Rose pattern, 205
Sunderland Pottery, 232, 233, 245, 246, 247, 251
Swansea, 46, 83, 84, 219-24, 245
Swinton, 251
Syntax, Dr., series, 168, 174, 202, 203

Tassie, James, 119
Tea-Plant pattern, 88
Tebo (or Thibault), Mr., 93
Teulon-Porter Collection, 242
Thorne, Atwood, 249
Tilley, Frank, 87, 88
Tin-glazed earthenware, 30, 229
Tin oxide in porcelain, 80
Toby jugs, 148-50
Toft, Thomas, 140
Tomlinson, Foster, Wedgwood & Co., 132
Toppin, Aubrey J., 104
Tortoise-shell ware, 25, 26, 122, 175
Tower pattern, 173, 176
Tower, Donald, 25, 38, 39, 230, 241
Transfer printing, 56, 57, 61, 94, 123, 161, 167-68, 169, 171-74, 175-77, 193, 208, 235
Translucence of porcelain, 105-08
Transmitted light, 105-08
Transylvania University, views of, 179, 180, 183
Tree-of-Life pattern, 226
Treviso earthenware, 124
Triangle period. *See* Chelsea

Trident china, 220, 222
Turner: John, 31, 125, 126, 130, 172, 249, 263; Thomas, 48, 83, 107, 167, 171, 172, 173, 176; William, 240, 249, 263
Twig baskets, 124

Unaker. *See* Cherokee china clay
Underglaze-blue printing, 48, 103, 172-73, 210, 211, 234, 235
Underglaze color-printing, 268
Unicorn and Pinnox Works, 132
Utschnieder factory, 243

Vase forms, antique, 119
Vauxhall Pottery, 259
Vedgwood [sic], 133, 134, 135
Venable, Mellor, & Company, 169
Views: 168, 174, 227; American, 167-68, 169, 174, 184-87, 188, 190-91, 198, 208, 211, 235, 269; American universities, 179-83; English, 167, 169, 174, 210-15, 227, 269; French, 167; German, 212; Greek, 173; Indian, 173, 174, 188; Italian, 167, 172, 175; Naval, 186, 191-92; Railroad, 196-97; Steamship, 193-96, 204
Vincennes porcelain, 278, 279
Vodrey, Jabez, 207, 208
Voyez, John, 145, 146, 147
Vyse, Charles, 282

Wainright, Samuel, 35
Walker, Samuel, 72, 219, 220, 222
Wall: Dr. John, 60, 104; W. G., 168, 194
Wall period, 60-62
Walpole, Horace, 57
Walton, John, 148, 149, 158
Warburton, Mrs., 42, 122, 123, 251
Watkins, John, 14
Watt, James, 110
Wedgwood: Enoch, 132, 133; John, 42, 43; Josiah I, 18, 19, 20, 25, 26, 27, 30, 35, 37, 40, 42, 43, 44, 98, 99, 110-12, 113-17, 118, 119, 120, 121, 123, 125, 128, 131, 132, 134, 159, 160, 210, 231, 232, 245, 249; Josiah II, 119, 250; Josiah C., 19; Ralph, 132, 134; Star, 252; Thomas, 24, 35, 43, 141

Wedgwood Institute, 110
Wedgwood wares: 34, 35, 36, 49, 50, 110-12, 113-17, 118-21, 122-24, 125-27, 185, 250, 271, 275, 281; age tests for, 128-30; imitators of, 131-35, 175
Wednesbury, 58
West Point Military Academy, views, of 179, 180, 183
Wheat-Sheaf design, 61
Whieldon, Thomas, 25, 26, 35, 44, 110, 122, 141, 144, 145, 147, 149, 153, 154, 155, 156, 175
Whieldon-Wedgwood ware, 27, 145
Wiegwood [sic], 133, 134, 135
Wilkie series, 202, 203, 205
Williams, Robert, 95
Williamsburg, Virginia: 15, 19, 23; Colonial Williamsburg, 26, 37-41, 46, 86-90
Williamson, Thomas, 188
Willow pattern, 48, 167, 171, 172, 173, 176
Wilson: David, 250-51; Robert, 130
Wood: Aaron, 141, 144, 146, 160; Enoch, 25, 126, 144, 146, 149, 160, 161, 166, 179, 180, 181, 183, 184, 186, 187, 190, 195, 197, 199, 210, 234; Enoch, Jr., 210, 215; Isaac, 220, 224; John, 132; Ralph I, 131, 144, 145, 146, 147, 148, 149, 150, 154, 156, 157, 160; Ralph, Jr., 144, 145, 146, 147, 148, 149, 150, 154, 156, 157, 160; Ralph II, 146; Ralph III, 146
Wood & Caldwell, 149, 250
Wood, Enoch, & Co., 46
Wood, Enoch, & Sons, 45, 46, 211, 213, 214, 232, 234
Worcester, 47, 60-62, 67, 68, 69, 70, 72, 73, 82, 83, 103, 107, 108, 172, 173, 177, 229
Wrench, Frank, 268

Yale College, views of, 179, 180, 182-83
Yardley, John, 58
Yates, John, 172
Yellow-glazed earthenware, 229-34, 235-39
York House, 56, 60
Young, William Weston, 219, 222, 224
Young Philosopher pattern, 212, 213

Zodiac, signs of the, 119